# MICHIGAN QUARTERLY REVIEW

Vol. XXII, No. 3                         Summer 1983

*A SPECIAL ISSUE*

# THE BIBLE AND ITS TRADITIONS

## EDITED BY

## MICHAEL PATRICK O'CONNOR
### AND
## DAVID NOEL FREEDMAN

MICHIGAN QUARTERLY REVIEW is published quarterly (January, April, July, and October) by The University of Michigan, Ann Arbor, Michigan. Subscription prices, $13.00 a year, $24.00 for two years; institutional subscriptions obtained through agencies $15.00 a year; $3.50 a copy; back issues, $2.00. Claims for missing numbers can be honored only within two months after publication.

Available on microfilm from Xerox University Microfilms, 300 N. Zeeb Rd., Ann Arbor, Michigan 48106, where full-sized copies of single articles may also be ordered. Reprinted volumes and back-volumes available from AMS Press, Inc., 56 E. 13th St., New York, 10003. Indexed or abstracted in Abstr.E.S., Am.Bib.Cent., Ann.Bib., Bk.R.Hum., Bk.R.Inc., P.A.I.S., P.M.L.A., Index of American Periodical Verse, Index to Periodical Fiction, American Humanities Index.

Editorial and business office, 3032 Rackham Bldg., The University of Michigan, Ann Arbor, Michigan 48109. Unsolicited manuscripts are returned to authors only when accompanied by stamped, self-addressed envelopes or by international postal orders. No responsibility assumed for loss or injury.

Second class postage paid at Ann Arbor, Michigan.

ISSN 0026-2420

Published with financial support from The Horace H. Rackham School of Graduate Studies

# CONTENTS

## VI. THE RELIGIOUS TRADITION

Cover Design by Carol A. Gregg

# CONTRIBUTORS

YEHUDA AMICHAI, generally considered one of Israel's best poets, has most recently published *Time* and *Love Poems*, both from Harper & Row.

MARGARET AVISON'S distinguished collections of poetry, *Winter Sun* and *The Dumbfounding*, have recently been returned to print by McClelland and Stewart. A third book, *sunblue*, was published in 1978 by Lancelot Press (Hantsport, Nova Scotia BOP IPO).

ARNOLD BAND, who teaches at the University of California at Los Angeles, recently translated *Nahman of Bratslav: The Tales* for the Paulist Classics of Western Spirituality series (New York, 1978). His study of the greatest of modern Hebrew writers, S. Y. Agnon, *Nostalgia and Nightmare*, was published by the University of California Press in 1968.

JOHN BRAND teaches literature and creative writing at the University of Northern Colorado, Greeley, Colorado.

EDNA AMIR COFFIN is Associate Professor of Modern Hebrew Language and Literature at the University of Michigan. In addition to articles on literature and linguistics, she has written extensively on language teaching and has published two widely-used textbooks, *Lessons in Modern Hebrew*, Level I (1977), and Level II (1978).

JOHN J. COLLINS is Professor of Religious Studies at De Paul University in Chicago. His publications include *Between Athens and Jerusalem: Jewish Identity in the Hellenistic Diaspora* (New York: Crossroad, 1982) and *The Apocalyptic Imagination in Ancient Judaism* (New York: Crossroad, 1983).

JOHN DOMINIC CROSSAN was born in Ireland and lives in Chicago, where he teaches at De Paul University. His books include *In Parables* (New York: Harper & Row, 1973), *The Dark Interval: Towards a Theology of Story* (Chicago: Argus, 1975), and *A Fragile Craft: The Work of Amos Niven Wilder* (Chico: Scholars Press, 1981).

WILLIAM VIRGIL DAVIS is a writer-in-residence at Baylor University; his book *One Way to Reconstruct the Scene* won the Yale Younger Poets prize in 1979. In addition to a doctorate in English, he has a divinity degree, from Pittsburgh Theological Seminary.

ROBERT A. FINK directs the creative writing workshop program at Hardin-Simmons University in Abilene, Texas. *Azimuth Points*, a chapbook, was the 1981 *Texas Review* Poetry Award Chapbook Winner.

DAVID NOEL FREEDMAN heads the Program on Studies in Religion at the University of Michigan and is editor of the Anchor Bible series published by Doubleday, for which he co-authored *Hosea*. His collected essays, *Pottery, Poetry, and Prophecy*, appeared in 1980 (Winona Lake: Eisenbrauns).

HERBERT B. HUFFMON, a native of Michigan and a graduate of the University (AB., 1954; Ph.D., 1963), now teaches at the Theological School of Drew University in Madison, New Jersey. His *Amorite Personal Names in the Mari Texts* has been complemented by other studies of ancient Mari; Huffmon has also been researching the modern history of biblical studies.

AIDAN KAVANAGH is a monk of Saint Meinrad's Archabbey in southern Indiana and professor of liturgics at the Divinity School, Yale University. He has published many essays on liturgy and its origins. Two of his recent books are *The Shape of Baptism* (1978) and *Elements of Rite: A Handbook of Liturgical Style* (1982). In preparation is *On Liturgical Theology*, to appear in 1984.

DIANE KIRKPATRICK is the author of a variety of scholarly articles in addition to a monograph on Eduardo Paolozzi (Greenwich: New York Graphic Society, 1969). She is Professor of the History of Art at the University of Michigan.

DAVID LEHMAN lectures at Wells College and has edited *Beyond Amazement: New Essays on John Ashbery* and, with Charles Berger, *James Merrill: Essays in Criticism*. His poems have appeared in a variety of journals and will soon be gathered together in a volume called *An Alternative to Speech*.

CLAYTON LIBOLT has taught at both Calvin College and Calvin Seminary and is now associated with the ministry of River Terrace Church in East Lansing.

J. LOUIS MARTYN is the Edward Robinson Professor of Biblical Theology at Union Theological Seminary in New York City and Adjunct Professor of Religion at Columbia University. He is co-editor of *Studies in Luke-Acts* (Abingdon, 1966; second edition Fortress, 1980) and author of two books on John and the forthcoming volume of the Anchor Bible on Paul's letter to the Galatian churches.

BERNARD McGINN gathered together diverse medieval materials in *Apocalyptic Spirituality* (New York: Paulist Press, 1979), a volume in the Classics of Western Spirituality series, of which he is an editor. He also wrote *Visions of the End: Apocalyptic Traditions in the Middle Ages* (New York: Columbia University Press, 1979). He teaches in the Divinity School of the University of Chicago.

CAROL MEYERS has done extensive archeological fieldwork in the Upper Galilee region and has written, in addition to numerous reports, a survey of the ancient evidence for *The Tabernacle Menorah* (Cambridge: American Schools of Oriental Research, 1978). She teaches at Duke University.

JAMES R. MOORE holds degrees in science, divinity, and history. He lectures in the history of science and technology at The Open

University in England, where he has prepared television and radio programs with the BBC. He has published *The Post-Darwinian Controversies* (Cambridge University Press, 1979) and is presently completing a monograph on Darwin's religious and social life.

JACOB NEUSNER is the University Professor and Ungerleider Distinguished Scholar of Judaic Studies at Brown University and Co-Director of Brown's Program in Judaic Studies. He is author of *Judaism: The Evidence of the Mishnah* and *Judaism: The Evidence of the Yerushalmi. Toward the Natural History of a Religion* (both The University of Chicago Press). Forthcoming is his *Midrash in Context. Exegesis in Formative Judaism* (Fortress).

JOYCE CAROL OATES, who teaches at Princeton University, is the author most recently of *A Bloodsmoor Romance* and *The Profane Art: Essays and Reviews.*

MICHAEL PATRICK O'CONNOR's *Hebrew Verse Structure* (Winona Lake: Eisenbrauns) appeared in 1980. His poem *Pandary* is forthcoming from L'Épervier.

PETER ORESICK recently completed an M.F.A. at the University of Pittsburgh. His book of poems *The Story of Glass* is available from West End Press of Minneapolis. "Receiving Christ" is based in part on a pre-communion prayer in the Divine Liturgy of St. John Chrysostom.

PAUL RABOFF lives in Israel and has published in a number of literary journals, as well as in *Voices from the Ark: The Modern Jewish Poets.*

RICHARD L. RUBENSTEIN is Robert O. Lawton Distinguished Professor of Religion at Florida State University and Co-Director of the University's Humanities Institute. Since *After Auschwitz* (1966) he has written a number of books related to Jewish history, the Holocaust, and modern history in general. Beacon Press has recently published his latest book, *The Age of Triage: Hope and Fear in an Overcrowded World.*

KATHARINE DOOB SAKENFELD is Associate Professor of Old Testament at Princeton Theological Seminary, Princeton, New Jersey, where she has taught for twelve years. She studied at Harvard Divinity School and at Harvard University. She is an ordained minister in the United Presbyterian Church, USA, and is active in its local and ecumenical work.

JON SILKIN has published seven collections of poetry since the appearance of his first volume, *The Peaceable Kingdom*, in 1954. Most recently, Routledge & Kegan Paul has issued *Selected Poems* and *The Psalms with Their Spoils* (both 1980). Silkin has also written a book of literary criticism, *Out of Battle* (Oxford, 1972). He is founder and co-editor of the literary quarterly *Stand.*

C. H. SISSON at the time of his retirement from the British civil service over a decade ago was among the most distinguished writers in England. The last decade has witnessed the publication of *In The Trojan Ditch: Collected Poems and Selected Translations* (1975) and *The Avoidance of Literature: Collected Essays* (1978, both Manchester: Carcanet), as well as translations of Horace, Lucretius, LaFontaine, and Dante.

WILLIAM STAFFORD has recently published *A Glass Face in the Rain* (Harper and Row), the first volume since his collected poems, *Stories That Could Be True*, in 1977.

CHARLES P. R. TISDALE, who teaches at the University of North Carolina at Greensboro, is currently at work on a book-length mixed genre work based on the myth of Eden and set in a modern context.

PHYLLIS TRIBLE is best known as author of *God and the Rhetoric of Sexuality* (Philadelphia: Fortress, 1978). She teaches at Union Theological Seminary in New York.

THEODORE WEISS's volume of selected poems, *Views and Spectacles* (1978), has been succeeded by a long poem, *Recoveries* (Macmillan) and a selection of essays, *The Man from Porlock* (Princeton).

GLORIA WHELAN's short stories have appeared in a number of literary magazines, including the Summer 1981 issue of MQR. A short novel appeared in a recent issue of *Redbook*, and a story will be included in *Prize Stories 1983: The O. Henry Awards*.

*Acknowledgments*

"The Bible to be Believed," by Margaret Avison, is reprinted from her volume *sunblue*, originally published in Hantsport, Nova Scotia, at the Lancelot Press in 1978; it is reprinted here with the permission of the author and the publisher. "The Words," by William Virgil Davis, is reprinted from *Pig Iron* (Youngstown, Ohio) # 2 (1976); it is reprinted here by permission of the author and Jim Villani, editor of *Pig Iron*. The lines from the book *Somewhere Is Such A Kingdom*, by Geoffrey Hill, published by Houghton Mifflin Company, Boston, Copyright © 1975 by Geoffrey Hill, are reprinted by permission of Houghton Mifflin Company. The passage appears in *King Log*, by Geoffrey Hill, published by André Deutsch and is reprinted by their permission.

# EERDMANS

## THEOLOGICAL AND BIBLICAL STUDIES

**·fall/winter·**
**·1982·**

**EERDMANS' HANDBOOK TO CHRISTIAN BELIEF**
*Edited by Robin Keeley*
In the tradition of the best-selling *Handbook to the Bible*, here is a clear and lively presentation of basic Christian beliefs. Cloth, $24.95, November

**MORE DIFFICULT SAYINGS OF JESUS** *by William Neil and Stephen Travis*
Brief but insightful discussions of 31 perplexing statements made by Jesus. Paper, $5.95, August

**THE WORSHIP OF GOD Some Theological, Pastoral, and Practical Reflections** *by Ralph P. Martin*
A compact guide to some of the main themes of the worship of God. Paper, $7.95, September

**MERE MORALITY What God Expects From Ordinary People** *by Lewis B. Smedes*
From the author of *Love Within Limits* comes a brilliant and searching look at the role of commandments in Christian moral decision-making. Cloth, $15.95, January

**ON BEING HUMAN Essays in Theological Anthropology** *by Ray S. Anderson*
Provides a biblical and theological understanding of the nature of human personhood. Paper, $9.95, December

**ORDINATION A Biblical-Historical View** *by Marjorie Warkentin*
Stimulating and provocative, this study challenges basic assumptions about the rite of ordination. Paper, $6.95, October

**THE LIGHT HAS COME An Exposition of the Fourth Gospel** *by Lesslie Newbigin*
Interprets the message of the *Gospel of John* for modern-day readers. Paper, $8.95, August

**THE NIGHT HE WAS BETRAYED** *by R.E.O. White*
A devotional commentary on the conversation of Jesus in the upper room. Paper, $5.95, January

*Karl Barth*

**A NEW ENGAGEMENT Evangelical Political Thought 1966-1976** *by Robert Booth Fowler*
A detailed, timely compendium of the development of political and social attitudes within evangelicalism in the decade from Vietnam to Carter. Paper, $12.95, November

**UGARIT AND THE OLD TESTAMENT** *by Peter Craigie*
This book relates the discovery and subsequent findings of the remains and libraries of the ancient city of Ugarit. Paper, $5.95, February

**A LATE FRIENDSHIP The Letters of Karl Barth and Carl Zuckmayer** *Translated by Geoffrey W. Bromiley*
Chronicles a remarkable friendship between theologian Karl Barth and poet-playwright Carl Zuckmayer. Cloth, $7.95, November

**LIVING WITH DEATH** *by Helmut Thielicke/Translated by Geoffrey W. Bromiley*
Theological probings into the meaning of death by world-renowned theologian Helmut Thielicke. Cloth, $15.95, February

**THEOLOGY OF THE NEW TESTAMENT, Vol. 2 The Variety and Unity of the Apostolic Witness to Christ** *by Leonhard Goppelt/Translated by John Alsup*
The last volume of a two-volume work by a major German New Testament scholar. Cloth, $15.95, January

**FOUNDATIONS OF DOGMATICS, Vol. 2** *by Otto Weber/Translated by Darell L. Guder*
The first English translation of a monumental classic in systematic theology. Cloth, $31.00, December

*Helmut Thielicke*

**SPIRITUALITY AND HUMAN EMOTION** *by Robert C. Roberts*
Psychological, theological, and ethical themes are brought together in this constructive reflection of what emotions are and how they can be educated. Paper, $6.95, January

**THE ORIGIN OF PAUL'S GOSPEL** *by Seyoon Kim*
This scholarly examination suggests that the basis of the apostle Paul's theology lies in the Damascus road event. Paper, $13.95, October

**NEW CENTURY BIBLE COMMENTARY**
**Forthcoming Releases:**
EZEKIEL *by John Wevers* Paper, $6.95, August
I PETER *by Ernest Best* Paper, $5.95, August
JAMES, JUDE, 2 PETER *by E. M. Sidebottom* Paper, $5.95, September

**THE BOOKS OF EZRA AND NEHEMIAH *(New International Commentary on the Old Testament)* by F. Charles Fensham**
This latest volume in the NICOT series examines two books which cover the last century of Old Testament Jewish history and mark the beginning of Judaism. Cloth, $12.95, December

**A CONCORDANCE TO THE APOCRYPHA/DEUTERO-CANONICAL BOOKS OF THE REVISED STANDARD VERSION**
The first concordance available to the *Revised Standard Version* Apocrypha. Cloth, $30.00, December

For more complete descriptions on these and other recent publications, write for a copy of the latest Theologist Catalog. Examination copies of most publications are available to qualified professors.

Prices subject to change.

At your bookstore, or write:

**WM. B. EERDMANS PUBLISHING CO.**
255 JEFFERSON AVE. S.E. / GRAND RAPIDS, MICH. 49503

# MICHIGAN QUARTERLY REVIEW
## Fall 1983 Issue

**Francis A. Allen**
*Nineteen Eighty-Four* and the Eclipse of Private Worlds

•

**Sven Birkerts**
Television: The Medium in the Mass Age

•

**Czeslaw Milosz and Carl R. Proffer**
A Conversation about Dostoevsky

•

**Albert Feuerwerker**
Academe in Contemporary China

•

**Charles Tilly**
Karl Marx, Historian

•

**Maxine Hong Kingston**
On the Imagination

•

Reviews by: Eric A. Bermann, Paul Roche, Burton Raffel, Martha Vicinus, Stephen Whitfield, and others.

---

☐ Begin my subscription with the Fall 1983 **MQR**. I enclose $13 (1 year).

☐ Please send only the Fall 1983 **MQR**. I enclose $3.50.

Name _____

Address _____

City/State _____ Zip _____

**Michigan Quarterly Review, University of Michigan**
**3032 Rackham Building, Ann Arbor, MI 48109**

# Academic and Professional Books from Augsburg

## NEW BOOKS

AUGSBURG COMMENTARY ON THE NEW TESTAMENT:
**JAMES**/R. A. Martin
**1 & 2 PETER, JUDE**/John H. Elliott
Clear, non-technical interpretation for students,
professors, pastors, lay people.          Kivar **$7.50**

**GROUNDWORK OF BIBLICAL STUDIES**/W. David Stacey
Background materials, including OT and NT facts and
archaeology. Companion volume to **Studying the OT**
and **Studying the NT.**          Paper **$12.50**

**STUDYING THE OLD TESTAMENT**/Henry McKeating
Analyzes the types of literature, key people and
themes.          Paper **$7.95**

**STUDYING THE NEW TESTAMENT**/Morna D. Hooker
Overview of each book. Includes study questions and
bibliography.          Paper **$7.95**

**READINGS IN CHRISTIAN HUMANISM**
Edited by Joseph M. Shaw, R. W. Franklin, Harris Kaasa,
and Charles W. Buzicky
Represents 50 writers from Biblical times to the
present: Augustine, Erasmus, Galileo, Luther, Calvin,
Wesley, Bunyan, King.          Paper **$19.95**

**SIGNPOSTS TO FREEDOM**/Jan Milič Lochman
**The Ten Commandments and Christian Ethics**
Discusses current problems in personal, sexual, and
social ethics in light of the Decalogue.          Paper **$8.95**

**THE COMMUNITY AND MESSAGE OF ISAIAH 56-66**
**A Theological Commentary**/Elizabeth Achtemeier
The first full-length commentary on Third Isaiah based
on results of current research.          Paper **$7.95**

**ETHICS FOR THE PROFESSIONS**/Darrell Reeck
**A Christian Perspective**
Surveys key issues confronting professionals, and
develops an ethic that can be applied to all
professions.          Paper **$8.95**

**THE AMERICAN POOR**
Edited by John A. Schiller
Analysis of poverty from the perspectives of
economics, social welfare, political science, biblical
studies, sociology, and ethics.          Paper **$9.95**

**THE CHRISTIAN CHURCH**/Hans Schwarz
**Biblical Origin, Historical Transformation, and
Potential for the Future**
A complete, up-to-date, comprehensive, ecumenical
study of the church.          Cloth **$19.95**

**LUTHER: WITNESS TO JESUS CHRIST**/Marc Lienhard
**Stages and Themes of the Reformer's Christology**
"The first book to trace the development of Luther's
Christology from its early to late stages"—Gerhard
Forde.          Cloth **$19.95**

**CONFESSING ONE FAITH**
Edited by George Wolfgang Forell and James F. McCue
**A Joint Commentary on the Augsburg Confession by
Lutheran and Catholic Theologians**
An international group of Protestant and Catholic
theologians examines key issues in the Augsburg
Confession.          Paper **$15.00**

**EVANGELICAL CATECHISM**
**Christian Faith in the World Today**
A comprehensive new resource for adult Christian
learning. Introduces and explores the major topics of
Christian faith and life.          **$4.95**

## RECENT EDITIONS

**AUGSBURG COMMENTARY ON THE NEW
TESTAMENT: ROMANS**
Vol. 1 by Roy A. Harrisville.          Kivar **$7.50**

**THE LETTER TO THE COLOSSIANS**
Eduard Schweizer's commentary from the
EKK.          Paper **$12.50**

**ESSAYS ON BIBLICAL THEOLOGY**
by Hartmut Gese.          Paper **$12.50**
**CHRISTIAN/MARXIST DIALOGUE IN EASTERN
EUROPE**
by Paul Mojzes.          Paper **$14.50**
**CREDO: The Christian View of Faith and Life**
by Gustaf Wingren.          Paper **$8.95**

At Your Bookstore or

Augsburg Publishing House, Minneapolis, MN 55440

# Chicago Studies in the History of Judaism

## Edited by **Jacob Neusner**

In this monumental undertaking, Neusner proposes a new model for the genuinely humanistic reading of religious texts and the reconstruction of a religious world view. To achieve this end, he has developed an innovative plan composed of three parallel and ongoing tracks: volumes in the first track will provide translations and explications of classical texts, beginning with the first translation of the Palestinian Talmud into English; those in the second, analyses of the texts for the purposes of social and historical inquiry; and, those in the third, interpretive studies with more wide ranging implications for the humanities in general.

## IMAGINING RELIGION

*From Babylon to Jonestown*
**Jonathan Z. Smith**

In seven provocative essays Smith develops a new approach to religious studies based on his perception of religion as conventional, anthropological, historical, and, above all, an exercise of imagination. His compelling analyses decisively alter the way religion must be studied and interpreted. Returning religion to the realm of human creation and invention, he opens new avenues for investigation, contemplation, and, ultimately, understanding.

Cloth   $15.00   184 pages

## JUDAISM

*The Evidence of the Mishnah*
**Jacob Neusner**

In this volume, Neusner relates the unfolding of the ideas of the Mishnah to the historical setting of the philosophers of the document, comparing context and concept and exploring the interplay between idea and social reality.

Cloth   $25.00   440 pages

## THE TALMUD OF THE LAND OF ISRAEL

*A Preliminary Translation and Explanation*
Translated and Edited by **Jacob Neusner**

These volumes are the first in a projected thrity-five volume translation of the Palestinian Talmud. It is the first translation of the Palestinian Talmud into English and will be the only complete and unabridged translation into any language.

Volume 33, Abodah Zarah
Cloth   $25.00   244 pages

Volume 34, Horayot and Niddah
Cloth   $25.00   256 pages

*forthcoming, Spring 1983*

## TAKE JUDAISM, FOR EXAMPLE

*Studies toward the Comparison of Religions*
Edited by **Jacob Neusner**
Cloth   March

# THE UNIVERSITY OF CHICAGO PRESS

*5801 South Ellis Avenue   Chicago, IL   60637*

# THE HISTORICAL APPROACH TO THE BIBLE

*Howard M. Teeple*

The Bible is widely misunderstood because unreliable methods and attitudes have guided the interpretation of it. This book presents a comprehensive, yet concise, survey of the history and methods of the historical approach, the only reliable way to understand the Bible. Concludes with an appeal for fuller use of the approach in order to raise the intellectual standards in religion. Written for laymen and students, full of factual information, yet readable in style. This work is the culmination of a lifetime of research, writing, and teaching in the fields of Bible and Christian origins.

The author received a Ph.D. in Bible from the University of Chicago, and has taught Bible at Bexley Hall seminary, West Virginia Wesleyan College, and Northwestern University.

". . . well researched, engagingly written, and timely" --JAMES H. CHARLESWORTH, Duke University

". . . a full and frank account of the way this method developed . . . demonstrates clearly how to use it" -- EDMUND F. PERRY, Northwestern University

". . . a magnificent job of synthesizing an enormous amount of material . . . no other recent book covers the whole range of historical critical methodology"--DAVID E. AUNE, Saint Xavier College, Chicago

A new quality paperback original, 1982 (series: Truth in Religion, 2), 334 pp., $7.50

RELIGION AND ETHICS INSTITUTE
P. O. Box 664
Evanston, IL 60204

# Good News Studies

*This new series aims to air and share the good work of modern biblical scholarship.* Consulting Editor: Robert J. Karris, O.F.M.

Vol. 1: **Call to Discipleship: A Literary Study of Mark's Gospel** *by Augustine Stock, OSB*
By showing that the structure of Mark falls neatly within the "plan" of a classical Greek drama, the author's study illuminates the method and message of Mark. $7.95

Vol. 2: **Becoming Human Together: The Pastoral Anthropology of St. Paul** *by Jerome Murphy-O'Connor, OP*
A new and enlarged edition of a focal and well-respected work. $6.95

Vol. 3: **Light of All Nations: Essays on the Church in New Testament Research** *by Daniel Harrington, SJ*
These unified essays present an important study of the church in the light of modern biblical studies. $7.95

Vol. 4: **Palestinian Judaism and the New Testament** *by Martin McNamara, MSC*
A large and important study. The good harvest of the author's long and meticulous research on the subject. $12.95

Vol. 5: **The Apocalypse: The Perennial Revelation of Jesus Christ** *by Eugenio Corsini* of the University of Turin.
Translated and Edited by Francis Moloney, SDB
$12.95

Vol. 6: **St. Paul's Corinth** *by Jerome Murphy-O'Connor, OP*
A very informative work on the social, cultural and architectural aspects of Corinth in Paul's time. $6.95

Other titles to follow

# Theotokos
## A Theological Encyclopedia of the Blessed Virgin Mary
*by*
*Michael O'Carroll, CSSp*

**Walter Burghardt, SJ:** "It will be a useful source book for students and scholars for decades to come."

Large cloth volume (8 1/2" x 11", double-column pages) ......$42

  **Michael Glazier, Inc.**

1723 Delaware Avenue, Wilmington, Delaware 19806

# Explore the Biblical World with a Trustworthy Guide— BIBLICAL ARCHAEOLOGIST

Combining reliability with readability, **BIBLICAL ARCHAEOLOGIST** presents news of archaeological discoveries and the results of ongoing historical research in clear, nontechnical language and an attractive format. Some of the topics you'll read about in BA include:

Current discoveries in the Middle East and the Mediterranean world

Enigmatic Bible passages; new vistas in biblical interpretation

Life in ancient Egypt, Syria-Palestine, Mesopotamia, and elsewhere

Decipherment of baffling scripts

Continuing work on the Dead Sea Scrolls, Nag Hammadi documents, and Ebla tablets

Judaism in antiquity

New research on the life and sayings of Jesus

The travels of Paul

The social world of early Christianity

—and more!

**BIBLICAL ARCHAEOLOGIST** is published quarterly by the American Schools of Oriental Research (ASOR), a nonprofit, nonsectarian educational organization with administrative offices at 4243 Spruce Street, Philadelphia, PA 19104. Founded at the turn of the century, ASOR has received international recognition for its leadership in the wider field of Near Eastern studies and, in particular, Near Eastern archaeology. Members of ASOR automatically receive **BIBLICAL ARCHAEOLOGIST** as one of their annual membership benefits.

# Studies Review

**Religious**

A publication like *Religious Studies Review* has been needed for a long time in our field. We now have in the *Review* a thoroughly responsible organ dedicated to reviewing the critical books in the field of religion and related disciplines—it is high time and many of us are very, very grateful for it.
Sally McFague, Vanderbilt Divinity School

*Religious Studies Review* is a sign of maturity in the discipline, and a guide to the wealth of resources now available. Its scholarly approach and critical stance provide perspective in an area tempted to live beyond its means.
Joseph C. McLelland, Dean, Faculty of Religious Studies McGill University

*Religious Studies Review* dramatically documents the extent to which American scholarship in religion has come of age after having achieved corporate self-consciousness only so recently. In the Review Essays each issue of *RSR* bristles with material relevant for anyone concerned with religious studies in its wider scope, while the Notes on Recent Publications, organized according to topic areas, provide prompt contact with the stream of books and monographs that continue to emerge from presses throughout the world. The listing of recently completed Dissertations in Religion is an added bonus.
Robert A. Kraft, Chairperson, Department of Religious Studies University of Pennsylvania

I have become an enthusiastic, regular reader of *Religious Studies Review*. It keeps me abreast of scholarly developments and current literature in my own and in other fields in a helpful, readable way.
Robert T. Handy, Academic Dean and Professor of Church History Union Seminary, New York, and Adjunct Professor of Religion Columbia University

## Annual Subscription Rates

Individuals belonging to member societies of the CSR: $12.00
Others (including institutions): $18.00

Make checks payable to **Council on the Study of Religion**, and mail to Council on the Study of Religion, Wilfrid Laurier University, Waterloo, Ontario N2L 3C5

# cholaRs PRess

## Augustine on Romans
### Propositions from the Epistle to the Romans
### Unfinished Commentary on the Epistle to the Romans
Paula F. Landes, editor and translator

The first English translation of Augustine's two early commentaries on Paul's letter to the Romans, which are particularly important in understanding Augustine's development as a biblical exegete and a theologian. An important work for historians and theologians interested in the development of biblical interpretation in the West generally and in Augustine's thought in particular.

Code: 06 02 23      Price: Paper $12.75 (8.50)°

## Sin and Judgment in the Prophets: A Stylistic and Theological Analysis
Patrick D. Miller

A study of the theme and characterization of judgment in the Prophetic literature with particular attention to the ways in which judgment is placed in correlation with sin. Primary attention is given to literary and stylistic matters as well as to the implications of this study for theology of judgment in the Old Testament.

Code: 06 00 27      Price: Cloth $19.50 (16.00); paper $16.00 (12.00)

## Humanizing America's Iconic Book
Douglas A. Knight, Gene Tucker, editors

Growing out of the centennial celebration of the Society of Biblical Literature, this collection of essays deals with the issues entailed in a humanistic approach to the Bible. The authors include: Gillian Feeley-Harnik, Langdon Gilkey, Hans Küng, Edmund Leach, Martin Marty, J. Hillis Miller, Hayim Tadmor, Yigael Yadin.

Code: 06 11 06      Price: Cloth $29.95 (21.50); paper $17.50 (11.50)

## The Bible and Social Reform
Ernest Sandeen, editor

An assessment of the impact of the Bible upon seven American movements in essays written especially for this volume: Indian missions by James P. Ronda; abolitionism by James B. Stewart, the Social Gospel by William M. King; women's place in the church by Barbara Brown Zikmund; peace movements by Charles Chatfield; Black churches by Peter Paris; and Catholic reform thought by William Miller. An introduction is provided by the editor.

Code: 06 12 06      Price: Cloth $12.95 (8.50)

°( ) denotes member price

St. Luke. From University of Michigan manuscript 22:123 verso (12th century).

# INTRODUCTION

In the centuries since the materials of the Bible began to assume their present shape, they have constituted both a living presence and a dominating monument among the peoples of the Book. The materials we have assembled here deal with some of the major aspects of that presence, that monument.

The bulk of this issue is taken up by essays written by scholars and addressed to the general reader. General readers, mythical creatures that they are, are not likely to read the Bible as scholars do. That is, in part, why we have gathered together these essays: scholars are edgy about the fact that general readers read the Bible on terms not set by scholars. Scholars tend to prefer to read the Bible *as* something, as a historical document, for example, or as literature. Speaking of non-scholarly readings of the Bible *as*, C. S. Lewis shrewdly remarked: "I cannot help suspecting, if I may make an Irish bull, that those who read the Bible as literature do not read the Bible." We hope Lewis overstated the case.

The central tension among the essays in the issue is the tension between those occasions on which the Bible is looked at in its ancient context, occasions of apparently pristine regard, and those on which the Bible is examined in alien contexts, contexts, that is, in which the Bible has the shape we know. The first set of occasions is that of biblical scholarship, a field of study which has established itself over the last century in the region of history, philology, archeology, and anthropology. An emblem of these occasions might be a remark from Moshe Greenberg, of the Hebrew University:

> The beginning of wisdom in biblical studies is the realization that the Bible is an exotic book about which modern readers understand very little.

The second set of occasions has no unifying rubric, for the Bible has been everywhere and done everything since it achieved its various identities. This everywhere, this everything is sometimes called tradition, a word easily fitted out with adjectives—religious, political, social, technological—though perhaps best fitted with the adjective Northrop Frye applies here:

> The Bible is clearly a major element in our own imaginative tradition, whatever we may think we believe about it. It insistently raises the question: Why does this huge, sprawling, tactless book sit there inscrutably in the middle of our cultural heritage . . . frustrating all our efforts to walk around it?

It would be a mistake to separate these sets of occasions too strictly—

though the first set dominates the opening two sections of the issue and the second, sections III, V, and VI—and a greater mistake to confuse the sets of occasions with methodologies or inquirers.

There are methodologies in evidence, most strongly in the first two sections. J. Louis Martyn interrogates Paul's Epistle to the Galatians as a historical document, asking what can be learned about the apostle's so-called opponents from Paul's own references to them. John J. Collins considers the last book of the New Testament as a capstone to that collection and as an example of a kind of writing associated with Jews and Christians in the troubled Hellenistic and Roman Levant. Bernard McGinn examines how that book, as a canonical document rather than a contemporary one, was scrutinized in the Middle Ages of western Europe, both before and after the great watershed of the late twelfth century, the era of the Crusades, the mendicants, and the Investiture Controversy. David Noel Freedman takes up the Bible from the other end, considering the ways in which the first canon of scripture was prepared and put to use. Literary methods are used in the essays of Phyllis Trible and J. Dominic Crossan, though the up-to-date labels of hermeneutics and feminism should not mislead us: the story of Jephthah's daughter and the parables of Jesus are actual parts of the Bible, not broken off on our terms but set always to break out on their own. Philology leads Katharine D. Sakenfeld into rereading two biblical stories and leads Michael Patrick O'Connor into considering Hebrew verse as part of the range of Mediterranean poetry.

The second set of occasions examined here leads us, for the most part, to the modern world, to the eighteenth and especially the nineteenth and our own centuries. To have considered the intervening period would have been too much for a single issue. Not all occasions have been examined, either: they are too many and too diverse, some more parochial and others more global than these essays consider. All of these occasions could be called religious—after all, the Bible is involved, is it not?—or political—the Bible is always associated with authority and therefore power, is it not?, but we have settled for three rubrics to accommodate our modern occasions, as well as several further ancient ones.

In the concluding section, each of the authors considers how the Bible has posed a problem to the religious tradition or some part of it and how the problem has been dealt with. Aidan Kavanagh, speaking of the common Jewish and Christian tradition, reflects on scripture as part of and as a precondition for worship and the worshiping community. Narrowing the focus to Judaism, Jacob Neusner considers how the tradition opens itself to a textual presence other than the Bible; that question first arose in Judaism in ancient times, apropos of the Mishnah, and Neusner discusses the ancient resolution, as Arnold Band discusses a similar, modern incident. Clayton Libolt treats the management of the biblical presence in the Protestant tradition, especially in America. C. H. Sisson, our senior contributor, raises the question of the Bible as an English book in the Anglican communion: Is it by linguistic means that we can guarantee that the monument of the Bible will also serve as a presence?

In the second last section, we have set cheek-by-jowl essays that look to the actual power structures of the corridor of land that stretches south from the Lebanon and Anti-Lebanon mountain ranges to the Aqaba/Elath ports. Carol Meyers reexamines a phase of the ancient history of the region, and Richard Rubenstein reflects on the ways in which that ancient history has been misapplied and misunderstood in modern times. Edna Coffin discusses the uses of patriarchal themes in Hebrew fiction since 1948, a body of writing as urgently conceived and received in our time as the Apocalypse was in its.

The central section treats topics which spill out of religion and politics into other realms. Arnold Band's essay on the Hasidic tale deals with a crisis of religious and political authority like Neusner's, but the central factor in the later crisis is literature (or, perhaps better, what we would call literature). James Moore writes on Creationism, an element in the crisis of religious leadership Libolt treats, though Creationism curiously presents itself as innocent of religious bearings. Moore's essay is centrally illumined by reflections from the last half of the last century, and Diane Kirkpatrick and Herbert Huffmon both deal with crises of the same period. In each crisis, something new confronted the Bible, put up a good fight, and lost. The new technology of photography raised the question, Is this medium appropriate to dealing artistically with Bible?, a question answered negatively only after some interesting experiments. The new lore of Assyriology raised the question, Is this material, as it seems to claim, of greater importance than the Bible?, a question also answered No!, though the question itself has a grim later history.

We have complemented this gathering of essays with some artistic images, both by major moderns and by younger contemporaries, and with some stories and poems. No aspect of the issue is definitive, though the terrain is well staked out, and all of the material is engaging testimony to the presence and the monument. In an interview given shortly before her death, the Anglo-Jamaican novelist Jean Rhys offered a distinctive piece of further testimony, with which we close:

> Before I could read, almost a baby, I imagined that God, this thing or person I had heard about, was a book. Sometimes it was a large book standing upright and half open and I could see the print inside, but it made no sense to me. Other times the book was smaller and inside were sharp flashing things.

❀     ❀     ❀

The transcription of foreign, especially Hebrew, words is inconsistent, both because the aims of the essays are diverse and the typographical resources at our disposal were limited. The bibliographical notes are largely the work of the editors. Several of the authors have preferred over B. C. and A. D. the abbreviations B. C. E., Before the Common Era, and C. E., Common Era, now widely used among scholars.

✿   ✿   ✿

The editors want to thank for their assistance in preparing the selection of biblical manuscripts Miss Harriet C. Jameson, Head Emerita of the Department of Rare Books and Special Collections of the University of Michigan Libraries, Mrs. Karla M. Vandersypen, Head of the department, Mrs. Helen S. Butz, Acting Head of the department, Mr. David Whitesell, of the department staff, Mrs. Louise C. Youtie, and Professor Ludwig Koenen,of the Department of Classical Studies of the university, and especially Mrs. Butz for granting permission to reproduce plates and Mrs. Youtie for arranging for preparation of the papyri plates. The selection of twentieth-century graphics was prepared with the assistance of Professor Diane M. Kirkpatrick, of the History of Art Department of the university, to whom we are grateful. We also want to thank Laurence Goldstein, the editor of MQR, for inviting us to prepare the issue, for soliciting several contributions, and for giving the contents their final shape, and Michael Long, of the MQR staff, and Jo Ann H. Seely, of the Program of Studies in Religion staff, for aiding and abetting.

WILLIAM STAFFORD

# SCRIPTURE

In the dark book where words crowded together,
a land with spirits waited; and they rose and walked
every night when the book opened by candlelight—

A sacred land where the words touched the trees
and their leaves turned into fire. We carried it wherever
we went, our hidden scene; and in the sigh of snow coming down,

In the city sometimes a people without any book
drove tunneling by in traffic, eyes measuring
chances ahead, the red light at the end of the block—

Then sprung over that city a dark word like judgment
arched, every face turned into a soul
wandering the shadow of the tabernacle world.

*ONE*

# THE HEBREW
# BIBLE

DAVID NOEL FREEDMAN

# THE EARLIEST BIBLE

Twenty years ago I proposed the thesis that the major components of
the Hebrew Bible in substantially the form in which they have come
down to us were organized and compiled, published and promulgated
during the Babylonian Exile and that therefore we could legitimately
speak of a first Bible, an authoritative and quasi-canonical work,
already functioning by the middle of the sixth century B.C.E. It contained the "Primary History," comprised of the Torah (Pentateuch)
and the Former Prophets (Joshua–2 Kings) as well as the bulk of the
prophetic works. This work was intended to serve many purposes for
the exilic community: standard and guide, rationale for and defense of
the faith, explanation of the past, instruction for the present, and
support for the future. But mainly it was designed to provide a context
within which the exiles could survive, maintain their identity, and
prepare for an ultimate return to the holy land.

The actual return, initiated in 538 under the reign of Cyrus the
Persian, added a new chapter to the recorded history of the people
who worshipped the God of Moses. As it changed their circumstances
dramatically, revisions in existing works and composition of new books
were required for the recently promulgated Bible. It is instructive,
however, that no such post-exilic additions or changes were apparently
made in the Primary History or in the books of the major prophets such
as Jeremiah and Ezekiel; these works must have already been fixed and
hence beyond the reach of continuators and supplementers. The new
and revised compositions may be recognized in exilic and post-exilic
Isaiah (chapters 40–66) and such prophets as Haggai, Zechariah, and
perhaps Malachi. Another example is an early edition of the Books of
Chronicles, an edition which arose out of the flurry of excitement and
expectation generated by the rebuilding of the Temple and the
emergence of Zerubbabel, the scion of the House of David, as leader
of the restored community.

As to the main thesis, not much has happened in the past two
decades. The central contention, about the date of the Primary History,
and its implications for the literary history of the several sources behind
the Torah have largely been passed by, and traditional positions have
been reaffirmed. There has been little reason, therefore, to modify or
alter the proposal, still less to retract it. Its chief merits are its simplicity
and prima facie plausibility. The burden of proof would seem to rest

upon those who would deny or dismiss it; I think it should be the point of departure for consideration of both the previous, early stages in the development of the authoritative literature of Israel and the subsequent course of canon and text.

The current paper will elaborate and expand on the original thesis and make further proposals concerning the compilation and promulgation of the literature under consideration.

## I

The key to the publication puzzle is to be found in the final paragraph of the Primary History (2 Kings 25:27–30). This passage provides the last and latest date in the work and serves as a colophon, stating the date and publication place of the current edition. The date is given as 27 Adar in the 37th year of the Exile (= 21 March 561 B.C.E.), during the accession year of the Babylonian king Awel-Marduk, the successor of Nebuchadrezzar II, who sacked Jerusalem. The occasion for the paragraph's inclusion was the release of the exiled king Jehoiachin from prison and the bestowal of allowances and perquisites appropriate to his royal status; in itself the item is of modest import. It is quite distinct from the preceding account (vv 22–26), which describes the death of Gedaliah, the governor of Judah, in 586. The absence of data for the intervening years (586–561) shows that the historical work effectively ended with the Fall of Jerusalem, the chaotic aftermath that resulted in the death of the governor, and the flight of many Judahites to Egypt (among them the prophet Jeremiah and the scribe Baruch, cf. Jeremiah 42–44).

The postscript, appended 25 years later, mentions the last surviving king of Judah, but adds nothing else of importance. Apparently it was the last piece of information available on the subject; nothing is said of the succession or of the next in line. While the passage refers to the remaining years of Jehoiachin's life, indicating only that the imperial stipend was bestowed as a lifetime annuity, it says nothing of his death or of the transfer of royal status. The precision of the imperial decree's date would lead one to expect similar detail about Jehoiachin's death if that information had been available. More important information would include a reference to the successor(s) of Awel-Marduk and subsequent renewals of or changes in the grant to Jehoiachin.

The text also bears no indication of the death of Awel-Marduk, although we know that he died in the second official year of his reign, between 7 and 13 August 560. The entry about Jehoiachin must then have been made before the death of Awel-Marduk; it may well have been written after the death of Jehoiachin, in view of the repeated references to "all the days of his life." In any case, the publication date for the entire work, in full and finally edited form, appears to fall between 21 March 561 and 13 August 560 B.C.E., a period of a year and five months.

The only differences between the published text of 560 B.C.E. and the preserved texts from the Middle Ages resulted from scribal errors and adjustments. Editorial changes of different kinds may also have taken place, as reflected, for example, in the varying Hebrew manuscripts and the versions, but these are of a minor nature for the most part, explicable in terms of divagations from a central and official text. The existence of the latter (of Babylonian origin, perhaps) is attested in the third century B.C.E. by the Dead Sea Scrolls, can be projected into the fourth century, and can plausibly be associated with the official text (of at least the Pentateuch) promulgated by Ezra in the fifth century B.C.E. It may be possible some day to trace the textual history of the Primary History and some of the prophetic books back to the sixth century, although documentary evidence is wanting.

## II

The immediate implication of such a hypothesis is that everything contained in the Primary History belongs to the period before 560 B.C.E., that nothing in it is to be attributed to a later date. That contention runs counter to long prevailing views of the composition of the Pentateuch or Hexateuch (the Pentateuch and Joshua) and of the dates of the later sources comprising that complex. These later sources are two in number: the Priestly Source (called P), which contributed to the Pentateuch most of the liturgical, genealogical, legal, and technical materials; and the Deuteronomic Source (called D), which comprises the bulk of the Book of Deuteronomy. Closely allied to D is the framework of the Former Prophets, the Books of Joshua, Judges, Samuel, and Kings, a body sometimes called the Deuteronomic (or Deuteronomistic) History. The standard assertions about the Priestly and Deuteronomic sources confidently assigning various editions to later and later post-exilic periods and circumstances need themselves to be questioned and tested, since in large degree the claims made are based upon reconstructions of the post-exilic settlement, themselves hypothetical.

Thus it is widely argued that the Priestly Document, with its sacrificial and sacramental orders, reflects the practices and procedures of the Second Temple and was in fact drawn up on the basis of those practices. It is certain that the liturgy and ritual of the Second Temple and Priestly Document have much in common, but that in itself proves nothing except that both derive from and develop out of the same community. Determining the chronological sequence and the direction of influence is much more difficult, perhaps impossible. Nonetheless, the proposed hypothesis about the Primary History has value in that it posits an answer to the question of priority and requires proponents and opponents to present their evidence and arguments.

It seems to me that the burden of proof is on those who defend a post-exilic date for P or even the Pentateuch as a whole and that none of the evidence so far adduced in favor of such a date is beyond question. The correlations between the Pentateuch and post-exilic practice (recorded or reflected in undoubted post-exilic works) not only fail to demonstrate priority but can in all cases be explained either as normal development from pre-exilic procedure or as evidence of post-exilic dependence on the protocols of P. Even to devise a provable test for any priority—if we do not accept the traditional chronology—would tax scholarly ingenuity, and to produce proof of any kind would seem beyond our capacity, at least at this juncture. Perhaps it will suffice to say that post-exilic practice deliberately imitated what was believed to be the pattern of the First Temple and that the Priestly writing, while purporting to record and reflect the liturgical experience of the wilderness wanderings of the earliest Yahwists, is in fact also rooted in the practice of the First Temple. There is no denying that some of the traditions in P are archaic, perhaps indeed deriving from the experience in the wilderness and even from the pre-Israelite traditions of Canaan.

What has been said about the P-work applies even more strongly to the D-work. Deuteronomy itself, or the bulk of it, has been regarded as pre-exilic in origin and date since the days of W. M. L. de Wette (1780–1849), whose identification of D with the document found in the Temple in the 18th year of Josiah (662/21) has survived critical testing for almost 200 years and remains one of the few relatively fixed points in biblical research. Whatever the original date of the Book of Deuteronomy or of its core (the ultimate sources and roots must reach far back in Israelite history), there is little double on anyone's part that it substantially reached its present form before the end of the Exile.

The same may be said of the Deuteronomic History, which comes to an end with the fall of Jerusalem in 586, excluding the postscript already discussed. (My view is that the postscript was never part of the Deuteronomic History; hence its omission from the Books of Chronicles, which follow the older source fairly closely in this material.)

There is no hint in the Deuteronomic History of subsequent events, especially the return from Exile in the specificity with which it is described in 2 Chronicles and Ezra 1–6. While the hope of a return is part of the deuteronomic credo as adumbrated in places in the sermons of Moses, these are hardly predictions after the fact, since the data are vague, imprecise, and inaccurate in detail.

The Deuteronomic History is certainly capable of creating *vaticinia ex eventu*, prophecies after the fact, as in the case of the prophecy at Bethel that names Josiah as the great future king of Judah about 300 years before his time. But it includes nothing like that in connection with the return from the Babylonian Captivity, nothing about the fall of Babylon, the rise of Persia, or the emergence of Cyrus. In the other case, the Deuteronomic History mentions Josiah as the fulfiller of the prophecy made to Jeroboam I both in the prophecy itself (1 Kings 13:1–3) and in the subsequent history (2 Kings 23:15–20). Had the writer known about the return from Exile, he would surely have been more specific in the wording of the prophecies of that event and would have recorded the actual return in confirmation of the ancient predictions. His failure to follow this pattern in the case of the return argues strongly for a pre-exilic or exilic date for the D-work.

Since we assign the postscript at the end of 2 Kings to the final editor or redactor of the Primary History (in 561/0), we may date the D-work to the period immediately following the fall of Jerusalem. The story ends with the departure of a large group for Egypt after the assassination of Gedaliah, an indication that the concern of the D-writer was at least as much with Egypt as with Babylon. Richard Friedman has recently suggested that Egypt was in fact the focus of the writer, who brings the story full circle, beginning with bondage in Egypt (reflected in the Mosaic sermons in D) and ending with the return to Egypt. The passage from Egypt to Egypt complements the movement from Bablyon, in Abraham's migration from Ur, back to Babylon, in the captivity. Friedman's arguments are persuasive, as is his proposal that an important link exists between the D-work and the Book of Jeremiah, also apparently a product of Egypt. The D-work and Jeremiah must both have been compiled there after 586 B.C.E. but well before the end of the Exile. We postulate a *terminus ad quem* for all such efforts in 561/0 B.C.E.

The last chapter of Jeremiah holds an important clue to the date of the book's compilation. This chapter consists of three parts: the first long section (vv 1–27) is equivalent to 1 Kings 24:28–25:21; a short entry (vv 28–30) follows, summarizing the numbers of captives and providing a series of dates that, like the numbers, are different from anything else about the captivity in the Bible; the final passage (vv 31–34) is essentially identical to the passage at the end of 2 Kings, the postscript discussed above.

The numbers and dates in the brief second section of the chapter appear reliable and seem to be derived from government (perhaps Babylonian) sources. Their incorporation into the Book of Jeremiah provides a terminus for this book as well, as they provide the latest dates in the book apart from the closing date, already assigned to the compiler of the Primary History. Whether this second unit and perhaps even the first were added by the editor in Egypt, Jeremiah's scribe Baruch, or by a Babylonian redactor, Seraiah, the brother of Baruch, is not a material consideration here, as in any case the information serves to close the book, thereby incorporating in it the violent anti-Babylonian prophecies of chapters 50–51 (probably by someone other than Jeremiah, whose attested views concerning Babylon and Nebuchadrezzar were very different).

We may, therefore, adopt 582/1 as the earliest possible date for the publication of the Book of Jeremiah. The addition of the postscript was intended to tie that book to the Primary History and to bring it under the same authority as the larger work. It is clear that the support of Jeremiah and of Ezekiel, the two major prophets of the period, was regarded from the inception of the process as necessary and important. The Primary History was constructed on the basic pattern of prediction and fulfillment, whether in the promises to the patriarchs realized in the conquests of Joshua or in the warnings of Moses fulfilled in the terrible judgments visited upon Israel. Buttressing the classic prophets from Moses through Samuel, Elijah, Elisha, and even Isaiah, the timely words of the two great contemporary prophets, Jeremiah and Ezekiel, conclude the work.

That observation leads to a consideration of the P-work, its place of publication and date. As to the place, the general opinion that this work takes its origins and derives its contents from the tradition of the priestly class and the experience of the Solomonic Temple seems most reasonable. Whether the work is pre-exilic, compiled in Jerusalem, or exilic and put together in Exile is difficult to decide, and there are legitimate arguments on both sides of the question. The solution may lie in a compromise, that is, in the recognition that large and significant components are clearly old, some ancient, and that probably some major sections belong to a pre-exilic work.

There is some difficulty in defining the limits of the work. Does it extend beyond the Tetrateuch (Genesis–Numbers)? If so, where does it end, and in what fashion? Traditionally P was thought to continue and complete the story begun in Genesis with the allocation of the tribal territories in Joshua, but that opinion has come into question in recent years. In all likelihood a decision here would have bearing on a judgment about the date of the whole work, as we lack both a date and a datable tag. I think that we can trace P through Numbers without great difficulty; after that the trail becomes uncertain.

I am sure there was a continuation of some kind, perhaps parallel to or even still contained in Joshua, because the promises in Genesis belong to P as well as to the earlier Yahwist and Elohist sources. The redactor of P knowingly incorporated all the patriarchal promises, which must find resolution or fulfillment in conquest or settlement in the promised land. That element is entirely lacking in the Tetrateuch, especially as the conquest in Numbers does not correspond territorially to the promises in Genesis. There must have been something more in the original P-work. Our conclusion about the compilation of the P-work is that the process began in Jerusalem and may have ended in exile in Babylon. The date is uncertain, but I believe that it is roughly contemporary with the D-work, although the process may have taken longer in the case of P.

Comparison with Ezekiel is indicated; the connections, linguistic, lexical, and conceptual, are obvious, but the questions of interaction, dependency, and the direction of influence are hard to determine. A consensus that Ezekiel in its totality is the later work seems to be emerging, holding that the prophet is ultimately dependent for basic attitudes and ideas on the Priestly tradition but not trying finally to settle the question of specific dependence or influence.

For the oracles of the Book of Ezekiel we have a series of explicit dates, ranging from the 5th year of the Exile to the 25th (40:1) year of the Exile (roughly 593/2–573/2). However, an editorial insertion in vv 17–21 of chapter 29 (itself dated to the 10th year of the Exile, 588/7) is dated to the 27th year (571/0). In this interpolation the prophet comments on his earlier prophecy, which he has not seen fulfilled. Here he offers an evaluation of the former prophecy and a revised oracle. This paragraph is a clear example of editorial work by the prophet, not entirely satisfied with the text and wishing to bring his comments on the matter up to date. There is no further comment about this particular prophecy, which appears in chapters 26–28, concerning Nebuchadrezzar's siege of Tyre; the new oracle speaks of an impending conquest of Egypt by Nebuchadrezzar as compensation for the failure to capture Tyre.

Ezekiel 1:1 contains a reference to the 30th year (568/7); if it belongs to the same chronological system as the rest of the dates, it would be the latest of all and might be intended or understood as the date of compilation or publication. The range between 571/0 and 568/7 is not large; we can leave the issue undecided. The minimum date would be 571/0. If we allow about three years for the completion of editorial work we come out about the 30th year, 568/7.

That leaves another seven years for the final work on the Primary History and its publication along with the two major prophets, Jeremiah and Ezekiel. We can summarize the proposal as follows:

|  | Minimum Date | Place |
|---|---|---|
| D-work | 586 | Egypt and Babylon |
| Jeremiah | 581 | Egypt and Babylon |
| P-work | Early 6th century | Jerusalem and Babylon |
| Ezekiel | 571 (or 568) | Jerusalem and Babylon |
| Primary History | 561 | |

These dates indicate that the final process of editing and compiling took place in a relatively brief interval and that the work was carried out in accordance with a general plan. We have dealt only with the final stages of a process that was both long and intricate. Internal evidence shows that the Book of Jeremiah went through a number of earlier phases, though the latter ones have to be conjectured and reconstructed. It is a roughly contemporary work, assembled during the lifetime of or shortly after the death of the prophet. The same may be said of the Book of Ezekiel, although we lack factual data about the way in which the work was carried out.

Both books reflect intense interest in dating and preserving prophetic oracles so that they could be checked against the later events for validity. This attitude and care were matters of great moment to the exilic communities, whether in Egypt or Babylon, and we can recognize the same process of preservation and consolidation in both locales without denying that the impulse and method derive from Jerusalem, with its royal and priestly traditions and archives.

### III

The intense editorial activity of this period no doubt reflects the extraordinary trauma that the people of Judah and Jerusalem experienced. Deprived of freedom and nationhood and bereft of Temple and Land, the only visible recourse was to the text. It was an idea of their own creation that a book of remembrance should serve in place of all that had been lost. It would provide for a distinctive manner of life to keep them separate from their gentile neighbors. It would also give hope for the future, a future which in the light of their sister Israel's experience a century and a half earlier as well as that of other small nations must have seemed exceedingly bleak and gloomy.

To give substance to that hope, it was necessary to explain at length and in detail just what had happened to this people and why. Simply to state the facts that a large empire had twice overwhelmed a small kingdom in the space of a decade was hardly enough. That could only confirm the exiles' worst fears and anguish. It was necessary to explain rather that their God, Yahweh, was not defeated but victorious, that he remained in sovereign control of the world that he had created and ruled since the beginning. Hence the elaborate proemium in Genesis 1–11, otherwise out of proportion to the story of a small people that follows. The same God who had created them a nation and given them a land in accord with solemn promises made to the patriarchs also judged and condemned them and finally destroyed them because they failed to obey the word and persisted in running after and serving other gods. They richly deserved their destiny. They had no one to blame but themselves. In this recognition of their own fault lay the basis of revival and restoration. The same God was not permanently alienated;

he was willing, even eager, to bring them back to the land from which he had torn them and to reestablish them as he had once before. Palace and temple, priesthood and kingship would all be restored, and that life of peace and security, prosperity and well-being to which they had been called and for which they had been instructed would be theirs, this time forever. Roughly speaking this promise was the message of the Book, of the first Bible, which consisted of the Primary History supplemented by Jeremiah and Ezekiel.

Other books or parts thereof doubtless existed at the same time, and some at least may have been authorized and pressed into official service. We can and should postulate an exilic collection of prophets, including, in addition to the two mentioned, the four eighth-century prophets (Amos, Hosea, Isaiah, and Micah), whose oracles were especially important for Jerusalem a century after Samaria had fallen. The later prophets, strongly influenced by the earlier ones, make frequent comparison between the two kingdoms using Israel (the northern kingdom) as an object lesson from which the southern sister could learn. Other books such as Nahum, Zephaniah, Habakkuk, and probably Obadiah can be listed as well, for all refer to the momentous events of the last century of Judah's existence.

Beyond the horizon of the first Bible lay the second, much enlarged edition. The dividing point and the stimulus for the new burst of literary activity was the end of the Exile and the return from captivity. This remarkable event required a revised history (the Books of Chronicles, the first edition of which goes through Ezra 3) and a new set of prophetic supplements (including books such as Haggai, Zechariah, and probably Malachi) for the last part of the sixth century. But the great prophet of the return and restoration comparable to the prophets of doom and destruction associated with the Primary History (Jeremiah, Ezekiel, and many of the Minor Prophets) was Isaiah—both or several of them in a single book. Without attempting to analyze or reconstruct the complex history that produced the book we have, it is clear that the Book of Isaiah was regarded as the appropriate companion piece to Chronicles, as both emphasized the decisive role of Cyrus, the continuity and authority of the house of David, the centrality of Jerusalem, and the inviolability of Zion.

*Bibliographical Note*

For the previous study of the Primary History, see "The Law and the Prophets" in *Supplements to Vetus Testamentum*, 9 (1963), 250–65, and the elaboration in the article, "The Canon of the Old Testament," in *The Interpreter's Dictionary of the Bible /Supplementary Volume*, ed. K. Crim et al. (Nashville: Abingdon, 1976), 130–36. For Friedman's work, see "From Egypt to Egypt," in *Traditions in Transformation*, ed. B. Halpern and J. D. Levenson (Winona Lake, Indiana: Eisenbrauns, 1981), 167–92.

PHYLLIS TRIBLE

# A DAUGHTER'S DEATH:
## FEMINISM, LITERARY CRITICISM, AND THE BIBLE

Like a pilgrim, the Bible wanders through history to engage a host of methodologies and perspectives. The journey is always compelling and never-ending, yielding varied applications of the text to diverse settings. In the current scene one manifestation of this process combines the discipline of literary criticism with the hermeneutics of feminism to reinterpret familiar passages, highlight neglected ones, and thus offer fresh understandings of both scripture and its readers.

Though biblical scholars have utilized literary critical methodologies for centuries, a renewed emphasis upon this discipline is now underway. Attention focuses upon an intrinsic reading of the text in its final form. The critic may trace general design and plot movement, pursue the unfolding of a single motif, key word, or particular stylistic device, or offer a close reading of a unit, examining in detail the interconnections of form and content. Some analyses stress the typicality of literature in order to locate a single text within a genre while others accent the uniqueness of each specimen. These many pursuits employ learned principles, procedures, and controls, but they also reside in the realm of art, following hints and guesses and welcoming intuition and surprise.

If literary criticism is a long-established methodology for interpreting biblical texts that is now enjoying a revival, feminism is a relatively new perspective. Indeed, only within the last decade has a sustained feminist critique emerged within the biblical guild. It works in a variety of ways. Some studies document the case against women in the Bible, evaluating the abundant evidence for their inferiority, subordination, and abuse. Others explore within scripture itself a counter-literature pertaining to women that stands over against the dominant patriarchal biases. The creation texts in Genesis 1–3 and the Song of Songs provide such a view, as does female imagery for God. Further, a feminist perspective may retell sympathetically stories of terror about women. Interpreting *in memoriam* challenges both the misogyny of scripture and its use in church, synagogue, and academy. In general, feminism is one current approach to the study of the Bible that calls forth new meanings. Joining this hermeneutic with the methodology of literary criticism, we offer here a case study: the story of the daughter of Jephthah (Judges 11:29–40).

## I. Setting the Stage

This story of terror belongs to the days of the judges. Israel lived in tribal societies free from the power of a centralized government and yet subject to threats of anarchy and extinction. Within this setting public and private events interlock to yield a saga of faithlessness, death, and mourning.

In the eleventh century, when Ammon becomes a kingdom in Transjordan with Rabbah as its capital city, that nation begins to oppress the children of Israel, specifically those living in the territory of Gilead with Mizpah as their central city. For the Deuteronomic editor-theologian of Judges, this military crisis is the work of the Lord, who is punishing Israel for its apostasy (Judges 10:6–16). After confessing their sins, the people seek a deliverer, one to lead the fight against the Ammonites (10:17–18).

Their savior, however, emerges in ambiguity (11:1–3). "Now Jephthah the Gileadite was a mighty warrior,"° one well trained in combat who could supply his own equipment as well as a contingent of soldiers. Yet beside these desirable credentials the storyteller places an irredeemable flaw: "But he (hû') was the son of a prostitute." Indeed, so uncertain was Jephthah's lineage that only the personified district of Gilead could qualify as his sire. Child of an unnamed harlot and an unknown father, Jephthah the mighty warrior suffered for the sins of his parents. The pure offspring of his generation expelled him from his father's house. With an ironic touch, the narrative reports that Jephthah then fled "from his brothers" to dwell in the land of Tob. In time, this outcast attracts friends from the dregs of society: "Worthless fellows collected round Jephthah and went raiding with him ('immô)."°

Having presented the future deliverer as an outcast, the storyteller proceeds to reunite Jephthah and his people in the face of Ammonite aggression (11:4–11). An external threat alters an internal division. Initiative comes from the elders of Gilead whose vacuous military establishment has left them no choice but to seek out the illegitimate one to save them. Thus, these elders "went to bring Jephthah from the land of Tob."° At first, they offer him only temporary authority during the forthcoming fight with the Ammonites: "Come and be our leader (qāṣîn). . . ."° But Jephthah challenges the elders with questions recalling his harsh treatment at their hands (11:7). Though the elders deny these accusations, their desperation impels them finally to offer him permanent authority:

---

°Biblical quotations identified by an asterisk (°) come from the Revised Standard Version. My own translations, designed to convey Hebrew style, vocabulary, and syntax, rather than felicitous English, are left unmarked.

> Now we have turned to you
>> that you may go with us
>>> and fight the children of Ammon;
>> that you may be for us Head (*lĕrō'sh*)
>> of all the inhabitants of Gilead. (11:8)

Amazingly, the elders award this enormous power to Jephthah without even specifying that he must win the battle.

Their revised offer brings Jephthah to the point of bargaining:

> If you (*'attem*) cause me (*'ôtî*) to return
>> to fight the children of Ammon
> and (if) Yahweh gives them to me,
> then I (*'ānōkî*) shall be
>> over you (*lākem*) Head (*lĕrō'sh*). (11:9)

The bargaining is shrewd. By appealing conditionally to Yahweh, Jephthah decreases further the power of the elders while enhancing his own authority. What they have just offered, he now proposes to earn on the battlefield, if the Lord so wills. Then, once the condition is fulfilled and the battle won, Jephthah alone will claim permanent power without reference to Yahweh. According to his words here, the deity who is useful in the bargaining process has no part in the aftermath of victory. And so the divine enters the story obliquely, neither speaking nor acting nor being addressed directly. Such religious language will in time exacerbate the terror and perplexity of all that happens. Meanwhile, in their reply to Jephthah, the elders acquiesce completely to his bargain. Faced with an external threat, Gilead has resolved its internal conflicts of both a public and private nature. With Jephthah as their "head and leader" (v 11), the children of Israel are now ready to confront the children of Ammon.

The initial confrontation is an exercise in diplomacy. On two occasions the enemies talk, with the narrator providing information and commentary (11:12-13, 14-28). Emissaries take Jephthah's words to the unnamed king of the Ammonites: "What is at issue between us that you have come to fight against my land?" (11:12). The answer is uncompromising. To the charge that the Ammonites have come "to fight against *my land*," the king counters that "Israel on coming from Egypt took away *my land*" (11:13). In a territorial dispute, the king seeks restoration. A second time Jephthah sends messengers to the monarch. They make a lengthy speech, in the style of a prophetic lawsuit where the standard formula, "Thus says the Lord," becomes instead, "Thus says Jephthah" (11:15). "But the king of the Ammonites would not heed the words of Jephthah which he sent to him" (11:28). The stage is now set for the battle that provides the occasion for our story.

## II. Joining the Battle

Although Jephthah, the elders of Gilead, and the narrator have all invoked the Lord, at no point thus far has the deity actually intervened. Striking, then, is the narrative report that commences the battle scene: "Then the spirit of Yahweh came upon Jephthah" (11:29). This formulaic speech clearly establishes divine sanction for the events that follow and predicts their successful resolution. But Jephthah himself does not evince the assurance that the spirit of Yahweh ought to give. Rather than acting with conviction and courage, he responds with doubt and demand. In the middle of the battle episode (11:30–31), he disrupts the narration (11:29, 32–33) to make yet another bargain. So serious are his words that the storyteller designates them a vow: "Now Jephthah vowed a vow to Yahweh." Unlike his earlier scheme addressed to the elders of Gilead, this one beseeches God directly, with pressuring language: "If you will *really* give. . . ," begins Jephthah. The use of the infinitive absolute in Hebrew (*nātôn*, translated here adverbially) may suggest that Jephthah is pushing the bargaining mode of discourse to its very limits. The chosen savior, endowed with the spirit of Yahweh, is nevertheless unsure of divine help and hence insecure about his own future among those who had once rejected him. Therefore, he implores the deity, "If you will *really* give the Ammonites into my hand. . . ." The intensity of this protasis leads to a resolute apodosis: "then whatsoever comes forth from the doors of my house to meet me upon my return in victory from the Ammonites shall belong to Yahweh; I will offer it as a burnt offering." In moving from condition to outcome, Jephthah switches from direct address to a third-person reference for the deity: "Whatsoever comes forth . . . shall belong to Yahweh." Though this third-person reference corresponds to usages of the divine name elsewhere in the story, its appearance in the apodosis of this sentence is special. Unlike Jephthah's earlier bargain (11:9), this vow implicates the Lord in the outcome of the condition. Beyond doubt, the sacrifice will be made *to Yahweh*.

The nature of the sacrifice, however, is as unclear as it is emphatic. Literally, the words read, "the comer-forth who comes forth," a compound expression of emphasis that is difficult to render in English. Moreover, the masculine gender of these terms is a standard grammatical usage that alone does not identify either species or sex. A certain vagueness lurks in these words of Jephthah, and we do well to let it be. Did he intend a human sacrifice, male or female? a servant perhaps? or an animal? The story fails to clarify the precise meaning of his words here; rather, we shall know Jephthah by his fruits.

In so thoroughly linking his private life with a public crisis, the savior figure has spoken on his own, for neither Yahweh nor the people of Gilead require the vow. Furthermore, his speech has disrupted the flow of the narrated discourse. It has broken in at the very center to press for divine help that ironically is already Jephthah's through the spirit of the Lord. The making of the vow is truly an act of unfaithfulness. Jephthah desires to bind God rather than embrace the gift of the spirit. What comes to him freely, he seeks to earn and manipulate. The meaning of his words, then, is doubt, not faith; it is control, not courage. To such a vow the deity tellingly makes no reply.

"So Jephthah passed over to the Ammonites to fight against them" (11:32). As we would expect, since the spirit of Yahweh is upon him, the outcome is victory. In reporting this result, however, the narrator borrows language from the vow itself. "If you will really give the Ammonites into my hand," Jephthah had implored. Now we read, "Yahweh gave them into his hand." Those words that earlier broke the narration here become part of it. Artistically, this reference to the Lord at the end of the scene balances the phrase "spirit of the Lord" at the beginning; yet the two statements are in tension. In the first, the spirit of Yahweh is a gift to Jephthah that by itself guarantees the desired outcome but is not subject to it. By contrast, the second statement, "Yahweh gave them into his hand," using the vocabulary of the vow, violates the language of unqualified gift. In other words, the working out of the vow to Yahweh has replaced the free bounty of the spirit of the Lord. Jephthah has gotten what he wanted in the way he wanted it, but he does not understand that to win is to lose. By appropriating Jephthah's speech, then, the storyteller heightens the efficacy of the vow, forecasts its continuing power, *and* alters the theological stance of the story.

After making this theological shift, the narrative supplies details of the victory (11:33). How very great was the slaughter; how very decisive the defeat! Even the syntax of the sentences discloses the changed status of the Ammonites. Whereas in earlier reports they were aggressors, most often subjects of active verbs (10:17; 11:4, 5), in this and subsequent episodes they become objects acted upon (11:32, 33) or talked about (11:36; 12:1-3). Those who "made war against Israel" (11:4) are now "subdued before the people of Israel" (11:33). Warfare has accomplished what words failed to do; it has resolved the opposition between Israel and Ammon that initiated the story.

### III. Reaping the Victory

Yet this scene is not finished. Slaughter begets sacrifice, for the vow of Jephthah must now be redeemed (11:34-39b). Appropriately, the location is Mizpah, the site of both Israel's encampment against the Ammonites and Jephthah's words before the Lord (11:11; perhaps also 11:29). Though once he dwelt in the land of Tob, the outcast-turned-deliverer is now well established in the central city of Gilead. His victory over the Ammonites leads him predictably to the threshold of his own home: "Now Jephthah came to Mizpah, to his home" (11:34). This introductory statement recalls Jephthah's vow, and so it evokes anticipation, even anxiety. What will meet him? The storyteller underscores the answer with the use of the emphatic Hebrew word *hinnēh*, usually rendered "behold," followed directly by the familial subject, "his daughter." We may translate, "Just at that very moment his daughter. . . ." The Hebrew words alone are chilling harbingers of the terror that is to unfold. The next words confirm the horror because they come directly from the vow of Jephthah. He had promised, "Whatsoever comes forth (*yṣ'*) . . . to meet (*qr'*) me" (11:31). Now we are told, "Just at that very moment his daughter came forth (*yṣ'*) to meet (*qr'*) him" (11:34). The ambiguity of Jephthah's vow disappears. His daughter is his sacrifice; she must die for his unfaithfulness. If Jephthah himself suffered for the sins of his parents, how much more shall this child bear because of the machinations of her father. Unfaithfulness reaches into the third generation to bring forth a despicable fruit.

"Just at that very moment his daughter came forth to meet him." Immediately, then, we know, but she does not. "With music (*tuppîm*) and dancing (*mĕḥōlôth*)," she comes forth to celebrate her father's victory. She moves freely, unaware that her joyful initiative seals her death. To those acquainted with the traditions of her people, her appearance and activity are no surprise. Long ago, after Yahweh brought back the water of the sea upon Pharaoh, his horses, and his horsemen, Miriam, the prophet, "took a timbrel in her hand; and all the women went out (*yṣ'*) after her with music (*tuppîm*) and dancing (*mĕḥōlôth*). And Miriam sang to them:

> Sing unto Yahweh, glorious is he!
> The horse and the rider he has hurled into the sea."
> (Exodus 15:19-21)

And centuries later, "when David returned from slaying the Philistines, women came out (*yṣ'*) of all the cities of Israel, singing and dancing (*mĕḥōlôth*) to meet (*qr'*) King Saul with timbrels (*tuppîm*), with songs of joy and instruments of music. And the women sang to one another as they made merry,

> Saul has slain his thousands,
> And David his ten thousands."*
> (1 Samuel 18:6-7)

To such an ancient and noble company of women belongs the daughter of Jephthah, coming out (*yṣ'*) "with timbrels and dances" to meet (*qr'*) her victorious father. Unlike them, however, she comes alone, and no words of a song appear on her lips. This difference accents the terrible irony of an otherwise typical and joyful occasion. Moreover, the narrator stresses the isolation of the child *and* the dilemma of the parent through an extraordinary accumulation of expressions: "She was his one and only child; beside her he had neither son nor daughter" (11:34). Once before in the traditions of Israel such language has occurred with comparable poignancy: "Take your son, your only one (*yĕhîdĕkā*), whom you love, Isaac . . . and offer him as a burnt offering . . ." (Gen 22:2, cf. vv 12, 16). But that utterance by God initiated a divine test of faithfulness; our description by the narrator belongs to a human vow of unfaithfulness about which God has kept silent. Jephthah is not Abraham; distrust, not faith, has singled out his one and only child. Furthermore, the son of promise, child of the mighty patriarch Abraham, had a name: Isaac. He also had a respectable family lineage: a mother named Sarai and a grandfather named Terah (Gen. 11:27, 29). By contrast, this daughter of the mighty warrior Jephthah is nameless. Her father is of illegitimate birth; her mother is never mentioned; her grandmother was a harlot; and her grandfather cannot be identified. Hence, this little girl emerges an isolated figure in the traditions of Israel as well as in this particular story. "She was his one and only child; beside her he had neither son nor daughter." If the narrator's description singles her out for pity, nevertheless, at the same time, it evokes sympathy for Jephthah whose own vow threatens now to destroy his most precious possession. Father and daughter are held together in the ambiguity of tragedy.

In coming forth from the house to meet the victorious warrior, the daughter fulfills the language of her father's vow. The horror of this situation is clear to the audience before the characters themselves confront it. When he does see her, Jephthah rends his clothes (11:35). It is a gesture of despair, grief, and mourning—but for whom? What the narrated words hint, the direct discourse boldly proclaims. Jephthah mourns for himself, not for his daughter. A cry of anguish leaves his lips, "Ah, my daughter!" to be followed, however, by strong words of accusation: "You have brought me low (*kr*'); you ('*at*) have become my calamity ('*kr*)." At the beginning of the first clause in Hebrew, the hiphil infinitive absolute (*hakrēa*') stresses the devastating deed of the daughter; at the beginning of the second clause, the independent pronoun *you* further accents her as the cause of the calamity; and between these two clauses a wordplay on the verb *bring low* and the noun *calamity* underscores yet again the censure placed on her. Altogether, five Hebrew words intensify the condemnation of the child by her father. Some ancient versions include still a third clause: "You have become a stumbling-block for me." Repeatedly, language triumphs; blame overwhelms the victim. At the moment of recognition and disclosure, Jephthah thinks exclusively of himself and indicts his daughter for the predicament. "I" (*'ānōkî*), he continues emphatically, "have opened my mouth to Yahweh, and I cannot turn back."

Faithfulness to an unfaithful vow has condemned its victim; father and daughter are now split apart in deed and destiny. Though in anguish he calls her "my daughter," he offers her neither solace nor release. His words diverge from the compassion of Abraham, who evasively yet faithfully assured Isaac, "God will provide himself the lamb for a burnt offering, my son" (Gen. 22:8). Unlike the father Abraham, Jephthah fails to evoke the freedom of the deity to avert disaster. Nor does he wish to die instead of his child, as did the father David (2 Sam. 19:1). Although his daughter has served him devotedly with music and dance, Jephthah bewails the calamity that she brings upon him. And throughout it all God says nothing.

With courage and determination the daughter answers her father (11:36). Though she is not told the specific content of his vow, the inevitability of his words is sufficient. She does not seek to deny or defy them; nor does she show anger or depression. No sentiment of self-pity passes her lips; instead, she feels for her father the compassion that he has not extended to her. "My father," she begins. Once Isaac uttered the very same word of intimacy (Gen. 22:7), but how different is that language now. Unlike Isaac, this child knows what the father must do, and yet she embraces him with speech. How different also is her address from her father's. "My daughter" yielded recrimination and self-concern; "my father" brings justification and courage. Both responses, however, testify to the inviolability of the vow spoken to the deity (cf. Num. 30:3; Deut. 23:22–24). "I have opened my mouth to Yahweh," said Jephthah, "and cannot turn back." The daughter's reply echoes that understanding:

> You have opened your mouth to Yahweh;
> do to me according to what goes forth from your mouth,
> since Yahweh has done to you deliverance
>     from your enemies, from the Ammonites. (11:36)

The word that has gone forth (*yṣ'*) from his mouth (11:36) has become the daughter who has gone forth (*yṣ'*) from his house (11:34). To her he must do (*'śh*) what he has declared to the Lord, because the Lord has done (*'śh*) for him what he asked.

## IV. Seeking a Respite

The little girl understands well; she holds her father to his vow. She does not pray that this cup pass from her. Nevertheless, hers is not quiet acquiescence. Within the limits of the inevitable she takes charge to bargain for herself. The victim assumes responsibility, not for blame but for integrity. "And she said to her father." This time, however, the narrator, not the daughter, uses the paternal vocabulary. The difference is distance. Having already embraced her father with words, the girl now steps back from the one who is to be her executioner. Her request makes clear this separation: "Let this thing (*dābār*) be done for me," she begins. The verb and its prepositional object play upon her earlier speech. "Do (*'śh*) to me (*lî*)," she had said, because the Lord "has done (*'śh*) to you (*lĕkā*)." First, however, "Let this thing be done (*'śh*) for me (*lî*)."

> Let me alone for two months
> that I may go and wander upon the hills
> and lament my virginity—I and my female friends. (11:37)

The request is for a respite, a time and place apart from her father and his vow. That time is to be filled with lamentation not for death itself but for unfulfilled life.

To be sure, death belongs to life: "We must all die; we are like water spilt on the ground, which cannot be gathered up again"* (2 Samuel 14:14). Nevertheless, this particular death defies all the categories of the natural and the expected. First, it is premature; life ends before its potential has unfolded. If King Hezekiah could weep bitterly that "in the noontide" of his days he must depart (Isaiah 38:3, 10), how much more this child must lament in the morning of her life. Second, her death is to be violent. Death by fire is itself bitter death, and more bitter still when its author is her own father. Third, her death will leave no heirs, because she herself is a virgin child. What alone designated fulfillment for every Hebrew woman, the bearing of children, will never be hers to know (cf. 1 Samuel 1:1–20). Truly, with no child to succeed her, she may be numbered among the unremembered, those "who have perished as though they had not lived" (Ben Sira 44:9). Premature; violent; without an heir: all the marks of unnatural death befall this child, and she is not even spared the knowledge of them. Hers is premeditated death, a sentence of murder passed upon an innocent victim because of the faithless vow uttered by her foolish father. These conditions shroud the request she now makes of her father, "that I may go and wander upon the hills and lament my virginity."

The closing words of her speech, however, introduce a new dimension to the story. Thus far emphasis has fallen upon her isolation. She is "the one and only child"; by herself she greets her father with music and dances; and now she requests that he let her alone for two months. But then she adds, "I (*'ānōkî*) and my female friends." At the time of her deepest sorrow, the very last days of her life, this child reaches out to other women. She chooses them to go with her to wander upon the hills and lament her virginity. Hence, in communion with her own kind, she transcends the distance between herself and her father. After this reference to female friends, the daughter speaks no more. Within the limits of the inevitable she has shaped meaning for herself.

Simply and succinctly the father grants the request (11:38). "Go," he says—his very last word in the story. From now on only the narrator speaks. Adopting the daughter's speech pattern, the storyteller reports the fulfillment of her plan: "He sent her away for two months, and she went, she and her friends, and lamented her virginity upon the hills" (11:38). In the company of other women who acknowledge her tragedy, she is neither alone nor isolated. She spends the last days of her life as she has requested.

## V. Returning to Death—with a Postscript

At the end of two months, the appointed time, the daughter returns to the father (11:39a). Quickly, without passing judgment, the narrator tells the deed: "He did to her his vow which he had vowed." How very different is this story from Abraham's sacrifice of Isaac where detail heaped upon detail slows down the narrative to build suspense for the climactic moment:

> When they came to the place of which God had told them, Abraham built an altar there, and laid the wood in order, and bound Isaac his son, and laid him on the altar, upon the wood. Then Abraham put forth his hand, and took the knife to slay his son.° (Genesis 22:9–10)

That suspense is bearable because Isaac is to be spared. At the last moment, the angel of the Lord negates the divine imperative, "Kill your child," with another command, "Do not lay your hand on the lad or do anything to him"° (Gen. 22:12). But in the story of the daughter of Jephthah, no angel intervenes to save the child. The father carries out the human vow precisely as he spoke it; neither God nor man nor woman negates it. Accordingly, the narrator spares us the suspense and agony of details; the despicable outcome is sufficient unto itself. Five Hebrew words tell the tale: "and-he-did to-her his-vow which he-had-vowed." Though the son was saved, the daughter is slain. Surely, "the victory that day was turned into mourning"° (2 Samuel 19:2).

The verb *do* has now completed its life in this episode. "Do to me," she had said, "according to what goes forth from your mouth, since Yahweh has done to you deliverance" (11:36). Thus, "he did to her his vow which he had vowed" (11:39b). Further, the vocabulary of the vow returns us to the beginning of the entire scene (11:30), thereby interlocking public and private crises in a composition of circularity. A vow led to victory; victory produced a victim; the victim died by violence; violence has, in turn, fulfilled the vow. From beginning to end, this faithless and foolish vow has been the subject; it controls both father and daughter, though in different ways. Moreover, in its presence even the deity to whom it was addressed remains silent.

Death and silence, however, are not the final words of this story. In fact, a narrative postscript (11:39c–40) shifts the meaning altogether from vow to victim; from the father who survives to the daughter who, dying prematurely and violently, has no child to keep her name in remembrance (cf. 2 Samuel 18:18). At the beginning of this postscript, the narrator reemphasizes her barrenness: "Now she had not known a man." The next three words have been translated, almost unanimously through the ages, as, "and it became a custom in Israel"° (11:39c). The verb in this clause is a feminine singular form of *be* or *become*. Since Hebrew itself has no neuter gender, such feminine forms may carry a neuter meaning so that the traditional reading, "it became," is certainly legitimate—but it may not be perceptive. Indeed, grammar, content, and context provide compelling reasons for departing from this translation. After all, the preceding clause has *she* as the subject of its verb: "Now she had not known a man." An independent feminine pronoun (*hî'*) even accents this subject. Accordingly, the feminine grammatical gender of the verb *become* may similarly refer to the daughter herself. Further, the term that is usually designated *custom* (*hōq*) can also mean *tradition*. The resulting translation would be, "She became a tradition in Israel."

In other words, the postscript reports an extraordinary development. Whereas the female who has never known a man, that is to say, the girl who dies childless, is typically numbered among the unremembered, in the case of the daughter of Jephthah, the usual does not happen. "Although *she* had not known a man, nevertheless she became a tradition in Israel." In a dramatic way this sentence alters, though it does not eliminate, the finality of Jephthah's faithless vow. The alteration comes through the faithfulness of the women of Israel, as the next line explains: "From year to year the daughters of Israel went to mourn for the daughter of Jephthah the Gileadite, four days in the year" (11:40). The unnamed virgin child becomes a tradition in Israel because the women with whom she chose to spend her last days have not let her pass into oblivion. They have established a living memorial: activities of mourning reiterated yearly in a special place. The narrative postscript, then, shifts the focus of the story from vow to victim; from death to life; from oblivion to remembrance. Remarkably, this saga of faithlessness and sacrifice mitigates, though it does not dispel, its own tragedy through the mourning of women.

### VI. Exploring the Tradition

"Is it nothing to you, all you who pass by?"° (Lam. 1:12). Sadly, the scriptures of faith have failed to perceive and interpret the nuances of

this story. Throughout centuries the practice of patriarchal hermeneutics has forgotten the daughter of Jephthah but remembered her
father, indeed exalted him. The earliest evidence follows immediately
upon the telling of the tale, when the scene shifts from the private crisis
of sacrifice to a public confrontation between tribes (12:1-6). Challenged by armed Ephraimites, Jephthah leads the Gileadites to a
resounding victory. Hence, the mighty warrior prevails uncensured;
the violence that he perpetrated upon his only daughter stalks him not
at all. In the end he dies a natural death and receives an epitaph fit for
an exemplary judge (12:7). Moreover, his military victories enhance his
name in the years to come. Specifically, the prophet Samuel proclaims
to Israel that "Yahweh sent . . . Jephthah and delivered you out of the
hand of your enemies . . ." (1 Samuel 12:11).

What the Old Testament begins, the Apocrypha continues. In
Sirach's litany of praise for famous men, we infer that Jephthah has a
place among

> The judges also, with their respective names,
>     those whose hearts did not fall into idolatry
> and who did not turn away from the Lord—
>     may their memory be blessed!
> May their bones revive from where they lie,
>     and may the name of those who have been honored
>     live again in their sons!\* (46:11-12)

What the Apocrypha continues, the New Testament concludes triumphantly. In the Epistle to the Hebrews Jephthah is explicitly named
as one "who *through faith* conquered kingdoms, enforced justice, . . .
escaped the edge of the sword, won strength out of weakness, became
mighty in war, put foreign armies to flight"\* (Hebrews 11:32-34, italics
mine). Jephthah is praised; his daughter forgotten. Unfaith becomes
faith. Thus has scripture violated the ancient story, and yet that story
itself endures to this very day for us to recover and appropriate.

Like the daughters of Israel, we remember and mourn the daughter
of Jephthah the Gileadite. In her death we are all diminished; by our
memory she is forever hallowed. Though not a "survivor," she becomes an unmistakable symbol for all the courageous daughters of
faithless fathers. Her story, brief as it is, evokes the imagination, calling
forth a reader's response. Surely words of lament are a seemly offering,
for did not the daughters of Israel *mourn* the daughter of Jephthah
every year? Now the biblical tradition itself provides both a model and
foil for just such an offering: the lament of David for Saul and
Jonathan, for a father and son who died prematurely in the violence of
battle (2 Samuel 1:19-27). Overcome by grief, David cried,

> Thy glory, O Israel, is slain upon thy high places;
> How are the mighty fallen!\*

Using these haunting words as point and counterpoint, let us in the spirit of the daughters of Israel remember and mourn the daughter of Jephthah.

Thy daughter, O Israel, is slain upon thy high places!
   How are the powerless fallen!
Tell it in Ammon,
   publish it in the streets of Rabbah;
for the daughters of the Ammonites will not rejoice;
   the daughters of the enemies will not exult.

Tell it also in Gilead
   publish it in the streets of Mizpah;
for the sons of Israel do forget,
   the sons of the covenant remember not at all.

Ye valleys of Gilead,
   let there be no dew or rain upon you,
   nor upsurging of the deep,
for there the innocence of the powerless was defiled,
   the only daughter of the mighty was offered up.

From the tyranny of the vow,
   from the blood of the sacrifice,
the unnamed child turned not back,
   the courage of the daughter turned not away.

Daughter of Jephthah, beloved and lovely!
   In life and in death a virgin child,
greeting her father with music and dances,
   facing his blame with clarity and strength.

Ye daughters of Israel, weep for your sister,
   who suffered the betrayal of her foolish father,
   who turned to you for solace and love.

How are the powerless fallen
   in the midst of the victory!

The daughter of Jephthah lies slain upon thy high places.
I weep for you, my little sister.
Very poignant is your story to me;
   your courage to me is wonderful,
   surpassing the courage of men.

How are the powerless fallen
   a terrible sacrifice to a faithless vow!

*Bibliographical Note*

An expanded version of this study, with full documentation, appeared as "A Meditation in Mourning," *Union Seminary Quarterly Review* 36 (1981), pp. 59–73. For further discussion of the feminist perspective in this article, see Trible, *God and the Rhetoric of Sexuality* (Philadelphia: Fortress, 1978), and Trible's article on "Woman in the Old Testament" in *The Interpreter's Dictionary of the Bible*, edited by Keith Crim et al. (Nashville: Abingdon, 1976), pp. 963–66, as well as "Feminist Hermeneutics and Biblical Studies," *The Christian Century* (3–10 February 1982).

KATHARINE DOOB SAKENFELD


# LOYALTY AND LOVE: THE LANGUAGE OF HUMAN INTERCONNECTIONS IN THE HEBREW BIBLE


The path of translation from one language to another winds cir-cuitously and is full of dangers. Those who dare upon it sometimes find themselves fleeing a lion, only to be met by a bear. Hazards known and unknown challenge each step toward the goal. How should any given sentence be translated? Dictionaries offer so many options for each word that a knowledge of grammar simply does not suffice to insure reliable results. Idioms unfamiliar to the translator, constructions or word usage which deliberately violate the norm to achieve an effect, special connotations of ordinary words, all conspire to challenge the translator. And a translator's slip at any of these danger spots serves eventually to confuse or mislead the reader. Especially vexing to the translator are those cases in which a word in the original text represents a concept for which there is no equivalent in the translation language (and yet some word must be chosen); equally problematic are cases in which the original language word has an accepted standard translation, but at times carries a connotation or valence which would never occur to the reader of the translation language. A major gap between the cultures of the two languages may greatly compound the difficulty of translation in such cases.

This essay first discusses the methodology used by scholars in ascer-taining the meaning of the vocabulary of human interconnections in the Hebrew Bible. A section sketching issues in kingship and family structure in Hebrew culture is followed by illustrations from two famous relationships: David and Jonathan, and Naomi and Ruth. The story of each of these pairs incorporates two words illustrating the problem cases identified above: (a) the Hebrew noun *hesed*, often translated "loyalty" but not properly equivalent to any English con-cept, and (b) the Hebrew verb *'āhēb*, almost always translated "to love" but often carrying connotations surprising to and unexpected by the English reader. We will see how understanding the words con-tributes to our appreciation of the stories, as well as how careful reading of the stories can help our recognition of special nuances in this vocabulary of human interconnection.

## I. Methodology

In seeking for the meaning of a word in the ancient biblical text, we have no native speakers to consult. Modern Hebrew differs markedly in syntax, vocabulary, and idiomatic usage from its ancient counterpart. Furthermore, the biblical text which is preserved constitutes a relatively limited corpus; perhaps half of the words are used as few as five times, and many words appear only once. The material took written form over a period of roughly eight hundred years; even a language which evolves slowly changes considerably over such a span. And in many instances the actual "reading" (the proper consonants) of the text is not certain. Normal kinds of scribal errors contribute to such uncertainty, as do the changes in spelling practices, word nuances, or grammatical constructions which may have caused an ancient scribe to "correct" a seeming "mistake" in the copying process, thus altering a more ancient reading. It should be noted as well that a full system of written vowels was added to the Hebrew consonantal text only after about the fifth century C.E. This system thus reflects the pronunciation tradition some six centuries after the last of the texts had been composed.

How do biblical scholars proceed in the face of these difficulties? Here we cannot examine the larger debates among linguistic theorists concerning the development and comprehension of language. We will simply outline the principal clues which scholars use in attempting to get at the meaning of the text. A first line of approach is the examination of ancient translations of the text, especially the Septuagint (Greek) translation tradition, but also other languages of the ancient world into which the Bible was translated (e.g., Latin, Syriac, Coptic). These ancient translations provide some indication of how a word or sentence was understood at the time the translation was made, so long as it appears clear that the translator worked directly from the Hebrew and that the phrase in question in that original Hebrew was the same as that preserved for us.

A second clue to interpretation lies in the study of literary remains from the ancient Near East, especially from other Semitic languages with cognate vocabulary. Ugaritic (a Canaanite dialect from the Syrian coast), Aramaic, and Akkadian sources are especially useful here. These languages (and others in the Semitic family) exhibit an interlocking pattern of consonant usage, so that it is possible to compare the meaning of a single "root" through the various languages. This procedure must be used with some caution, since the meaning of a given root may have developed very differently in the cognate languages; still, comparison suggests options for our evaluation. Comparative material also can function more generally through examination of the usage of translational equivalents and idiomatic expressions, even where vocabulary is not strictly cognate.

Any such comparative linguistic aids must be used only in conjunction with careful study of the pertinent biblical materials themselves. Relevant passages need to be assessed by subcategories such as date, author, idiomatic expression, and secular versus religious intention, in order to avoid misleading generalization. While each sentence, each passage, may have its own special nuance, grouping those which are relatively similar provides clues to meaning. A study of related nouns, verbs, and adjectives built upon a single root is often undertaken, as well as some effort to distinguish nuances between synonyms.

The study of the language of human interconnections requires more than the study of the general vocabulary of human interaction. It must include also an understanding of the basic social institutions of a society. The terms for king or judge or wife or husband or slave may be quite clear as individual vocabulary words, but the pattern of human interconnections involved in the institutions of kingship or marriage or slavery will vary greatly across time and cultures. Here the text of the Bible provides the primary resource, with appropriate recognition of cultural change over the long history of its composition. The text must be used with some caution, however. First of all, the authors' purposes did not usually include informing us about such sociological subjects. Much that is institutional is presumed and must therefore be inferred. Moreover, the Bible tends to preserve narratives about unusual situations, exceptional people, and the elite classes of society; thus one cannot casually assume that the stories typify the structure and life of the society as a whole. The legislative material can occasionally be helpful, but what has been preserved is scattered, incomplete, not reliably datable, and perhaps not always reflective of actual practice.

For further guidance in describing the biblical culture, scholars again turn to the use of extra-biblical evidence. The materials adduced range from second millennium B.C.E. texts of Mesopotamian, Egyptian, and Hittite cultures to nineteenth-century Bedouin practices catalogued by soldiers, explorers, and missionaries, to broadly typical characteristics of pre-industrial peasant societies developed by macro-sociologists. Given the breadth and diversity of this material, it is little wonder that consensus has not been reached and that research continues. The reliability of analogies drawn from such comparative material must be assessed by general category and also by detailed case-by-case consideration of the specific evidence.

The preceding review of methodology, deliberately cautious and even skeptical in tone, is not intended to suggest that we cannot know anything about human interconnections in ancient Israel. Rather, the reader is invited by this review to appreciate the complexity of our investigations, the tentative character of our conclusions, and the caution with which popular handbooks on "life in Bible times" should be used.

## II. Social Organization: Kingship and Family

The institution of kingship was the longest-lived political structure of ancient Israel's life in the land, and it remains the best attested. Before the era of Saul and David (ca. 1000 B.C.E.) the people were organized tribally and governed by some combination of elders, itinerant "judges," and charismatic military leaders. Scholars continue to debate both the extent to which Israel was unified in this premonarchical period and also the role of religious faith and practice in whatever unity existed. After four centuries of kingship, the institution came to an end (in practice if not as an ideal) with the destruction of Jerusalem and the First Temple by Nebuchadrezzar of Babylon (587 B.C.E.); after that time Judah and Samaria were provinces in a series of empires. The religion of Judaism continued but political autonomy was never restored.

The Bible offers diverse sources for understanding Israel's theory of kingship and its actual practice. The histories recorded in Samuel-Kings and in Chronicles narrate those four centuries from particular theological perspectives, and these can be supplemented by materials from the psalmody of the Jerusalem temple and from the comments of various prophets about kingship. From the time of David onward, kingship was basically conceived of as a hereditary dynasty, with a son succeeding his father. The king, unlike the Pharaohs of Egypt, was never viewed as divine. Nevertheless, as in Mesopotamia, the king was understood to be the channel for God's blessing upon the people: both the fruits of nature (critical against famine in a subsistence agricultural economy) and the basics of societal justice were associated with the reign of the king (see, for example, Psalm 72). It is interesting to note that although various kings promoted administrative or judicial reforms, not one is recorded to have promulgated a law code. According to biblical tradition, all law was given by God to the people at Mt. Sinai, long before the era of kingship. While we cannot argue from silence that no king attempted to codify ancient case precedents, the theological symbolism of the tradition is clear: every king was subject to the will of God, which was for justice in the whole community. The king was not "above the law."

Once the kingdom divided (after Solomon, ca. 922 B.C.E.), however, the separate kingdoms of Israel in the north and Judah in the south appear to have held different conceptions of dynastic succession, related to different conceptions of the relationship between obedience and the right to rule. Both retained the father-son hereditary pattern, but under different assumptions. In Judah there emerged the theology of God's everlasting and irrevocable choice of the Davidic line; no matter what crimes (apostasy or injustice to subjects) an individual king might commit, the line would continue (see, for example, Psalm 89). In the north, by contrast, the Book of Kings suggests that dynastic preservation was viewed as contingent upon the obedience of each ruler to God's will, especially in the matter of exclusive worship of the LORD, but also in matters of community justice. Prophets arose to proclaim in God's name the end of one dynasty and the establishment of its replacement. The tradition of prophet as kingmaker and king-breaker which had its roots in the era of Samuel and Saul (see 1 Samuel 10, 15, 16) was thus preserved in the north.

Both the extended kinship categories of clan and tribe and also the more immediate family unit of parents, children, and close relatives have recently received fresh attention. Our focus here is upon the smaller unit and particularly upon marriage customs as background for the story of Ruth and her mother-in-law Naomi. The rise of feminist concerns in the United States has evoked interest in the influence of biblical tradition on western values and practices in marriage and family life; curiosity about family life and the role and status of women generally in ancient Israel has accompanied this interest. Here we may only paint the picture of Israelite marriage in broadest strokes, descriptively and without value judgment.

A general picture is necessitated not only by limitations of space, but also because it is not possible to create a single or comprehensive picture from the biblical evidence. The legislative material gives but a sampling of case decisions; the inconsistencies in detail among various biblical laws probably point to an even greater inconsistency in practice over time and in different regions. Narrative materials are likewise variable. Thus there are some stories (e.g., Jacob, Samson) which have been taken as indicators of matriarchal marriage; but most scholars would regard these as doubtful (or at best vestigial or exceptional) examples in an overwhelmingly patriarchal marriage and family structure.

Although polygamy was not forbidden (and is presumed in the legislation of Deuteronomy 21:15-17), monogamy existed as well and may have been more typical practice. It is not certain exactly how marriages were arranged, but it is clear that the husband and father was head of the household, with sons probably regarded as more important than the wife. The mother was responsible for the nurture of small children; in a village agricultural economy women would participate along with the men in food production, probably with traditionally assigned tasks. The well-known portrait of the "ideal wife" in Proverbs 31 must be regarded as atypical in that it presumes an elite and wealthy household (probably within the top five percent of the socio-economic structure).

Evidence concerning divorce is scanty. Divorce appears usually to have been permitted at the husband's initiative, but the allowable grounds are unclear and became the subject of later rabbinic disagreements. Within the patriarchal structure the divorced woman would be left without real status, a burden to her own father's household if indeed she could return there. Instances of divorce are rare in the preserved materials, however.

Probably the more likely calamity to befall a woman of ancient Israel was the death of her husband; and especially disastrous would be his premature death before the birth of male offspring. The Bible's oft-reiterated special concern of God and obligation of the community to care for widows and orphans reflects a traditional motif of ancient Near Eastern culture, but it also reflects realistically the dire straits in which a widow probably found herself, particularly if there were no sons through whom a claim to (agricultural) land or property could be established.

The custom of "levirate" marriage, wherein a brother of the deceased husband, or a more distant male relative, was called upon to marry the widow, was one mode of Israel's response to this problem. Known also in the cultures of some of Israel's neighbors, the practice seems to have had three interrelated functions: to care for the widow, to keep property within the family, and to carry forward the name and lineage of the deceased husband through a son born to his widow. When we turn to the story of Ruth, we will see that care for the widow looms large in the understanding of the terms loyalty and love.

## III. Loyalty and Love

### A. *David and Jonathan*

In much of Judeo-Christian culture the paired names David and Jonathan evoke the image of strong friendship between two men, even though the details of the story may be vague to the hearer. Recorded in 1 Samuel, especially in chapters 18-23, their story is one of a personal bond in the midst of agonizing pressures to split them apart. Son-in-law and son to King Saul, they must contend with Saul's inconsistent but eventually murderous intentions toward David. Jonathan struggles with the tension between allegiance to his father and to his friend and brother-in-law. He aids David's escape from Saul but eventually dies alongside his father. The complexity of this personal dimension is compounded by the issue of royal succession. Is Jonathan as Saul's son the legitimate heir, as Saul and a typical notion of hereditary dynasty would suppose? Or is David the legitimate successor? The author of the narrative believes in and argues for David's legitimacy; the story of David and Jonathan is a part of his case.

The history of the development of the 1 Samuel narrative is complicated, to say the least. Probably there were at least three "stages:" a first period when small sections concerning the ark of the covenant, King Saul, and David were circulating separately; a second stage in which these three components were combined and expanded to provide an early theological defense of David's legitimate rule over all Israel, both north and south (perhaps composed during David's own reign); and a third stage in which this longer material was incorporated into the great work of the Deuteronomic Historian, our present books of Deuteronomy-Joshua-Judges-Samuel-Kings (quite likely during the reign of King Josiah, ca. 620 B.C.E.).

The story line of 1 Samuel has been analyzed in two main ways. One perspective, taking its cue from the historical development outlined above, sees a first main section (chaps. 1-7) dealing with the emergence of the prophet Samuel as a major force, a second part (chaps. 8-15) focusing on the beginning of kingship and the immediate complications occasioned by Saul's act of disobedience and God's rejection of him, and a third section (chaps. 16ff.) relating David's rise to power as a replacement for the rejected Saul. An alternative outline places the major break of the book not at chap. 15 but rather at chap. 12, in which Samuel addresses the people concerning the requirement for obedience even within the structure of kingship. But even on this outline, chaps. 13-15 (recording Saul's disobedience and rejection) would appear to function as a preface to the anointing of David as king-to-be in chap. 16, the event which sets in motion the story of David's rise.

The David and Jonathan material which concerns us falls within this last section of the book. The narrative includes five scenes in which David and Jonathan meet: 18:1-5; 19:1-7; two in 20:1-42; 23:15-18. The vocabulary in which we are focally interested occurs in chaps. 18 and 20; but the materials of 19 and 23 provide narrative clues for understanding the key words, to which we now turn.

The term *hesed* has proved notoriously difficult to translate, with the English options proposed ranging from "duty" to "mercy." Although in this essay we have opted for the translation "loyalty," it must be noted that *hesed* is regularly used as object of the verb "to do"; hence the focus is on an *act* of *hesed* or loyalty. The objective here is not to defend the choice of a particular English word—which is at best only an approximation—but rather to open up to the reader the nuances of the Hebrew term.

In the case of this particular word the Greek and other versions are not of much help for interpreting the Hebrew. The Greek most often uses "mercy," but seems to reflect a post-exilic nuancing of the Hebrew word. The Syriac uses "goodness," which is too general to be useful. Nor is there help to be gained from the cognate Semitic languages. The usual meaning of this triliteral formation in Targumic Aramaic and Syriac has to do with something "shameful" or "disgraceful"—clearly not pertinent to an interpretation of the main Hebrew usage. The word is not found in any ancient extra-biblical texts of the biblical period or earlier. Thus we must rely principally upon the biblical material itself.

An examination of all secular uses of the term (that is, those not in explicitly religious or theological settings) in prose narrative turns up no significant variations by period or author within pre-exilic times. The situations and relationships in the stories in which the term appears can be classified into two main types. On the one hand, there are cases in which no basis is stated for the doing of an act of *hesed*. There exists a close personal relationship between the parties involved in the request for an act of *hesed*, but the relationship between the parties is never cited in the dialogue; the existence of the relationship is presumed as the basis for the responsibility of one party to undertake loyal action for the other. Examples include the relationship of husband and wife (Abraham and Sarah, Genesis 20:13), king and adviser (David and Hushai, 2 Samuel 16:17), kinsmen (Abraham and Laban, Genesis 24:49), and father and son (Jacob and Joseph, Genesis 47:29).

In the second group of cases, the doing of an act of *hesed* is explicitly tied to the mention of some prior action taken by the party now requesting *hesed*. Here the relationship between the parties is much more tenuous and may even be adversarial; thus it seems important to demonstrate that the relationship between the parties is in good repair. Examples include two men in prison (Joseph and the Cupbearer, Genesis 40:14), two kings (Ahab and Ben-Hadad, 1 Kings 20:31), spies and a resident of the city under their scrutiny (Joshua 2:12-14; Judges 1:24).

Although the narrative examples fall into these two general types, they have as a set a series of features in common. First of all, *hesed* is always requested and carried out within the context of some publicly identifiable relationship. It is an act of loyalty to the other party in the relationship, and it is generally an action or series of actions, not merely an abstract attitude or verbal promise of loyalty. The situation in which an act of *hesed* is requested is not a casual one, however. Examination of the stories reveals these features: (1) Individuals requesting an act of loyalty are unable to fulfill their need on their own. The obstacle may be death, human frailty, or political exigency—but the request is not optional. (2) The action requested is genuinely necessary to the person in need: descendants, homeland, life itself are at stake. (3) The need is such that there is one, and only one, person conspicuously able to provide the needed assistance. No one else can replace that person, given the circumstances. (4) As a consequence of the first three features, the person in need is not in a position to exercise any control or compulsion over the person to whom the request for *hesed* is made. Thus the person who is asked to perform the act of loyalty is completely in control of the situation; that person is "situationally superior" to the other, regardless of who is superior/inferior within the everyday relationship of the parties involved.

Against the backdrop of this general interpretation of the word, we turn to its use in the David and Jonathan story. In 1 Samuel 20:8a David requests *hesed* of Jonathan on the basis of the covenant established between the two of them (as reported in 18:3). Protection of David from Saul is obviously the central concern here. Essentially Jonathan's act of *hesed* will consist in making excuses for David's absence, developing a ruse for discovering Saul's intentions, and then by another ruse letting David know what to do. A relationship, a situation impossible to handle on one's own, a matter of life and death, a person uniquely capable of filling the need—all are characteristic of this occasion. The single Hebrew word powerfully evokes all the facets of David's need and Jonathan's freedom.

But the narrator continues in a remarkable vein. In the very next paragraph, in the course of the same encounter and before Jonathan undertakes his action to aid David, we find the roles reversed, with Jonathan asking David for *hesed* (20:14-15). One must begin by observing that the Hebrew text of vv 11-17, and especially vv 14-15, is extraordinarily difficult. Translators are forced to resort to numerous emendations in order to work from a grammatical and sequentially coherent text. Nonetheless the broad outlines of this unusual situation appear reasonably clear. Jonathan's comments presume that David will be the next king (espcially in v 13b: "And may the LORD be with you as he was with my father"). Jonathan requests that David always deal loyally with him or, if he dies, with his household. This vague request seems mysterious until we recognize that it functions as the narrator's anticipation of a specific action (recorded in 2 Samuel 9) which David undertakes as king, after the death of Jonathan. There we read that David, desiring to do *hesed* for the houshold of Saul for Jonathan's sake, seeks out Jonathan's crippled son Meribaal (or Mephibosheth) living in a sort of exile in Transjordan, and offers him his ancestral family land and a "place at the king's table." Whatever political motives may have lain behind such an invitation, the narrator uses it to bring full circle the story of the relationship between Jonathan and David. In death and in change of dynasty they are not separated.

Remarkably and yet appropriately, the David and Jonathan narrative does not fit neatly into either of the two types of *hesed* relationships outlined above. Theirs is presented to us as an intimate personal friendship. Jonathan was "bound up with David" (18:1); they wept together (20:41). And yet we are told repeatedly of a "covenant" or treaty between them (18:3; 20:8; 20:16 [though the Hebrew here is probably corrupt]; 23:18)—a term which regularly carried political rather than personal overtones. And this covenant which Jonathan initiated is referred to as the explicit basis for David's request for *hesed*. This combination of personal friendship and political allegiance allows Jonathan to function as a bridge figure in David's rise to kingship. In 18:4 we read that Jonathan gave his own robe and armor to David; many interpret this action as a proleptic recognition of David's eventual kingship, which Jonathan implies again in 20:13 and states explicitly in 23:17. And yet one would expect Jonathan to be his father's successor, as Saul himself urges in 20:31. Since Saul was Israel's first king, no principle of succession had been established. It has been proposed that David was regarded as a legitimate successor under a principle which passed the rule to a son-in-law rather than to a blood son. While this theory might explain why Jonathan assumes David will succeed Saul, two other explanations are equally plausible. The handing over of clothing may symbolize Jonathan's voluntary giving up of his hereditary right. Moreover, from the narrator's theological perspective it is obvious that God has chosen David (1 Samuel 16) when the prophet Samuel anoints him. And even if the anointing was done in secret, Samuel has already explicitly and publicly announced God's rejection of Saul and his line (1 Samuel 15). It is the reality of God's choice of David over Saul (and hence over Jonathan) which the entire story of David's rise is intended to demonstrate. Jonathan's support of David would be the most powerful argument against any remaining supporters of a Saulide dynasty after the death of Jonathan. Thus Jonathan's recognition and support of his friend and political ally are pivotal in the narrative, for even Saul's "logical" heir does not share his father's desire to destroy David. In fact, Jonathan even contributes to David's rise—by his act of *hesed* in preserving David alive. David's act of *hesed* after Jonathan's death confirms the mutuality of their personal and political ties and again makes clear that David gained and held the throne by the will of God rather than by destroying Saul's line.

The verb *'āhēb*, "to love" appears eight times in the story of David's rise (1 Sam 16:21; 18:1, 3, 16, 20, 22, 28; 20:17) and again in David's beautiful poetic lament over the death of Saul and Jonathan (2 Sam 1:26). In every one of these texts except 1 Sam 20:17, it is David who is loved by someone else; and there are excellent textual reasons for preferring the Septuagint version of 20:17 which makes Jonathan the subject and David the object of the verb *'āhēb* in this instance as well. David is said to be loved by Saul (16:21), by Saul's servants (18:22), by Saul's daughter Michal (18:20), by all Israel and Judah (18:16), by all Israel (18:28, following the Septuagint), and of course by Jonathan (18:1, 3; 20:17; 2 Sam 1:26). David's love for Jonathan (or for anyone else) is not explicitly mentioned.

The usual English meaning of the word "love" (e.g., Webster's "A

feeling of strong personal attachment induced by sympathetic understanding, or by ties of kinship; ardent affection") satisfies the intention
of *'āhēb* in most of its biblical occurrences. In the story of David,
however, one may suspect that more is at stake. The question is raised
by the one-sidedness of the usage even with Jonathan, the extension of
the term to all Israel and Judah as a group who could know David only
by reputation, and the statement that Michal loved David before she
even met him personally. The word must be extended at least to
include admiration for, perhaps captivation by, David's good appearance, his musical ability, and his military prowess against the Philistine
giant.

There is good evidence, however, for yet another level of meaning
for the word in this story. William Moran has demonstrated that in
extra-biblical sources ranging from the early second millennium down
to seventh century B.C.E., the translational equivalent of *'āhēb*
(Akkadian *ra'āmu*) appears in political and treaty contexts in the
meaning "to recognize, to show loyalty to." The word belongs as much
to the area of diplomacy as to that of personal relationships. As we
view the David-Jonathan texts with this extra-biblical usage in mind,
we can readily see that the verb *'āhēb* carries the same double notion of
personal relationship and political commitment which was characteristic of the use of the term *hesed* in this narrative.

1 Sam 18:1–3 reports that "Jonathan loved David as he loved himself
. . . and made a covenant with him because he loved him as himself,"
after which Jonathan bestowed his clothing and armor upon David.
The rest of the chapter seems intended in part to show how everyone
else except Saul (who "loved" David at 16:21 but is now "his enemy,"
18:29) followed Jonathan's lead. Then in 1 Sam 20:17 (reading with the
Septuagint) Jonathan swears to help David know Saul's plan, swearing
"by his [Jonathan's] love for him [David], because he [Jonathan] loved
him as he loved himself." Political overtones of loyalty and formal
recognition are suggested for the use of *'āhēb* here by the association
with the term "covenant" in 18:3 (referred to also in 20:8 and 23:18; see
above). The seemingly personal phrase "as he loved himself" which
appears in both of these passages may further confirm this political
nuance, for Michael Fishbane has pointed out a striking parallel to this
expression in an extra-biblical treaty context. The key role of Jonathan
in the narrator's legitimation of David as Saul's successor is apparent
here as it was in our discussion of *hesed*. Jonathan and David have a
relationship of deep personal affection; but Jonathan goes further and
offers David political loyalty as well, recognizing him as the future
king. David flees after Jonathan confirms Saul's intention to kill him,
and the two men meet secretly just once more (chap. 23), reiterating
their covenant, before Saul and Jonathan die in a battle against the
Philistines.

In David's elegy he says of Jonathan, "Your love to me was wonderful, passing the love of women" (2 Sam 1:26). In these lyrics the poignancy of the personal affection between the two men seems to come to the fore. We are reminded of the tearful embrace and the clandestine rendezvous. But that affection cannot be divorced from its context, Jonathan's casting of his political lot with David rather than seeking his own glory.

(There have been arguments advanced for the possibility of a homosexual relationship between David and Jonathan. The text comparing Jonathan's love to the love of women and the references to physical affection are key elements of the discussion. As the preceding paragraphs indicate, however, the present writer interprets the themes of love, loyalty, and covenant in quite a different direction.)

In summary, we have seen that the several references to Jonathan's love (*'āhēb*) for David express not only personal affection and deep admiration but also a political statement crucial to David's rise to kingship. This political statement is one key to the narrator's demonstration of how God's will (known in the prophet Samuel's rejection of Saul and anointing of David) comes to fruition in the course of historical events. Just as Jonathan's act of *hesed* preserves David's life, so his love for David demonstrates his support for David as successor to Saul. At the same time the act of loyalty (*hesed*) which David performs for Jonathan after his death serves to highlight the strength of their mutual relationship, a bond of responsibility which is able to take risks and which persists even beyond the grave.

## B. *Ruth and Naomi*

Our presentation of the themes of loyalty and love in the story of Ruth and Naomi can be much briefer, since much of the groundwork for understanding the terms has been laid in the preceding section. We may begin with a review of the story line. Naomi accompanies her husband and sons from their home in Bethlehem to the foreign country of Moab, where the sons marry Moabite women, Ruth and Orpah. The death of all three men creates a crisis. Orpah returns to her family; Naomi and Ruth go back to Bethlehem. Ruth goes to glean in the fields, and meets Boaz, who is a kinsman of Naomi's. Initiative by the women eventually results in Boaz's marriage to Ruth under the levirate law treated above. A son is born to them, Obed, the grandfather of King David.

But the power of this exquisitely crafted little narrative (only four chapters) lies in the detailed nuances of the telling more than in the story line itself. The three appearances of the term *hesed* and the single use of *'āhēb* give some clues to the relationships among these women in crisis.

The first use of the word *hesed* comes in 1:8, as the two daughters-in-law are starting to Bethlehem with Naomi. Naomi urges them to return home and says, "May the LORD do *hesed* with you, as you did with the dead and with me." Here we encounter God as the one who is called upon to act loyally. This frequent usage extends the secular connotations of the term to the theological realm. God is called upon to fulfill a significant need which cannot be provided through any usual human agency. The freedom of God and the dependence of the petitioner are lifted up together in such a request for the *hesed* of God. Naomi's particular expression appears to belong to a special "benedictory" category in which the *hesed* of God is invoked as a way of concluding a relationship (cf. 2 Samuel 2:6; 15:20). Ruth and Orpah have shown their care for Naomi in starting out on the journey with her. Now Naomi's words do more than commit the women to God's keeping; she signifies her intent to free them of responsibility to her. They are to remarry—to establish a different family bond, a different personal relationship. If they follow her, she says, they cannot really do any good for themselves or for her, for the levirate duty cannot be fulfilled. And so it is that Orpah does what is reasonable and expected. Ruth's insistence upon accompanying Naomi is remarkable and foolhardy. As Phyllis Trible puts it, "One female has chosen another female in a world where life depends upon men. There is no more radical decision in all the memories of Israel."

The second occurrence of *hesed* in the narrative (2:20) most likely refers also to the *hesed* of God, although the Hebrew is ambiguous. Ruth returns from gleaning and informs Naomi she has been in the field of Boaz. While the narrator has informed the readers of Boaz' relationship of kin to Naomi (2:1), Ruth does not know it, and (for reasons unknown to us) Naomi has either forgotten or discounted Boaz and the relationship as a source of assistance. At this word from Ruth, however, Naomi bursts into praise of God and blessing of Boaz: "Blessed be he by the LORD who has not abandoned his *hesed* with the living or with the dead." Ruth's choice of a field for gleaning, which had appeared to be by chance, was really a part of the hidden *hesed* of God. Through God's bringing Ruth into contact with Boaz, the way is opened for the protection and sustaining of the widows and for the continuation of the family line. But although the *hesed* is God's act, the agency of fulfillment will be Boaz and Ruth, both of whom will act "loyally" within the familial structure, even though quite free to do otherwise.

The perceptive reader will have observed the characteristics of an act of *hesed* in Ruth's decision to accompany Naomi to Bethlehem. And this reality is recognized in the final use of the word in the narrative. Having heard that Boaz was kind to Ruth, the once despairing Naomi is galvanized to develop a daring plan which Ruth carries forward. Ruth arranges to encounter Boaz as he sleeps at the threshing floor. But rather than simply offer herself to him sexually, she challenges him explicitly to carry out his levirate responsibility as one who is "next of kin." Boaz replies, "May you be blessed by the LORD, my daughter. You have made your latter act of *hesed* better than the former, in that you have not gone after the younger men, whether poor or rich" (3:10). The "former" act of *hesed* is surely Ruth's loyalty to Naomi, witnessed by her very presence with her mother-in-law in Bethlehem. The "latter" act consists in approaching the older Boaz so that the interests of Naomi and the deceased father-in-law and husband are held central. And Boaz willingly agrees to meet the responsibility Ruth lays before him, as the narrator shows us Ruth's *hesed* to Naomi coming to fruition.

The word *'āhēb* appears just once in the Book of Ruth, at the very conclusion of the story. A son is born to Ruth and the women gather around grandmother Naomi to rejoice. They bless God, who has not left Naomi without a redeemer. In a delightful ambiguity of Hebrew pronouns, the celebration of the LORD and of the new child are joined together as restorer of life and sustainer in old age. And the women conclude, "for your daughter-in-law who loves (*'āhēb*) you has borne him, and she means more to you than seven sons" (4:15).

Here by contrast to the David and Jonathan story, there are no political connotations to the term *'āhēb*. The setting is strictly familial. But here, as there, the story itself illustrates what love is all about. It involves the kind of bond which calls forth acts of *hesed*, the kind of bond which is willing to fulfill the other's need without regard for repayment or public recognition or personal convenience. Such love from a daughter-in-law is more precious than the traditional love from one's own son—indeed, even from seven sons.

In the lives of two women, as in the lives of two men, love enables radical decisions, acts of loyalty which break with established convention and everyday expectations. The describing of such love in the *men*'s story as "passing the love of *women*" (2 Samuel 1:26), and in the *women*'s story as "more than the love of *sons*" (Ruth 4:15), should be held in tandem. One set in a lament in time of death, the other set in a rejoicing in time of new life, both expressions appear in lyrical contexts and may be traditional metaphors. But they point us to what is quite untraditional about each of the stories they summarize. The acts of loyalty done here may lie within the realm of the ideally expected from a moral point of view. But they go far beyond what most people actually expect in everyday life, thus giving us some picture of what a "really real" life might be like. And so it is that David and the women around Naomi must push beyond the conventional imagery for love—

wife to husband, son to mother—good as these are, to express the depth of the relationships portrayed in these narratives. The scholars' labors unravel the connotations of the vocabulary of human inter-connections. But it is the narrators' art which finally gives the words their power.

*Bibliographical Note*

The interpretation of the term *'āhēb* (love) developed here is especially indebted to two essays which are suggested for further reading: William L. Moran, "The Ancient Near Eastern Background of the Love of God in Deuteronomy," *Catholic Biblical Quarterly* 25 (1963) 77-87; and J. A. Thompson, "The Significance of the Verb *Love* in the David-Jonathan Narratives in 1 Samuel," *Vetus Testamentum* 24 (1974) 334-38. The discussion of *hesed* (loyalty) is developed in greater detail in Sakenfeld, *The Meaning of Ḥesed in the Hebrew Bible*, Harvard Semitic Monographs 17 (Missoula: Scholars Press, 1978). See also M. Fishbane, "The Treaty Background of Amos 1:11 and Related Matters," *Journal of Biblical Literature* 89 (1970) 314.

For further reading in the complex textual and historical issues of 1 Samuel, the reader is referred especially to the recent commentary by P. Kyle McCarter, Jr. in the Anchor Bible series (Garden City: Doubleday, 1978). For further reading on the literary, cultural, and theological issues in the Book of Ruth, see the commentary by Edward F. Campbell, Jr. in the Anchor Bible series (Garden City: Doubleday, 1975), and Phyllis Trible, *God and The Rhetoric of Sexuality* (Philadelphia: Fortress, 1978).

MICHAEL PATRICK O'CONNOR

# UGARIT AND THE BIBLE

Poetry does not in general hide itself, and yet it seems poetry does hide itself in the Hebrew Bible. In the text as it is written in Hebrew, little of the poetry betrays itself; in the Authorized (or King James) Version, none of it is set off. There are a few relevant verbal signs in the text, references to singing or lamenting or "lifting up" a parable, but these are not infallible markers of poetry. Yet in modern editions and translations, there is a great deal of poetry set off.

*hiddenness of poetry in Bible*

There are three ways to approach the apparent hiddenness of poetry in the Hebrew Bible (the poetry of Christian scripture presents altogether different problems). We can read it as it hides itself, that is, we can read the Bible as a seamless whole, seeking not to apply pressure at the boundaries between various genres of writing. This is how the bulk of Christian and Jewish tradition has read the text; this is the believer's as well as the theologian's reading. Northrop Frye contends that it is also the poet's reading, and he has attempted to capture the essence of that reading in *The Great Code: The Bible and Literature* (1982). Such a reading cannot, as Frye allows, be pure. Job has always been read, for example, as a text of a different sort than Isaiah, a fact reflected as much in the exclusion of Job from the traditional Roman Catholic liturgy as in William Blake's devotion to it.

(1)

Another approach to the hiddenness of Hebrew verse is keyed to its issue; poems beget poems, and one way of recognizing the poems of the Bible is to look for their offspring in other poems. If we were to begin with the language of the Bible itself, we would need to grasp the complexities of Hebrew's long history. T. Carmi, an American-born Israeli poet, has marshalled the appropriate resources in *The Penguin Book of Hebrew Verse* (1981), a bilingual volume which is yet the only anthology which samples *all* of Hebrew verse. As we read through the six hundred pages of Carmi's anthology, we can see the poetry of the Bible as Hebrew poets have read it. The same task could be carried out for other languages, due allowance being made.

(2)

There is a third approach, one which has yielded the editions and translations I mentioned earlier. If, for example, we open the third and last volume of the new Jewish Publication Society translation of the Hebrew Bible, *The Writings* (1982), we find that, in contrast to the corresponding portions of the Authorized Version, nearly two-thirds of the pages are presented as verse. The recognition involved here is due

(3)

in large part to the northern European poets of the eighteenth and nineteenth centuries who stimulated the philological study of Hebrew verse. One of the great developments in the recent course of that study was the discovery of Ugarit over fifty years ago, and it is the character of Ugaritic studies that I am concerned with here. We will not confront the hiddenness of Hebrew poetry directly; rather we will examine a major resource in the confrontation. The literature of ancient Ugarit must be taken on its own terms, and thus our exposition will not adhere to a strictly biblical agenda.

*philol.*
*defined*

   Philology involves acts of compilation and editing, commentary and annotation, translation and glossing; none of these acts is particularly accessible. In seeking to expose one realm of philological acts and actors, I will be forced to take a circuitous path. I will begin by describing the city of Ugarit, the archeological source of a body of poetry closely allied to Hebrew poetry, and then the body of texts in that city's language. I will then return to the notion of philology in general and explore the cultural roots of that activity. Finally, I will review the work of three philologists who have devoted their lives to the study of the texts from Ugarit.

## I. The City of Ugarit

   The north Syrian city of Ugarit is located south of the mountain passes that lead into Anatolia and east of the easternmost point on Cyprus. It is a Mediterranean city accessible to the Aegean region and the Levant, as well as to Egypt and Mesopotamia. The city was founded in the Neolithic period before pottery came into general use and lasted six millennia before it was largely abandoned in the crisis associated with the transition from Bronze to Iron Ages, around 1200 B.C.E.

   Like the ancient sites of Mari, Qumran, and Nag Hammadi (and radium, yoghurt, and Uranus), Ugarit was discovered accidentally. The first part of the Ugaritian complex to emerge was the city's port: the peak of a tomb there collided with a peasant's plow in 1928. In early April of 1929, Claude F.-A. Schaeffer began excavating at the port and a month later turned his attention to modern Ras Shamrah nearby, where he found the city of Ugarit proper. The area of Ugarit that has so far been unearthed includes two major shrines and their libraries, and three palaces, complete with archives. The largest of the palaces covers 9,000 square meters and has between five and eight dozen rooms—not Peking's Forbidden City of 999 rooms, but the largest palace known in the ancient Near East. Only five days after he went to Ras Shamrah, on 14 May 1929 (a Tuesday, at around 5 p.m.), Schaeffer picked up the first of 4,000 tablets so far exhumed.

   The tablets belong to Ugarit's last and greatest period, the last phase of the Late Bronze Age (1375–1190 B.C.E.). This is the age of Amarna internationalism and of its catastrophic reversals: in northwestern Anatolia, Homer's Trojan War; in central Anatolia, the collapse of the Hittite empire; all along the Syro-Palestinian littoral, the destruction stimulated by the Sea Peoples, the biblical Philistines. At virtually every stratified site in the Near East, a layer of ashes is associated with the years around 1200 B.C.E. Out of the ashes emerge only minor states in the Levant, including, in the far south, Israel and Judah. Joshua's "conquest" of Palestine was part of the process that also "burned the topless towers of Ilium," though those processes are caricatured if they are described only in military terms. The attendant transformations ripped apart social organizations of international reach; the commercial center of Ras Shamrah was among the most cosmopolitan of them.

Wherever there are money and power, there are scribes for hire. If the money and power are drawn from an international base, the scribes will be trained in a variety of languages. Just as joint degree programs in business and modern Near Eastern languages are becoming more common in America, so at Ugarit there were scribes who knew many languages and wrote many scripts. The first tablet Schaeffer picked up was written in an unknown script, made up of the wedges of Sumerian writing handled in a distinctive way. The signs were alphabetic, and they recorded a previously unknown language. Though the script is still generally called Ugaritic, as is the language, we now know that the script was used over a much larger area than Ugarit controlled. The use of the script along much of the southwestern Asiatic coast tells us that before the linear (Phoenician-Greek-Latin) alphabet took over the scene in the Iron Age, alphabetic literacy, the cornerstone of democratic culture, had started on its way in the Late Bronze Age.

The cultural matrix of such literacy is best examined at Ugarit, amid the rich archeological and epigraphic finds. All the intelligible remains make some contribution, but the texts in the Ugaritic language constitute the major reason for the site's importance. The vocabulary of Ugaritic is small, and much of it is so obscure as to make the reading of some passages impossible. The number of gods attested is great, and we know nothing of most of them. Even the major gods are not well understood in themselves or as a pantheon. Nonetheless there is a great deal to read.

There are economic texts, manumissions from slavery, calendars, letters between kings, lists of wine deliveries, rosters of palace personnel, and there are the literary texts. These include charms and rituals, and myths and legends. Some are small, others medium-sized, a few large. Some are well-preserved, and others have gotten smashed in ancient or modern times.

The greatest of the literary texts fall into three groups. The major mythic texts concern the god Baal, the ruler of the cosmos. He appears in contests with his rivals, Yamm (the sea), Athtar (an upstart cousin), and Mot, who is, as St. Paul calls him, "the last enemy to be overcome," Death himself. Baal goes into battle aided by his sister Anat; later it is she who overcomes Death after he has killed Baal. In other texts, Baal seeks and eventually gets a palace from which to reign. The other groups of literary texts are legendary. The Keret cycle concerns a king who needs a wife and children and acquires them with divine aid. The Aqhat poems focus on King Daniel, who gets an heir and then loses him when the boy Aqhat angers a goddess. It is easy to see the subject of the literary texts: kingship. This is evident in the topics: a ruler-god, his rivals, and his palace; Keret begetting children, and Daniel losing his son. Ugarit was a monarchy and the apparat that produced the forms we have of the originally oral texts existed to support the monarchy. As we shall see, however, there is more to Ugaritic texts than propaganda.

The riches of a literature are proper to those who use its language. We work at a disadvantage in studying literature in a dead language, a language that is only written. There are aspects of usage, however, that live across languages, and many such vivify ancient Mediterranean and southwestern Asiatic literature and make it accessible to us. A few examples may help to make the point.

One temptation of the hero in these literatures is the goddess who lies, who tries to win him by promising him the world. The hero meets this temptation only if he says she is lying. He must first find the lie, the promise of immortality, and recognize it as a lie. He must say, "I am dying; that is how I shall live."

In Book Five of *The Odyssey*, Kalypso, having been warned by Zeus' messenger to send Odysseus on his way home, feeds the hero well and lies to him anyway.

> Son of Laertes and seed of Zeus, resourceful Odysseus,
> are you still so eager to go back to your own house
> and the land of your fathers? I wish you well, however you do it,
> but if you only knew in your own heart how many hardships
> you were fated to undergo before getting back to your country,
> you would stay here with me and be the lord of this household
> and be an immortal. (5.203–209; trans. Richmond Lattimore)

She is lying. She cannot make him an immortal. He knows it, and he says so (nicely; Odysseus knows nothing if not how to lie). The Mesopotamian goddess Ishtar greets the hero Gilgamesh and similarly propositions him with lies.

> Come, Gilgamesh, be thou my lover!
> Do but grant me of thy fruit.
> Thou shalt be my husband and I will be thy wife.
> I will harness for thee a chariot of lapis and gold,
> Whose wheels are gold and whose horns are brass.

Thou shalt have storm-demons to hitch on for mighty mules.
In the fragrance of cedar thou shalt enter our house.
When our house thou enterest,
Threshold and dais shall kiss thy feet!
Humbled before thee shall be kings, lords, and princes!
The yield of hills and plain they shall bring thee as tribute.
Thy goats shall cast triplets, thy sheep twins,
The he-ass in lading shall surpass thy mule.
Thy chariot shall be famed for racing,
Thine oxen under yoke shall not have rival.
    (6.7–21; trans. E. A. Speiser)

Gilgamesh sees the lie for what it is and says so, less politely than Odysseus; he grounds his refusal in precedent by citing Ishtar's many dead lovers, to whom the same offers were presumably made.

The subtlest version of this story occurs at Ugarit. The goddess Anat here asks not for sexual satisfaction directly but by synecdoche—she asks for the magic bow possessed by the beautiful youth Aqhat. She offers money, and he says, "Let me get you the stuff you need to make a real fine bow for yourself." She comes back—she wants *his* bow— and she is lying.

Ask for life, O Aqhat the Youth.
Ask for life and I'll give it thee,
    For deathlessness and I'll bestow't on thee.
I'll make thee count years with Baal,
    With the sons of El shalt thou count months.
And Baal, when he gives life, gives a feast,
    Gives a feast to the life-given and bids him drink;
Sings and chants over him,
    Sweetly serenades him:
So give I life to Aqhat the Youth.
    (UT 2 Aqht=CTA 17.6.27–33; trans. H. L. Ginsberg)

Aqhat recognizes the promises and says simply, "You're lying—I will die whatever you do." The clarity of his answer has a consequence. Odysseus leaves Kalypso, Gilgamesh slips away from Ishtar, but not so lucky Aqhat. Anat kills him.

This figure of the lying goddess is one of the basic forms of ancient Semitic and Aegean literature, a form closely shared among Greek, Akkadian, and Ugaritic stories. The biblical counterpart to these goddesses is mortal; she is the loose woman of lying lips that boys are so often warned against in the first seven chapters of the Book of Proverbs.

A listing convention shared among these literatures involves the use of sequential numbers in story-telling and wisdom recitation. The author of Proverbs 30, a chapter full of number sayings, explains:

listing
convention

> Under three things the earth shudders,
>   There are four it cannot tolerate:
> A slave who has become king;
>   An obstinate fool when he is filled with food;
> An unpopular woman when she gets a husband;
>   And a slave girl when she supplants her mistress.
>   (Proverbs 30:21–23; trans. R. B. Y. Scott)

Similarly the god Baal in an Ugaritic story uses numbers in stating his pet peeves (he refers to himself in the third person).

> Baal hates two sacrifices
>   Three, the Rider of Clouds [that is, Baal again]:
> The sacrifice of shame
>   And the sacrifice of baseness
>     And the sacrifice of the abuse of handmaids.
>   (UT 51=CTA 4.3.17–21; trans. C. H. Gordon)

The use of the pair $x$ and $x + 1$ in story-telling is not surprising. Children put billion after million as often as they add jillion after billion. But the convention endures strongly in the Near East and its cultural dependencies. A modern Palestinian Arab storyteller tells of a young man who, when asked how many children he has, says, "Three or four." The force of verbal habit that aided the author of Proverbs has apparently overpowered the storyteller. In a recent *New Yorker* piece, James Stevenson related a breakfast-time incident from a diner in rural Virginia.

> Old customer says something derogatory about cook; waitress concurs.
> Cook: "They's three things I can't stand—and you's two of them."

The cook here has bested the tradition, if unwittingly. Whether she was consciously quoting the language of Proverbs or not, she bears out the truth of C. H. Gordon's remark, "What the Greek and Latin classics are to modern Europen literature, Ugaritic is to the Old Testament."

Major motifs are also common. The stories of Noah, Job, and Daniel (the Ugaritic, not the biblical, Daniel) cited in Ezekiel 14 all refer to offspring, unfaithful or lost, as do the Aqhat and Keret poems. Gordon has alleged that the quest for Helen of Troy stimulates both Ugaritic Keret in his epic regaining of a lost wife and biblical Abraham in his recovery of Sarah from Pharaoh and the king of Gerar.

The closest contacts of Ugaritic and biblical literature appear in the psalter, perhaps most notably in Psalm 29, but the contacts go further and deeper than any single text or group of texts can show. Poetic form—line structure and word usage—is comparable at Ugarit and in early Israel. Given these similarities, other links are easily appreciated. For example, Israelite and Ugaritic kings were both expected to tend to widows and fatherless children, and to act on comparable ideas of filial piety. In both literatures, a chief god controlled the weather and fought off an evil twisting sea-serpent, Leviathan in Israel, Lōthan at Ugarit.

How can we explain the intimacies embracing Ugarit in its world? Some scholars look chiefly at Hebrew-Ugaritic similarities and explain the phenomena linguistically and literarily. Others refer to a framework of parallel developments in the eastern Mediterranean resulting from similar social and geographical conditions. Still other students tie Homer and Hebrew together through the agency of Minos, the legendary king of Crete. Before we consider these themes of interpretation, however, let us reflect on the processes of interpretation.

## II. Philology

Philology, the love of words, is a discipline out of sorts. The process of taking seriously the most learned members of society has continued in the centuries since learning itself grew to be taken seriously, but the philologist has little standing in the assembly these days. It is scientists, in the broad sense of those who confront the real directly, who have pride of place. Isaac Newton's prestige would suffer were it widely known that he spent more of his life studying biblical chronology (especially in Daniel and Revelation) and alchemy than he did considering physics.

The scientist, though absorbed in learning, is not chained to books. He attends to things through observation, Galileo staring at stars and van Leuwenhoeck gazing at specks under the microscope. Even Newton (the physicist!) has been made to fit the pattern: he is appropriated to the iconography of heroism as a young man allowing himself to be hit on the head by an apple. The scientist-hero has offspring everywhere, most obviously in science fantasy, from Hawthorne's "Rappaccini's Daughter" to current pulp; and in fictional investigation of out-of-the-way human behavior: detective stories deal not with detectives but urban scientists.

Indeed, the greatest storybook detective of the nineteenth century was a scientist proper. Sherlock Holmes could recognize ashes from all kinds of cigars and soils from every corner of the British Isles. He imagined from all this knowledge a science of crime and sought to forge it in the heat of confronting the mad criminal, the abandoned wife, the distressed child. Holmes himself was greater than philologists but not above their pursuits, it might be noted. During an enforced retreat in Cornwall because of ill health, Dr. Watson tells us Holmes turned philologist.

> The ancient Cornish language had . . . arrested [Holmes's] attention and
> he had, I remember, conceived the idea that it was akin to . . . Chaldean

[i.e., Aramaic], and had been largely derived from Phoenician traders in tin. He had received a consignment of books upon philology and was settling down to develop this thesis when suddenly, to my sorrow and his unfeigned delight, we found ourselves . . . plunged into a problem at our very doors which was more intense, more engrossing, and infinitely more mysterious than any of those which had driven us from London. ("The Adventures of the Devil's Foot," from *His Last Bow*, 1917)

And, needless to say, more engrossing than philology, though it is just as well we were spared Sherlock Holmes on Anglo-Levantine connections. It does not seem philology would have been his forte.

What of the learned besides scientists? Why has the popular imagination so largely resisted assimilating their modes of life, their modes of study? It has made allowances. Whether as a result of an appreciation of Claude Lévi-Strauss's autobiographical *Tristes Tropiques* or Michael C. Rockefeller's unexplained disappearance in New Guinea in 1961, there is abroad some sense of the anthropologist as hero (to borrow Susan Sontag's phrase for the Frenchman). Indeed, there is a monument to this sort of hero: Nelson Rockefeller donated his collection of "primitive" art to the Metropolitan Museum, to be housed in the Michael C. Rockefeller Memorial Wing. This is a restricted sort of assimilation, since the admiration is directed toward the ethnographic fieldworker, toward Lévi-Strauss in his days in the interior of Brazil (and to a lesser extent in his visions of laboratories for coordinating vast funds of data); toward Rockefeller, dying and dead, suffering the ultimate fate of being lost in the encounter with the real. This popular view of the anthropologist-hero as a sort of scientist is distinct from the vision of *The Beautiful Contradictions* (1970), a long poem by Nathaniel Tarn, who is both an ethnographer and a poet. Tarn in that poem vividly depicts a scholar-poet who bridges cultures in order to assemble humankind.

This figure is not far from the true image of the philologist, despite his being denied heroic status in the popular understanding. The philologist studies cultures not in contrast, especially through the great contrast of industrialization, as anthropologists usually do, but with regard for their texture. This texture involves historical study and political, social, economic, artistic, religious, moral, and intellectual considerations, but refers chiefly to texts. It is thus proper to high cultures, which endure through written texts, rather than preindustrial cultures, which preserve themselves through oral traditions.

Philology is distinguished from its godchild linguistics in being bound to texts. Linguistics, especially as a historical discipline, is a byproduct of philology's labors and must continue to refresh itself in the oceans from which it was drawn. The greatest linguist of our time, the late Roman Jakobson, devoted himself not only to considering universal aspects of language but also to close philological study of traditional Slavic epics and modern poems.

Though the philologist is rarely acknowledged a hero, there are villain philologists. In the last quarter of the eighteenth century, advocating the study of grammar in connection with the Hebrew Bible מִשְׁפָּטִים was a sure sign of heresy or even apostasy in Eastern European Jewish communities. The enlightened or Maskilim, who threatened to find a system of language within the holy tongue, were liable thereafter (it was erroneously thought) to attack religion on every possible front. There are more powerful and enduring villains, too. Of the greatest philologist-villain, Sir Hugh Lloyd-Jones writes, "Nietzsche's achievement in professional scholarship is trivial in comparison with his general understanding of Greek life and thought." And further, that he is "a greater writer than any philosopher since Plato." In other words: although few philologists would care to admit the fact, it is possible in philology, as elsewhere, to have all the details wrong and still be, in some sense, right. It was of Nietzsche that William Arrowsmith, the American classicist, remarked, "The pretensions of philologists are apparently boundless." Helga Wingler adds: "One can read from the political history of our century just how Nietzsche's theory of irrationality turned into the practice of inhumanity."

Though popular culture resists philology, modern imaginative literature does not, not least because until recently the core of education was philology. At least up until 1925, all English-language poets had some knowledge of classical philology and used it, whether as alienating kitsch or genuine grist. These writers lived in greater kinship than we do with the tradition that allowed philology's objects to animate culture. Nero, not a figure known for finesse or discretion, was philologist enough to say, when presented with some texts found on Crete during his reign, presumably inscribed a millennium and a half earlier with Linear A, that they should be given to Phoenicians for decipherment. Scholars have only recently realized he may have been right about the language of the tablets.

More recent writers have found the figure of the philologist proper to their imaginations, and we shall look at one imaginary philologist at work before we turn to three live ones. Philology for him is joined to archeology as a cognate discipline because philology is no longer, as it once was, the study of *received* texts; it concerns *all* texts, whether exhumed from the soil, from museums, or from traditions. The British poet Geoffrey Hill opens his sequence of poems "The Songbook of Sebastian Arrurruz" (1968) with the speaker picturing himself as a philologist at work on the data of his life.

> Ten years without you. For so it happens
> Days make their steady progress, a routine
> That is merciful and attracts nobody.

Already, like a disciplined scholar,
I piece fragments together, past conjecture
Establishing true sequences of pain;

For so it is proper to find value
In a bleak skill, as in the thing restored:
The long-lost words of choice and valediction.

In a later poem in the sequence, Arrurruz writes from the Near East as an archeologist, considering both ceramics and ethno-botany, both burn layers and necropolises.

I turn my mind
towards delicate pillage, the provenance
of shards glazed and unglazed, the three
kinds of surviving grain. I hesitate amid
circumstantial disasters. I gaze at the
authentic dead.

"Sequences of pain" belong to the inauthentically living, who need a philologist's passion to know why or how they said goodbye. Authenticity belongs to the dead, surrounded by the evidence of the acts of gods and enemies.

## III. Three Philologists Reading Ugaritic

Semitic philology has not, since the revival of learning in Europe, been foreign to the core of humanistic study. Recent work in women's history reminds us that the Italian Elena Cornaro, the first woman to receive a doctorate, when she was examined at Padua in 1678, offered knowledge not only of classical and modern European languages but also of Hebrew, Aramaic, and Arabic. Her contemporary Anna van Schurman of Utrecht knew Hebrew, Aramaic, and Syriac and wrote an Ethiopic grammar. The curriculum in our century has changed. The development of intellectual concerns and approaches has been rapid enough in itself, and archeological finds have accelerated the rate of change in Semitic philology far beyond that characteristic of most humanistic fields.

The wear and tear of the speed-up is taken out on the individual scholars who mediate texts, traditions, students, and readers. In any generation, in any area of scholarly concern, the lead falls to a few people, and the leaders in Ugaritic research from the thirties to the present are a trio of English-speakers who, in concert with an international array of scholars, have sought to make sense of the texts: T. H. Gaster, H. L. Ginsberg, and C. H. Gordon. This trio is intriguing because each member has operated with the Ugaritic texts from a distinct vantage point, and made the process of reading from and back into the context as vigorously fruitful a process as possible. To appreciate them best we must look to these vantage points.

Theodor Herzl Gaster, Harold Louis Ginsberg, and Cyrus Herzl Gordon were all born in the first decade of this century; they also share close ties to New York City. Ginsberg taught at the Jewish Theological Seminary from 1941 until his recent retirement. Gaster has taught at Columbia University and Barnard College, a few blocks away from the Seminary, for the latter portion of his teaching career. Since his retirement from Brandeis University, Gordon has taken a teaching position at New York University. All three remain active scholars.

The three scholars have reached this common ground of Manhattan maturity by different routes. Of the three, only Gordon was born in the United States. Ginsberg was born in the Jewish quarter of Montreal made famous in Mordechai Richler's *The Apprenticeship of Duddy Kravitz*. Gaster's family background is the most philologically interesting. His father, Moses Gaster, was born in Bucharest and taught and wrote extensively about Rumanian literature, both before and after his expulsion from Rumania for protesting mistreatment of Jews. At the time of his son's birth, Gaster was not only lecturing in Slavic languages at Oxford; he was also serving as rabbi of the English Sephardic community. Beyond his pastoral and educational duties, he was an active and combative supporter of Herzl; the conference which resulted in the Balfour Declaration was held in his house, although he later broke off his official Zionist activities. As a scholar, Moses Gaster ranged far beyond Rumania, covering folklore and magic, medieval romance and Hebrew apocrypha; his work on the Samaritan community in postbiblical times is still basic.

The most direct path from the Orient to the Occident is the biblical tradition, and H. L. Ginsberg's contextualization of the Ugaritic materials has relied on showing how complex that path is. Gaster and Gordon, too, have devoted much study to the Hebrew Bible, along with most scholars who have worked on Ugaritic, but Ginsberg has most assiduously cultivated the texts themselves. He has done this publicly in his capacity as co-editor (1956–1962) and editor-in-chief (1962–1977) of the Jewish Publication Society translation of the Bible, mentioned earlier. His duties involved the translation of the Latter Prophets, and much of his scholarly work has been devoted to the book of Isaiah. His preoccupation with translation also shaped his work on the texts of Daniel and Qoheleth, which he has contended are difficult in part because they are ancient translations between Hebrew and Aramaic, done by scribes with insufficient grasp of the languages.

Ginsberg's greatest labors of translation, however, involved the Ugaritic literary texts, which he translated first into Modern Hebrew, and later into English. Ginsberg laid the foundations for his translations in numerous scholarly articles. His treatment of points he regards as settled is sometimes abrupt; he footnotes a translation of one difficult poetic passage with the remark, "The Hebrew cannot mean" (he here supplies another translation) "and that is that." This illustrates, at least in part, the phrase used of him by a colleague: he is "prudent without being pusillanimous."

Cyrus Gordon's work, like Ginsberg's, has involved a range of materials associated with the Ugaritic texts, which are at the center of his career. Out of his initial concern with Ugaritic grew an interest in what he called in the title of one essay *The Common Background of Greek and Hebrew Civilizations.* Ugarit, he proposes, is a Janus culture which turns one face toward the Aegean, specifically the Minoan civilization of Crete, and the other toward the southern Levant, with its intellectual and moral center in Jerusalem.

Gordon's first Ugaritic efforts involved producing the basic reference work in the field; he has kept it up-to-date for over a quarter century. In parallel works he has furnished translations of the texts. It was in praising Gordon's translations that Ginsberg uttered an aphorism exemplifying the Spartan comforts of scholarship: "The only people who have never made mistakes in Ugaritic philology are those who have never engaged in it."

The historical thesis which Gordon has been led to by his work in Ugaritic involves a careful scrutiny of the whole of the eastern Mediterranean in the mid-second millennium. The occurrence of Mycenean objects at a site where a Northwest Semitic language was spoken is not merely the byproduct of commerce or coincidence. Rather, it offers palpable witness to a cultural blending of Aegean and Asiatic spheres, a blending evidenced elsewhere at Ugarit. The instances of the lying goddess we quoted above we owe to Gordon, who has studied the very different poetry of Homer and the Bible in terms of the Ugaritic texts on a variety of levels. He has attended to phenomena in the societies which produced the texts and to purely textual phenomena. He has also studied the conditions of literary production which can be triangulated from these. In this work he continues, at the ground level, the necessary task of reworking Matthew Arnold's now-dated alignment of the Hellene and Hebrew sides of our civilization with columns marked sweetness and light.

Theodor Gaster's work in many respects continues that of his father, both in the English tradition of folklore studies and in the focus on Semitic texts. The term folklore was coined in 1846 to replace the phrase "popular antiquities" in describing folk rituals and customs and the stories and explanations that go with them. In many ways, the material of folklore studies is that of cultural anthropology, though folklorists are often especially concerned with the survival of fragments of rituals and legends in vastly changed cultural contexts. Current concern with oral history and "old ways" is an offshoot of folklore. The greatest folklorist was Sir James G. Frazer (1854-1941), and Gaster is an important continuer of Frazer's studies in his *New Golden Bough* (1959) and *Myth, Legend, and Custom in the Old Testament. A Comparative Study* (1969).

*Thespis*, first published in 1950 and revised in 1961, is the core of Gaster's achievement, a major essay in understanding the relationships among ritual, myth, and drama. In the book Gaster presents ancient Near Eastern texts which he proposes reflect religious rituals keyed to the workings of the seasons, texts in Egyptian, Hittite, and Ugaritic. The rituals, often associated with major seasonal festivals, are not widely attested outside Egypt. Rather, older rituals seem to have provided a shaping structure for the extant texts, which may have been used for performance or in which the seasonal shaping may have been "mere literary convention."

Some Ugaritic texts, Gaster proposes, manifest a science of the weather. Thus, the Baal texts can be fitted together in a cycle covering the entire course of a year. The story of Aqhat is the tale of a god whose summertime disappearance leads to drought. The Poem of the Gracious Gods, another Ugaritic text, preserves some ritual rubrics in which Gaster has recognized the framework for the burlesque of seasonal ritual that survives in mummers' plays. Here is a harvest song from the poem.

> Death-and-Rot may sit enthroned,
> firm ensconced in regal sway,
> in his either hand a rood—
> Loss of Children, Widowhood;
> yet, when men do prune the vine,
> 'tis *he* they prune away;
> when they come to bind the vine,
> *he* it is that they entwine;
> when they grub the soil round,
> beneath *his* feet they tear the ground.
> (UT 52 = CTA 23.8–11; trans. T. H. Gaster)

Features of seasonal rituals survive also in the secular Greek dramatic tradition and in some texts in the Bible, notably Psalms 93 and 89. The concerns that motivate these texts are often the concerns of the seasonal rituals.

Just as passages in Ugaritic texts remain obscure, and new philological puzzles appear with new excavations, so questions of tactics in doing and using philology continue to get different answers, and continue to need new ones. If Gaster, Ginsberg, and Gordon seem to have undertaken different labors for philology, they are entirely aware of the circumstance, and have expressed both admiration of and disquiet, if not dissatisfaction, with features of one another's work from time to time. Indeed, a single issue of *Commentary* some years ago had Gaster reviewing harshly the Jewish Publication Society Torah which Ginsberg had worked on, and Ginsberg reviewing harshly a book by Gordon; Gordon replied in those pages later.

If these philologists have not been entirely happy with each other, attentive and perspicacious outsiders, though appreciative, have not been altogether satisfied either. Charles Olson, more than any other recent American poet, took the ancient world seriously and studied it so as to bring its congruences into conjunction with those of our eastern coast. Olson, writing of the kind of philological frameworks we have isolated here, remarks:

> It is this business of taking the edge off new discovery when the stuff hasn't even been taken into the bloodstream of the present which makes literacy as it is now practiced suspect.

It is also what makes extensions of literacy possible, even extensions which are apparently only reconsiderations of texts which have never failed to be central in our tradition.

*Bibliographical Note*

The Ugaritic translations of H. L. Ginsberg are published in *Ancient Near Eastern Texts Relating to the Old Testament*, edited by J. B. Pritchard (Princeton: Princeton University Press, 1969); those of C. H. Gordon are most accessible in *Ugarit and Minoan Crete: The Bearing of Their Texts on the Origin of Western Culture* (New York: Norton, 1967); those of T. H. Gaster are incorporated into *Thespis: Ritual, Myth, and Drama in the Ancient Near East* (New York: Harper & Row, 1961). Gaster's remarks on the JPS translation of the Torah appear in "Translating the Bible," *Commentary* 36 #4 (1963), pp. 305–11, and Ginsberg discusses Gordon in "Hebrews and Hellenes," in the same issue, pp. 333–36. Olson's remark is from an essay, "Homer and the Bible," reprinted in *Human Universe and Other Essays*, edited by Donald Allen (New York: Grove, 1967). For other aspects of the philological study of Hebrew poetry, see O'Connor, *Hebrew Verse Structure* (Winona Lake, Indiana: Eisenbrauns, 1980); for discussion of the treatment of verse in recent English translations, see the lively essays collected by Lloyd R. Bailey in *The Word of God: A Guide to English Versions of the Bible* (Atlanta: John Knox, 1982).

# TWO

# THE CHRISTIAN
# SCRIPTURES

WILLIAM VIRGIL DAVIS

# BEATITUDES

And he opened his mouth and said unto them:
Blessed are the stones for they shall know wholeness.
Blessed is the light which keeps the evil one away.
Blessed are the beasts of the fields and all creeping things
    for they have been made by the hand of God.
Blessed are they who hope and fear me for they hope for
    that which is to come and have nothing to fear.
Blessed are all children.
Blessed are all men who love stones.
Blessed are bones.
Blessed are they who wait.
Blessed are the dead, who live.
Blessed are all who are persecuted for they are true prophets.

J. LOUIS MARTYN

# A LAW-OBSERVANT MISSION
# TO GENTILES:
# THE BACKGROUND OF GALATIANS

## I

That the early church was intensely and passionately evangelistic is clear to every reader of the documents that make up the New Testament. Equally clear, or so it would seem, is the scholarly consensus that when Christian evangelists took the step of reaching beyond the borders of the Jewish people, they did so without requiring observance of the Jewish law. The work of these evangelists, in turn, is said to have sparked a reaction on the part of firmly observant Jewish Christians, who, seeing the growth of the Gentile mission, sought to require observance of the Law by its converts. Struggles ensued, and the outcome, to put the matter briefly, was victory for the mission to the Gentiles, for the Law-free theology characteristic of that mission, and for the churches produced by it.

In broad terms such is the standard portrait of early Christian missions. That portrait was codified, so to speak, at the beginning of our century by the great German theologian Adolf von Harnack (1851-1930); with minor alterations it is still to be found in the standard handbooks. A clear indication of its hegemony is the use of the definite article before the expression "Gentile mission." Every college student in the standard course on early Christianity hears a lecture on "the Gentile Mission," thus learning that the branch of early Christian evangelism directed to Gentiles was essentially monolithic. However varied the Gentile mission may have been in minor regards, in respect to the Jewish law all *primary, evangelistic* efforts toward Gentiles were the same: *the* Gentile mission was the mission loosed from observance of the Law.

This portrait is not arbitrary. Harnack and his successors drew it on the basis of (1) primary evidence in the letters of Paul, (2) traditions and editorial material in the Acts of the Apostles, and (3) other traditions scattered throughout the New Testament, notably in the gospels. The evidence in Paul's letters is basic, because those letters were written during the sixth decade of the first century, right in the midst of what is termed the Gentile mission. Most influential is a paragraph in Paul's letter to the churches of Galatia, in which, speaking of the leaders of the Jewish-Christian church in Jerusalem he says,

> ... they came to see that I had been entrusted [by God] with the gospel to the Gentiles, just as Peter had been entrusted with the gospel to the Jews (Galatians 2:7).

From Paul's own mouth, therefore, we have a picture that presents two distinguishable developments along two parallel lines; the context of the quotation makes it clear that one of the lines is Law-observant, while the other is not: Peter pursues *the* mission to the Jews (Law-observant); Paul pursues *the* mission to the Gentiles (Law-free). Thus, the standard portrait of *the* unified, Law-free mission to the Gentiles is responsibly drawn on the basis of primary evidence stemming from that mission itself.

Luke wrote the Acts of the Apostles a number of years after the earliest missions, a fact that makes his testimony less historically valuable than that of Paul. Moreover, at numerous points one sees the effects of his own editorial policy, not least in his determination to show that the Christian movement expanded along a single line. Given this tendency on Luke's part, one is not surprised to see that he has no place for the two parallel lines that were so important to Paul in Galatians. On the contrary, he shows the Jewish mission and the mission to the Gentiles to have been two distinguishable segments of one line, the Gentile mission proving to be the *successor* to the mission to the Jews.

In the matter of our present inquiry, however, Luke agrees with Paul: there was one mission to the Gentiles (with several fragmentary beginnings) and that mission was loosed from observance of what any Jew would have known to be the Law, that is to say, observance of circumcision, the sabbath, dietary rules, and so forth. (The "council" in Acts 15 is a different matter.) Luke shows that the transition to this mission repeatedly generated conflict, and when he gives the reason for the struggle, that reason proves to be the Law-free character of the Gentile mission. The same thing can be said of references made elsewhere in the New Testament to evangelistic activity directed toward Gentiles (e.g., Mark 7:14-30; Matthew 10:5; 28:19; Luke 14:15-24).

The standard portrait of an essentially unified mission to Gentiles, free of observance of the Law, is, then, well founded, being drawn from traditions formulated in the very early years of the church's history. As a sort of *double entendre*, referring both to the writings of the New Testament and to the writings of Harnack and other highly influential modern historians, one might say that this portrait is *canonical*.

## II

Is it also fully accurate? A major responsibility of the historian is to pose that question at least once each day. To do so in the present instance is to be assailed by doubt, for if one ponders, even momentarily, the possibility that at least some early Christian preachers directed their *evangelistic* message to Gentiles without surrendering observance of the Law, then one can think immediately of reasons why Paul and Luke would have suppressed evidence pointing to such activity.

If Paul is passionate about anything as he writes to the Galatian churches—and Galatians is his most hot-tempered letter—it is to show that God has brought about *one* mission to the Gentiles, and that that mission is loosed from the Law. Paul can tolerate, and even recognize as God's doing, a *parallel*, Law-observant mission to the Jews, so long as that mission is and remains truly parallel, that is to say, so long as it does not infect the Gentile mission with the demand for Law-observance. Nothing would have been further from Paul's mind than to indicate that there was a Law-observant mission to Gentiles, considered by at least some members of the church to be authorized by God.

Writing some years later, Luke is not driven by quite the same passions. But he does live in a church that was produced by the Law-free mission to Gentiles, *and* he is passionate to show that that church is *the* church. The point at which our question is focused is, then, a point at which we cannot be confident of our primary sources, because of their evident biases.

And what about our confidence in Adolf von Harnack and his successors? Being a representative of modern, scientific historiography, so-called, Harnack was supposed to be largely free of bias. But, in fact, he was a human being, considerably influenced by his own setting; one aspect of that setting suffices by itself to draw the standard portrait of early Christian missions under suspicion. Along with his contemporaries and his successors, Harnack lived and worked in a culture that was religiously dichotomous. If one actively espoused a religion, one was either an observant Jew, in some sense, or a Gentile Christian. And if one was a Christian, one belonged to a church that was descended over the span of twenty centuries from the Law-free mission to Gentiles. In one's own milieu one had no neighbors and colleagues who were Law-observant Gentile Christians. The particular form of religious polarization that informed Harnack's culture may also have informed his historical research, however unconsciously. Between the Jewish synagogue and the Christian church there was in Harnack's setting no palpable middle group of Law-observant Gentile Christians. Small wonder, then, that it did not occur to him that there might have been such a group in Paul's time.

## III

Doubt takes on significance when it can give birth to a new vista. In the present case, a fresh angle of vision may emerge when one recognizes that, viewed against the background of Jewish Christianity, the New Testament is the collection of the documents of the victorious party. If there was an active and effective Law-observant mission to Gentiles, and if it left literary remains, these must lie—at least for the most part—outside the New Testament. Have any such remains been in fact preserved?

A few highly important sources from Jewish Christianity have indeed come down to us, notably two that are embedded in the Pseudo-Clementine literature, *The Ascents of James* and *The Preachings of Peter*. *The Ascents* seems to have been written in or near the city of Pella, in Transjordan, not long after the middle of the second century. The author lived in a community of persons we will do well to call Christian Jews, because they say about themselves that they differ from their Jewish kinsfolk in one regard only: they have been led to identify Jesus as the Messiah. From that statement it is clear that members of this community of Christian Jews understand themselves to be fully Law-observant. It is, therefore, striking that they pointedly affirm a mission to the Gentiles:

> It was necessary that the Gentiles should be called into the place of those [Jews] who did not believe [in Jesus as the Messiah], so that the number might be filled up which had been shown [by God] to Abraham. Thus, the preaching of the blessed Kingdom of God is sent into all the world (Clementine *Recognitions* 1. 42. 1).

It is true that the author of the *Ascents* knows of Paul. Indeed, he believes that some sort of activity by Paul had the effect of reducing the number of Jews who came into the church. Thus, when he says that the motivation for preaching the gospel to the Gentiles arises from the fact that numerous Jews did not believe, and had, so to speak, to be replaced, he portrays a Gentile mission that is in a distant and roundabout way reactive to Paul. Two points are nevertheless worthy of note: (1) Since there is no hint that the author's community of Christian Jews requires of Gentile converts less than it does of itself, we probably have a second-century witness to a Law-observant mission to Gentiles; and I see no indication that this mission is designed *to correct* the sort of Gentile mission that Paul carried out. (2) The motivation for preaching the gospel to Gentiles rests *theologically* on God's promise of a massive number of progeny to Abraham. In order for that number to be filled out, the Law-observant gospel is to be taken to the Gentiles.

*The Preachings of Peter*, the second of these Jewish-Christian sources, was probably written, near the end of the second century in

Syria, for a community living in effective isolation from the emerging church of the west. Again we are dealing with a group that perceives itself to be fully observant of "the Law of God which was made known by Moses and was confirmed by our Lord in its everlasting continuance" (*The Epistle of Peter to James* 2.5). Moreover, like the community reflected in *The Ascents of James*, this group affirms a Gentile mission. Indeed, the author (speaking fictitiously in Peter's name) mentions two missions to the Gentiles, one that is Law-observant, and one that is not. The former is Peter's word of truth, his "Law-observant preaching," and it is the *first* message that went out to the Gentiles. Subsequently, "the enemy man" (Paul) began his mission to the Gentiles, preaching a "Law-less and absurd doctrine." In a word, the second-century author of *The Preachings* claims that already in Peter's lifetime there was a Law-observant mission to Gentiles, and that that mission antedated the Law-less mission of Paul.

Our sortie outside the New Testament has taken us to two second-century sources from Jewish Christianity (or Christian Judaism) that portray a Law-observant mission to Gentiles. It would be a mistake to infer that because they are non-canonical these sources are free of bias. Doubtless their authors, along with all other human beings, have their own axes to grind. One is impressed, however, with the fact that there seems to be no literary relationship between the two documents. Each portrays, independently of the other, a Law-observant Gentile mission, and one document pointedly claims that that mission is chronologically prior to Paul's Law-free mission. It is true that the claim to chronological priority is a standard element in struggles over the definitions of orthodoxy and heresy. Perhaps we should be wary, therefore, of taking it at face value in this instance. But even so, we have the probability that our Jewish-Christian authors give true reflections of second-century Law-observant missions to Gentiles, carried out independently of the Great Church. That leads to our final question: Could it be that the evangelistic efforts portrayed in these second-century documents are descended from a Law-observant mission pursued by Jewish Christians in the first century?

## IV

Re-reading Paul's Galatian letter with that question in mind may lead one to borrow a note from Queen Gertrude, by suggesting that the Apostle "doth protest too much, methinks." Psychoanalysts are not alone in knowing that a heated denial may reflect the accuracy of what is denied. In any case, Galatians, the major witness to the existence of a single, Law-free mission to Gentiles, might prove, upon inspection, to reflect a picture rather more complex than is customarily assumed.

We can best make our renewed attempt to look behind Paul's letter by asking about the setting in which the Galatians first heard it, as Paul's messenger read it aloud to them. Clearly there have been new developments since Paul's departure from Galatia. At present some people are active among the congregations in ways that have aroused intense anger on Paul's part. Modern scholars customarily refer to these people as Paul's "opponents"; and that usage is readily understandable: Paul makes it clear that he views them as opponents, and there are indications that to a considerable degree they view him in the same manner. But a moment's reflection will suffice to show that this appellation prejudices the matter we are investigating by implying that these people derive their identity from their opposition to Paul, and, therefore, that their work is a reaction to his. In order to keep open the possibility that they have their own mission, independent of that of Paul, we will refer to them as "the Teachers."

As Paul shapes his letter, he takes for granted that the listening context in which his Galatian congregations will hear it is crucially marked by the activity and influence of the Teachers. Paul knows that the Galatians will listen to his letter with the Teachers' sermons still ringing in their ears, and probably with the Teachers themselves at their elbows. It follows that in order to make an entrance into this highly charged atmosphere we must have a reliable portrait of these people and of their teaching.

Do the pertinent data in the letter offer us clues sufficient in number and clarity to enable us to draw the picture we need? Paul refers explicitly to the Teachers in five passages, while at several other points he alludes to their gospel in revealing ways. We have, then, cause for some degree of optimistic confidence.

Obviously two extremes are to be avoided. On the one side lies the temptation to be overly bold in our detective work, falling unawares into massive speculation, reconstructing an entire face, so to speak, on the basis of the cut of the mustache. Some of Paul's polemical statements may have been formulated by him solely for the sake of rhetorical emphasis. We cannot assume that there lies behind every one of them a statement of the Teachers. On the other side lies the temptation to be too modest, limiting ourselves to points which can be "scientifically" demonstrated beyond doubt. Exegesis itself is more an art than a science, although it partakes of both. It is by asking at crucial points how the Galatians are likely to have understood the text in front of us that we shall acquire both the scientific control and the poetic fantasy needed for our own understanding of the text.

### A.

We begin with the five explicit references to the Teachers, for they form a secure basis on which to build (Galatians 1:6-9; 3:1-2, 5; 4:17; 5:7-

12; 6:12-14); in fact the picture which emerges shows enough internal coherence and a sufficient number of motifs paralleled in traditions connected with Jews, Christian Jews, and Jewish Christians to cause us to believe that that picture is indeed reliable.

Paul consistently differentiates the Teachers from the members of his Galatian congregations. He addresses the Galatians quite directly as "you," whereas he always refers to the Teachers by such terms as "some persons," "they," "those people." With considerable probability we can infer that the Teachers are outsiders who have only lately come into the Galatian churches.

Since we may assume that Paul very likely knows the Teachers' names or at least some of the epithets by which they identify themselves, we can conclude that, instead of using their names and epithets, he employs such colorless expressions as "some persons" in order to indicate disdain. We must also note, however, that he does employ three descriptive terms in direct references to them:

(1) those who frighten you (1:7, cf. 5:10);
(2) those who stir you up into a state of mental agitation (5:12);
(3) those who are circumcised (6:13).

We shall return to the first two of these in a moment. The third almost certainly tells us that the Teachers are Jews. We thus have a group of Jews who have come into the Galatian churches from somewhere else.

What, precisely, are they doing in these congregations? The standard picture of early Christian missions portrays them as interlopers who, in reaction to Paul's Law-free mission, dog his trail in order to lay on his converts the requirements of the Law (hence "Judaizers"). But when we look carefully at Paul's initial reference to them (1:6-9), another possibility emerges. Paul says that under the influence of the Teachers the Galatians are turning their allegiance to "another gospel." And then, having said that, he has to correct himself by insisting that in reality there is no "other gospel." Why does he take the route that requires self-correction? Surely it would have been easier to avoid associating the Teachers with the term "gospel," by saying that under their influence the Galatians are turning *away from* the gospel, in that they are giving their allegiance to a false teaching (cf. Revelation 2:14-15) or to an impotent philosophy (cf. Colossians 2:8; 2:23). It seems highly probable that Paul takes the path requiring self-correction because he knows that the Teachers are in fact referring to their message as "the gospel." It follows that, no less than the Apostle himself, the Teachers are in the full sense of the term evangelists, finding their basic identity not as persons who struggle against Paul, but rather as those who preach God's good news. They are, then, Jews who have come into Galatia proclaiming the Gospel.

To learn precisely what they consider God's good news to be is our major concern, and the direct references carry us a considerable distance toward that goal.

1) We have already seen that they speak of the good news as the gospel of Christ. Apparently without fear of contradiction, Paul repeatedly portrays the Teachers as those who find in the Law the absolute point of departure for their theology (e.g., 5:3-4). It is probably they who coined the expression "the Law of Christ" (6:2), intending by it to say that their good news *is* God's Law as it has now been affirmed and perhaps also interpreted by God's Messiah.

2) For whom is the Messiah's Law good news? It is apparently the vocation of the Teachers to make it clear that the Law is good news for the Gentiles, and they do that with a vision which we may assume to be, in their view at least, no less universalistic than that of Paul (3:8). We have, then, another reason to avoid referring to the Teachers as "Judaizers," as has so frequently been done. The term "Judaizer" usually refers to someone who wishes to hem in Gentile Christians by requiring them to live according to "narrow" Jewish practices, whereas the Teachers are embarked on an ecumenical mission under the genuine conviction that, through the law of his Messiah, God is now reaching out for the Gentiles and thus for the whole of humankind.

3) God's doing so is marked by the fact that he bestows his Spirit even on communities of Gentiles if their communal life is ordered by correct exegesis of scripture and thus by true observance of his Law. In 3:1-5 there are several strong hints that Paul is contrasting the type of worship service the Galatians first knew under his direction with the type of worship service they are now experiencing at the hands of the Teachers. Both services have about them certain aspects of the theater. In his preaching Paul clearly portrayed before the Galatians' eyes the dramatic picture of Christ as he suffered crucifixion (3:1). Presented with this theater, the Galatians found that faith was elicited in them and that the Spirit fell upon them. Now a new acting company has arrived on the scene, presenting a novel and highly effective drama. In the services of worship conducted by the Teachers, the Galatians see extraordinarily masterful exegetes who quote and interpret the scriptures with the firm conviction that out of true exegesis will flow mighty manifestations of the Spirit (3:5). And, indeed, developments in Galatia seem to confirm this conviction. In their dramatic services the Teachers demonstrate to the Galatians the impressive connection between the true interpretation of the Law and the miraculous dispensation of the Spirit. It follows that God is to be known as the one who supplies the Spirit to those who are both true exegetes of his Law and faithful observers of it.

4) This laying down of a strict condition for the true and dependable granting of the Spirit is surely a token for the conditional nature of the whole of the Teachers' good news. We can now return to the fact that

Paul twice characterizes the Teachers as persons who frighten the Galatians (1:7; 5:10). How are we to understand these two references? Help may come from Paul's comment in 4:17, where, employing the image of a gate, he says that the Teachers threaten to shut the Galatians out of salvation. Like the other pictures Paul paints of the Teachers, this one is decidedly negative. But there are positive Jewish traditions about the value of Gentiles becoming proselytes in order to *enter* the people of God, thus becoming participants in God's promise of life to Israel. When the Teachers encounter Gentiles who have been misled by Paul, they must wake them up with threats. With other Gentiles, they can presumably employ the image of the gate in a positive way, understanding themselves to be gatekeepers intent on ushering Gentiles through the gate into full participation in the people of God.

5) How is a Gentile to pass through this gate? We notice that one of the major foci of the Teachers' preaching is the subject of circumcision (6:12). It is a subject which properly belongs to proselytizing, for a Gentile passes into the people of the Law by belonging to a family the males of which submit to circumcision. Circumcision is the commandment par excellence, the commandment which signifies full participation in the people of God. The Teachers are, then, themselves circumcised Jews who preach circumcision to Gentiles as the act appropriate to the universal good news of God's Law, the observance of which will bring God's Holy Spirit to the Gentiles.

6) We may further summarize these five points by asking, finally, what the Teachers say about Christ. However difficult it may be to answer this question with the detail we would desire, the major point is quite clear: they necessarily view God's Christ in the light of God's Law, rather than the Law in the light of Christ, and this means that Christ is secondary to the Law. Paul thus seems to have no fear of being contradicted when he repeatedly says they avoid taking their theological bearings from the cross. Presumably they understand Christ's death to have been a sacrifice for sins, perhaps even those of Gentiles (cf. Galatians 1:4a and Romans 3:23-25), a sacrifice in harmony with God's Law. In any case, we can be sure that they consistently avoid every suggestion that God's Law and his Messiah could even partially conflict with one another. In their own terms they are clearly certain that the task of the Messiah can be seen in such words as are attributed to him in Matthew: "I have come to fulfill the law and the prophets. . . . Till heaven and earth pass away, not an iota, not a dot, will pass from the Law until all is accomplished" (5:17f). In a word, when they speak of the law of the Messiah, they do so in a way which takes for granted that the Messiah is the Messiah of the Law. In all likelihood he derives his identity from the fact that he confirms (and perhaps normatively interprets) the Law. If he is involved in the Teachers' commission to preach to the Gentiles, that must be so because he has deepened their

passion to take to the nations God's gift of gifts, his Spirit-dispensing Law. Thus, the Teachers are "first cousins" of those Jews who pursue among Gentiles the proselytizing mission referred to in the Gospel of Matthew (23:15).

These six points would seem to encapsulate most of what Paul reveals about the Teachers' gospel in his direct references to them. He has more to say in these references, particularly by way of maligning the Teachers' motives, seeking to show the Galatians that the Teachers are not true friends to them, do not really have their interests at heart, and are only superficially impressive rhetoricians. But these and similar jabs constitute the sort of outbursts one commonly finds among competitive preachers, especially, but not exclusively, in the Hellenistic age. There is no reason to think the Teachers refrained from saying similar things about Paul; such mutual mudslinging tells us nothing of importance about the Teachers' gospel.

### B.

There are, however, other data quite revealing of the Teachers' gospel, for since Paul has one part of his mind on the Teachers through the whole of the letter, his direct references to them are accompanied by numerous allusions to them and to their work. Carefully interpreted, these allusions fill out in important ways the picture we receive of these evangelists, and especially of their gospel.

One of the most revealing of these allusions emerges in Paul's highly developed retelling of the Abraham story in Galatians 3:6-29. The passage is a carefully structured and tightly argued piece of exegesis, however difficult it may be to trace Paul's line of argument at every juncture. Writing the whole of it with his eye firmly fixed on a series of Old Testament texts, Paul does not explicitly mention the Teachers; indeed, numerous interpreters have been able to comment on the passage without making sustained reference to them. But there are, I think, clear indications that as he formulates his interpretation of Abraham, Paul has them very much in mind. Indeed it is likely that in carrying out his own exegesis Paul is to a large degree reformulating one of the Teachers' key scriptural retellings and that he is doing so by quoting some of their key texts and by employing some of their favorite expressions.

We begin by noting Paul's initial exegesis. After giving as his lead text Genesis 15:6,

> Abraham had faith in God, and his doing so was recognized as righteousness.—

Paul provides his interpretation:

> You know therefore that those whose lives flow from faith, these are the descendants of Abraham (Galatians 3:6-7).

This is a very strange exegesis, and its strangeness cannot be fully explained by saying that Paul is following what may seem to us to be some odd, first-century rule of interpretation. The word "therefore" clearly tells the hearer that a consequence is being drawn from the quoted text. But Paul draws this "consequence" by placing his major emphasis on an expression which is not to be found in the text, "the descendants of Abraham." And he clearly designs his interpretation to answer a question which is not posed by the text: Who is it who can truly be said to be the descendants of Abraham?

If the text itself (Genesis 15:6) has provided neither the emphasized expression nor the key question to be answered, these must arise from some other source. What might this source be? In pondering this question one is helped by asking another: How can Paul assume the Galatians will understand such a strange exegesis of Genesis 15:6? One hypothesis is that he can make this assumption because both the expression "descendants of Abraham" and the question "Who is it who can truly be said to be the descendants of Abraham?" are components of the context in which the Galatians will interpret his letter. In other words, this hypothesis would run, Paul can move from Genesis 15:6 to this strange exegesis because he knows that the Galatians are currently hearing a great deal about Abraham and about the identity of his descendants.

In order to test this hypothesis we may note first that the problem of identifying Abraham's descendants emerges not only in Paul's opening exegesis of Genesis 15:6 but also in his closure of the scriptural section, at which point he asks, in effect, how can the Galatians know whether they are descendants of Abraham? Paul answers definitively:

> If you belong to Christ, then you are descendants of Abraham . . . (3:29).

It thus becomes clear that while the exegetical catena of 3:6-29 touches a number of issues, the major one is that of the identity of Abraham's descendants.

Is this Paul's issue? Obviously he takes it as his own, but there is at least one good reason for thinking that he borrows its key terms from some development in the Galatian churches: as far as we can reconstruct Paul's initial preaching in the Galatian cities and in cities such as Philippi, Thessalonica, and Corinth, he gave no place either to Abraham or to the expression "descendants of Abraham." A paragraph or section on Abraham does not seem to have been part of Paul's "gospel." It begins to seem quite probable that both Abraham and the expression "descendants of Abraham" have entered the Galatian milieu in the sermons of the Teachers.

What did the Teachers say about Abraham and his descendants? We cannot answer with certainty, but it is probable that they spoke at some length about "the blessing of Abraham," indicating that when God blessed Abraham, he did so in such a way as eventually to bless those Gentiles who by circumcision and Law observance become Abraham's true descendants. After providing what we have characterized above as the rather strange exegesis of Genesis 15:6, Paul proceeds to introduce a quotation from Genesis 18:18 (cf. 12:3):

> And the scripture, foreseeing that God justifies the Gentiles through faith, preached the gospel beforehand to Abraham, saying: "In you shall all the Gentiles be blessed" (Galatians 3:8).

Again several points are notable: nowhere else in the letters which have come down to us does Paul cite this text from Genesis or in any way express interest in it or in its motifs. When he deals with Abraham in Romans 4, he does not use this quotation from Genesis 18:18. Similarly he connects the noun "blessing" with the name Abraham only in the present passage (3:14). When Paul is composing more or less freely, he speaks of "the promise to Abraham" (Romans 4:13; cf. Galatians 3:16, 18), not of "the blessing of Abraham." Again, therefore, we have to wonder whether we are not dealing with an expression and a motif which have made their way into the Galatian scene via the sermons of the Teachers.

Is there corroborating evidence for this conclusion? We know that the first of the two expressions, "descendants of Abraham," was greatly significant among Christian Jews of the first century. Aside from Galatians 3 we encounter that formula as a self-designation in 2 Corinthians 11 and in John 8. In both of these passages we see Christian Jews who proudly denominate themselves as descendants of Abraham. Moreover, the same thing is clearly presupposed by the Christian Jew who authored the second-century *Ascents of James*, mentioned above. He shows that the true line of religion extends from Abraham to his descendants.

Similarly the blessing God bestowed on Abraham plays a significant role in the same document. Indeed for the author of the *Ascents* God's blessing of Abraham provides the motivation for the Law-observant mission to Gentiles.

Returning to the Teachers in Galatia, we can now say with great probability that by making considerable use of the traditions in Genesis 18:18, 22:15-18, 28:3-4, etc., they placed at the center of their good news a well-developed exegesis of traditions about Abraham. And the point that requires emphasis is that in regard to this weighty matter—nothing less than the issue of identifying that act of God from which the impulse to evangelize the Gentiles springs—it is Paul who is doing the reacting, not the Teachers. There is no indication that they have developed interpretations of the Abraham texts in order to counter the effects of Paul's Law-free mission. On the contrary, Paul takes up the traditions about Abraham in hopes of neutralizing their Law-observant mission. We ought, therefore, to take with utter seriousness the independence of their work, if not its chronological priority.

Indeed the theology underlying the Teachers' Law-observant mission is so important for our understanding of Christian origins that it deserves to be displayed in its own right, and as fully as possible. True enough, the actual wording of the Teachers' sermons is lost to us, since we have no sources written by them. But the clear hints in Paul's letter, amplified by similar and closely related motifs traceable to Christian Jews of the first two centuries, suffice to suggest the outline of a significant part of their evangelistic theology. The safe and prosaic route at this point would be to list a number of theological motifs, taking account of variant understandings of the biblical texts (the Teachers apparently did not care that Ishmael was circumcised). The better route, I think, is to try, with a pinch of fantasy, to reconstruct a sermon fragment similar to one we may imagine the Teachers to have preached.

## The Sermon

Listen, now. It all began with Abraham. He was the first human being to discern that there is but one God. Because of that perception he turned from the service of dumb idols to the worship of the true God. Therefore God made him the father of our great nation; but that was only the beginning, for God made to Abraham a solemn utterance which through our mission has begun to find its fulfillment in the present time. Speaking through a glorious angel, God said to Abraham:

> In you shall all nations of the world be blessed . . . for I shall multiply your descendants as the stars of heaven. . . . Come outside, and look toward heaven, and number the stars, if you are able. . . . So shall your descendants be . . . for I speak this blessing to you and to your descendants.

What is the meaning of this blessing which God gave to Abraham? Pay attention to these things: Abraham was the first proselyte. As we have said, he discerned the one true God and turned to him. God therefore made an unshakable covenant with Abraham, and as a sign of this covenant he gave to Abraham the commandment of circumcision. He also revealed to Abraham the heavenly calendar, so that in his own lifetime our father was in fact obedient to the Law, not only keeping the commandment of circumcision, but also observing the holy feasts on the correct days.

Later, when God actually handed down the Law at Sinai, he spoke once again in the mouths of his glorious angels who passed the Law through the hand of the mediator, Moses (Galatians 3:19). And now the Messiah has come, confirming for eternity God's blessed Law, revealed to Abraham and spoken through Moses (6:2).

And what does this mean for you Gentiles? We know from the scriptures that Abraham had two sons: Isaac and Ishmael (4:22). On the day of the feast of the first fruits Isaac was born of Sarah the freewoman, and through him have come we Jews, who are descendants of Abraham. Ishmael was born of Hagar the slave girl, and through him have come you Gentiles. Thus also you are descendants of the patriarch. We are in fact brothers!

We also know from the scripture we have just quoted that God made his indelible promise to both Abraham and his descendants, saying: "In you shall all the nations be blessed. The inheritance of salvation is to your children's children!" That fact faces us all with the crucial question: Who is it who are the true and therefore blessed descendants of Abraham (3:7, 29)? And the answer is equally clear from the scriptures: Abraham himself turned from idols to the observance of the Law, circumcising himself and Isaac. As we have said, he even kept the holy feasts at their precisely appointed times. And not least, by keeping God's commandments, he avoided walking in the power of the Evil Impulse (5:16, cf. Genesis 6:5). It follows that the true descendants are clearly those who are faithfully obedient to the Law with faithful Abraham (Galatians 3:6-9). At the present holy time God has been pleased to extend this line of true descent through the community in Jerusalem, the community which lives by the Law of Christ (6:2), the community of James, Cephas, and John, *and* through the community which we represent (2:1-10).

What are you to do, therefore, as Abraham's descendants through Ishmael, the child of Hagar the slave-girl? The gate of conversion stands open (4:17; 4:9)! You are to cast off your enslavement to the Evil Impulse by turning in repentance and conversion to God's righteous Law as it is confirmed by his Christ. Follow Abraham in the holy and liberating rite of circumcision (6:13); observe the feasts at their appointed times (4:10); keep the sacred dietary requirements (2:11-14); and abstain from idolatry and from the passions of the flesh (5:19-21). Then you will be true descendants of Abraham, heirs of salvation according to the blessing which God solemnly uttered to Abraham and his descendants (3:7, 8).

You say that you have already been converted by Paul? We say that you are still in a darkness entirely similar to the darkness in which not long ago you were serving the elements, supposing them, as Abraham once did, to be gods that rule the world (4:3, 9). In fact the fights and contentions in your communities show that you have not really been converted, that Paul did not give you God's holy guidance. Paul left you, a group of sailors on the treacherous high seas in nothing more than a small and poorly equipped boat. He gave you no provisions for the trip, no map, no compass, no rudder, and no anchor. In a word, he failed to pass on to you God's greatest gift, the Law. But that is exactly the mission to which God has called us. Through our work the good news of God's Law is invading the world of Gentile sin. We adjure you, therefore, to claim the inheritance of the blessing of Abraham, and thus to escape the curse of the Evil Impulse and sin (5:16). For, be assured, those who follow the path of the Evil Impulse and sin will not inherit the Kingdom of God (5:21). It is entirely possible for you to be shut out (4:17). You will do well to consider this possibility and to tremble with fear. For you will certainly be shut out unless you are truly incorporated into Abraham (3:29) by observing the glorious and angelic Law of the Messiah. Turn therefore in true repentance, and come under the wings of the Divine Presence, so that with us you shall be saved as true descendants of our common father Abraham.

## V

The standard portrait of early Christian missions is surely in need of modification. We cannot be sure that the Teachers in Galatia are historical progenitors of the communities of Christian Jews we see reflected in the second-century sources cited. With a high degree of probability we can say, however, that like the evangelists in those later communities the Teachers pursue their own Law-observant mission among Gentiles. In the main it is not they who are reacting to Paul's theology, but rather he who is reacting to theirs. To be sure, the Galatians heard Paul's gospel first and only later that of the Teachers. But the finely formed theology of the Teachers is best understood on the hypothesis that the order of events in Galatia is for them atypical. Elsewhere they will have worked in virgin fields, impelled not by a desire to correct Paul, but by a passion to share with the entire world the only gift they believed to have the power to liberate humankind from the grip of evil, the Law of God's Messiah. In the full sense of the expression, therefore, they represent a Law-observant mission to Gentiles, a mission inaugurated not many years after the death of Jesus.

*Bibliographical Note*

The standard accounts of early Christian missions are those of A. von Harnack, *The Mission and Expansion of Christianity in the First Three Centuries* (German, 1902; English, 1908), and J. Weiss, *The History of Primitive Christianity* (German, 1914; English, 1937). A somewhat more nuanced picture emerges in the recent work of H. Koester, *History and Literature of Early Christianity* (German, Berlin: de Gruyter, 1980; English, Philadelphia: Fortress, 1982), but one notes that Law-observant efforts made among Gentiles by Jewish Christians are still seen to be *reactive* to Paul's Law-free mission (p. 203).

Two recent books on Paul are worth mentioning: Leander E. Keck, *Paul and His Letters* (Philadelphia: Fortress, 1979) and J. Christiaan Beker, *Paul The Apostle* (Fortress, 1980).

On the New Testament as the collection of the documents of the victorious party (Law-free Gentile Christianity), see H. J. Schoeps, *Jewish Christianity* (1969). Regarding sources behind the Pseudo-Clementine literature, see G. Strecker, "On the Problem of Jewish Christianity," in W. Bauer, *Orthodoxy and Heresy in Earliest Christianity* (1978), pp. 241-285. On the term "descendants of Abraham," see J. Louis Martyn, *The Gospel of John in Christian History* (1978), pp. 109-115, with reference also to the work of D. Georgi.

The basic dimensions of this essay were laid out in the spring of 1978 as I was working on the introduction to the Anchor Bible commentary on Galatians. The material was presented in lecture form to the Rainbow Group of New York, 7 March 1982, and to the faculties of the Jewish Theological Seminary of America and the Union Theological Seminary, 21 April 1982.

JOHN DOMINIC CROSSAN

# THE HERMENEUTICAL JESUS

Jesus' parable of *The Great Supper* has been transmitted to us in three different locations and in three different versions. The parable's transmissional plurality will be considered here as an entrance into the problem of the historical Jesus and as a move towards the solution of the hermeneutical Jesus.

## I. Transmissional Analysis

Of the three accounts of the parable, two are intracanonical, being contained in Matthew 22:1–14 and Luke 14:16–24. The other version is extracanonical, appearing in the *Gospel of Thomas* 64. I shall consider them separately rather than simultaneously but develop the comparisons between them as I proceed.

### A. The Parable in the *Gospel of Thomas*.

1. Context. One could think of catholic Christianity as emerging toward its fourth century Constantinian consummation with a more conservative legal Christianity as its right wing and a more radical gnostic Christianity as its left. Options on the right wing, however, were shortly and sharply limited by the Roman destruction of Jerusalem's Temple in 70 C.E. and by the subsequent ascendancy of the Pharisaic vision within and even as official Judaism. Options on the left wing remained fluid for a much longer time but there too it was imperial Roman power, albeit now baptized, which clarified the boundaries and doomed gnostic Christianity to the status of persecuted heresy.

Sometime in that fourth century a sealed jar was buried in the dry sands of Upper Egypt, near the modern town of Nag Hammadi, just north of Luxor. It contained about fifty tracts and represented a small gnostic Christian library. This *may* have been secreted by monks expelled for gnosticism from nearby monasteries as these institutions were being brought more firmly under orthodox control from Alexandria. It was unearthed in December of 1947 at the base of the Nileside cliffs by local peasants digging for fertilizer for their fields.

The tracts were written in Coptic, Egyptian written with the twenty-four letters of the Greek alphabet and seven other letters from the indigenous demotic script. Among the tracts was one which began by announcing that "These are the secret words which the Living Jesus spoke and Didymos Judas Thomas wrote," and which ended with the title "The Gospel according to Thomas." The terms Thomas and Didymos mean Twin respectively in Aramaic and Greek, so the gospel is attributed to Jesus' twin-brother Judas, a figure of very great importance in the Syrian church around Edessa.

This Coptic gospel was translated from a Greek original, and three different fragmentary versions of that Greek were unearthed in the rubbish dumps of Oxyrhynchus, halfway between Nag Hammadi and the Delta, around the turn of the present century. Those fragments, numbered as Oxyrhynchus Papyri 1, 654, 655, push the date of the gospel's composition well back into (at least) the second century.

In form the gospel is very different from the narrative mode so common in the canonical gospels. It is far closer to the discourse mode characteristic of the gnostic gospels, but in *Thomas* it is still the earthly Jesus who speaks and who can be questioned not only by his disciples but also addressed by others as well. The text, then, is composed of aphorisms and parables, questions and answers, and these are assembled sequentially with no concern for overall order, pattern, or development. The gospel is a series of small sections introduced mostly by "Jesus said" and numbered by scholars at 114 units. The only connections are short verbal or formal contacts, as, for example, the sequence of three parables in *Gos. Thom.* 63, 64, 65, which have similar openings in Coptic. Context, therefore, is of no significance.

There is still controversy over the relationship between this newly discovered gospel and the four canonical ones. Is it a dependent conflation of their discourse materials or does it represent an independent strand of the Jesus tradition? Two reasons persuade me of the second alternative. First, there is the question of order or sequence. When you compare the sequence of units in *Thomas* with their parallels in any of the four canonical gospels there is absolutely no coincidence of order whatsoever. In itself this does not prove independence, *if* one could indicate contextual or compositional reasons why *Thomas* might have changed the borrowed materials so radically. But, since *Thomas* itself is absolutely without overall compositional sequence or overall sequential development, such complete reordering becomes inexplicable if not impossible. Second, there is the question of content within the individual units. Here, unfortunately, as controversy came in the door, methodology went out the window. There is little real profit in comparing the content of a unit in *Thomas* and, say, Matthew, and then arguing which came from which. Any decent exegete should be able to furnish several reasons in either direction. Correct method demands the prior separation of what is traditionally given from what is redactionally personal in Matthew. If the former is present in *Thomas*, one has proved nothing, but if the latter, or any such canonical redaction, is discovered in *Thomas*, then and only then can one argue for this gospel's dependence on the canonical four. And it is precisely such editorial additions and redactional elements that are lacking in *Thomas*. Those two reasons taken together persuade me that this recently discovered gospel is an independent transmission of the Jesus tradition.

2. Text. This means that *Thomas'* version of *The Great Supper* must be considered as an independent account of that parable.

The parable in *Gos. Thom.* 64 opens with the usual "Jesus said" and then moves immediately to the first element in the story, *The Situation*:

> A man had guest-friends, and when he had prepared the dinner, he sent his servant to invite the guest-friends.

One immediately senses a possible problem. In this version there is no forewarning of the banquet. It is as if you or I decided on a Saturday morning to have a party that very night and, with preparations fully underway, started to telephone around to various friends. . . . Also, there is only a single servant involved, and he will have to make the full circuit before he can report back on any part of it.

The second element in *Thomas'* parable is what happens with *The Former Guests*. I shall give the text here in parallel columns:

| FIRST GUEST | SECOND GUEST | THIRD GUEST | FOURTH GUEST |
|---|---|---|---|
| He went to the first, he said to him: "My master invites thee." He said: "I have some claims against some merchants; they will come to me in the evening; I will go and give them my orders. I pray to be excused from the dinner." | He went to another, he said to him: "My master has invited thee." He said to him: "I have bought a house and they request me for a day. I will have no time." | He came to another, he said to him: "My master invites thee." He said to him: "My friend is to be married and I am to arrange a dinner: I shall not be able to come. I pray to be excused from the dinner." | He went to another, he said to him: "My master invites thee." He said to him: "I have bought a farm, I go to collect the rent. I shall not be able to come. I pray to be excused." |

There are two points worth noting about the element concerning *The Former Guests*. First, the dialogue between servant and guest is recorded in direct address. This means that we can actually hear their excuses for ourselves and we can hear that they are quite detailed, very reasonable, and extremely polite: "I pray to be excused." The master, having called a dinner without warning, finds that each of his proposed guests has a perfectly valid reason why he cannot come on that specific evening. All takes place within the rubrics of the possible and the plausible. Second, the case of the second guest is distinct from the other three in its dialogue. In that case the servant says, "My master has invited thee," rather than "My master invites thee," as with the other three guests. And in that case the guest gives a three-part rather than a four-part answer, since he omits the terminal apology which is given by the other three guests. I shall return to this second point below.

Next comes the third element in the parable's narrative, *The Latter Guests*. Once again we are in direct discourse, but now between master and servant:

> The servant came, he said to his master: "Those whom thou hast invited to the dinner have excused themselves." The master said to his servant: "Go out to the roads, bring those whom thou shalt find, so that they may dine."

With all the expected and invited guests unavailable, the master simply fills the dinner at random with the unexpected and the uninvited, not with his friends but with strangers.

3. Interpretation. There is, however, one final element appended in the *Gospel of Thomas*. In this *Conclusion* it is Jesus who is now speaking outside the narrative world of the parable and not the master inside it: "Tradesmen and merchants shall not enter the places of my Father." That final sentence serves to interpret the parable as *Thomas* sees it. The ascetic or gnostic Christian is warned not to be like the business people in the story. And this reflects back on the case of the second guest noted above. In the Western story-telling tradition one expects things to happen in threes, for example, *The Three Bears*. And Jesus' parables usually stay clearly within this triadic convention. Think, for example, of the three servants in *The Talents* of Matthew 25:14–28, and the path, rocky ground, thorns in *The Sower* of Mark 4:3–8, or the Priest, Levite, Samaritan in *The Good Samaritan* of Luke 10:30–35. One expects, therefore, triple but not quadruple phenomena in his parables. Most likely, then, *Thomas* added the second guest to increase the overall number to four and to double the "I have bought" between the second and fourth guest. For *Thomas* it is precisely material interests which kept the guests from the dinner and which could keep the gnostic from "the places of my Father."

## B. The Parable in the Gospel of Luke.

1. Source. As noted earlier, *The Great Supper* parable appears in both Matthew 22:1–14 and Luke 14:16–24.

The relationships in order and content between, on the one hand, Matthew, Mark, and Luke, and, on the other, Matthew and Luke, have persuaded scholars that there is some direct literary linkage between those gospels. The solution to this "synoptic problem" which I accept is called the Two-Source Theory because it postulates that Matthew and Luke, apart from their own separate sources, used two common sources. One of these was a narrative gospel which we still have, that of Mark. The other was a discourse gospel which we now have only as it can be reconstructed from behind Matthew and Luke. If this ever had a title, it might have been something like, "The Sayings of the Lord Jesus." But scholars call it Q (for *Quelle*, the German word for Source), a title about which one can only say that it is at least better than X.

It is from this second common source, the discourse gospel known as Q, that Matthew and Luke took their versions of *The Great Supper* parable. Each of them developed the parable in such a different way that this common origin might well be denied in this specific instance. But, as we shall see, it is most likely that their different contexts rather than their different sources better explain those differences.

2. Context. Luke 14:1–24 has grouped a series of Jesus' sayings concerning meal situations in an actual meal situation itself. There are four units involved and each one opens with a reminder of the symposium situation. First, in 14:1–6, there is a healing "one sabbath when he went to dine at the house of a ruler who belonged to the Pharisees." Second, in 14:7–11, he speaks of places of honor "to those who were invited." Third, in 14:12–14, "He said also to the man who had invited him, 'When you give a dinner or a banquet, do not invite your friends or your brothers or your kinsmen or rich neighbors, lest they also invite you in return, and you be repaid. But when you give a feast, invite the poor, the maimed, the lame, the blind, and you will be blessed, because they cannot repay you. You will be repaid at the resurrection of the just." Fourth, in 14:15–24, the parable of *The Great Supper* is introduced by this dialogue: "When one of those who sat at table with him heard this, he said to him, 'Blessed is he who shall eat bread in the kingdom of God.'"

This general context and especially the presence of that immediately preceding third element concerning "the poor, the maimed, the lame, the blind," will be of significance in discussing Luke's interpretation of the parable itself.

3. Text. Like *Thomas*, Luke opens by giving the first element, *The Situation*, in 14:16–17:

> A man once gave a great banquet, and invited many; and at the time for the banquet he sent his servant to say to those who had been invited, "Come; for all is now ready."

But here you notice two differences from *Thomas'* opening. First, the meal has escalated from a dinner with four (or three) guests to a "great banquet" with "many" guests invited. Second, the culpability of the guests is now greatly increased since they had been forewarned and had presumably accepted the invitations proffered earlier. The situation is now as if one's friends had accepted a future dinner invitation but upon being telephoned with a reminder when the actual day came, all then made excuses.

Next, in Luke 14:18–20, comes the second element, the excuses of *The Former Guests*. Once again I shall give them in parallel columns:

| *FIRST GUEST* | *SECOND GUEST* | *THIRD GUEST* |
|---|---|---|
| The first said to him, "I have bought a field, and I must go out and see it; | And another said, "I have bought five yoke of oxen, and I go to examine them; | And another said, "I have married a wife, |
| | | and therefore I cannot come." |
| I pray you, have me excused." | I pray you, have me excused." | |

One notices immediately that the guests here are the conventional triad, as was suggested for the pre-Thomistic version. But each guest does not get a complete dialogue, a complete invitation and answer in direct discourse. Instead, there is recorded a single general invitation, "Come; for all is now ready," and then each guest replies individually. More interestingly, the excuses are no longer four-part responses, as in *Thomas*, but only three-part ones, and yet, as I have indicated in the parallel columns, a four-part process can still be discerned across the triad: (1)— I have bought . . . (2) I must go . . . (3) I cannot come . . . (4) I pray to be excused. . . . Once again, the excuses are plausible and possible, realistic and polite.

We next find a new element, one that was not present in *Thomas*, that is, *The Host's Reaction*. In Luke 14:21 it is noted almost in passing as the element of *The Latter Guests* is being recorded:

> So the servant came and reported this to his master. Then the householder in anger said to his servant, "Go out quickly to the streets and lanes of the city, and bring in the poor and maimed and blind and lame."

Because of the forewarning, this anger is quite understandable in Luke's version. And by the same token the excuses of the guests are no longer understandable. Indeed, their politeness now seems like hypocrisy. But the most important development so far concerning *The Latter Guests* is how the four categories of suffering from Luke 14:13 are now introduced in 14:21: they have moved from context into text.

Next follows an even more interesting difference in that *The Latter Guests* now involve a second sending of the servant, in Luke 14:22–24:

And the servant said, "Sir, what you commanded has been done, and still there is room." And the master said to the servant, "Go out to the highways and hedges, and compel people to come in, that my house may be filled. For I tell you, none of those men who were invited shall taste my banquet."

4. Interpretation. This double sending for *The Latter Guests* is best seen as a factor in Luke's interpretation of the parable. He reads the story not just as a general warning, as does *Thomas*, but as a specific allegorical description of early Christianity's relationship to Judaism, that is, as the opening dialogue puts it, of those "who shall eat bread in the kingdom of God" (Luke 14:15). In Luke's interpretation those who refused to come to the banquet would be "the lawyers and Pharisees" among whom Jesus is sitting and to whom he is speaking: see 14:1-2 and 14:15. They are replaced, first, by the suffering outcasts of Israel from "the streets and lanes of the city," and, second, by believing Gentiles, that is, by those farther away, from "the highways and hedges." If ascetic morality dominates *Thomas'* reading, historical allegory dominates Luke's interpretation.

### C. The Parable in the Gospel of Matthew.

1. Context. Just as the Lukan context of 14:12-14 has deeply affected the Lukan parable in 14:16-24, so also has the Matthean context of 21:33-44 even more deeply affected the Matthean parable in 22:1-14. When contextual influence is accepted on both versions, it is possible, but not much more, to presume a common Q text behind them, as suggested before. But, admittedly, it only shows directly now in such slight contacts as the same Greek words for "farm/field" in Matt 22:5=Luke 14:18 or for "thoroughfares/highways" in Matt 22:9-10= Luke 14:23.

It is clear, however, what Matthew has done. He has formed a parabolic diptych of two stories, one concerning a householder and his tenants (*The Wicked Tenants*) in 21:33-44, and the second concerning a king and his guests (*The Great Supper*) in 22:1-14. And he has placed as their hinge the following statement in 21:45-46: "When the chief priests and the Pharisees heard his parables, they perceived that he was speaking about them. But when they tried to arrest him, they feared the multitudes, because they held him to be a prophet." Within this diptych context, the former parable has infiltrated the Matthean version of the latter parable. For example, in the parable of *The Wicked Tenants* the householder "sent his servants" and "again he sent other servants" in Matt 21:34, 36; so also in that of *The Great Supper*, instead of the single servant of *Thomas* and Luke, the king "sent his servants" and "again he sent other servants" in Matt 22:3, 4. And also: just as servants were "killed" in Matt 21:36, so are they now "killed" in 22:6.

2. Text. Matt 22:2–3a begins immediately with *The Situation*:

> The kingdom of heaven may be compared to a king who gave a marriage feast for his son and sent his servants to call those who were invited to the marriage feast.

First, the escalation of situation continues: from a "dinner" in *Thomas*, to a "great banquet" in Luke, to a wedding feast for a king's son in Matthew. Second, there is again forewarning, as in Luke but not as in *Thomas*, and, of course, the royal occasion renders refusal much more serious. Third, the messengers are now appropriately plural.

Next follows the refusal of *The Former Guests* in 22:3b–6:

> But they would not come. Again he sent other servants, saying, "Tell those who are invited, Behold I have made ready my dinner, my oxen and my fat calves are killed, and everything is ready; come to the marriage feast." But they made light of it and went off, one to his farm, another to his business, while the rest seized his servants, treated them shamefully, and killed them.

This is clearly a very different case from either *Thomas* or Luke. First, as noted above, there are twin sendings of plural servants for *The Former Guests* in Matthew. Second, we have no direct dialogue but hear instead the voice of the king himself, "Behold, I have made ready—come." Third, instead of politely plausible excuses, there is now abuse and murder.

After such a lethal response, one is not surprised that the newer element of *The Host's Reaction*, absent from *Thomas*, cited simply as anger in Luke, is now fully developed in Matt 22:7:

> The king was angry, and he sent his troops and destroyed those murderers and burned their city.

It is now a separate and independent element in the story's narrative sequence.

Then there comes the element of *The Latter Guests* in 22:8–10:

> Then he said to his servants, "The wedding is ready, but those invited were not worthy. Go therefore to the thoroughfares, and invite to the marriage feast as many as you find." And those servants went out into the streets and gathered all whom they found, both bad and good; so the wedding hall was filled with guests.

Like *Thomas*, but unlike Luke, Matthew has only one sending here, but the new guests are specified as "both bad and good." There is nothing about Luke's own particular mention of "the poor and maimed and blind and lame."

Finally, in Matt 22:11–14, there is a brand new element. In *Thomas* we had a three-element plot: Situation, Former Guests, Latter Guests. In Luke a fourth element, *Host's Reaction*, started to appear. This was fully developed in Matthew, and now comes a new one, so that Matthew's plot is a five-element sequence. The fifth and final element is *The Wedding Garment* in 22:11–14:

> But when the king came in to look at the guests, he saw there a man who had no wedding garment; and he said to him, "Friend, how did you get in here without a wedding garment?" And he was speechless. Then the king said to the attendants, "Bind him hand and foot, and cast him into the outer darkness; there men will weep and gnash their teeth." For many are called, but few are chosen.

It has been suggested that we might have here the debris or the summary of a quite separate parable concerning *The Wedding Garment*. While this is quite possible, I am more inclined to see all of 22:11–14 as a creative part of Matthew's own reading of the parable itself.

Matthew 22:11–14 has three parts. The first part concerns the wedding garment in 22:11–12. Notice that while *Thomas* and Luke allowed direct discourse on the lips of servant, guest, and host, Matthew in 22:4, 8, and 12 allows direct discourse only on the king's lips. So 22:11–12 could be purely his. The second part is in 22:13. This is one of Matthew's dearly loved phrases, and, in full panoply, it has three subunits: (a) bound hand and foot, (b) cast into outer darkness, (c) there men will weep and gnash their teeth. Matthew has that third subunit in Matthew 13:42, 50, and he has added it on to Q/Matthew 24:51=Luke 12:46. Matthew has added on the second and third subunits of the phrase to Q/Matthew 8:11–12=Luke 13:28–29 and Q/Matthew 25:29–30=Luke 19:26–27. Finally, here in Matthew 22:13 he has appended all three subunits of the phrase. Clearly, then, 22:13 is pure Matthew. The third part is in 22:14. This is not a statement of the king within the narrative frames of the parable but is an aphorism placed on the lips of Jesus by Matthew to serve as a *Conclusion* for all of 22:1–13. The aphorism is independently known from the anonymous treatise traditionally called the *Epistle of Barnabas*, which dates from the early thirties of the second century. This work, which employs an allegorical interpretation of the Old Testament in the tradition of Philo and Alexandria, warns at *Barn.* 4:14, "And consider this also, my brethren, when you see that after such great signs and wonders were wrought in Israel they were even then finally abandoned;—let us take heed lest as it was written we be found 'many called but few chosen.'"

I conclude, therefore, that all of Matthew 22:11–14 is due to Matthew's own creative reading of Jesus' parable. It is not necessary to postulate an originally independent parable in 22:11–13.

3. Interpretation. For Luke the parable was an allegory of the history of early Christianity. So also for Matthew but in a much more detailed fashion. Indeed, both the diptych parables of Matthew 21:33–44 and

22:1–14 are allegories of earliest Christianity as far as Matthew is concerned.

God has invited, has twice invited, possibly through the earlier and later prophets or maybe even through the prophets of old and the apostles more recently, his people to come to the marriage feast. They have lethally refused, in Matthew's view, and the destruction of "their city," presumably of Jerusalem by Titus in 70 C.E., was the punishment. Now the Gentiles have taken their place at the feast. But, and here comes something characteristically Matthean, even among those at the feast there are "both good and bad." On the last day, at the final judgment, God will review the guests and then it will not be enough simply to be at the feast, it will be necessary to be properly attired for the feast as well. Matthew, in other words, knows certain members in the church whose ultimate fate he does not consider to be eternal happiness. Possibly their attitude towards the Mosaic Law is one of which he disapproves. So also, in the preceding parable of *The Wicked Tenants*, the new tenants who replaced the old ones must make certain to "give him the fruits in their seasons" (21:41). And in an earlier parable, recorded in Matthew 13:24–30 and the *Gospel of Thomas* 57, but interpreted only in Matthew 13:36–43, Matthew knows that there are both wheat and weeds in the kingdom, but "at the close of the age," in the last judgment, "the Son of man will send his angels, and they will gather out of his kingdom all causes of sin and all evildoers, and throw them into the furnace of fire; there men will weep and gnash their teeth" (13:40–41). Within the narrative of the parable, it may have seemed unfair for the king to demand sartorial elegance from guests pulled in off the streets, but within the history of Matthew's own community, the threat was for the future and was, no doubt, quite clear.

## II. Transmissional Emphases

The process which I have just completed follows fairly standard scholarly methodology. It is variously termed traditio-critical or traditio-historical or history-of-traditions analysis. I prefer to avoid hyphens and call it simply transmissional analysis. But it has not been underlined as much as it should have been in past scholarship that *exactly the same transmissional analysis can be the basis for three quite different transmissional emphases.* My second section will explore these three options in both their adequacy and their implications. But I would insist immediately that all can start from a similar transmissional analysis.

## A. Primal Emphasis.

In primal emphasis the concern is with the original parable of the historical Jesus. It would be vastly imprudent to speak of *ipsissima verba*, that is, the precise and verbatim words of Jesus, since Jesus was an oral teacher and within such a sensibility one can speak only of original structure rather than original syntax. Indeed, oral sensibility could be defined as the triumph of structure over syntax, of linguistic structure over sequential syntax. But, in the parable just studied, I would be relatively certain of the original *plot outline*: A host decides on a sudden dinner and by the time his servant returns with the news that none of his friends is available he has everything ready and so brings in anyone he can find. It is a perfectly plausible everyday possibility but it results in a most paradoxical situation: all the expected guests are absent and only unexpected guests are present. The King-dom of God, says Jesus, is like that paradoxical image.

A scholar interested in primal emphasis seeks to recover that original parable. The function of the transmissional analysis is to remove what later writers have added and to see again that original version. Such an emphasis may speak quite pejoratively of those additions, may call them changes or alterations, cobwebs or debris. But, in any case, they are studied only to be removed.

A primal emphasis cannot be dismissed simply because it concerns a scholarly reconstruction, the reconstituted original parable of the historical Jesus. If reconstruction alone invalidated it, much more would be thereby invalidated as well, for example, the very Greek text of the New Testament itself. There is, however, a much more serious problem with primal emphasis and this will be discussed later.

## B. Final Emphasis

In final emphasis the concern is with the ultimate text present on the page. A scholar, for example, might undertake a transmissional analysis not because of any primal emphasis but in order to understand genetically what a given author actually and finally produced. Indeed, a final emphasis may sometimes even dismiss the whole idea of trans-missional analysis and claim exclusive concern with the text as it now stands in final context. This is probably not a good strategy, however, because one tends to look from the corner of the eye at those other versions. Can one really speak of "the Lord's Prayer" without facing the fact that there are two versions of it within the New Testament itself? Can one really speak of "the Beatitudes" without facing the fact that there are two versions of them within the New Testament itself? But, once again, there is a more serious problem with final emphasis, just as earlier with primal emphasis, and this will be considered in the final section.

### C. Hermeneutical Emphasis.

Both those previous emphases were on product, on either the primal and original product of the historical Jesus or the final and scribal product of the individual author. The third emphasis is not on product but on process, not on initial or terminal product but on the entire process which flows from one to the other and also beyond that to all others as well. I term it hermeneutical emphasis and I consider that it is the only adequate emphasis within a transmissional analysis of the Jesus tradition. This can be seen by comparing it with the two preceding emphases and by underlining their weaknesses in comparison with it.

Imagine that we have carefully reconstructed the plot outline of Jesus' original parable by removing what is proper to the versions of a *Thomas*, a Luke, a Matthew. What we have removed are not accretions and alterations but interpretations and applications. It is the intrinsic nature of the successful parable not just to be repeated but to be interpreted. The genre itself provokes hermeneutics, and multiple interpretations are intrinsic to its being. The fact that interpretations are given internally and textually rather than externally and contextually is of minor importance. They are the parable's destiny and, having carefully removed them, we would immediately have to restore them. In parable, original product includes hermeneutical process.

A similar problem arises with final emphasis. First of all, there is an extracanonical and an intracanonical interpretation. Can one simply ignore the former as having no bearing on the latter? And even if one could, there are two interpretations within the canonical books themselves. It is not possible to discuss these versions as canonical products without also raising the question of hermeneutical process. Once again, a product emphasis is inadequate within a situation of hermeneutical process. Indeed, one begins to suspect that what has been canonized by such multiple interpretations of the same parable is not this or that interpretation *but the very necessity of interpretation itself*.

Primal emphasis is sometimes called historical, and final emphasis is sometimes called canonical. But not even those terms can save both emphases from being ultimately absorbed within a hermeneutical emphasis. The modes and genres of Jesus' language, such as, for example, the parable or the aphorism, render hermeneutics imperative, so that transmissional analysis which is both historical and canonical becomes eventually and necessarily hermeneutical analysis.

One final point. In product emphases, whether initial or terminal, the present respondent stands somewhat outside the situation. But when the emphasis is on hermeneutical process the present reader or hearer is pulled inside the phenomenon itself. The parable reaches out through all its earlier interpretations to provoke the present anew.

The search for the historical Jesus has resulted in the discovery of the hermeneutical Jesus. We knew that Jesus hung something on a wall in Galilee. We thought it was a picture of the Kingdom and worked diligently to remove the dust of the ages from its surface. Underneath, however, we found not a picture but a mirror, and the dust of ages was but the images of our ancestors. In a mirror, however, we see not just ourselves but ourselves *looking*. We see our eyes before we see all else. In a parable we see not just ourselves but ourselves *thinking*, ourselves interpreting, ourselves being interpreted. We see our minds before we see all else. It is in such hermeneutical wrestle that the Kingdom is experienced and the fact that the mirror is overlaid with images, with multiple interpretations, is not our failure but its success.

*Bibliographical Note*

The most serious and sympathetic study of the religious ethos of the Nag Hammadi materials, though it predates full analysis of them, is Hans Jonas's *The Gnostic Religion* (Boston: Beacon Press, 1966). A more popular and up-to-date treatment is John Dart's *The Laughing Savior: The Discovery and Significance of the Nag Hammadi Gnostic Library* (New York: Harper and Row, 1976). The only complete translation of the texts is *The Nag Hammadi Library in English*, edited by James M. Robinson (New York: Harper and Row, 1977).

JOHN J. COLLINS

# THE APOCALYPTIC CONTEXT OF
# CHRISTIAN ORIGINS

"Apocalyptic was the mother of all Christian theology." This bold assertion by the German New Testament scholar Ernst Käsemann has been the subject of much controversy among biblical scholars and theologians. Few can deny that it has some basis in fact. There were, at least, notable apocalyptic elements in early Christianity. Yet many have been reluctant to admit that these elements could have had central importance. In a reply to Käsemann, another German theologian, Gerhard Ebeling, cautioned that "according to the prevailing ecclesiastical and theological tradition, . . . apocalyptic is, to say the least, a suspicious symptom of tendencies towards heresy." The best known apocalypse, the New Testament Book of Revelation, has always been especially attractive for groups on the fringes of Christianity and has been used to fuel emotional and irrational beliefs about the imminent end of the world. More orthodox Christians are often embarrassed by the possibility that such speculation played a significant part in the origins of their religion, and are at a loss as to what to do with this part of their heritage. Moreover the apocalyptic books are full of strange imagery and cryptic signs which are highly confusing for the uninitiated. If it is true that familiarity breeds contempt, it is no less true that excessive strangeness is repelling. Many Christians, theologians and lay, would gladly relegate the apocalyptic literature to the shadowy realm of New Testament "backgrounds." Anyone who wants to understand Christianity, however, must recognize that this strange material is an integral part of the tradition, which cannot be left out of account.

## I. The Genre "Apocalypse"

Since the adjective "apocalyptic" is commonly misused as a noun, it may be well at the outset to clarify our terminology. The basic point of reference for any discussion of apocalpytic matters is the literary genre apocalypse. The word apocalpyse, Greek *apokalypsis*, means "revelation," but it is usually reserved for a specific type of revelation, characterized by distinctive form and content. *In form*, the revelation is mediated by an otherworldly being to a human recipient. Usually the recipient is said to be a venerable ancient figure, such as Enoch or Abraham, although some early Christian apocalypses depart from this convention (notably the Book of Revelation). In one type of apocalypse this human figure sees visions, which are then interpreted for him by an angel. In the other main type, the human being is elevated to the heavens and given a guided tour, again by an interpreting angel. The mediating angel distinguishes the apocalypses from most prophetic revelations, where the message is received directly from God. *In content*, the apocalypses always involve a supernatural world, which may be described in cosmological detail, or may be indicated primarily by the activity of angels. They also involve some form of eschatological salvation, which includes provision for the judgment of the dead. One group of apocalypses, the "historical" type, envisages a pattern in history leading up to a final judgment. Other apocalpyses pay little attention to history but are concerned rather with the judgment of the individual. Some form of final judgment is essential to the kind of revelation we call an apocalypse. This point is very important, since ancient Israelite religion, as attested in the Old Testament, did not envisage a judgment of the dead. Most scholars agree that the only reference to resurrection in the Hebrew Bible is found in the apocalyptic Book of Daniel. (There are a few disputed passages in earlier books.) It would seem that the notions of resurrection and judgment of the dead first entered the Judeo-Christian tradition through the apocalyptic literature.

The literary apocalypses provide the touchstone for the broader use of the word "apocalyptic." The adjective apocalyptic may be applied to ideas and motifs which are typical of apocalypses, although this usage will inevitably be loose. "Apocalypticism" is the ideology of a movement characterized by apocalyptic ideas. The Essenes of Qumran, the people of the Dead Sea Scrolls, provide a relevant example. Finally, apocalyptic eschatology is the kind of eschatology found in apocalypses, but which may also be found in other genres. Its most distinctive feature is a focus on the judgment of the dead.

Only two books in the Bible are apocalypses: the Book of Daniel in the Old Testament (strictly, only Daniel 7–12) and the Book of Revelation in the New. A few other biblical passages are sometimes called apocalypses, notably Isaiah 24–27 and Mark 13, but they lack the distinctively apocalyptic form of revelation which we have described above. The main corpus of apocalypses is found outside the Bible, in Jewish books attributed to Enoch, Ezra, Baruch and Abraham, and later Christian apocalypses of Peter, Paul, John, James and Mary. In the past scholars have often assumed that the canonical apocalypses came first and that the noncanonical ones were second-class imitations. We now know that this is not so. The Book of Daniel was written about 164 B.C.E. Fragments of books of Enoch have been found among the

Dead Sea Scrolls which date from the first quarter of the second century, or may even be earlier than 200 B.C.E. These discoveries have changed our understanding of the apocalyptic literature appreciably. The earliest Enoch books, the Book of the Watchers and the Astronomical Book, diverge more sharply from the biblical tradition than is the case in Daniel. It becomes more difficult then to view the apocalypses simply as an outgrowth of biblical prophecy.

The nature of the apocalyptic literature may be most easily understood if we illustrate it from two early examples, the Enochic Book of the Watchers (1 Enoch 1–36) and the visions of Daniel.

## II. The Book of the Watchers

The Book of the Watchers takes its name from the story of the fallen angels (the Watchers). In a brief and enigmatic passage in Genesis 6 we are told that the sons of God saw that the daughters of men were fair, came in to them and begat children. In 1 Enoch 6–11 this story is elaborated. Here the Watchers form a conspiracy before they descend. They not only beget giants but also teach the women charms and spells. The giants devour all that mankind can produce and spread violence and lawlessness. Then some angels take the complaint of the earth to God, and he commands them to imprison the Watchers and cleanse the earth.

Enoch now enters the story. The Watchers ask him to intercede for them. Enoch is lifted up to heaven on the clouds and is admitted to the divine throne. The petition of the Watchers is rejected. Enoch is given a message for them: "You were in heaven but its secrets had not yet been revealed to you and a worthless mystery you knew. This you made known to the women.... You will not have peace" (16:3–4). By contrast, the secrets of heaven are now revealed to Enoch. He is taken on an extended tour, guided by angels. He is shown the storehouses of the winds, the cornerstone of the earth and all the mysteries of creation. He is also shown "the prison for the stars of heaven and the host of heaven" (18:14) and the place where the Watchers will be judged. He also sees the places which are prepared for "the spirits, the souls of the dead" (chap. 22), paradise and the valley of Gehenna. His vision extends to the ends of the earth and moves him to praise God.

The Book of the Watchers serves as an interesting introduction to the apocalypses in several respects. First it is obviously an imaginative, even fantastic composition. The biblical Enoch allegedly lived before the Flood. His adventures here are evidently pseudonymous—Enoch is not the real author but a fictional surrogate. In large part the story is extrapolated from the terse allusion to the sons of God in Genesis and from the statement in Genesis 5:24 that Enoch walked with 'ĕlohîm, which is usually translated "God" but more probably refers to angels.

Undoubtedly, Genesis already presupposes a legend about Enoch but the highly developed account in the Book of the Watchers depends on the biblical text. There is also evidence that the portrayal of Enoch incorporates motifs which were associated with legendary Babylonian heroes, especially the seventh Babylonian king, Enmeduranki. The motif of ascent to heaven was fairly widespread in antiquity, and indeed in world religions in general. What is important for our present purpose is that the entire story in the Book of the Watchers is an imaginative construct, woven from various traditional motifs but ultimately a work of fiction. No one would argue that the book recounts actual experiences of Enoch, or that it provides reliable information about cosmological matters or future events.

This is not to say that the Book of Watchers is simply a work of fantasy, unrelated to historical experience. Unlike some other apocalypses, such as Daniel or Revelation, the book gives no clear indication of the circumstances in which it was written. Yet scholars have assumed, with good reason, that the story of the Watchers is a veiled way of alluding to contemporary events. Specifically, the fallen "sons of God" have been seen as an allegory for the Greek princes who ruled the Near East after Alexander the Great and who often claimed to be divine. If indeed the story originally referred to the Greek princes, then the Book of the Watchers can be seen as a complaint against the influx of Hellenistic culture in the third century B.C.E. There is nothing to indicate persecution or any specific historical crisis. The condition of the Jews under Hellenistic rule at any time in a period of more than a hundred years could have given rise to this apocalypse.

The Book of the Watchers does not refer explicitly to the Hellenistic princes or to any other historical figures. Such evasiveness is characteristic of apocalyptic writings. It is not a result of fear that open criticism of the pagan authorities would bring persecution. There is no suggestion of persecution in the Book of the Watchers. When persecution was a factor, as in the Book of Daniel, the authors did not seek to avoid it, but welcomed martyrdom. Rather, the use of allegory is an intrinsic aspect of apocalyptic rhetoric. The apocalypse furnishes imagery to articulate any situation where affairs are out of control, and violence and sin are rampant. The story of the Watchers provides a mythic paradigm which illustrates a type of situation which can recur at various times. The problems of the Hellenistic age, then, are not unique or even novel; they are an actualization of the mythic paradigm. The evil in the world is not ultimately due to Greek princes but to fallen angels. The outcome of the myth is known: it ends with the judgment of the Watchers. Accordingly one may anticipate that the problems of the present will be resolved in a similar way.

The allegorical application of the story of the Watchers is not the only means which this book provides for dealing with problems. The worthless mysteries of the Watchers are contrasted with the secrets of heaven revealed to Enoch and now revealed to the reader too. Enoch's tour of the heavens and the extremities of the earth puts the problems of the present in context. Evil may be rampant on earth, but we now know that the places of judgment, and of reward and punishment, are already prepared. The present success of the Watchers is of lesser importance in the light of the knowledge that their fate is sealed. Moreover, the mysteries of heaven, and the sight of the divine throne itself, induce a sense of wonder which culminates in the praise of God. While everything may seem chaotic, God is in his heaven and all will ultimately be well.

The Book of the Watchers suggests on the one hand that there is a pattern in history, which can be illustrated by the story of the Watchers, and, on the other hand, that there is a structure in the universe and that provision has already been made for the eschatological judgment. Any problem will be shrunken in significance because of the larger view provided by the revelation. It is characteristic of the apocalypses that this revelation is not accessible to everyone. It was given to Enoch, long ago, with the assistance of angels. It involves knowledge which is out of this world.

### III. Daniel

The visions of Daniel may be more familiar to the average reader than the story of the Watchers, but the imagery is scarcely less bizarre. In Daniel 7 we read that Daniel had a dream and visions of his head as he lay in his bed. He saw four great beasts come up out of the sea, one like a lion with eagles' wings, one like a bear, then a leopard with four wings and finally a beast with ten horns, from which another little horn then sprouted. As Daniel watched, an "ancient of days" took his seat on a fiery throne. The fourth beast was slain and burned with fire, while the dominion of the other beasts was taken away. Finally "one like a son of man" came on the clouds of heaven and was presented before the Ancient of Days, and was given a kingdom which would never be destroyed. An angel then gives Daniel a partial explanation. The four beasts are four kings (7:17) but the fourth is a kingdom and each of the horns represents a king (7:23–24). The little horn will make war on "the holy ones of the Most High" and prevail for a time, but in the end "the holy ones of the Most High" will receive the kingdom (7:18) and "the greatness of the kingdoms under the whole heaven" will be given to "the people of the holy ones of the Most High" (7:27).

Here, as in the Book of the Watchers, there is no explicit mention of historical figures. In this case, however, the original referents are not in doubt. The four kingdoms can only be the Babylonians, Medes,

Persians, and Greeks. In fact, the Medes never ruled either Babylon or Judea, but the sequence of Medes and Persians had become a fixed schema, as we know from classical sources. Accordingly, the little horn must be the eleventh king of the Greek era. While there is some uncertainty as to how the Greek kings should be counted, the allusions to persecution make clear enough that the little horn is Antiochus IV Epiphanes, the king whose defilement of the Jerusalem temple precipitated the Maccabean revolt.

The vision of the beasts from the sea and the "one like a son of man" provides here the allegorical dress for the conflict between the Hellenistic powers and the Jews. The imagery has ancient associations. In the Old Testament there are scattered allusions to a battle between Yahweh and the monsters of the deep: "Was it not you that cut Rahab in pieces? that pierced the dragon? Was it not you that dried up the sea, the waters of the great deep?" (Isaiah 51:9–10; cf. also Psalms 74:13–17; 89:9–11; Job 26:7, 12–13). In the so-called Apocalypse of Isaiah the battle is still in the future: "In that day the Lord with his hard and great and strong sword will punish Leviathan the fleeting serpent, Leviathan the twisting serpent, and he will slay the dragon that is in the sea" (Isa 27:1). Usually the battle is assumed to have taken place in primordial times. No battle between Yahweh and a sea-monster is ever described in the narrative books of the Bible, but the allusions have been clarified by the discovery of the Canaanite texts from Ugarit. There we read of a battle between the god Baal and the Sea (Yamm) and its monsters. Evidently the old Canaanite myth had been adapted in ancient Israel so that Yahweh, not Baal, is the victorious deity. The Canaanite material is directly relevant to Daniel 7, however. In the Ugaritic myths, Baal is the rider of the clouds, an epithet which is reserved for Yahweh in the Old Testament. In Daniel 7 the "one like a son of man" who comes with the clouds is clearly distinct from the Ancient of Days, who must be identified as Yahweh. The imagery suggests that both the Ancient of Days and the one like a son of man are divine beings. The apparent discrepancy is best explained if we assume that Daniel is adapting a Canaanite scene in which the ancient god was the high god El and the rider of the clouds was Baal, exalted in victory over the sea and its monsters.

The rhetorical effect of the vision derives from the allegorical use of this imagery. The four kingdoms are not merely human powers. They are beasts which come up out of the sea, embodiments of the chaotic forces symbolized in the ancient myths. Equally they are not overcome by a human power but by divine judgment and by the exalted figure of "one like a son of man."

The identity of the "one like a son of man" who plays the role of Baal in Daniel's adaptation of the myth, has been one of the most keenly disputed questions in biblical interpretation. According to the interpretation the kingdom is given to "the holy ones of the Most High" and "the people of the holy ones of the Most High." While these are not identified with the "one like a son of man," there is obviously a correspondence between them. The question is complicated by the ambiguity of the term "holy ones." In the great majority of cases in the Old Testament and Dead Sea Scrolls the holy ones are angels. In Daniel 7 "the people of the holy ones" are clearly the persecuted Jews but this very terminology suggests that they have the support of the heavenly host, to counter the demonic power of the beasts. The "one like a son of man" should not be simply identified with the holy ones but is their leader and representative. Elsewhere in Daniel, figures who have the appearance of a man are found to be angels (e.g., 8:15; 10:18). In light of the parallel account in Daniel chaps. 10–12, the "one like a son of man" can be most plausibly identified as the archangel Michael, leader of the heavenly host.

The technique of Daniel's vision is analogous to that of the Book of the Watchers. On the one hand, the allegory reduces the persecution of Antiochus to the recurring pattern of the myth. The outcome is assured by the traditional pattern. On the other hand, the conflict is viewed as a struggle between supernatural, mythic forces. The human dimension of the conflict is thus put in perspective. The hope of the Jews does not depend on their own strength but on the judgment of God, and on the "one like a son of man."

The apocalyptic vision of Daniel is more clearly expressed in chaps. 10–12. There Daniel sees an angel who explains to him that there is an ongoing battle between the angel himself, aided by Michael, "prince" of Israel, and the angelic "princes" of Persia and Greece. Chapter 11 describes the wars between the Hellenistic princes. No names are mentioned, but the identifications can be easily supplied. The story comes to a climax with the persecution of the Jews by Antiochus Epiphanes. Then, we are told, "the people who know their God shall stand firm and take action, and those among the people who are wise shall make many understand, though they shall fall by sword and flame, by captivity and plunder for some days. When they fall they shall receive little help . . . and some of those who are wise shall fall, to refine and to cleanse them and to make them white . . . " (11:32–34). The narrative goes on to describe how the king would come to his end "between the sea and the glorious holy mountain"— i.e., in the land of Israel. The eschatological conclusion follows: "At that time shall arise Michael, the great prince who has charge of your people. And there shall be a time of trouble . . . but at that time your people shall be delivered, every one whose name shall be found written in the book. And many of those who sleep in the dust of the earth shall awake, some to everlasting life, and some to shame and everlasting contempt. And those who are wise shall shine like the brightness of the firmament; and those who turn many to righteousness, like the stars for ever and ever" (12:1–3).

This lengthy discourse by the angel throws much light on the logic of apocalyptic thought. First, it is quite clear that two levels of action are distinguished. Behind the struggles of the Hellenistic rulers lies the ongoing battle of the angels. The decisive action is not on the earthly level, but is the victory of Michael. Second, the focus of the entire revelation is evidently the crisis brought on by the persecution of Antiochus. The long review of Hellenistic history is designed to show that this crisis is near the time of the end. The accurate account of the Hellenistic wars inspires confidence that the final predictions are accurate too. In fact, they are only accurate down to the time of the persecution. Antiochus did not die in the land of Israel. From this we know that the prophecy was actually composed after the outbreak of the persecution but before the king's death. Finally the promise of resurrection plays a crucial role. The wise teachers can withstand Antiochus even at the cost of their lives because they are assured that they will rise again and "shine like the stars," which, in apocalyptic symbolism, means that they will become companions of the heavenly angelic host.

It should be clear that Daniel is no less a work of imagination and fantasy than the Book of the Watchers in 1 Enoch. Many conservative Christians are unwilling to grant this, mainly because the book is included in the Bible. Daniel was ostensibly a Jew who lived during the Babylonian exile, not an obviously legendary character like Enoch. In fact, however, the stories about Daniel in chaps. 1–6 of the book are riddled with historical problems. (E.g., a prominent role is assigned to "Darius the Mede." No such king ever existed.) The stories of the fiery furnace and lions' den are the stuff of legend, not of history. The visions too are clearly fictions, which do not give factual information but are powerful poetic expressions of hope in a time of despair. The Book of Enoch provided an alternative to the disorder of the present by imagining the cosmology of a transcendent world. Daniel's visions place their main emphasis on the axis of history and project the resolution of the present conflict. The details of this projection proved unreliable, but the Book of Daniel was by no means discredited in the Jewish community. More important than the time and location of the death of Antiochus was the conviction that the crisis would pass and that the persecuted Jews would be vindicated. In this more general sense, the prophecy of Daniel could be said to be fulfilled. A crucial part of Daniel's prediction, however, concerned the resurrection and judgment of the dead, which could neither be verified nor disproved. Daniel's vision of the future invited the Jews to stake their lives on a hope which went beyond this world and adjust their values accordingly.

## IV. The Qumran Scrolls

The Book of the Watchers and the Book of Daniel were composed more than two hundred years before the New Testament, but the genre flourished throughout this period. Some of the greatest Jewish apocalypses (4 Ezra, 2 Baruch) were composed in the period after the destruction of Jerusalem in 70 C.E., roughly contemporary with the gospels and the Book of Revelation. Somewhat earlier, perhaps contemporary with the Epistles of Paul, are the Similitudes of Enoch, which are notable for their emphasis on a heavenly figure who is referred to as "that Son of Man." Besides the literary apocalypses, the central ideas of Daniel and Enoch had become fairly widespread in Judaism by New Testament times. Much light has been thrown on this period by the discovery of the Dead Sea Scrolls, the library of an Essene community which lived at Qumran from roughly 150 B.C.E. to 68 C.E. The Essenes preserved several copies of Daniel and the Enoch literature, but, as far as we know at present, did not compose any apocalypses. Yet they may fairly be described as an apocalyptic community. According to their Community Rule, the world is in the grip of an ongoing struggle between a spirit of light and a spirit of darkness, which fight even within the hearts of men. "God has established the spirits in equal measure until the final age ... but in the mysteries of his understanding and in His glorious wisdom, God has ordained an end for falsehood, and at the time of his visitation he will destroy it forever." The Qumran War Scroll anticipated a final battle between the Sons of Light and the Sons of Darkness when this conflict would finally be resolved. The Scrolls repeatedly emphasize the mysterious character of the world and of history, but the mysteries are revealed to the Teacher of Righteousness, the founder of the community. In particular the scriptures were viewed as coded mysteries which referred to the last generation. In their commentaries (*pěsharîm*) the scribes of Qumran interpreted the scriptures with reference to the events of their own time, on the assumption that the final generation was now at hand. So they explain, with regard to Habbakuk: "And God told Habbakuk to write down that which would happen to the final generation, but he did not make known to him when time would come to an end. And as for that which He said, *That he who reads may read it speedily*, interpreted this concerns the Teacher of Righteousness to whom God made known all the mysteries of the words of His servants the prophets." So, while the Qumran community did not write apocalypses, it shared many basic ideas which were characteristic of the genre: the world is mysterious and can only be interpreted by means of special revelation; history is subject to supernatural powers and the final age is at hand. The last point is not essential to all apocalypses but it is typical of the "historical" type exemplified by Daniel.

## V. The New Testament

We may now return to Käsemann's dictum that "apocalyptic was the mother of all Christian theology." There is only one full-blown apocalypse in the New Testament, the Book of Revelation. It is a relatively late work, composed in the last decade of the first century. Its historical significance is considerable, and it heralded a rapid growth of Christian apocalypses in the second century. Yet it could hardly be described as a central New Testament work. Käsemann's argument was evidently not based on the centrality of Revelation. Rather, the issue is whether the earliest stages of Christianity involve ideas which are especially characteristic of the apocalypses and share an apocalyptic view of the world.

The importance of apocalypticism for Christian origins centers on the most basic of all Christian beliefs, the resurrection of Jesus from the dead. The resurrection was never viewed as an isolated miracle but rather as a revelatory event which provided a new perspective on life and history. The new perspective could be articulated in various ways, and in time was found to be compatible with various theological and philosophical systems. In the earliest stages of Christianity, however, the context in which the understanding of the resurrection developed was distinctly apocalyptic. This point can be illustrated by considering two major witnesses to early Christianity, the letters of Paul and the "Son of Man" passages in the three Synoptic Gospels. In both illustrations, the major affinities of the New Testament are with the "historical" apocalypses of Daniel's type rather than with the otherworldly journeys of Enoch.

### Paul

The earliest discussion we have of the resurrection is provided by St. Paul in 1 Corinthians 15. His argument is striking, since he makes no mention of an empty tomb. Rather, he mentions the apparitions of Jesus to the apostles, to "more than 500 brethren at one time" and to Paul himself. Yet even the visions are not regarded as conclusive proof, for "if there is no resurrection of the dead, then Christ has not been raised" (1 Cor 15:13). An empty tomb or visions can be explained in various ways and cannot convince anyone who denies a priori that resurrection is possible. For Paul, the resurrection of Jesus is not an isolated event. It is not enough to believe that God could raise a privileged individual as he had taken Elijah up to heaven according to the Old Testament. Rather, Christ is the "first fruits of those who have fallen asleep," and his resurrection is as fateful for humanity as the sin of Adam had been. In short, Paul argues that the resurrection of Jesus must be understood in the context of a general resurrection, and since one person has already been raised the rest cannot be far behind. The end is at hand. This reasoning is also apparent in Peter's speech in the second chapter of Acts. There the phenomenon of speaking in tongues is taken as evidence that prophecy is being fulfilled and that the "day of the Lord" is imminent. Again, the underpinning of Peter's argument is that God raised up "this Jesus; of that we all are witnesses. Being therefore exalted at the right hand of God and having received from the Father the promise of the Holy Spirit, he has poured out this which you see and hear" (Acts 2:32–33). Belief in the resurrection implies that the "last days" are at hand.

The hope of resurrection had been introduced into the Jewish tradition in the apocalyptic writings. By the first century C.E. it had become fairly widely disseminated in circles which could not be categorized as "apocalyptic" such as that of the Pharisees. Whether or not an author or group is "apocalyptic" depends not only on whether they attest apocalyptic ideas or motifs, but whether those ideas occupy a central place in their thought. In Paul, the resurrection and the transformation of creation which it brings are absolutely pivotal. It is accompanied by a sense of urgency which underlines the affinity with the "historical" type of apocalypses. At least in the earlier part of his career Paul expected that the second coming of Christ would take place in his own lifetime: "Lo! I tell you a mystery. We shall not all sleep but we shall all be changed, in a moment, in the twinkling of an eye, at the last trumpet. For the trumpet will sound, and the dead will be raised imperishable, and we shall be changed" (1 Cor 15:51–52). The first letter to the Thessalonians is more explicit: "We who are alive, who are left until the coming of the Lord, shall not precede those who have fallen asleep. . . . The dead in Christ will rise first; then we who are alive, who are left, will be caught up together with them in the clouds to meet the Lord in the air and so we shall always be with the Lord" (1 Thess 4:15–17). We may infer from 2 Thessalonians chap. 2 that at least some circles had no difficulty in believing that the end was at hand. Instead, it was necessary to calm them down: "We beg you brethren, not to be quickly shaken in mind, or excited, either by spirit or by word, or by letter purporting to be from us to the effect that the day of the Lord has come." The passage goes on to explain how the "lawless one" must yet be revealed and the Lord Jesus will slay him with the breath of his mouth. (2 Thessalonians was probably not written by Paul himself.)

Much of Paul's practical theology is colored by the sense of imminent expectation. So he writes to the Corinthians: "I mean, brethren, the appointed time has grown very short; from now on let those who have wives live as though they had none, and those who mourn as though they were not mourning, and those who rejoice as though they were not rejoicing, and those who buy as though they had no goods, and those who deal with the world as though they had no dealings with it. For the form of this world is passing away" (1 Cor

7:29–31). The impact of Paul's advice on Christian spirituality would be felt long after the sense of imminent expectation declined.

The significance of the resurrection for Paul was not only in the urgent sense of an ending which it triggered. It also provided a model for Christian life. The death of Jesus showed that salvation must be sought beyond this life in resurrection. The way to salvation was henceforth to be like Christ: "Do you now know that all of us who have been baptized into Christ Jesus were baptized into his death? We were buried therefore with him by baptism into death, so that as Christ was raised from the dead by the glory of the Father, we too might walk in newness of life. For if we have been united with him in a death like his, we shall certainly be united with him in a resurrection like his" (Romans 6:3–5). In Daniel, the martyrs who lose their lives in this world are precisely those who shine like the stars in resurrection. The example of Jesus has evidently far greater force for Paul and becomes a normative example for Christians so that the death and resurrection of Jesus becomes an allegory for the pattern of Christian life. The new event of Jesus' death holds a central place in Paul's theology, but its significance is viewed in an apocalyptic context, in so far as it points the way to the resurrection.

## The Son of Man

The belief in the resurrection of Jesus led the early Christians to the conviction that the end was at hand. It also led to new ideas of who Jesus was. After the crucifixion the followers of Jesus searched the scriptures for anything that would make sense of the death of their leader. The messianic passages of the Old Testament must now be read in a new light, and the key was provided by the apocalyptic hope of resurrection. Daniel had made sense of the death of the righteous martyrs by affirming that they would be resurrected. Now the shocking death of Jesus could be explained in the same way, and the explanation found confirmation in the visions of the disciples. Jesus was not regarded as just another martyr, but as the messiah, and so the early Christians sought support for their beliefs in the prophecies of the Old Testament. The process is exemplified in Acts 2. There Psalm 16 ("For thou wilt not abandon my soul to Hades, nor let thy holy one see corruption") is read in a novel way, as a prophecy of the resurrection of the messiah. Again, Psalm 110 ("The Lord said to my lord, Sit at my right hand") is taken to mean that the messiah is exalted to the right hand of God in heaven. The exegetical method here is similar to that practiced in the Qumran commentaries and shows no regard for the original historical context of the prophecies. Given the belief that Jesus was exalted to heaven, it was inevitable that he would also be identified with the "one like a son of man" of Daniel. The sequence of associations is apparent in Stephen's vision in Acts 7: "Behold, I see the heavens opened and the Son of Man standing at the right hand of God." In several passages in the Synoptic Gospels the emphasis is on the future coming of Jesus as "Son of Man" on the clouds of heaven.

It is possible that Jesus used the expression "son of man" to refer to himself, as a circumlocution for "I" (e.g., "The son of man has nowhere to lay his head"), but the belief that he would come again on the clouds of heaven presupposes both the resurrection and the ascension. Only when Jesus had gone up to heaven did it make sense to expect that he would come on the clouds. The expectation of the Son of Man was not only a belief that the end was coming. As in Daniel, the figure on the clouds is the vindicator of those who are buffeted in the present: "They will deliver you up to councils and synagogues . . . you will be hated by all for my name's sake . . . but in those days, after that tribulation, the sun will be darkened . . . and then they will see the Son of Man coming in clouds with great power and glory. And then he will send out the angels, and gather his elect from the four winds, from the ends of the earth to the ends of heaven" (Mark 13). The pattern of crisis/persecution followed by the triumphant coming of the Son of Man is similar to Daniel 7; it can serve as a paradigm for any crisis in which Christians may find themselves. In Matthew 25 the Son of Man sits on his throne of glory and presides over the final judgment. The assignment of judgment to the Son of Man marks a development over Daniel 7 but is paralleled in the Similitudes of Enoch, a Jewish apocalypse from the first century C.E.

The identification of Jesus with the "Son of Man" in Daniel serves nicely to illustrate the blend of apocalyptic tradition and new experience which went into the formation of Christianity. In Daniel, the "one like a son of man" was a heavenly figure, most probably the archangel Michael. In Mark he is also a heavenly figure, but he has a different history, since he is identified with the man from Nazareth who was crucified. Jesus is a role model for the persecuted Christians of the first century in a way that Michael could never be for their Jewish ancestors. Yet the Son of Man in Mark 13 comes in power and glory. He is not only a model for the Christians, but he is the heavenly power that ensures their final triumph.

## VI. Conclusion

Neither the Synoptic writers nor St. Paul use the literary form of "apocalypse" which we outlined at the beginning of this essay. It is also true that the unifying element for Christian theology is not apocalypticism but the focus on the person of Jesus of Nazareth. Apocalyptic elements are by no means the only factor in earliest Christianity. Käsemann's claim should therefore be modified. Yet it also has a substantial basis. Insofar as the resurrection of Jesus was understood to imply that the general resurrection was at hand and formed the basis for the rise of Christology, the apocalyptic elements in the New Testament occupied a place of central importance. Consequently the Book of Revelation cannot be viewed as an oddity in the New Testament; rather it develops, with its own distinctive emphases, basic ideas and themes that are found in Paul and the Gospels. From the second century on, Christianity increasingly found the apocalyptic genre to be a congenial medium of expression, although the emphasis moved away from the urgent expectation of the New Testament to the more speculative apocalypses of the heavenly journey type.

What significance can now be attached to the apocalyptic character of early Christianity? The expectation of the imminent second coming of Christ proved to be mistaken. Yet there is little indication that Christianity suffered any significant crisis of credibility for this reason. As we have seen in Daniel, apocalyptic literature does not give exact information about times or places. Paul's scenario for the rapture in 1 Thessalonians ("We who are alive . . . will be caught up . . . to meet the Lord in the air") is a tour de force of the imagination, just as much as Enoch's heavenly journey. The abiding value of such poetic flights lies not in their pseudo-information, but in the underlying conviction that this world is passing away. Even if the physical universe endures forever, there is no doubt that the social and cultural, man-made worlds we inhabit are constantly crumbling. Christianity, like the Jewish apocalypses, involves a challenge to affirm transcendent values, those things which we should affirm even when the world around us collapses. The pervasive sense of transience finds its counterpart in the Christian conviction that death was not the end of Jesus of Nazareth. Something endures, however difficult it may be to express exactly. Beyond the thresholds of life and of this world we can only see as in a glass darkly, in the Pauline phrase. The apocalyptic revelations are symbolic attempts to penetrate the darkness. They provide ways of imagining the unknown, not factual knowledge. Christians should have learned by now to be wary of the naive apocalypticism which is obsessed with factual prediction, especially when it is combined with dogmatic fundamentalism. Yet Christianity could scarcely retain its identity without some form of the transcendent perspective and sense of the transience of this world which it inherited from the Jewish apocalypses.

*Bibliographical Note*

On apocalypses most generally, see *Apocalypse: The Morphology of a Genre*, ed. J. J. Collins (Semeia 14; Missoula, Montana: Scholars Press, 1979). On Daniel, see J. J. Collins, *The Apocalyptic Vision of the Book of Daniel* (Missoula: Scholars Press, 1977), and, in a more popular vein, in the Old

Testament Message series *Daniel, 1 and 2 Maccabees, With An Appendix on the Apocalyptic Genre* (Wilmington, Delaware: Michael Glazier, 1981). On the New Testament Apocalypse, see Adela Yarbro Collins, *The Apocalypse* (New Testament Message; Wilmington: Michael Glazier, 1979).

The work of Käsemann and Ebeling can be sampled in *Apocalypticism*, ed. R. W. Funk (Journal for Theology and the Church 6; New York: Herder, 1969). The Qumran passages are cited from Geza Vermes, *The Dead Sea Scrolls in English* (Baltimore: Penguin, 1968).

BERNARD McGINN

# SYMBOLS OF THE APOCALYPSE
# IN MEDIEVAL CULTURE

Fifty years ago George Bernard Shaw issued an original, if highly
abbreviated, commentary on the Bible and Western religious tradition
under the guise of a Voltairian moral tale. *The Adventures of the Black
Girl in Her Search for God* (1932) possessed the virtues of brevity and
boldness, though not that of sympathy with Christianity. One cannot
but be amused by the panache with which Shaw summarized the
various parts of the Bible, and especially by his dismissal of its final
book as " . . . a curious record of the visions of a drug addict which was
absurdly admitted to the canon under the title of Revelation. . . ."
   Saint John the Junkie has exercised a more potent attraction on other
twentieth-century writers, such as D. H. Lawrence, whose early
education was at least as biblically-formed as that of Shaw. Lawrence's
*Apocalypse* (1931), his last work, was the result of lifelong interest and
considerable ambivalence. Lawrence was at once appalled by the
Apocalypse and fascinated by it—appalled by what he took to be its
appeal to vengeance as the ultimate religious motivation, fascinated by
the way in which the work summed up the collective religious values
that had dominated Western society. He concludes:

> The Apocalypse of John is, as it stands, the work of a second-rate mind.
> It appeals intensely to second-rate minds in every country and every
> century. Strangely enough, unintelligible as it is, it has no doubt been the
> greatest source of inspiration of the vast mass of Christian minds—the
> vast mass being always second-rate—since the first century, and we
> realise, to our horror, that this is what we are up against today; not Jesus
> nor Paul, but John of Patmos.

Lawrence's lack of sympathy for the most noted of apocalyptic
works and for the whole apocalyptic mentality is widespread today.
But despite Lawrence's hostility to apocalypticism, *Apocalypse* remains an important book, if only because Lawrence was one of the first
modern students to take the symbolic power of John's Apocalypse into
account. Perhaps his most telling insight concerned the special appeal
of the book to the collective aspect of religious experience, but here a
fatal flaw in his interpretation also becomes evident. For Lawrence, the
symbols of the Apocalypse convey "the revelation of the undying will-
to-power in man, and its sanctification, its final triumph." He sees the

symbols as conveying a message about the arrogant collective thirst for power and vengeance on the part of second-rate minds, but in reality the essential message of the Apocalypse is not about man's power, but about God's, and the fundamental human reaction evoked is awe, not arrogance.

Investigations of the symbolic dimensions of the Apocalypse and of apocalyptic literature in general, while not unknown, have scarcely been plentiful in the fifty years since Lawrence's book appeared. Rather than concentrate primarily on the meaning of the symbols of the Apocalypse within their original context, as biblical scholars do, I wish to look at the way in which these symbols shaped and were in turn shaped by Western culture. Obviously, this story is far too long and complex to be summarized here, but aspects of the dynamics of the role of biblical symbols in Western culture can be illustrated by a study of some uses of the Apocalypse in the Middle Ages.

# I

Apocalyptic eschatology or apocalypticism—broadly understood as a sense of the meaning of history that sees the present as inexorably tied to the approaching final triple drama of crisis, judgment, and vindication—necessarily works through the use of symbols and the symbolic mentality. By symbol I mean some material object or image presented through word or picture that not only stands for something else, but that also manifests multiple meanings within the very material form itself. This understanding, while not explicitly a medieval formulation, is not far distant from some medieval notions of *symbolum*. By the term "symbolic mentality," I refer to that aspect of human intentionality which is concerned with the creation, presentation, and understanding of symbols. Its special character is perhaps best understood through its contrast with the logical discursive mode of thought so much studied in Western philosophy since the days of Aristotle. A logical concept, however much it may begin in sense perception, abstracts from sensible images in order to present its content; but a symbol's message is always revealed in and through the image itself. For example, there is a whole range of meaning present in the picture of the Great Harlot painted in the Apocalypse that is not and cannot be conveyed by the bald statement, "The prophet despises the Roman Empire." Further, a symbol attempts to convey multi-leveled meanings rather than a single unambivalent message. A symbol is deliberately polyvalent insofar as it attempts to manifest diverse aspects of a reality that by definition cannot be fully grasped by the human intellect. A consequence of this is that symbols are not bound by the laws of Aristotle's logic or poetics; that is, they do not observe the principle of contradiction or the classical idea of narrative development. Any symbol worth its salt means many things and frequently contradictory things, and if John's Apocalypse had a clear beginning, middle, and end, it would never have been the subject of so many debates about its structure.

Recently Richard Bauckham has pointed out the intensely visual way in which John, the "seer" par excellence, conveys his message. In comparison with other contemporary Jewish and early Christian apocalypses, he claims, John's revelations are far less auditory and less subject to editorial explanation. John of Patmos had a visual imagination of remarkable power; the striking images and scenes he presents, while not always easy to picture, are frequently unforgettable. In other words, John was a master symbolist.

One of the ways in which John reveals his mastery of the symbolic mode of discourse is the manner in which he uses mutually opposed symbolic images as a crucial part of the structure of his work. The striking oppositions between key animal, human, temporal, and spatial figures are evident throughout the book. The Lion who is really the Lamb of chapter five stands in fundamental opposition to the Great Dragon of chapter twelve. On the anthropological level, the image of the Woman with the Sun and Moon under her feet (the Queen of Heaven in chapter twelve), she who is attacked by the Dragon, cannot but call up the portrait of that "other woman," the Great Harlot Babylon in chapter seventeen.

If we turn to spatial and temporal symbolism, the same dynamic of mutual opposition is found. Unlike a number of early Jewish apocalypses, John's revelation does not contain a review of world history, but temporal symbolism is found throughout the work, especially in the tendency to order events in terms of sevens (e.g., seven seals, seven trumpets, seven bowls). If sevens form the order that God *intends* for chastisement, however, the opposing time that he *allows* for the domination of evil is expressed through half-seven, or 3½ years (42 months—1260 days), the famous apocalyptic "time, times, and half a time" that appears throughout the book. The frequent repetition of these contrasting numbers indicates a structural and not an adventitious symbolical feature. In the realm of spatial symbolism, opposed pairs are also portrayed. The most significant for the form and meaning of the book seems to be the opposition between the earthly Babylon and the heavenly Jerusalem. The earthly Babylon is symbolically the same as the Great Harlot herself, upon whose forehead was written "Babylon the Great, mother of harlots and of earth's abominations" (Apocalypse 17:5). The geographical structure of Babylon is not described—we are merely reminded of its seven hills (17:9) and its three parts (16:19). This forms a signal contrast to the elaborate descriptions of the quadrate shape, ideal dimensions and symbolic materials of the heavenly Jerusalem in chapters twenty-one and twenty-two. The key to this contrast would seem to be that Babylon, the city of chaos, has no describable order—it can only be pictured in terms of its effect upon those who, bound to her by fornication, are thrown into despair upon her destruction (18:2–24).

Each of the symbolic opposites in the pairs above has its own meaning and purpose; there is no suggestion that the opposing symbols are to be resolved into some higher coincidence of opposites. The opposition itself is central—it serves to highlight the contrast between good and evil and to invite moral decision—the choice between Lamb and Dragon, *Mulier* and *Meretrix*, Jerusalem and Babylon. This is a crucial feature of the symbolism of the Apocalypse and it also was a potent element in its subsequent influence.

These opposed symbols of the Apocalypse provided paradigms or models—we might even say objective correlatives—for interpreting events both personal and public at the time of the book's composition and for many subsequent generations of believers. The three pairs of symbols, which we can classify as the theriomorphic, the feminine, and the spatial, functioned not only as revelations (that is, "apocalypses" in the original sense of the word) of eschatological realities, but also as forces presently at work in the world that manifest the teleological implications of all the choices between good and evil confronting people. The Dragon lurks behind every evil; the Great Whore who is also the city of Babylon is a part of every temptation. On the other side, the Lamb who reigns triumphant in heaven controls the course of history, as his opening of the seals shows. His mother, the Queen of Heaven, may be persecuted by the Dragon, but cannot be conquered; his followers form the living stones of the Heavenly Jerusalem that is the Spouse of the Lamb (see chapter 21).

As archetypal manifestations of the irreducible conflict between God and Satan, these symbols shaped the imaginations of generations of Christians and were themselves reshaped, extended, and enriched by these later adaptations. The source of this rich development is to be found not only in the polyvalence of the symbols themselves, but also in the fact that precisely because of their presence in the Bible they were seen as calling out for multiple interpretation and direct application to the present. All medieval exegetes, whatever their disagreements, were in accord in holding that God's word contained an inexhaustible wealth of meanings and that it was immediately addressed to all people of every age. The medieval interpreters did not read the Bible to uncover its historical-critical meaning, what it had signified to an audience at some originating moment in time; rather, they read it to explore the diversity of significations that God had placed there in such overwhelming abundance (his work was by definition unfathomable). Medieval artists and poets did not take up biblical symbols so much for their attractiveness as for their truth: the artist's prime responsibility was seen as the presentation of truth in a pleasing fashion. In sum, during the medieval centuries, the Bible was not so much one book, even the most important, to be read; it was rather a universal language to be used—a way of seeing and interpreting the world that gave meaning to every level of culture. A brief survey of some uses of our theriomorphic, feminine, and spatial symbols from the Apocalypse will illustrate this dynamic role of the Bible in the Middle Ages.

## II

The witness of exegetes and theologians, to a large degree corroborated by that of artists and poets, indicates that we can distinguish two major periods in the use of these apocalyptic symbols in the Middle Ages. From roughly 300 to about 1100 A.D., the images from the Apocalypse tended to be read primarily in a spiritual sense, that is, as symbols of the present life of the Church and its members, and only secondarily and intermittently as prophecies of present events or those of the coming final crisis of history. From about 1100, however, there was a resurgence in historicizing and prophetic uses of the symbols; interpreters became increasingly willing to identify current persons and events with precise details of the symbolism of the book and to find in its images clear predictions of what was soon to come upon the world. The spiritualizing line of interpretation did not die out—the weighty authority of Augustine was enough to guarantee its continued vitality—but its employment was made more complex by this return to a more properly apocalyptic use of the symbols. These two periods are evident both in the history of medieval apocalypticism in general, and in use of our three pairs of opposed images from the Apocalypse itself.

The spiritualizing, or better, ecclesiological-moral, use of the Apocalypse was the main reason why the book enjoyed such great favor in the West as compared with the Byzantine East, where it entered the canon with difficulty and to this day has never been a book for liturgical use. The history of the domestication of the Apocalypse in fourth-century Latin Christianity explains this fact. In the early Church, the Apocalypse had been read in a largely literal way, as in the case of the account of the thousand-year reign of Christ and the saints on earth (the chiliastic kingdom), found in chapter 20:1-6. This literal reading, with its anti-Roman and chiliastic emphases, came under fire from the end of the second century on. Some wished to reject the book; others, more numerous, tried to correct the literal or "Judaistic" reading of the Apocalypse, that most Old-Testament-like book of the New Testament. This task was particularly imperative after Constantine's conversion, when the anti-Romanism of the Apocalypse became not only exegetically unenlightened, but politically suspect as well.

Latin exegetes and theologians of the fourth century worked out a spiritual reading that enabled the Apocalypse to be appropriated for the service of the Church even by those who no longer shared an apocalyptic world-view. The process began about the year 300 with the martyr bishop Victorinus of Pettau, who wrote a commentary that, while still fairly literal and even chiliastic in its interpretation of the later chapters of the book, saw in the early chapters a series of images about the life of the Church, or of the union between the Old and the New Testaments. About a century later, Jerome revised Victorinus's commentary to remove vestiges of chiliasm. This version of the work became an important source for later medieval exegetes. An even more important commentary was that of the Donatist Tyconius, written about 380. This African scholar, though himself convinced that the end of history was near and that the Apocalypse was in part a message about this end, provided a thorough account of the book and its images that saw it fundamentally as a revelation of the struggle between good and evil forces during the entire history of the Church. The symbolism of the Apocalypse in Tyconius's account became universalized and internalized; it was essentially a message about the nature of the Church in the time between the first and the second comings of Christ and about the way in which true members of the Church are to conduct themselves in their struggle against evil. Tyconius's reading of the Apocalypse was seized upon by Augustine, the most resolute anti-apocalypticist of all, especially in his account of the end of history in the final books of *The City of God*.

It is important to note that the ecclesiological-moral reading of John's Apocalypse never completely overcame the sense that the book also contained a message about the coming end of time, nor did the fact that the Apocalypse was not usually read apocalyptically mean that apocalyptic views of history died out in the early Middle Ages. A host of visions, historical accounts, and other sources shows us that many still believed that the signs of the times pointed to the imminent end of the world.

## III

At the same time that Western exegetes were working out the ecclesiological-moral interpretation of the Apocalypse, the vibrant images of the book also began to appear in Christian art and literature. At the risk of some over-simplification, we can say that the parts that appealed to the the artists from the fourth century on were especially the great theophanic visions, such as the picture of the worship of God by the four living creatures (the tetramorph) and twenty-four elders in chapter four, and the revelation of the Lamb opening the sealed book in chapter five. In this era of the imperialization of Christian art, the heavenly tableaux and liturgies of the Apocalypse provided the most adequate pictures of the true imperial court, that of the Pantocrator, or Ruler of the universe. Art historian Yves Christe has argued that the images of the Apocalypse that were so popular in Latin Christian art but absent in the East are not to be interpreted in a prophetic or apocalyptic sense, but they are to be seen as images of the present reign of Christ and his Church. As he puts it: "The expression of the BASILEIA TOU THEOU [Kingdom of God] in its timeless reality alone dominates the triumphal imagery." The point serves as strong confirmation for the picture that we get from reading the Latin exegetes and Church writers who were responsible for the dominant interpretation of the book.

To pick but one iconographical motif as illustration, let us reflect on an image common in the Christian art of the fifth century and beyond, that of the Lamb. The heavenly Lamb glimmers in many of the splendid Christian mosaics of this period (e.g., such as the arch of the apse of San Vitale in Ravenna, c. 550 A.D.), where it serves as a symbol of the struggle between good and evil on earth through the unloosing of the seals. The Lamb and the twenty-four elders of Apocalypse 5 appeared on a lost mosaic on the facade of Old St. Peter's, probably of seventh-century date, and it seems that portrayals of Christ as Lamb tend to be more influenced by the iconography of the Apocalypse from the ninth century on; but there is little or no evidence that these images were intended to have any more properly prophetic sense than they had in the interpretation of the contemporary exegesis of the Apocalypse.

The evidence drawn from the early Christian poets is more varied. The first known Christian Latin poet, Commodian, who appears to have lived in the mid-third century, was a pronounced apocalypticist and chiliast, but this does not seem to be the case with the greatest of the Late Antique Christian poets, Prudentius, writing toward the end of the fourth century. Prudentius made use of the images of the Apocalpyse in a number of places in his works. Especially striking is the magnificent summary he gives in the "Hymn Before Sleep" of the Apocalypse's vision of the conflict between the triumphant Lamb and the bloody monster that is Antichrist:

> The best-loved evangelist
> when Christ threw open the clouds,
> saw many things that were dark
> before his teacher taught him.
> The Lamb of God, Thunderer,
> stained with the blood of his death,
> alone has the strength to open
> the book which tells the future.
> In his strong hand he carries

a double-edged blade threatening
two strokes at once: it flashes
as he waves it in the air.
    Only he can see into
both body and soul. The blade
which is doubly fearful is
death for both body and soul.
. . . . . . . . . . . . . . . . .
    He is the great destroyer
of Antichrist and over
that monstrous being he wins
a victory easily.
    This is the beast whose hunger
devours all peoples, he is
that most bloody Charybdis
whom John's writings have condemned.

> *Cathemerinon* VI, lines 77–92, 101–08 (trans. H.
> Isbell, *The Last Poets of Imperial Rome*,
> Penguin, 1971)

The poetic portrayal is a powerful one, especially in its dramatic emphasis on the inalterable opposition between the two symbolic figures; but it is quite generalized. There is no evidence from this passage or others that Prudentius expected an imminent end of the world. Poetic references to the Last Judgment, with or without use of the symbols of the Apocalypse, are by no means uncommon in the early Middle Ages. They testify to continued Christian belief in the coming dread day, but they rarely give evidence of more than general eschatological hopes and fears.

Apart from the symbol of the Lamb, which early took on an independent life, most appearances of the other major opposed symbols from the Apocalypse—the Dragon, the Woman and the Harlot, Babylon and Jerusalem—occur within the context of illustrated Apocalypses or in programs closely related to them. These Apocalypse cycles, whether in the form of illuminated manuscripts or in mosaic, fresco, or stone are among the most impressive remains of early medieval art.

In his *Life of the Holy Abbots*, the Venerable Bede records that in the late seventh century Benedict Biscop brought back an illustrated Apocalypse from Rome to Northumbria as a model for church decoration. From the early ninth century, beginning with a manuscript now found in Trier (Stadtbibliothek MS. 31), we have a series of illustrated Apocalypses whose exact relationship to lost earlier books and church decorations is not fully clear. The most noted of these Apocalypse cycles is connected with the Commentary on the Apocalypse by Beatus of Liébana, a late eighth-century Spanish monk who wrote a lengthy exposition in the spiritualizing style of Tyconius. The

*Plate 1.* The Great Harlot riding on the Seven-Headed Beast and Holding the Cup of Abominations (Apocalypse 17) as portrayed in the Bamberg Apocalypse, f. 43$^r$. The figures above are the seer John and the revealing angel. Reproduced from F. Van der Meer, *Apocalypse*, p. 155.

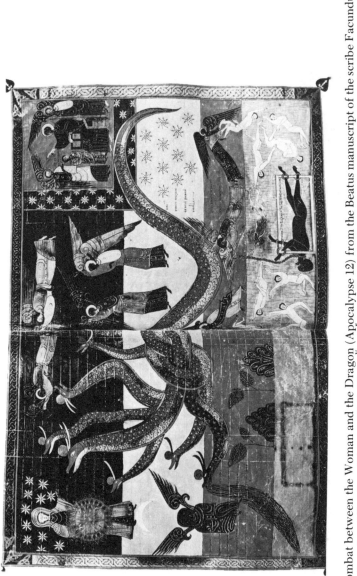

*Plate* 2. The Combat between the Woman and the Dragon (Apocalypse 12) from the Beatus manuscript of the scribe Facundus written for Ferdinand and Sancha of Leon in 1047 (ff. 186$^v$–187$^r$). The Woman adorned with the sun, moon and stars is attacked by the Dragon, who is in turn beset by angels. Immediately below the moon, the Woman is given wings for her flight into the desert. On the right we see the throne of heaven above and the devil chained in hell below. Reproduced from Henri Stierlin, *Le Livre de Feu. L'Apocalypse et l'art mozarabe* (Paris: La Bibliothèque des Arts, 1978), pp. 154-55.

earliest surviving example of the Beatus type, MS. 644 of the Pierpont Morgan Library in New York, has illustrations dating from about 950. Splendid examples continued to be produced right through the twelfth century. Other surviving books, such as the magnificent Bamberg Apocalypse produced for the German Emperor Henry II shortly after the year 1000, also highlight the important role of the illuminated Apocalypses in early medieval art. Monumental programs based on the Apocalypse were also fairly common. Those found in the mosaics of Roman churches centered on the Adoration of the Lamb by the elders and on the Heavenly Jerusalem. The finest surviving examples are in Saints Cosmas and Damian (c. 530) and Saint Praxedes (c. 820). A series of eleventh- and early twelfth-century programs from northern Italy (e.g., at Novara, Castel Sant'Elia, San Pietro di Civate) seem to be influenced by the cycles of manuscript illumination. Apocalyptic themes are also found in French church decoration—in capitals and lost frescos from the eleventh-century porch of the great abbey of Fleury, in the twelfth-century frescos at Saint Savin, and in the famous tympanum at Moissac.

These and the other surviving pictorial presentations drawn from the Apocalypse all give evidence of how powerful the attraction of our contrasting theriomorphic, feminine, and spatial symbols were in this era. The Trier Apocalypse from the early ninth century, with its seventy-four full-page illustrations, has frequent portrayals of the Lamb, and it also pays special attention to the career of the Harlot (Plate 1) and to the descent of the New Jerusalem. The conflict between the Dragon and the Woman (aided by Michael and the Heavenly Host) is a favorite of these programs. Among its most magnificent depictions are some of those found in the Beatus manuscripts (Plate 2), and in the large fresco over the entrance of San Pietro di Civate. The latter church also contains on its narthex roof the most evocative portrayal of the Heavenly Jerusalem found in the early Middle Ages (Plate 3).

When we ask what these presentations of the symbols of the Apocalypse meant to their original audiences, our most trustworthy (though by no means exhaustive) guides are the Apocalypse commentaries that continued the traditions laid down by Victorinus, Jerome and Tyconius. A survey of the most popular of these, such as those of Bede (c. 705), Ambrose Autpert (c. 760), Beatus (786), and Haymo of Auxerre (c. 850), shows the predominance of the ecclesiological-moral line of interpretation. For these authors, the Apocalypse tells the story of the church in its continuing struggle against the powers of evil. By their contemplation of pictorial symbols of the Apocalypse, individual believers were encouraged to ratify their membership in the society of the saved through personal victory over sin so that they, too, might one day share in the rewards of the Heavenly Jerusalem. The

*Plate 3.* The Heavenly Jerusalem (Apocalypse 21 and 22) from the vestibule roof of the Church of San Pietro al Monte above Civate (c. 1100 A.D.). Christ is portrayed as both Pantocrator and the Lamb from whom flows the river of life (22:1). On either side of the river are the trees of life (22:2). Reproduced from Otto Demus, *Romanesque Mural Painting* (New York: Abrams, 1970), Plate 13.

Woman of chapter twelve is almost invariably seen as a symbol of the church, the *ecclesia militans* persecuted through history by the Dragon who represents both Satan and the body of evildoers. The New Jerusalem could be seen as both a present and a future reality, as the use of the symbol in Christian Latin poetry indicates.

At the beginning of the period, Prudentius in his "Psychomachia," lines 800–887, describes how Queen Faith and her companion, Concord, after their victory over the vices, lay out the temple of the restored soul according to the model of the Heavenly Jerusalem, in preparation for the descent of the Son of Man. More typical is the eschatological hope expressed in a hymn of Bishop Fulbert of Chartres (c. 970–1028).

May the choir of New Jerusalem
Give forth a new sweet song
Celebrating the Easter feast
With sober joys.

On this day Christ, the unconquered lion,
Rises and overthrows the Dragon
While he cries out with a loud voice
And raises the dead from death.

> "Chorus Novae Jerusalem," lines 1–8 (*The Oxford Book of Medieval Latin Verse* #128, Oxford: Clarendon, 1959)

## IV

The late eleventh century and especially the twelfth saw some major shifts in the history of medieval apocalypticism. Among these must be noted an interest in using the symbols of the Apocalypse as prophetic manifestations of current events. Once again, apocalyptic images with their mythic dimensions and polyvalent symbolism were being employed, not just to reveal the nature of the Church and the conflict between virtue and vice in the hearts of men, but political conflict as well, the clash of opposed positions, parties, and armies.

For example, the interpretation of the epic story of the seven-headed Dragon of chapter twelve that was standard in the ecclesiological reading of the early Middle Ages is well illustrated in Bede's Commentary:

> "*And behold a great red dragon*" (12:3). The devil, bloody with savagery, is armed against the Church by the might of the earthly kingdom. In the seven heads John signifies all his kings, in the ten horns his every kingdom. "*And his tail was dragging down a third part of the stars of heaven*" (12:4). He points to the power and evil of the enemy which the Church conquers with God's aid. The enemy has cast down an uncounted part of angels or men by insidious fraud in the manner of a tail, because a tail is a blind and unclean thing covering unclean matters with its veil lest they be seen. Tyconius in his usual way interprets the third part of stars that fell as false brethren, another third as the Church, and external foes as a third.

Compare this very general reading with a poem written, it seems, by the well-known Benedictine monk, Rupert of Deutz, about 1095. Rupert and his abbot, strong supporters of the reforms of Pope Gregory VII, had been compelled to flee their monastery of St. Lawrence at Liège by ecclesiastical supporters of the anti-papal imperial party. Rupert puts this event within the context of the whole international conflict we know as the Investiture Controversy, and he presents it in the form of a poetic retelling of chapters twelve and thirteen of the Apocalypse.

I.    Now the bellicose dragon wages war.
Woe to me! The tail of the dragon laden
With such great spoils drags a third of the
Stars in bondage.

IX.    ... Now the ancient enemy arises from the sea
And rules as victor over the seven hills.
He fights and with a huge millstone
Strikes the already broken head.
Do you not see where Simon sits,
Relying on Nero, so like a king?
His lambs are fashioned like horns
And become like dragons.
They have to put to flight the six guardians
Who had protected your city;
They have put false prophets in their place,
Dragging away everything sacred for a price.
The Supreme Pontiff who persecuted crimes
And dared to attack the "kingly disease"
Fled from the See of Rome
And was buried in exile.

> "Calamitates Ecclesiae Leodiensis," *Monumenta Germaniae Historica. Libelli de lite* 3.624 (trans. B. McGinn, *Visions of the End,* New York: Columbia, 1979)

The apocalyptic symbols are historicized here in a way unknown to Bede, but without losing their symbolic value. The Dragon is Satan; his tail, the persecuting emperor, Henry IV. The third part of the stars dragged down by the tail (Apoc 12:4) signifies the bishops who followed Henry into schism. The emperor's conquest of Rome in 1083 is seen as the victory of the beast, the "ancient enemy" arising from the sea (Apoc 13:1). Rupert would not have denied the universal moral reading of John's Apocalypse (his own extensive Apocalypse commentary shows that), but unlike Bede or most other early exegetes, he was also willing to make specific application of the imagery of the book to the decisive events of his day. We may argue over whether or not Rupert saw the attack of Henry IV as a sign of the imminence of the end; there can be no question that later twelfth-century authors, notably Joachim of Fiore, did.

Rupert's poem is significant not only for the basic concerns it manifests, but also for its date. We may ask why interest in the prophetic import of the symbols of John's Apocalypse began to increase at the end of the eleventh century. The reasons are complex and difficult to prove in any definitive way, but I would argue that the root cause is to be found in the great debates over the nature of the church that began in the second half of the eleventh century and that were to continue uninterrupted into the Reformation period. In contrast to the early Middle Ages, when views of the church, while not static, were relatively stable, from the time of the Great Reform beginning c. 1050 essential elements in traditional understanding of the *ecclesia* came under dispute. The church's very structure and chief institutions could be seen undergoing rapid change and development. Since the fourth century, the Apocalypse had been the book of the church, the prime New Testament source, along with Matthew's Gospel, for that branch of theology later to be called ecclesiology. Is there any wonder, then, that as circumstances and debates moved Christians to acquire a better sense of the church's historical character, a more historicized and prophetic reading of the Apocalypse also became a real option?

The most creative proponent of the new historicizing, prophetic, and millenarian reading of the Apocalypse was Joachim of Fiore (d. 1202), whose *Exposition on the Apocalypse* is the greatest of all medieval commentaries, a theology of history equal in scope, if quite different in intention, to Augustine's *City of God*. Joachim also has the unique distinction of being the first apocalypticist who was his own iconographer. In his famous *figurae*, symbolic images he created to illustrate his complex thought, he provides a fascinating example of the interaction between apocalyptic thought and its artistic presentation. Only one of the *figurae* is drawn directly from the symbols of the Apocalypse, though all of them illustrate aspects of the vision of history that is revealed most fully in the final book of the Bible. This *figura* is Joachim's image of the seven-headed Dragon, a perfect illustration of the revived historico-prophetic reading (Plate 4).

As found in the surviving manuscripts of the *Book of Figures*, a compilation of Joachim's symbolic designs and accompanying texts that appears to have been put together by his disciples shortly after his death, the Dragon symbol has become a pictorial summary of the whole history of the church's persecution. The seven heads are identified with seven evil rulers: Herod, Nero, Constantine the Arian, Mohammed, Mesemoth (probably a North African ruler), Saladin, and the "Seventh King, who is properly called Antichrist, although there will be another like him, no less evil, symbolized by the tail." The commentary makes it clear that the abbot expected only a brief time to intervene between the persecution of his contemporary Saladin and that of the Antichrist. Joachim not only historicized the symbol to give meaning to the crises of his own time, but he also molded it to suit his own apocalyptic theories. It is well known that the abbot expected a time of the peaceful triumph of the church on earth after the imminent defeat of the Antichrist, marking the Dragon's seventh head; but this third state of history, the time specially ascribed to the Holy Spirit, would itself close with another persecution, that of Gog, the ultimate Antichrist, an event which Joachim saw pictured in the Dragon's tail.

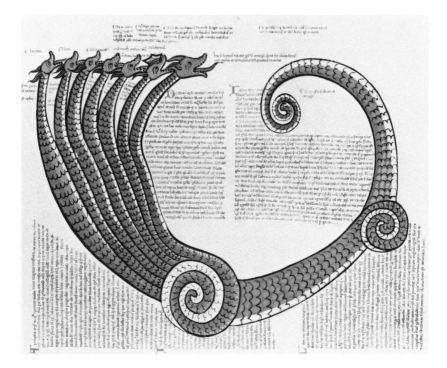

*Plate 4.* Joachim of Fiore's *figura* of the Seven-Headed Dragon from Apocalypse 12 with accompanying text. Reproduced from Leone Tondelli, Marjorie Reeves and Beatrice Hirsch-Reich, *Il Libro delle Figure dell'Abate Gioachino da Fiore* (Turin: SEI, 1953), Vol. II, Tavola XIV.

Comparable virtuosity in adapting the oppositional symbols of the Apocalypse to new situations, both endowing them with precise historical identifications and also, by that very fact, frequently modifying the symbols themselves, can be found in many other late medieval uses of apocalypticism, both in text and in picture. Once again, though, we must insist that these new accommodations did not drive out the more spiritualizing use of apocalyptic symbols that had characterized the early Middle Ages. Among the wealth of materials, space allows for only one further illustration.

The great poetical *summa* of medieval culture, Dante's *Divine Comedy*, is shot through with eschatological and apocalyptic themes. The Florentine's genius so transformed and enriched anything he touched that we should not be surprised at the difficulty in giving an adequate interpretation of all aspects of his symbols. His adaptations of the Great Harlot of chapter seventeen, here seen as married to evil popes, is a case in point.

The Harlot first appears in Canto XIX of the *Inferno*, when Dante and Vergil visit the circle reserved for the simoniacs. The upside-down punishment meted out to these sinners recalls the legendary fall of Simon Magus, their scriptural ancestor, whom tradition had come to view as an Antichrist figure. The evil popes punished here had inverted truth by selling spiritual things for crass gold, and thus had made themselves members of the Antichrist. Their association with the final apocalyptic foe is enhanced by Dante's evocation of the Great Harlot:

> It was you and your like the Evangelist had in mind
> When he saw her who sitteth on many waters
> Committing fornication with the kings of the earth;
>
> She that was born with the seven heads
> And had her argument from the ten horns
> As long as virtue was pleasing to her husband.
> > *Inferno* XIX, lines 106–11 (trans. C. H. Sisson,
> > *The Divine Comedy*, Chicago: Regnery, 1981)

In this passage, Dante combines the images of the Harlot and the city Babylon-Rome (symbolized in Apocalypse 17:3 by the seven-headed beast upon which the Harlot sits), but this fusion is not at all foreign to the way in which the Apocalypse presents these symbols. What is distinctive of Dante's appropriation is the way in which he highlights that the Harlot Babylon-Rome is actually the church gone bad, the "beautiful woman" (*bella donna*, *Inferno* XIX, line 57) who was once pleasing to her Divine Master by her virtue. This trenchant criticism of contemporary popes and the corrupted church brings Dante within hailing distance of the apocalyptic broadsides directed against Babylon, the "carnal church," by the more radical of the Spiritual Franciscans.

The second appearance of the Great Harlot (*magna meretrix* of Apoc 17:1) is more enigmatic. Cantos XXXII-XXXIII of the *Purgatorio* recount the pageant of the chariot of the church in its course through history, and contain some of the most abstruse lines in the whole *Divine Comedy*. In Canto XXXII, the chariot is joined to the tree of the knowledge of good and evil in the earthly Paradise by the Griffin, who represents Christ. This picture of the ideal state of the relations of church and state is symbolically negated by what Dante sees after he awakens from a convenient poetic slumber, as lines 109–160 tell the sad tale of the real history of the chariot, buffeted by an eagle, attacked by a she-fox and then a dragon, and bizarrely transformed by the growth of monstrous heads. The precise meaning of these details is still subject to some debate, but there can be no doubt that the poet is presenting a depressing sketch of the church's history. As a final indignity, the chariot is commandeered by a "shameless harlot" (*puttana sciolta* of line 149) and a lustful giant:

Securely, like a city set on a hill,
Appeared to me a harlot, her clothes loose,
And casting her eyes about her all the time.

And as if to ensure that no one carried her off,
I saw a giant beside her, standing upright;
And from time to time they kissed one another.
                    Purgatorio XXXII, lines 148–53 (trans. C. H.
                    Sisson)

When the saucy harlot turns her eyes on Dante himself, the giant
scourges her and then drags the chariot off into a wood, scenes which
attracted the attention of some of the illustrators of the *Comedy* in the
fourteenth century (Plate 5). It seems quite clear that the shameless
harlot here is an incarnation of the *magna meretrix* of Apocalypse
chapter seventeen, and thus another forceful critique of how far evil
has come to dominate the church. The identity of the giant is more
problematic. A traditional political interpretation would identify him
with the French monarchy and its illicit connection with papal
Avignon, but there is nothing distinctively French about the giant. It

*Plate 5.* The Giant and the Harlot in the Chariot of the Church, illustrating The
    Divine Comedy, Purgatorio XXXII, lines 148–60. In the picture on the left,
    Dante beholds the Giant and the Harlot; in the one on the right, he watches
    as the Giant leads the Harlot off in the Chariot. Found in MS. Holkham Hall
    514, p. 110 (Italian, 3rd quarter of the fourteenth century) and reproduced
    from Peter Brieger, Millard Meiss and Charles S. Singleton, *Illuminated
    Manuscripts of the Divine Comedy* (Princeton: Princeton University Press,
    1969. Bollingen Series LXXXI), Vol. II, Plate 419a.

has also been pointed out that Antichrist in medieval art and myth was frequently viewed as a gigantic figure, and so the giant appears to have definite apocalyptic overtones which do not necessarily exclude a secondary application to France, since Antichrist has many members and predecessors. In fine, Dante's poetic variations on the Great Harlot, especially his use of the symbol as a polemical weapon against corruption in the church, provide excellent illustrations of the kind of expansions and functions that traditional apocalyptic symbols from John's vision acquired in the second age of medieval apocalypticism.

John's Apocalypse has been called by Austin Farrer "the one great poem which the first Christian age produced." If the Apocalypse can be seen as a great poem, its genre seems close to that of the epic, and like the major epics, its symbols have invited both pictorial presentation and a wide variety of later interpretations and adaptations. This brief glance at some of the dynamics of medieval uses of the symbols of the Apocalypse suggests that not only does the symbol give rise to thought, in Paul Ricoeur's famous phrase, but that it also gives rise to a constant process of resymbolization as a part of our experience of the world.

*Bibliographical Note*

Some useful materials in English are Richard Bauckham, "The *Figurae* of John of Patmos," *Prophecy and Millenarianism. Essays in Honour of Marjorie Reeves* (Longman: Essex, 1980), pp. 107–25; John J. Collins, "The Symbolism of Transcendence in Jewish Apocalyptic," *Biblical Research* 19 (1974), pp. 5–22; Richard K. Emmerson and Ronald B. Herzman, "Antichrist, Simon Magus, and Dante's 'Inferno' XIX," *Traditio* 36 (1980), pp. 373–98; Robert E. Kaske, "Dante's Purgatorio XXXII and XXXIII: A Survey of Christian History," *University of Toronto Quarterly* 43 (1974), pp. 1–24; and Bernard McGinn, *Visions of the End. Apocalyptic Traditions in the Middle Ages* (Columbia University Press: New York, 1979), and "Symbolism in the Thought of Joachim of Fiore," *Prophecy and Millenarianism*, pp. 143–64.

Also see Yves Christe, "Traditions littéraires et iconographiques dans l'interprétation des images apocalyptiques," *L'Apocalypse de Jean. Traditions exégétiques et iconographiques III$^e$-XIII$^e$ siècles* (Droz: Geneva, 1979), pp. 109–34; and Ugo Vanni, "Il simbolismo nell'Apocalisse," *Gregorianum* 61 (1980), pp. 461–506.

WILLIAM VIRGIL DAVIS

# THE WORDS

If there were words to be spoken I will speak them
Let the poor man turn from his hunger
Let him eat his hunger
Have the young girl her thimble of pain
Have her treat it with the patience of a blemish
Let it scar her for life
Or let it blend in with the wrinkles of her age
If mothers cry listen to them
If mothers cry they can still laugh
To fathers the stone is patient
To fathers the stone is the first thing
Let brothers grow like trees
Let brothers have voices like trees singing

If there are words to be spoken let them speak
Let everything in heaven and earth glorify me
Let heaven and earth glorify my name
Have names for things unborn
Have names for things undiscovered
Let them be named discovered
Or let them be discovered unnamed
If winds blow do not hide
If winds hide bless them for hiding
To all small creatures that move give forth my hand
To all the dead who have ceased to move my hand give
Let life and dying stand for themselves
Let ending beginning again

# BIBLICAL MANUSCRIPTS FROM THE UNIVERSITY OF MICHIGAN COLLECTION

Although classical studies have been an integral part of the University of Michigan since its founding in 1817 and Oriental studies have been actively pursued for over a century, the University's greatest activity as an acquirer of manuscripts and artifacts and as a sponsor of archeological research dates to the 1920s and 1930s. In the years between the two world wars distinguished faculty and librarians traveled in the Near East, incidentally acquiring manuscripts for a fraction of what a good forgery would bring today. Greek papyri formed a major focus of the collecting activity, and the University is one of the great papyrological centers in the world. Literary manuscripts comprise only a small portion of the papyri collection, but several of the biblical texts at Michigan are of unique significance. The rare book collection of the University includes a variety of Bibles, lectionaries, and other parts of the Bible.

The four biblical manuscripts illustrated here span a millennium and a half of book making. The latest of them, the unpointed Hebrew scroll (Figure 4), illustrates the most archaic form, the parchment or papyrus scroll, a long single sheet with its two ends attached to poles. This scroll form is the traditional one for Synagogal reading texts, and the scroll shown here was made for that purpose. Two of the other manuscripts take the form of a codex, the ancestor of the modern book; the Pauline collection (Figure 1) is among the earliest codices preserved and thus testifies to the early Christian adoption of the codex, part of the church's struggle to set itself over against Rabbinic Jewish practices. The eminent convenience of the codex insured that it was eventually adopted by Jews, and the Hebrew codex (Figure 3) is a medieval study text. The fourth text (Figure 2) is fragmentary but was probably also part of a codex.

*Figure 1.* A leaf showing the end of Ephesians (6:20-24) and the beginning of Galatians (1:1-7), from a collection of Paul's epistles to the churches, dated around 200. The codex from which the leaf is drawn is the oldest witness to the text of Paul's epistles; part of the codex is held in Ann Arbor (30 leaves) and part in Dublin, in the Chester Beatty Collection (56 leaves), and the whole is thus called the Beatty-Michigan Manuscript (Gregory-Aland P⁴⁶; P. Mich. 6238). Among the important features of the text is its unusual ordering of the letters (Romans—Hebrews—the Corinthian correspondence—Ephesians—Galatians—Colossians—the Thessalonian letters)—generally Hebrews, not now regarded as Pauline, follows the other letters, and Ephesians follows Galatians, thus breaking the pattern of decreasing length which this codex observes. Also striking is the separation of Paul's letters to groups from his personal letters, those to Philemon, Titus, and Timothy. Each page of the manuscript is numbered, and each epistle is preceded by a note on its length, measured in lines of writing or *stichoi*. This leaf is folio 78 (numbered 158) of those preserved, and it records that Galatians has 375 lines.

*Figure 2.* One fragment of a leaf, probably from a codex, perhaps of the Four Gospels, dated around 300. Despite the small size of this fragment, which includes Matthew 26:19-52 (part of the Passion Narrative), the text provides a valuable witness to the form of the New Testament used in early Christian Egypt. The papyrus is Gregory-Aland P[37] and P. Mich. 1570; the recto, shown here, has Matthew 26:19-37.

*Figure 3.* A page showing the second half of the Song of the Sea (Exodus 15), from a tenth-century codex of the Pentateuch. The codex is among the oldest annotated texts of the Hebrew Bible; an annotated text includes the vowel and accent marks for the biblical texts, and the Great and Small Traditions, Aramaic commentaries on the text written in the margins. The system of annotation developed during the first millennium A. D., and all pre-Christian biblical texts, notably those from Qumran, are unannotated. The Michigan Codex (Mich. MS 88) was probably written within a century of the Aleppo Codex, the oldest such text in existence. Most of the Pentateuch is prose and is written as such; the verse portion shown here is among those traditionally written as verse. The leaf containing the first portion of the Song is missing; this page, folio 51a, begins at Exodus 15:10, and ends at Exodus 15:23, in the succeeding prose.

*Figure 4.* A column showing the Song of the Sea, with preceding and following prose passages (Exodus 14:28-15:23), from an early modern Torah scroll (perhaps 17th century). Scrolls of this shape and format remain in continuous use and production today; the writing of this verse portion (column 77) is particularly regulated.

*Bibliographical Note*

For a general orientation to biblical manuscripts, see B. M. Metzger's *Manuscripts of the Greek Bible: An Introduction to Greek Palaeography* (New York: Oxford University Press, 1981). On the Michigan collection, see M. M. Parvis, "The Importance of the Michigan Manuscript Collection for New Testament Textual Studies," in *New Testament Manuscript Studies*, ed. Parvis and A. P. Wikgren (Chicago: University of Chicago Press, 1950). On P[46], see J. D. Quinn, "P[46]—The Pauline Canon?," *Catholic Biblical Quarterly* 36 (1974), 379-85. On Mich. MS 88, see Eleazar Birnbaum, "The Michigan Codex, "*Vetus Testamentum* 17 (1967), 373-415.

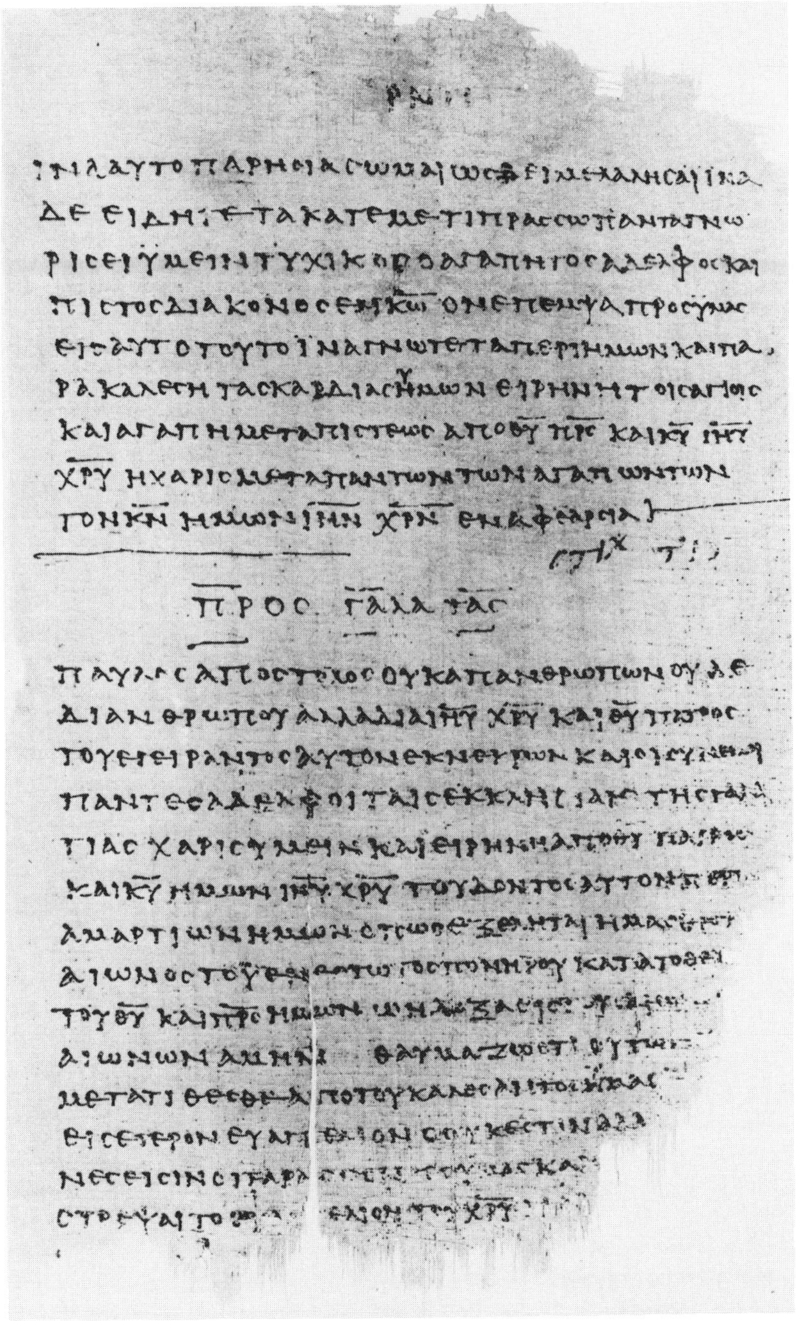

Fig. 1: P. Mich. 6238 (Gregory-Aland P⁴⁶), folio 78. ca. 200 A. D.

Fig. 2: P. Mich. 1570 (Gregory-Aland P³⁷). ca. 300 A. D.

**Fig. 3:** Mich. MS 88, leaf 51a. 10th century A. D.

הבאים אחריהם בים לא נשאר בהם עד אחד ובני ישראל הלכו
ביבשה בתוך הים והמים להם חומה מימינם ומשמאלם ויושע
יהוה ביום ההוא את ישראל מיד מצרים וירא ישראל את מצרים
מת על שפת הים וירא ישראל את היד הגדלה אשר עשה יהוה
במצרים וייראו העם את יהוה ויאמינו ביהוה ובמשה עבד—ו

אז ישיר משה ובני ישראל את השירה הזאת ליהוה ויאמרו

לאמר | אשירה ליהוה כי גאה גאה | סוס
ורכבו רמה בים | עזי וזמרת יה ויהי לי | לישועה
זה אלי ואנוהו | אלהי
אבי וארממנהו | יהוה איש מלחמה יהוה | שמו
מרכבת פרעה וחילו ירה בים | ומבחר
שלשיו טבעו בים סוף | תהמת יכסימו ירדו במצולת | כמו אבן
ימינך יהוה נאדרי בכח | ימינך
יהוה תרעץ אויב | וברב גאונך תהרס | קמיך
תשלח חרנך יאכלמו כקש | וברוח
אפיך נערמו מים | נצבו כמו נד | נזלים
קפאו תהמת בלב ים | אמר
אויב ארדף אשיג | אחלק שלל תמלאמו | נפשי
אריק חרבי תורישמו ידי | נשפת
ברוחך כסמו ים | צללו כעופרת במים | אדירים
מי כמכה באלם יהוה | מי
כמכה נאדר בקדש | נורא תהלת עשה | פלא
נטית ימינך תבלעמו ארץ | נחלת
בחסדך עם זו גאלת | נהלת בעזך אל נוה | קדשך
שמעו עמים ירגזון | חיל
אחז ישבי פלשת | אז נבהלו אלופי אדום | אילי
מואב יאחזמו רעד | נמגו
כל ישבי כנען | תפל עליהם אימתה | ופחד
בגדל זרועך ידמו כאבן | עד
יעבר עמך יהוה | עד יעבר עם זו | קנית
תבאמו ותטעמו בהר נחלתך | מכון
לשבתך פעלת יהוה | מקדש אדני כוננו | ידיך
יהוה ימלך לעלם ועד | כי בא
סוס פרעה ברכבו ובפרשיו בים | וישב יהוה עלהם את מי
הים | ובני ישראל הלכו ביבשה בתוך | הים

ותקח מרים הנביאה אחות אהרן את התף בידה ותצאן כל הנשים
אחריה בתפים ובמחלת ותען להם מרים שירו ליהוה כי גאה
גאה סוס ורכבו רמה בים | ויסע משה את ישראל
מים סוף ויצאו אל מדבר שור וילכו שלשת ימים במדבר ולא מצאו מים
ויבאו מרתה ולא יכלו לשתת מים ממרה כי מרים הם על כן קרא שמה

Fig. 4: Mich. MS 85, column 77. 17th century A. D. (?).

*THREE*

# LATTER-DAY ADAPTATIONS: FOUR STUDIES

ARNOLD BAND

# THE POLITICS OF SCRIPTURE:
# THE HASIDIC TALE

The "politics of scripture" is no oxymoron, but rather a straightforward assertion that even texts deemed scriptural are the products of circumstances which can properly be termed political. This assertion collapses the traditional opposition between the political and the spiritual by calling attention to the obvious facts that one grants authority to the text, and authority implies power. I prefer the term "authority" rather than the more current term "privilege" since it embraces both semantically and etymologically the notion of author, whether assumed to be divine or human. In the same conventional spirit, I mean by the term "scripture" precisely what users of English have generally meant by it, that is, a text to which a certain audience attributes divine authorship or inspiration. Here, too, I am constrained to call attention to my traditional usage of a simple English term since we live in a period during which avant-garde critics of Romantic poetry habitually refer to their subjects as visionaries or prophets while even a more conservative critic like Northrop Frye can write a book called *The Secular Scripture*, an oxymoron in more traditional parlance. This oxymoron obviously betrays an acute sense of cultural, and hence semantic, displacement which must engender both psychological and linguistic anxiety.

If there is any anxiety which I want to deal with in this essay, it is not that of the secular reaching out for an elusive source of authority, nor is it the anxiety of influence often discussed by Harold Bloom; rather it is the anxiety generated within a religious, scripturally-based society by the creation of a new authoritative text, a new scripture. I shall take for my prooftexts the opening tales of the first and foremost collection of Hasidic tales, *Shivhe HabBesht (In Praise of the Baal Shem Tov)*, first published in 1815, but probably circulated either orally or in manuscript around 1780, if not earlier, during the lifetime of the Baal Shem Tov himself (1700–1760). The specific problem I shall attempt to confront is how the early masters of the Hasidic tale made the accommodation between their notion of the sanctity of the tale (*qedushat hassipur*) and the prior, immutable sanctity of the scriptural text, the traditional Hebrew Bible.

The need for such accommodation is, to be sure, one of the pervasive problems of a scripture-based religion, particularly one in which the Lord created the world by what we call today "a speech act," and, in a counterpoised episode, shattered both the linguistic (and topographic) unity of mankind when it tried to transcend its nature by building a huge tower on the flat plains of Shinar. Most biblical scholars today would argue that the entire redactional process of the Hebrew Scripture was shaped in some way by reverence for the sanctity of text and language. When scripture officially became Scripture (for shorthand I refer to Nehemiah 8), the power of language, of the text, was both increased and diminished by institutionalization: increased through the permanence of bureaucracy and text; diminished by the mediation of the *same* social forces. The various accommodations with Scripture would constitute a veritable catalogue of the genres of Jewish—and for that matter, Christian and Islamic—literature through the ages, ranging from allegory, to midrash, to exegesis of all sorts. All this is well known and needs no elaboration here. What, however, we may ask, happens when a new genre of composition suddenly emerges within the scripture-based religion and almost instantaneously becomes an independent scripture without even pretending to be a commentary upon previous scripture? This is what happened in the case of the Hasidic tale, an argument forcefully advanced both by Joseph Dan (1975) and Gedalya Nigal (1981), the authors of the two most recent works devoted to this genre, which has received little scholarly attention to date.

## I

Hasidism, the religious and social movement which has embraced and revitalized much of Jewish spiritual life from the eighteenth century until today, has not been a neglected area of research and debate. Though several generations of intense research into the origins of the Hasidic movement have produced a host of contradictory theories regarding the nature and purpose of the original sects which appeared in the southwestern Ukraine in the early decades of the eighteenth century, several uncontestable facts have emerged. During these decades, there appeared a variety of individual groups led by forceful, pious men, many of whom did not fit the mold of traditional rabbinical leadership, which prided itself on the interpretation of the sacred law. While some of these new leaders were prodigiously learned, others were not; some adhered strictly to the traditional rabbinical norms of authoritarianism, but others indulged in charismatic practices including faith healing; some stressed asceticism, while others preached service of the Lord through joy and ecstasy. Their followers also varied: some were learned and wealthy; others were ignorant and poor. Within these divergent currents, two religious phenomena seem to be constant. Each group developed an extraordinary allegiance to its specific leader, whose authority derived more from personal charisma than formally ordained traditional practices.

This new allegiance slowly replaced the traditional structure of Jewish communal life which had rapidly disintegrated during the wars and social upheavals in Eastern Europe during the latter half of the seventeenth century. And though these new leaders did not preach reform or even outwardly challenge the status quo in either praxis or belief, they did convey, often in vastly popularized form, many of the basic notions of Lurianic mysticism which had developed in Palestine in the late sixteenth and early seventeenth centuries and had rapidly spread from the Ottoman Empire into the Kingdom of Poland, with which it was contiguous.

The Lurianic portrayal of the catastrophe of creation and the possible redemptive process was dazzling in its complexity but even in its popularized versions sufficed to give the masses of downtrodden Jews, often recent exiles, some sense of the meaning of the world, an understanding of their repeated exiles, and hopes for redemption through prayer and praxis. It certainly helped prepare tens of thousands of Jews to accept the messianic claims of Shabbetai Zevi, the "false messiah" who later converted to Islam in 1666 and, despite the normative rabbinic reaction to all signs of messianic claims usually identified with Shabbateanism in the late seventeenth and early eighteenth centuries, it could infuse the early, often isolated groups of early Hasidim with religious ardor. This new ardor, coupled with the comforting sense of belonging to a cohesive sect led by a self-assured, forceful religious leader, contributed significantly to the emergence of dozens of these groups in the southwestern Ukraine, specifically in Podolia.

By the third and fourth decades of the century, many of these groups coalesced under the charismatic leadership of Israel Baal Shem Tov, usually called "The Besht," the zadik (tsadik) or holy man considered by all later Hasidim—and historians—as the founder of the movement.

Gershom Scholem has summarized, in his characteristic authoritative manner, the history and meaning of the Besht's title.

> The technical term *ba'al shem* "Master of the Divine Names," literally: "Possessor of the Name," was the title given in popular usage and in Jewish Literature, especially in Kabbalistic and Hasidic works, from the Middle Ages onward, to one who possessed the secret knowledge of the Tetragrammaton and the other "Holy Names" and who knew how to work miracles by the power of these names. . . . In the 17th and 18th centuries the number of *ba'ale shem* who were not at all talmudic scholars increased. Such a *ba'al shem* was often a combination of practical Kabbalist, who performed his cures by means of prayers, amulets and incantations, and a popular healer familiar with *segullot* ("remedies") concocted from animal, vegetable, and mineral matter. . . . There is a variety to the title *ba'al shem* known as *ba'al shem tov*. The Besht, the founder of Hasidism, is the most famous bearer of this title. . . .

A popular though far from ignorant charismatic healer who employed amulets and magic spells, the Besht attracted masses of adherents who came to be cured and join him in ecstatic prayer, one of the special characteristics of his religious praxis. Precisely because of the dynamic relationship between the zadik and his follower, the term "Hasid," which formerly meant simply "pious," developed the connotation of "pious adherent of a certain charismatic leader, of a certain Rebbe or zadik." Both the Besht and his Hasidim clearly believed in his supernatural powers and visions, which were featured in a wealth of anecdotes narrated either by the master himself or by his Hasidim. The Hasidic tale, in fact, was one of the prominent literary genres spawned by the Hasidic movement, though it did not neglect more traditional genres such as exegesis and homily. By the time of his death in 1760, the Besht had left behind him a group of dedicated disciples and other, more tangential sects which were attracted to his charismatic posture but had not yet adopted all his practices or the unquestioning adulation of his saintly figure.

The Hasidic tale was certainly not the first hagiographic tale to emerge in the long history of Jewish literature, but it did succeed in changing the prevalent attitude toward the tale and the very act of telling tales. If, within the rabbinic tradition, tales, even hagiographic tales, were not accorded the dignity of other genres such as halakha, homiletics, or exegesis, the Hasidic tale was endowed with dignity and sanctity even in the lifetime of the Besht. Part of this new valorization is due to the simple sociological fact that the zadikim themselves told these tales or were the heroes in them. Joseph Dan has presented a more profound, theological explanation for the sanctity attributed to the Hasidic tale. He argues that the telling of the tale was the narrative correlative of the performance of commandments to which the individual—according to Lurianic doctrine—was to commit himself in order to contribute to the coming of the Messiah. In Lurianic Kabbalah the creation of the world is described as a catastrophic process, the violent clash of forces within God himself, a rending apart called *shevirat hakkelim* ("the breaking of the vessels"). This rending can be mended by the process of *tikkun* (remedying or repairing), in which man can take part by intense prayer, categorical belief, or fervent praxis.

The sanctity of the tale is encapsulated in an oft-quoted statement attributed to the Baal Shem Tov himself: "When one tells stories in praise of the zaddikim, it is as though he were engaged in 'Ma'aseh Merkavah'." The term *Ma'aseh Merkavah*, originally "throne mysticism," implied by this time some type of participation in the mystical act intended to cleanse the upper divine sphere through prayer and contemplation; the attribution of such dynamic effects to an activity, the telling of tales, which had not been held in high regard in previous generations, attests to a radical revision in values. I have demonstrated elsewhere that these stories are evidence of an impressive expansion and refinement of literary sensibility in the Jewish world and must be included in any consideration of "the making of the modern Jewish mind." What I would like to demonstrate now is that these tales, or rather their dissemination and parts of their structure, display a sophisticated social and political awareness, an awareness which is manifest in the attempts not only to reconcile two conflicting claims to personal authority but also to accommodate the scripturality of the later text with that of the former, biblical text, whose primacy can never be denied or challenged. We are therefore talking of politics in two senses: the literal, referring to the power struggle between two groups, in this case both Hasidic; the metaphoric, referring to the intellectual tension, the anxiety which a new scripture must generate in a community inextricably bound to an old, venerable scripture—not the "anxiety of influence" but an "anxiety of non-influence" spawned by the realization, or even the unarticulated intuition, that something has been violated by endowing the new text with sanctity. While we would argue that the metaphorical sense of politics is essentially meaningless divorced from the literal, political situation, it is the politics of scripturality which interests us here.

## II

While one can agree that these tales do not embody the theoretical richness of Hasidic thought, it is difficult to accept the notion that they have no other didactic purpose than the hagiographic presentation of the zadik. It is no accident that both *Shivhe HabBesht* (*In Praise of the Baal Shem Tov*), and the Bratslav Tales, the second major collection of classic Hasidic tales, were published in the same Hebrew calendrical year, 1814–15. By that time the Hasidic movement was well established in the Ukraine, in southern Volhynia, in eastern Galicia, and even in Belorussia. It had already encountered fierce opposition in Lithuania from the established rabbinic authorities and suffered some feeble attacks from the early maskilim (westernized, enlightened Jews). By 1815 we are talking not of small, isolated and secretive prayer sects, but of many well-organized courts, some large, some small, controlling masses of people, their way of life and their markets. Ironically, precisely at this period, both the compiler of *Shivhe HabBesht*, Dov Ber ben Samuel of Linitz, and its printer, Rabbi Israel Yoffe, felt that the movement had reached a critical juncture which required the collection and publication of these tales, tales which they had been reluctant to publish before. Though both express their hesitation about committing these holy tales to print, each gives a different reason.

Dov Ber ben Samuel, the compiler, states: "I myself have noticed that in the time between my youth and my old age miracles have become fewer every day and marvels have begun to disappear. This happens because of our many sins." The concept of decline is fairly normative for a pietist working within the confines of a traditional religious culture. Had he been able to conceive of his period as of historical value equal to that of the biblical patriarchs, or all subsequent rabbinic tradition, we would be forced to interpret this new valorization as a challenge to the sacred tradition or even as some form of messianism. The underlying difference between the Hasidic notion of new scripturality and that of the apostle Paul will be discussed further on; at present we shall simply note that this difference obviously must shape the respective attitudes toward allusions to the previous scripture. Modern historians of Hasidism, however, tend to discount Dov Ber's pessimism and see in Hasidism a revitalization of Judaism and a dynamic restructuring of social forms. Precisely during the most dynamic period of Hasidic expansion, the compiler of the most authoritative text of Hasidic tales perceives that there has been a religious decline, hence there is need for such a compilation to buttress the faithful. These varying perceptions of the state of affairs, that held by modern historians and that held by an authoritative contemporary, lead one to wonder how to weigh the valuations of each.

Rabbi Israel Yoffe, the printer, is troubled by another phenomenon, this one perhaps more political than religious, though it is couched in religious terms. The printer, in his preface, tells a tale worth quoting in full:

> I heard, moreover, from the people of the Holy Land, that the first time there was a plague in the Holy Land, God forbid, the holy Rabbi Menahem Mendel (of Vitebsk), blessed be the memory of this righteous and holy man, locked himself in his home with a minyan. During all the time they were secluded, their prayers were successful. However, on the holy Sabbaths, he did not say Torah at the third meal as was his custom: instead he used to sit at the dinner table with his companions who hearkened to his voice. There was an old man with him, one of the Besht's disciples, who told stories in praise of the Besht. One time the rabbi, the Maggid, blessed be the memory of this righteous and holy man, appeared in a dream of Menahem Mendel and said to him: "Are you not *my* disciple? Why do you not tell tales in *my* praise also?" So he agreed to tell tales in praise of our Great Rabbi during the third meal. When Menahem Mendel began to relate the wonders of the Great Maggid, the old man began to tell him about the Besht, as was his custom. Menahem Mendel did not let him continue, and immediately realized that he would be punished for it. Indeed it happened that after the meal he became sick with an intestinal disease. In a few days he passed away.

In concluding this tale, the printer asserts: "The profundity of these things is easily understood." Attempting to understand the profundity of these things, we should consider the following facts. Menahem

Mendel immigrated to the Land of Israel in 1777 and died in 1788. By that time, it was already a custom among Hasidim to substitute pious tales about the Besht for the customary Torah reading at the third Sabbath meal, late on Saturday afternoon; the tale, that is, had already assumed a quasi-ritual function and could be substituted for the Torah lesson. Menahem Mendel was thus practicing a custom known among Hasidim and given ritual status. When he attempted to substitute for a tale about the Besht, a tale about his own Rebbe, the Great Maggid of Mezeritsh, the second major leader of the Hasidic movement, he was severely punished and died. The contesting demands for honoring the memory of the two departed, saintly rabbis reflects a broader contest within the Hasidic movement in general. While we do not have a clear picture of the relationship between the Besht, who ruled until his death in 1760, and the Maggid, who led and spread the movement between 1760 and 1772, we do know that by the 1780s there were tensions between the biological descendents of the Besht and those who could claim authentic discipleship either from the Besht directly or through the Maggid, the first major theoretician of the movement. This conflict over legitimacy of succession is not unparalleled in religious movements and often erupts in the third generation.

This conflict, I would suggest, explains the peculiar organization of the first seven tales of *Shivhe HabBesht*, those prefaced to Dov Ber's manuscript by the printer, Israel Yoffe, at the behest of his Rebbe, Shneour Zalman of Lyady. That these prefatory tales were added to the manuscript on the instructions of Shneour Zalman (1745–1813) is of major import. He, as the leader of Belorussian Hasidism, was engaged in bitter struggles with the leading opponent of the movement, the famous Gaon of Vilna (Elijah ben Solomon Zalman, 1720–1797), and also rivaled Baruch ben Jehiel of Medzibezh (1757–1810), who, as grandson of the Besht, regarded himself as the legitimate leader of all Hasidim. The Gaon of Vilna had excommunicated Hasidim, burned their books, closed their prayer rooms, and in 1772 refused to meet for discussions with Menahem Mendel of Vitebsk and Shneour Zalman, whose beliefs and practices he considered heretical. Shneour Zalman, in fact, was imprisoned by Czarist authorities in both 1798 and 1801 on charges raised by followers of the Gaon. Within the Hasidic camp, Shneour Zalman was one of the paradigms of the charismatic leader whose authority derived from personal spiritual and intellectual virtues, not from family lineage. In struggles with both the Gaon and Baruch, Shneour Zalman was engaged in the historic contest over legitimacy and "privilege"—a contest which, I would argue, underlies the composition of the added passages, certainly the first seven stories, which, unlike the material collected by Dov ben Samuel of Linitz, pays scrupulous attention to chronology and sequence of events.

The first three tales are devoted to the miraculous adventures of

Rabbi Eliezer, the father of the Besht: his kidnapping, his sagacity, his chastity, his miraculous delivery by the Lord, and the promise of a remarkable son as a reward for his chastity in captivity. Chapter four relates the well-known story of the Besht's childhood and adolescence. Chapter five and six introduce an entirely different figure, the miraculous Rabbi Adam, "from whom the Besht received the manuscripts. Rabbi Adam had found these manuscripts containing the hidden secrets of eethe Torah in a cave." In the seventh chapter we learn of the involved mystical process through which Rabbi Adam tested the Besht and transmitted these manuscripts to him rather than to his own son, whom he told: "I have manuscripts here which hold the secrets of the Torah. But you do not merit them."

The delicate balance of this cycle of seven tales is no accident: it stressed the fact that the Besht actually has two fathers: his biological father, the saintly Rabbi Eliezer, and his mystical mentor, the miraculous and shrewd Rabbi Adam. I would suggest that this narrative cycle is an adroit attempt on the part of Shneour Zalman to heal the wounds incurred in the ideological conflict between the two camps claiming legitimacy of succession. The cycle says, in effect, that both are legitimate heirs of the charisma of the Besht. Like his contemporary Nahman of Bratslav, Shneour Zalman obviously realized that there are times when the telling of tales is the most effective way to communicate the truth of the Lord and, no less important, to preserve the integrity of the community. Not only among maskilim, but also among Hasidim, literature had established itself as a moving force in the life of Eastern European Jewry. Some scholars, in fact, would argue that Hasidism was the most cohesive force in Jewish communal life between the dissolution in 1754 of the Council of Four Lands, the representative assembly of Jewish notables in the Kingdom of Poland, and the politicization of Eastern European Jewry at the end of the nineteenth century. If this is so, the function of the Hasidic tale in enhancing this cohesiveness is a cardinal sociological factor in modern Jewish history.

### III

What we call the "politics of scripturality" can only be demonstrated by reference to a specific text, and so we turn to the first three tales of *Shivhe HabBesht*. Though these tales were told in Yiddish, they were transcribed in both Yiddish and Hebrew. The transcription and collection of the tales in Hebrew immediately lent them the status of a conventional pious text and it is in this form that they were widely circulated and read. In the Hebrew text there are no titles or paragraphing; the paragraphing used in the English translation both facilitates discussion of the text and demonstrates the structure of the story.

### RABBI ELIEZER

*Rabbi Eliezer, our teacher, the father of the Besht, lived in the state of Walachia near the border. He and his wife were old. Once bandits came to the city and captured him, but his wife managed to escape to another town. She was so poor that she became a midwife and in this way earned her living. Rabbi Eliezer's captors took him to a remote country where there were no Jews and sold him. Rabbi Eliezer served his master faithfully. His master liked him and he appointed him overseer over his house. He asked his master to allow him to observe the Sabbath and to rest on that day, and his master granted his request. And it came to pass that he remained there a long time. He wanted to escape and save himself, but a dream came to him: "Do not be too hasty, since you must still remain in this country."*

*It came to pass that his master had dealings with the king's viceroy and as a gift he gave him the rabbi, our teacher, our rabbi, Eliezer. He lavished praise on him and extolled him. As soon as he came to the home of the king's viceroy, he found favor in his eyes and was given a special chamber in which to stay. He had no duties to perform at all, except that when the king's viceroy came home Rabbi Eliezer would welcome him with a bowl of water to wash his feet, since this was the custom accorded to great men of state. During all that time he studied the Torah and prayed in his special chamber.*

*Once the king became embroiled in a great war and he sent for his viceroy to counsel him on tactics of attack and defense. Because it was difficult for the viceroy to grasp the actual situation, he did not know what to say. The king stormed with rage because the viceroy could not help him in this time of trouble. The king's viceroy went home dejected. When he arrived, Rabbi Eliezer, the rabbi, our rabbi and teacher, welcomed him as usual with a bowl of water, but the king's viceroy rejected it and lay down on this couch in a troubled mood. Rabbi Eliezer said to him: "My master, why are you so troubled? Please tell me."*

*The king's viceroy scolded him, but Rabbi Eliezer was a faithful servant to his master and wanted him to be treated justly. He endangered his life and repeatedly urged him until the king's viceroy was forced to tell him what had happened. And he said to his master: "Do not interpretations belong to God? The Lord is a man of war. I will keep fasts and I will ask the Lord, blessed be He, for this secret since He is a revealer of secrets." And he asked a dream-question and it was answered. All the tactics of war were revealed and clearly explained to him.*

*The next day he came to his master and told him the advice that had been revealed to him from heaven. The king's viceroy was very pleased with the information and he joyfully hastened to the king. And*

*he said, "Oh, my master, this is the advice I have to give." And he
answered every question.
    When the king heard all the viceroy's words, he said: "This is
marvelous advice. It is not from a human mind—unless it comes from a
holy man who had inspiration from gods whose dwelling is not with
flesh or from one who had contact with the Evil Spirit. Since I know
that you are by no means a godly man, you must be a sorcerer." The
king's viceroy was forced to confess the truth and tell him what had
happened.*

    The narrative devices employed to domesticate this new scripture,
i.e., to make the crucial accommodation between it and the traditional
Hebrew Scripture accepted by the audience, are varied and effective.
Before the narrative in the Hebrew text we find this statement by the
printer, Israel Yoffe:

> Since in the manuscripts from which I have copied these tales the
> sequence of events and the revelation of the Besht—may his merit
> protect us, amen—are not in the right order, and because I heard
> everything as it came from *Admor* [Shneour Zalman], whose soul rests in
> heaven, in the proper order and with the proper interpretation, I will
> print them first as I heard them from his holy lips, and after that point in
> the story I will include what has been written in the manuscripts.

This attribution of source, though much longer than that of the stories
in the main portion of the manuscript, is typical of the tales in *Shivhe
HabBesht*: almost all of them begin with the statement: "I heard this
from so-and-so," thus establishing the authenticity of the tale by
attributing it to a respected authority and deliberately disclaiming all
originality.
    Once the actual tale begins, "Rabbi Eliezer, our teacher, the father of
the Besht . . . ," the audience is immediately introduced into a familiar
world. The themes and even the diction is that of the patriarchal
narratives in the book of Genesis or of *midrashim* elaborated from
them. We learn that Eliezer and his wife were old (like Abraham and
Sarah) and presumably childless—a fact explicitly mentioned only in
the third tale. Eliezer's capture by the brigands, his sale to a master in a
distant land, his master's affection for him, all evoke memories of the
Joseph story and are even climaxed by a direct quote from Genesis 39:4
where Potiphar appoints Joseph overseer in his house. The motifs
patently culled from the Joseph story serve several purposes at once:
they assure the reader that this tale is indeed within the patriarchal
tradition; they identify Eliezer with Joseph, perhaps even suggesting
that Joseph is a traditional model for Eliezer; they prepare us for
accepting Eliezer's wondrous capacity to "interpret dreams," to have
access to knowledge not given to ordinary men, even kings. Eliezer,
furthermore, is portrayed as a saintly person in the rabbinic tradition

which embellished the biblical characterization of Joseph: he requests permission to observe the Sabbath, and he studies Torah in the seclusion of his room. Even the instructions he received in his dream when he wished to escape—"Do not be too hasty, since you must still remain in this country"—echo the narrative technique of the Joseph story, which is self-consciously structured with a control of episodes paralleling divine control of human affairs. In the Joseph story, this parallelism is concealed until Joseph declares to his astonished brothers that the Lord has all along controlled their behavior, hence the flow of the plot. Here, the theme of divine intervention in the plot is more obvious and is repeated in the second tale.

What the audience cannot know upon first exposure to this tale is that precisely those features that appear to be so conventional as to enhance the acceptability of the tale embody elements of the Hasidic claims to the legitimacy of the movement and its specific tenets. The patriarchal ambience endows Eliezer with the authority of the biblical patriarchs that pervades all Jewish literature. The identification with Joseph, so seemingly innocuous, might very well allude to messianic pretensions since the belief in the imminent appearance of the Messiah son of Joseph (as opposed to the Messiah son of David) was by no means a dormant issue in the Jewish world in the seventeenth and eighteenth centuries: the Shabbatean upheaval of the 1660s and the Frankist turmoil of the 1750s and 1760s generated by the heretical instigations and apostasy of Jacob Frank, were still fresh in the collective memory and are alluded to in *Shivhe HabBesht*. Even more crucial is the evidence of the fourth tale of this collection where we find clear intimations that the Besht might have the power to bring the Messiah—a very Lurianic notion. Satan, we are told, wanted to kill the young child who was to become the Besht since he "was afraid that the time was approaching when he would disappear from the earth," i.e., the prayers of the child might bring the Messiah, who would annihilate Satan.

Eliezer is endowed with the gift of "interpretation," a gift associated with Joseph and Daniel (many echoes of the Daniel stories are evident in the tale and at least two direct quotes from Daniel are inserted in the text), the two prototypical "interpreters of dreams." This visionary gift has a broad range of manifestations: sensing the depression of the viceroy, divining military tactics, receiving in dreams instructions that the time to escape his captivity has not yet come. Throughout this collection of tales, the Besht is known to possess a variety of super-human characteristics, many associated with the power of "interpretation" rooted in the traditional capacity of the "baal shem" to master the Divine Names. One decisive, hence controversial aspect of mastery of the Divine Names is the ability to interpret the truths embedded or hidden in the Torah; these "truths," though possibly new or even subversive of older truths, are in consonance with the Torah since they are demonstrably integrated in it and extractable by a "master of Divine Names."

That the time to escape has not yet come is more than an echo of the narrative device of Genesis since the correct time to escape captivity, i.e., to be redeemed from exile, is a pervasive theme in traditional Jewish thought and was given special urgency by Lurianic speculation. In *Shivhe HabBesht*, the specific time for revelation is transferred to the personal, biographical plane: the Besht, we are told, did not reveal his true self until 1736 when he was already 36 years old. Before that date, he lived as a humble worker or teacher, often humiliated, struggling to keep his secret until instructed to reveal it—a theme obviously central to the Hasidic tradition and touched on in this collection in several forms, including tales 14 and 15, the last two of the tales admittedly added by Israel Yoffe. The doctrine of the hidden zadik was prevalent both before and after the appearance of the Besht.

The saintliness and piety of Eliezer is necessary to establish the credentials for his son, who is to be the founder and authoritative source of a new religious movement; the pious father is a recognizable feature in hagiographies. From the point of view of narrative structure, these qualities are both given special importance and, in turn, actually shape the seemingly strange ending of the story. We would expect Eliezer to be rewarded for his services to the state in the final paragraph of the first tale, but this does not happen until the first statement of the second tale. Instead we are treated to a conversation between the king and his viceroy (Eliezer's master) who had just brought the king the brilliant military plan which, we understand, is to win the battle. The king remarks shrewdly:

> This is marvelous advice. It is not from a human mind—unless it comes from a holy man who had inspiration from *gods whose dwelling is not with flesh* [Daniel 2:11] or from one who had contact with the Evil Spirit. Since I know that you are by no means a godly man, you must be a sorcerer.

This statement, mouthed by a gentile king, is a perceptive encapsulation of fairly standard Kabbalistic doctrine which would have been widely known after the dissemination of popular Kabbalistic texts in the seventeenth century. It distinguishes between normatively human knowledge and that derived from superhuman sources; among superhuman sources, it distinguishes between God and the Evil Spirit and, on the earth, the corresponding agents of superhuman power, the godly man and the sorcerer. The king's logic is impeccable: the viceroy is not a godly man and since he has received this marvelous advice, he must be a sorcerer. The viceroy, confronted with this analysis, must confess the source of his inspired information.

This denouement subtly informs the audience that what has begun as a seemingly conventional retelling of a pious tale leaning heavily on biblical allusions, concludes with a logical, theological statement which both describes and legitimizes the charisma of the zadik figure in general, and the Besht in particular, since it refers to his father, Eliezer. This statement is dramatized in narrative form in the fourth tale where we find both oppositions, that between human and divine knowledge, and that between the saintly man and the sorcerer who is an incarnation of Satan.

## IV

The second tale both artfully reinforces the themes of the first and advances the plot.

### RABBI ELIEZER AND THE VICEROY'S DAUGHTER

*The king elevated him and made him his battle commander, for he perceived that the Lord was with him and that all that he did prospered. He won every battle that the king sent him to fight. During this time Rabbi Eliezer became concerned about what would happen to him, and he thought that it might be the time to flee to his native land. It was then revealed to him from heaven: "You must still remain in this country."*

*Then it happened that the viceroy died, and since Rabbi Eliezer had found favor in the king's eyes the king appointed him as his advisor. He also gave him the viceroy's daughter as his wife. Yet with God's help, the rabbi did not touch her. He devised various ways to avoid remaining at home, and even if by chance it so happened that he was at home, he refrained from touching her.*

*It so happened that no Jew was allowed to live in that country. When they found a Jew, there was only one verdict—that he be put to death. It had been so for several years. Once, his wife asked him, "Tell me, what fault do you find in me that you do not touch me and you do not make me your wife?"*

*He said to her, "Swear to me that you'll not reveal this to anyone, and I'll tell you the truth." She swore to him, and he told her: "I am a Jew."*

*She immediately sent him home with a rich treasure of silver and gold. But on the way thieves robbed him and he lost everything that he possessed.*

The parallel to the biblical Joseph is conveyed by (a) the elevation of Eliezer to general, then to viceroy (marked by a direct quote from Genesis 39:3), (b) a novel version of the temptation of Joseph, an episode with a rich midrashic history, Joseph's saintliness manifested in his resisting temptation, and (c) the awareness that the hero, for all his prestige, is an alien in a foreign land, an exile. Again we find the explicit manipulation of the plot by an external, divine force. Complementary to this thematic reinforcement, we find an ingenious concatenation of conventional themes: unlike the young bachelor Joseph, who is impor-tuned by his master's wife, Eliezer, an elderly married man, is given the viceroy's daughter as wife. Instead of the lust of Potiphar's wife, we have the natural expectations of the new wife that the marriage be consummated sexually, a deed which Eliezer, a traditionally pious Jew, refuses to do. This complication of plot is designed to motivate Eliezer's release from his land of exile—precisely the opposite of Joseph's incarceration when false charges are brought against him by the woman he spurned. The separation of Hebrews and Egyptians in the Joseph story is radicalized and given contemporary, concrete substance: there were, indeed, European lands where Jews were not allowed to reside. Eliezer's piety is rewarded by his disappointed wife—clearly an instrument of divine will—with release from bondage which echoes the Exodus from Egypt: he leaves laden with wealth. In a purposeful surprise ending, this wealth is robbed from him by thieves, and he arrives home destitute, clearly setting the scene for the climactic dispensation: the appearance of Elijah at the beginning of the third tale, which brings us to the birth of the charismatic leader of the new movement.

## THE BIRTH OF THE BESHT

*While he was on his journey, Elijah the Prophet revealed himself to him and said: "Because of the merit of your behavior a son will be born to you who will bring light to Israel, and in him this saying will be fulfilled: Israel in whom I will be glorified."*

*He came home and with God's help he found his wife still alive. The Besht was born to them in their old age, when both of them were close to a hundred. (The Besht said that it had been impossible for his father to draw his soul from heaven until he had lost his sexual desire.)*

*The boy grew up and was weaned. The time came for his father to die, and he took his son in his arms and he said, "I see that you will light my candle, and I will not enjoy the pleasure of raising you. My beloved son, remember this all your days: God is with you. Do not fear anything." (In the name of Admor, I heard that it is natural for a son and a father to be closely bound, for as our sages, God bless their memory, have said: "The talk of the child in the market place is either that of his father or of his mother." How much closer then are ties between parents and children who are born to them in their old age. For example, Jacob loved Joseph because he was born to him in his old age, and the ties between them were very great, as it is said in the holy Zohar. And it was true here. Although the Besht was a small child, because of the intensity and sincerity of the tie, the words were fixed in his heart.*)

The tale relating the actual birth of the Besht is carefully constructed to maintain a balance of the traditionally acceptable and subtly insinuated new ideology and problematics. The appearance of Elijah the Prophet to an individual—particularly alone on a road—is by no means an exceptional occurrence in Jewish folk literature nor is the annunciation of the birth of a child who will bring light to Israel (an obvious play on the Besht's personal name, which was Israel). And the audience would not be surprised by the old age of the parents—almost 100 years—since this is one of the traditional ways to suggest divine involvement in the birth process of an important personality in Jewish history. The early orphaning of the Besht might indeed have been based on fact and could evoke, either in real life or in the folk narrative, the death-bed blessing: "God is with you. Do not fear anything."

Since this tale must function as the narrative transfer of charisma from Eliezer to his son (subsequent tales in the collection do not deal with this issue), the very act of transfer should be the theme. And it is. As Eliezer recedes from the center of our interest, the Joseph story features disappear completely. The biblical Joseph, after all, was not the progenitor of the main line of the Israelites. We sense here a slight disruption in the line of succession. While Israel is clearly Eliezer's child, he is portrayed both there and in the following tale as an orphan whose father dies soon after the child has been weaned. The narrator finds it necessary to comment upon two aspects of transmission; one biological, the other spiritual. The miraculous birth of a child to elderly parents elicits an explanation, attributed to the Besht, that "it had been impossible for his father to draw his [the Besht's] soul from heaven until he [Eliezer] had lost his sexual desire." The problematic of spiritual transmission is handled in what looks like a traditional rabbinical explanatory note attributed here to Shneour Zalman himself. In attempting to explain how the son who had just been weaned could have comprehended and remembered his dying father's behest, Shneour Zalman asserts that it is natural for a son to be close to his father, particularly a son born to elderly parents. These common-sensical insights, however, are confirmed by three prooftexts: one from the Talmud; one from the patriarchal narratives in Genesis (Jacob and Joseph are cited as models, but not as an analogue to Eliezer and Israel); and one from the Zohar.

In telling the story of the birth of the charismatic leader of the new movement, the narrator both adorns his narrative with traditional, recognizable features, such as the annunciation by Elijah, and subtly insinuates the issue of both biological and spiritual legitimacy which interests him. After establishing Eliezer as a patriarchal figure, Shneour

Zalman must insist upon the demonstrable legitimacy of his son, the Besht.

The recourse to prooftexts to prove the possibility of a narrative item is not limited to this tale alone and indicates the tentativeness of the narrative: it cannot stand alone, free of the supports of traditional texts and traditional methods of reading them. Similarly, the crucial figure of Eliezer cannot stand alone but must be integrated with features from the Joseph story even when they are inverted or subverted in the narrative. I have therefore deliberately avoided in my analysis the term "prefiguration": Joseph here is not a *figura* (as described so lucidly by Auerbach) and the type of interpretation involved is not "figurative," since Joseph is not posited as an independent trans-textual reality in history.

## V

In a seminal essay on Nahmanides' symbolical reading of history, Amos Funkenstein has demonstrated the relative paucity of typological interpretation in the Jewish exegetical tradition. Even when this mode was employed by so sophisticated an exegete as Nahmanides, it was limited to the patriarchs, thus omitting Joseph who, in Christian typology, prefigures Jesus. Nahmanides, Funkenstein argues, was certainly aware of the implications such typological interpretations had for "the Church Fathers [who] employed these images . . . to define the continuity and progress from the Old Testament to the New Testament." For Paul, too, the Old Testament was a series of prefigurations of Christ.

While Nahmanides' awareness of Christian exegesis and his sensitivity to its implications can be established, Hasidism seems to have been more introverted and reacts primarily to previous Jewish assumptions and practices. To my knowledge, no Hasidic thinker considered the teachings of the Besht or the Maggid a new dispensation which replaced the older dispensation; rather the teachings were taken as a legitimate continuation of the Jewish tradition, if anything an enrichment of that tradition by the intensification of piety through adherence to charismatic leaders, fervent prayer, and devotions.

When the narrator of the first tales of *Shivhe HabBesht* relies heavily upon features and language from the Joseph story in order to portray Eliezer, he is presenting Joseph not as a prefiguration of Eliezer in the Pauline sense, but rather as a legitimizing literary forebearer. The Joseph imagery in these tales does not prefigure or predict the coming of the Besht, the charismatic zadik who leads this new movement, but rather legitimates his father Eliezer by attaching him both to the patriarchal tradition, broadly conceived, i.e., Abraham and Joseph, and the late prophetic or apocalyptic tradition, by reference to Daniel. While exegetes of the New Testament, following the Pauline tradition, claim that the new scripture is a fulfillment of the older scripture, Shneour Zalman's version of these crucial tales implies that this new sacred text—which I take the liberty to call scripture—should be regarded as a sacred text in the tradition of prior Jewish sacred texts.

In sum, Shneour Zalman's claims are reverential, apologetic—and cautious. If Nahmanides was cautious because he was aware of the Christian usage of typological interpretation, Shneour Zalman was probably cautious because he had been engaged in the bitter struggle with the Gaon and his followers and, on the other hand, realized the dangers inherent in the pretensions of his younger colleague, Nahman of Bratslav, who rashly denigrated the authenticity of all other Hasidic zadikim while hailing the true zadik (himself), whom he describes as *behinat Moshe*, of the essence of Moses. Nahman claimed that he was the fifth of great Jewish masters of the spirit: Moses, Simeon bar Yohai (second century C. E.), Isaac Luria, the Besht, and Nahman himself. Since these historical persons are chronologically remote from one another, the connection between them must be on another plane, probably the figural. This claim was clearly unacceptable to Nahman's contemporaries. Nahman, furthermore, had strayed in another direction: he, too, told tales which were considered holy scripture by his followers; they were printed in 1815, the same year which witnessed the publication of *Shivhe HabBesht*.

*Bibliographical Note*

There are few serious analytical studies in English of the Hasidic tale. The reader might consult the introduction to the English translation of *Shivhe HabBesht: In Praise of the Baal Shem Tov*, translated and edited by Dan Ben-Amos and Jerome Mintz (Bloomington: Indiana University Press, 1970); the introduction to Band, *Nahman of Bratslav: The Tales* (New York: Paulist, 1978) and also Band, "The Function of the Enigmatic in Two Hasidic Tales," *Studies in Jewish Mysticism*, ed. Joseph Dan and Frank Talmage (Cambridge, Mass., 1982), pp. 185–210. All quotes from *Shivhe HabBesht* are taken from the Ben-Amos/Mintz translation, which also has a fine bibliography on Hasidism and the Hasidic tale. The lengthy quote from Gershom Scholem defining the term "ba'al shem" was originally published in the *Encyclopedia Judaica* (Jerusalem, 1972), IV, pp. 6–7; it can also be found in his *Kabbalah* (New York: Quadrangle, 1974), pp. 310–11.

The two most complete books to date on the Hasidic tale are the Hebrew works of Joseph Dan, *HaSippur HaHasidi* (Jerusalem, 1975), and Gedalya Nigal's *HaSiporet HaHasidit* (Jerusalem, 1981). I have used the Hebrew texts, both the 1947 Horodetzky edition cited by most scholars and reprints of the first (Kapust) edition of 1815; for the first three tales, the variations are minor. The numbers and names of the stories are those of Ben-Amos/Mintz; they do not appear in the Hebrew texts. I do not deal with the variant reading of the second tale (2a) since it adds nothing to my argument. Though Ben-Amos casts some doubt on the authenticity of the attribution of tales 5–8 to Shneour Zalman, I do not.

HERBERT B. HUFFMON

# BABEL UND BIBEL: THE ENCOUNTER BETWEEN BABYLON AND THE BIBLE

Between January 1902, and October 1904, Friedrich Delitzsch (1850–1922), the most famous Assyriologist of his time, delivered a series of lectures entitled "Babel und Bibel," or "Babylonia and the Bible"; these lectures gave rise to a very extensive and heated controversy, which spread well beyond the borders of the German Empire and was conducted in many languages. This controversy had an impressive setting, both historically and physically. In 1902 German scholars had just begun their entrance into the archeological domain of Assyriology, with the initiation of the excavations at Babylon (in 1899), to be followed by excavations at Asshur (in 1903). The earlier dominance of British and French scholars in philology had previously given way to German leadership under the sway of Eberhard Schrader and his student, Friedrich Delitzsch himself. Yet Germany remained without serious representation in the excavations, which meant that the German scholars had no source material—no tablets—of their own and were dependent upon the tablet collections of such repositories as the British Museum. This blow to German pride had just recently begun to be remedied with the commencement of excavations in Mesopotamia under the auspices of the young German Oriental Society (which Delitzsch played a role in founding in 1898) and the patronage of Wilhelm II, the German Emperor. Delitzsch himself had recently returned from reviewing the German work in Mesopotamia when, at the request of the Oriental Society, he delivered his first lecture under the soon-to-be-famous title, "Babel und Bibel."

The Oriental Society assembled on 13 January 1902, in the Singakademie of Berlin, in the presence of the Emperor himself. At the emperor's request the lecture was repeated 1 February 1902, at the royal palace in Berlin. These were awesome conditions for a lecture by an Assyriologist.

The speaker, Friedrich Delitzsch, then in his early fifties, was an impressive figure. He was the son of the illustrious Franz Delitzsch (1813–1890), the most beloved Old Testament scholar in the Germany of his day. Coming from a conventional Lutheran family, Franz was noted for his Lutheran piety, his embracing of an encounter with modern Judaism, his philological and exegetical acumen, and his brilliant and imaginative interpretation of the Bible. As the son of such a beloved and orthodox figure, Friedrich could expect to be listened to attentively by a wide-ranging audience. In his own right, moreover, Friedrich had established himself as the recognized leader among the Assyriologists of his day. He had already published the standard Assyrian reading book, grammar, and dictionary of that period, and had made a major contribution to the study of biblical geography. His students were numerous and famous themselves. Among them were Heinrich Zimmern (Leipzig), Peter Jensen (Marburg), David Gordon Lyon (Harvard), Robert Francis Harper (Chicago), Ira M. Price (Chicago), Carl Bezold (Heidelberg), Paul Haupt (Johns Hopkins), Franz Weissbach (Leipzig), Robert W. Rogers (Drew), Richard Gottheil (Columbia), Carl W. Belser (Michigan), and James A. Craig (Michigan). Moreover, Delitzsch had recently returned from a visit to the Near East, where he had been able to see the results of the latest archeological work.

The German Oriental Society had invited Delitzsch to address them, and he in turn suggested several possible topics. The one they chose was "Babel und Bibel," i.e., the discoveries in Babylonia as they illustrate and affect the interpretation of the Bible. Once the topic had been announced, Delitzsch was assured of a large and attentive audience. There was great interest in what archeological discoveries might do to illuminate the Bible, an interest nurtured by a number of Assyriologists who had emphasized ways in which the new discoveries confirmed the Bible, figures such as A. H. Sayce in Britain and Fritz Hommel in Germany. In 1875 George Smith published his *Chaldean Genesis*, presenting as the Chaldean (i.e., Babylonian) account of Genesis descriptions of the creation, the fall, the flood, the tower of Babel, and so forth, extracted from tablets in the British Museum; the volume stirred a tremendous popular response. In 1887 the bulk of the Amarna tablets, with the correspondence in Babylonian between the king of Egypt and the great kings of the time as well as with local kings in Syria and Palestine, was found in Egypt; these tablets, some from Palestine, dated not long before the coming of the Israelites. (And at the very moment of the first lecture the stela containing the laws of Hammurabi was being discovered in Persia.) Delitzsch's potential audience was vast. There would be many for whom whatever he said would be new.

From the beginning Delitzsch intended to deliver a series of three annual lectures in order to explore his topic properly. His plan for the first two lectures was "to show in how many and various questions of a geographical, historical, chronological, linguistic, and archaeological type Babylon proves itself an interpreter and illustrator of the Bible, especially of the Old Testament." Delitzsch planned to emphasize the parallels concerning ideas about the flood, creation, the sabbath, and life after death, and then to turn to parallels in style and ideology (e.g., self-revelation of the deity and legal traditions). The third lecture, then, was to explore, in the light of recent research on Babylonia and the Old Testament, how the honoring of one God, Yahweh, led up to the new truth of Christianity. More specifically, Delitzsch intended in this final lecture to show "how the moral-religious demands of the noble spirit of Babylon completely coincide with those of the noble spirit of Israel."

## I. The First Lecture

As Delitzsch began his first lecture, the audience was expectant. Many surely anticipated that this eminent son of an eminent father would continue the tradition of those Assyriological scholars who argued that the discoveries in Babylonia could serve not only to illuminate but also to authenticate the Bible. Many also anticipated being able to note with pride the entrance of Germany into Mesopotamian archeology, and doubtless this was especially true of Emperor Wilhelm, who had granted funds to help launch the German archeological work. Indeed, one of the Society's obvious reasons for sponsoring the lecture was to seek support for German archeological work in Mesopotamia.

The very opening sentences of the lecture were no disappointment to the audience:

> What is the reason for these efforts in remote, inhospitable, and dangerous lands? What is the reason for this expensive rooting through rubble many thousands of years old, all the way down to the water table, where no gold and no silver is to be found? What is the reason for the competition among nations to secure excavation rights to these deserted mounds, and the more the better? Moreover, what is the source of the ever-increasing, self-sacrificing interest, on both sides of the Atlantic, allotted to the excavations in Babylonia and Assyria?
>
> To these questions there is one answer, even if not the whole answer, which points to what for the most part is the motive and the goal, namely, the Bible.

(One notes here the potential problem for a discipline studying great civilizations of the past that is largely viewed by others as ancillary to the study of the Bible.) Delitzsch turned immediately to the marvel of recovering from the ancient Near East, especially from Babylonia, records referring to persons and events mentioned in the Bible. But passing by the fascinating data about persons such as the Assyrian kings Sargon and Sennacherib, previously known almost exclusively from the Bible, Delitzsch moved on to his primary topic, the parallels between Babylonia and the Bible.

In reviewing the parallels that Babylonian and Assyrian texts offered to the biblical accounts of the flood, of creation, of the institution of the sabbath, and to the ideas of life—or nonlife—after death, Delitzsch covered material familiar to scholars though largely unknown to the wider lay audience he reached. (My copies of the first two lectures indicate printings of 60,000 and 45,000 respectively, and there were subsequent printings.) He then pressed on to his more important, underlying thesis. Not only was Babylonia an interpreter and illustrator of the Bible, it was also a great civilization in its own right. Indeed, Babylonia was culturally dominant in Palestine during most of the biblical period. Palestine was "a domain completely pervaded by Babylonian culture." Taking note of the "beautiful mantle from Shinar," i.e., Babylonia, mentioned in Joshua 7:21 as arousing Achan's greed, Delitzsch went on to state that "it was not only the commerce, but also the trade, law, custom and science of Babylon that set the fashion in the land [of Palestine]." His point became clearer as he indicated that it was not just a matter of *parallels* between Babylonia and the Bible; rather Babylonia was itself the *source* of many of the key ideas and institutions in the Bible.

Whereas the audience appreciated his opposition to the derivation of Old Testament ideas of God from fetishism or animism, they were less enthusiastic about his particular argument. He argued that the word for god meant "the Goal—the Being to whom as to a goal the eyes of man looking heavenwards are turned"; this Being was called, by "the nomad Semitic tribes" (i.e., the Amorites) of the time of Hammurabi, God or El. This was monotheism, "since this goal can naturally be only one" (or, in later editions, "since the Divine Essence was viewed by them as a unity"). Even more was involved, however, for among the names of persons from these North(west) Semitic tribes are found names such as "Yahwe is God," i.e., names featuring the particular name of the God known to Israel, Yahweh; this meant that Yahweh, Israel's God, "was the spiritual possession of those same nomad tribes out of which after a thousand years [according to the chronology of that time] the children of Israel were to emerge." (This claim was subsequently modified as referring only to the *name* Yahweh.) The religion of these tribes in Babylonia "quickly succumbed before the polytheism" of Babylonia, a polytheism that "continued throughout three thousand years to be the Babylonian state religion," even though "free and enlightened spirits taught that Nergal and Nebo, the Moon God and the Sun God, the God of Thunder, and all the other gods, even those of neighboring peoples, were one with Marduk, the god of Babylon." The Babylonian idea of divinity was very sophisticated, but polytheism was dominant.

Delitzsch closed his lecture with a plea for the continuation of the work of the German Oriental Society in Babylonia: "Out yonder on the ruins of Babylon, it is working ceaselessly, from morning till night, in heat and cold, for Germany's honor and for Germany's learning."

The response to the first lecture was immense. Although much of what Delitzsch had said was not new to scholars, prestigious circumstances and wide distribution brought his comments before a wide circle largely unfamiliar with what the scholars knew. Some scholars, however, were dismayed by many of his points. Objections were raised to his insistence on Babylonian cultural dominance in Palestine and the associated implication—or claim—that many key biblical ideas and institutions were borrowed from Babylonia. Objections were also raised to his interpretation of some personal names as containing the name of Israel's god, Yahweh, several hundred years before the time of Moses, thereby implying another breach in biblical originality (cf. Exodus 3:15, 6:3). The other main area of objections concerned his reference to a kind of Marduk monotheism. Objections came from Assyriological and biblical scholars in the form of letters in the press, articles, and pamphlets.

There were also some areas which were not prominent in the early discussion but which could be seen more clearly in the light of subsequent lectures and writings by Delitzsch. First, the lecture clearly heralded German nationalism (including as an aside the suggestion that Asshurbanipal's wife, to judge from the extant representations, was perhaps "a princess of Aryan blood"). Second, the lecture contained many elements of an unfavorable verdict on the life and theology of ancient Israel. Delitzsch attacked "those naive anthropomorphic and anthropopathic views of the deity which are peculiar to the youth of the human race; . . . a heathen sacrifical cultus; with external forms of law, which did not prevent the people of pre-exilic times from continuous backsliding . . . and, above all, . . . Israelite *exclusiveness*." All these difficulties ended only with Jesus. Delitzsch was preparing for his later assertion that not only was Babylonian culture dominant in Palestine, it was also religiously and morally superior. (In spite of the superiority of Babylonia, however, he allowed that ideas borrowed from there should not be theologically binding on us.)

## II. The Second Lecture

The second lecture to the German Oriental Society followed a year later, on 12 January 1903, again in the Singakademie of Berlin and in the presence of Emperor Wilhelm II, who was joined by the Empress.

In the second lecture, originally intended to parallel the first, it soon became clear that Delitzsch was advancing some new arguments and making some intimations much more explicit. The lecture begins by referring to those who objected even to his title, "Babylonia and the Bible," affirming that it should have been "The Bible and Babylon" (as in the reply vehemently presented by the conservative Old Testament scholar, Eduard Koenig), in spite of the historical priority of Babylonian civilization. Delitzsch moved on to question those who would "ban discussion" of some key matters concerning the Bible by

invoking "original revelation" or by asserting that "the ethical monotheism of Israel" was "an unassailable . . . bulwark," instead of rejoicing in the new discoveries, so many of which illuminated and even,
in a sense, supported the Bible. As Delitzsch also observed, however,
the historical authenticity of the Old Testament should not need
"corroboration at every turn by the cuneiform documents."

In the preface to the lecture, in its earlier form (the various editions
of the lectures incorporate a variety of small revisions, especially in the
notes), he began by quoting Isaiah 63:1-6 as an example of Israel's
"unquenchable hatred directed against surrounding peoples," even in
prophets "at their most advanced stage." He comments further:

> Instead of immersing ourselves in "thankful wonder" at the providential
> guidance shown by God in the case of our own people, from the earliest
> times of primitive Germany until today, we persist—either from
> ignorance, indifference, or infatuation—in ascribing to those old-Israelite
> oracles a "revealed" character which cannot be maintained, either in the
> light of science, or in that of religion or ethics. The more deeply I
> immerse myself in the spirit of the prophetic literature of the Old
> Testament, the greater becomes my mistrust of Yahweh, who butchers
> the peoples with the sword of his insatiable anger; who has but one
> favorite child, while he consigns all other nations to darkness, shame, and
> ruin.

In the course of the lecture Delitzsch concentrated upon a deroga-
tion of the Old Testament, especially vis-à-vis Babylonia, and upon a
negative evaluation of its theological role. He varied from emphasizing
the parallels between Babylonia and Israel ("How utterly alike
everything is in Babylon and Bible!") to stressing the contrasts ("In the
case of the Babylonians all this was managed differently and better,"
with reference to the status of women).

The points Delitzsch selected were in part rather curious, such as his
apparent dismay that the Sabbath Commandment has one motivation
statement in Exodus and another in Deuteronomy, and the difficulty he
found in "seeking for the mountain in the Sinai range which corresponds in all respects with what the accounts tells us" of Mt. Sinai, as
if he were unfamiliar with other descriptions of the numinous. He also
states that if mankind was created in the image of God, as Genesis 1
declares, God is conceived of materially, which is not different in kind
from the images of Babylonian gods so ridiculed in the Old Testament,
here arguing as if he had not read his father's commentary on Genesis.

Delitzsch approves of the Church's scholarship having "unanimously
abandoned . . . the doctrine of the verbal inspiration of the Old
Hebrew Writings, and . . . acknowledg[ed]. . .the absolutely non-
binding character of the Old Testament Scripture as such upon our
faith, knowledge, and recognition," but he cannot understand the
continuing emphasis on "the ethical monotheism of Israel." After all,

the conduct of warfare in ancient Israel was not noticeably less cruel than in Babylonia, and the condemnations of the biblical prophets show that the people and the kings were guilty of "grave corruption." To this he contrasts the justice demanded by King Hammurabi in his laws, so recently discovered. In sum, the "national, particularistic monotheism" of ancient Israel is unworthy of praise or emulation.

The second lecture, then, marked a significant shift of emphasis. Delitzsch had moved from Babylonia as interpreter and illustrator of the Old Testament to a general attack on the religious value of the Old Testament for the modern German. This attack was far more than an Assyriologist's resentment of the subordination of his field of study, the great civilizations of ancient Babylonia and Assyria (and also, as Delitzsch belatedly recognized, ancient Sumer, having abandoned his brief espousal of the notion that there was no such language as Sumerian), to the study of the Bible. Delitzsch was apparently caught in the difficulty of sustaining a somewhat naive and unsophisticated approach to the Old Testament, partly in keeping with the rather conservative ideas of his upbringing, whereas he was far from naive in his analysis of Babylonian civilization. Perhaps he was also misled by his philological brilliance into thinking that he had nothing to learn from exegetes of the Old Testament. (After all, he knew Hebrew better than they did.) Yet his father, the great Franz Delitzsch, was, though conservative, neither so theologically naive nor so insensitive to religious language as the learned son. Moreover, whereas Franz Delitzsch was especially known for his concern for effective interchange between Christians and Jews, and his high regard for Judaism, it is difficult to grasp the source of Friedrich Delitzsch's confidence that nothing of what he said about the negative religious value of the Old Testament could "be considered injurious or even insulting to Judaism, least of all to the modern Jewish faith." In his notes to the lecture, Delitzsch stated that surely, in the search for truth, agreement with his views "in even the Jewish camp proper, will gradually . . . be attained." As various remarks suggest, Delitzsch was caught up in German nationalism.

Delitzsch was not asked to repeat this lecture at the royal palace, although he was invited there for a private conversation. In fact, Emperor Wilhelm II issued a public reply to the lecture in the form of a letter to the president of the German Oriental Society, Admiral Hollmann. In this letter he advised Delitzsch to stick to Assyriology and not inflict on the public or on the Oriental Society his views concerning theology and Christology. After all, "we carry on excavations and publish the results in behalf of science and history, but not to confirm or attack religious hypotheses. Professor Delitzsch, the theologian, has run away with Professor Delitzsch, the historian; his history is exploited merely for the benefit of his theology."

Adoph Harnack, the famous church historian and Delitzsch's colleague at Berlin, replied to the Emperor that Delitzsch had said nothing new, either in his affirmation of the Babylonian origin of many of the ideas and customs in ancient Israel or in his negative characterization of Old Testament religion. Indeed, there were Christian theologians (such as Harnack) who had expressed similar ideas.

The response from America was somewhat muted. Many prominent scholars familiar with the debate had little if anything to say about it. In New York, *The Catholic News* advised its readers that Delitzsch's attack had significance only for Protestants, and its success may be seen "in the total disintegration of all Protestant belief," with its emphasis on the Bible. Catholics, however, could stand comfortably in theological matters on the authority of the church. They were not dependent on the vagaries of higher criticism. From Chicago, Paul Carus, manager of the Open Court Publishing Co., which was responsible for the American edition of Delitzsch's first two lectures, wrote in Delitzsch's favor and in defense of what he saw as science versus faith.

K. Kohler published a reply in the *Year Book* of the Central Conference of American Rabbis, 1903, arguing that Delitzsch gave a one-sided presentation, misleading both as to Babylonia, for which he stresses its best features, and as to ancient Israel, for which he stresses the worst features. Kohler is not unaware of Babylonian grandeur and influence, but neither is he naive about the Bible and critical scholarship.

Delitzsch stirred up a storm of literature. He reports that by 1904 the German literature alone, leaving aside "some clearly worthless items," amounted to 1350 short and 300 long newspaper and journal articles, and 28 pamphlets. There were also responses in many other languages, for the first two lectures were translated into English, Italian, Danish, Swedish, Hungarian, and Czech. These responses ranged from pious rejections of his ideas to violent attacks; there were learned disputes from Assyriological colleagues, some of them his own students, to whom Delitzsch had to concede some points, though he was generally able to support his Assyriological opinions; biblical scholars also advanced many arguments against various of his theses. Some conservative scholars, such as Eduard Koenig, sought to dispute Assyriological matters, wherein they were no match for Delitzsch. Other scholars, such as the brilliant Hermann Gunkel, welcomed new Assyriological light but pointed out Delitzsch's naivete in dealing with questions of the history of religion and biblical interpretation. Expertise in Hebrew philology is no guarantee of understanding Israelite religion. For Gunkel, Delitzsch had said nothing of significance about ancient Israel.

## III. Delitzsch's Review and Preview

If Delitzsch made no significant contribution to understanding the Bible, he nonetheless had significant influence on the public debates of that time. He pressed on toward his third and concluding lecture, but first he published an interpretative pamphlet, *Babel und Bibel. Ein Rückblick und Ausblick* (*Babylonia and the Bible. A Review and a Preview*) in 1904. Like his third lecture, this was not translated into English. Public attention was starting to fade as Delitzsch shifted his focus away from Babylonia as interpreter of the Bible.

In the pamphlet, Delitzsch recorded the vast range of reaction to his first two lectures and indicated something of the background and nature of his plan for the three lectures. He reiterated his view that Israel had been greatly influenced by Babylonia. Although the Babylonian traditions had been put through a purification process, these purified traditions should not be theologically binding on us. He went on to state that he wanted to exclude from the Christian Canon that which has only historical or archeological value for Judaism, or only literary value. He wanted to concentrate on what he saw as essential to all religions, "heart-felt communion with God."

Delitzsch went on to say that if one were to defend retaining the Book of Job and the Song of Songs in the canon because they could be claimed to be among the most appealing books of world literature, the same logic would lead one to take up the German works that are gems of world literature into "our Christian-German Book of Religion," which would be a foolish request. (Delitzsch subsequently commended such a step, a step taken by the German-Christians of the Third Reich.)

The pamphlet also argued that ancient Israel's history provided only bad examples of behavior for God's people; their actual conduct was not more edifying than that of the Phoenicians, the Babylonians, or the Greeks. (He did not comment on the history of the Christian Church as a political and military force, but made his comparisons with Jesus.)

At the end of the pamphlet, Delitzsch quotes with favor from J. E. Baron von Grotthuss: "The concept of God and the morality of the old Jews which derives therefrom are in rather essential, indeed decisive principles not only not the same as ours [i.e., German], but even directly opposed to them."

## IV. The Third and Concluding Lecture

The third lecture did not have an auspicious setting. The German Oriental Society was no longer an eager audience, and the Emperor was not on hand. Delitzsch delivered the final lecture to the literary societies of Barmen and Köln, on 27 and 28 October 1904, respectively. Instead of repeating his lecture at the royal palace, as with his first venture, he repeated it on 9 November 1904, to the Association for Geography and Statistics in Frankfurt!

In this lecture Delitzsch shifted more and more to a negative treatment of ancient Israel and of the Old Testament, even though he said that the best of Israel and the best of Babylonia would generally match. One of his first points was to emphasize the mixed population of Galilee following the eighth-century incorporation of that area into the Assyrian provincial system. That is to say, the population of Galilee included many Babylonians, who (Delitzsch argued) were not purely Semitic but included some Aryan stock. He approaches here the notion of an Aryan Jesus, but is content to remark that many of the ideas, sayings, and deeds of Jesus the Galilean easily remind one of Babylonian comparisons, such as reference to "the Son of Man," an expression Ezekiel borrowed from the Babylonians, or the use in Jesus' baptism of the Babylonian adoption formula, "You are my son."

Similarly, Delitzsch notes that in the parable of the Good Samaritan Jesus commends the Samaritan, claimed to be a Babylonian (!), as a model of neighborliness. And he connects that with the Babylonian willingness to incorporate foreigners, whereas Israel sought to exclude them.

He is concerned to argue that the limitations of Israelite and Babylonian religion are rather parallel, especially with reference to nationalistic ideas of deity. It was Jesus who broke through the nationalism, but it was the three wise men (also claimed to be Babylonians) who, in the Gospel of Matthew, are the first to present their homage at the Cradle of Christianity.

## V. The Aftermath

The extensive discussion that followed Delitzsch's lectures, especially the first two, did not lead Delitzsch to change his mind on any matter which he regarded as central. Some years later Delitzsch published a two-part work, *Die Grosse Täuschung*, or *The Great Deception* (the first part was essentially complete in 1914; a new edition of part one and the first edition of part two appeared in 1921), in which he took up many of the same issues, though he regarded the Babel-Bibel time as over. The "Great Deception" was the Old Testament. He emphasized the many seemingly exaggerated claims and numbers in the biblical texts, the numerous minor variations in names and other specific data, the unfulfilled divine promises, the lowly cultural level of the Hebrews ("robbing and murdering nomads"), the false attribution of writings to Moses, the false assertion that Yahweh, Israel's particular god, was God. All these points led him to the conclusion that the Old Testament was no book of Christian religion and should be excluded from Christian theology.

In keeping with his German nationalism, Delitzsch recommends replacing the Old Testament with Wilhelm Schwaner's *Germanen-Bibel* (4th edition, 1918), which includes the thoughts of German heroes concerning God, eternity, and immortality. This is much better, says Delitzsch, than the "barbaric" qualities of the Ten Commandments! Delitzsch in this book has become an opponent of Judaism; Jews, "as a homeless or international people, present a great danger for all the other people of the earth." He saw "the Jewish question" as the most decisive issue for the German people of his day. Finally, Friedrich Delitzsch represented almost a complete reversal of his father, Franz Delitzsch. His theme was no longer Babylonia as interpreter of the Bible or even Babylonia versus the Bible. It is ironic that he ends his diatribe with what he regards as the essence of Jesus' teaching: "God is love, and whoever abides in love, abides in God and God in Him" (1 John 4:16). Jesus teaches us, but then Jesus was a Jewish proselyte, not a Jew. Being from Galilee he was actually a Babylonian and therefore not even a pure Semite but probably in part Aryan.

In dealing with Assyriological matters, as Delitzsch did in his first two lectures, he combined scholarship with special pleading; in dealing with Old Testament materials, Delitzsch mixed learning with considerable naivete; in dealing with the New Testament, or, more specifically Jesus, Delitzsch displayed naivete and perfidy.

The controversy concerning Babylonia and the Bible is associated with the distinct but related intellectual movement known as "Pan-Babylonianism." This movement made immense claims for Babylonian influence in the ancient world and beyond. Some of its leading proponents were students of Delitzsch, such as P. Jensen and A. Jeremias, who, in Jensen's case in particular, disputed many of Delitzsch's *Babel und Bibel* arguments. But Pan-Babylonianism is another story. The sentiments behind these publications by Friedrich Delitzsch ultimately played into the hands of the *Deutsche-Christen* movement, a key feature in the sad story of Christian collaboration with the Third Reich.

*Bibliographical Note*

The first two lectures were translated into English by C. H. W. Johns (London: Williams and Norgate, 1903) with a commendatory introduction; they were also translated by Th. J. McCormack and W. H. Carruth (Chicago: Open Court, 1903), together with extensive notes by Delitzsch and selections from the responding literature. There were many editions of the first two lectures in German. The pamphlet *Babel und Bible. Ein Rückblick und Ausblick* appeared in 1904 (Stuttgart: Deutsche Verlags-Anstalt; I have a printing in the third thousand), and the third lecture appeared from the same publisher in 1905 (seventh to tenth thousand, in my copy). *Die Grosse Täuschung* appeared from the same publisher in 1921 (a new edition of the first part, thirteenth and fourteenth thousand, and the initial publication of the second part). For discussion, note Helmut Weidmann, *Die Patriarchen und ihre Religion* (Göttingen: Vandenhoeck & Ruprecht, 1968). Emil Kraeling, *The Old Testament Since the Reformation* (New York: Harper & Brothers, 1955), contains serious errors.

For a review of the Babel-Bible question by an eminent Assyriologist, see Jacob J. Finkelstein, "Bible and Babel: A Comparative Study of the Hebrew and Babylonian Religious Spirit," *Commentary* 26 (July-Dec. 1958) 431-44.

JAMES R. MOORE

# INTERPRETING THE NEW CREATIONISM

> Most men have no time for speculation. They have too many immediate
> worries. Ideas are of no use to them unless they provide means of dealing
> with the things that worry them. They feel insecure. They have to make a
> living, and they are constantly menaced by this and that, by drought and
> plagues, by wars and oppressions, by disease and death. An easy and
> tolerant skepticism is not for them. They want ideas which they can
> count upon, sure cures, absolute promises, and no shilly-shallying with a
> lot of ifs and perhapses. . . .
> A man can only begin to be disinterested when he has ceased to be
> hungry and uncomfortable and frightened. I was free because I wanted
> so little. You were free because you wanted nothing more. But people are
> never free who want more than they can have. Their wants create
> worries, their worries create prejudices, their prejudices demand guaran-
> tees, and under freedom of thought nothing is guaranteed.
>
> Walter Lippmann ("Socrates"), *American Inquisitors: A
> Commentary on Dayton and Chicago* (1928)

How shall we understand and challenge the New Creationism? In
this essay I want to propose that everything we say, or are ever likely to
say, about the New Creationism will address the general problem of a
"critical hermeneutics": that is, *How do interpreters understand texts
within particular social contexts?* This problem arises first of all when
we read the Neo-creationist literature from our differing cultural and
national standpoints. And no doubt in the near future—what with at
least 15 books on the New Creationism in the offing—there will be
distinguished scholarly gatherings where sociologists and historians
will argue about their interpretations. Equally, however, the problem
of a critical hermeneutics arises when we examine the intellectual
credentials of the New Creationism. Here there is primarily one text in
question: the Book of Genesis, or rather its first eleven chapters. The
social context is late twentieth-century America, and the interpreters
run the gamut from Semitic philologists to electronic preachers and
evangelical apologists.

## I

Let me consider these three elements in turn. The Book of Genesis,
clearly, is both a prime piece of ideological property, and a strategic

territory for turning to further ideological account. Starting at the beginning, as the uninitiated are apt to read the Bible, Genesis is the first document they encounter. And every story, without exception, that they read in the first eleven chapters can be—indeed, has been— understood to furnish some rationale, or etiological explanation, for the existing arrangements of nature and society. The uniqueness of human beings (1:26-27; 2:7, 21-23), their warrant to populate and dominate the earth (1:28), their willfulness as the source of natural and moral evil (3:1-22), and their obligation to labor hard as the penalty for sin (3:17-19)—these are the fundamental doctrines. Then on this basis of Creation and Fall an entire social system takes shape: marriage and the family (2:24; 4:1-25; 5:1-5), sexual modesty (2:25; 3:7, 11, 20; 9: 22-27), the subordination of females (2:18; 3:16) and of negroes as slaves (9:22-27), sabbath-day observance (2:1-3), retributive justice (3:14-19; 4:11-12; 6:7, 12-13), and capital punishment (8:21-22; 9:11-17), all within a promised secure natural order (8:21-22; 9:11-17). Notice that a fictitious Fall can't explain actual human corruption; mythical people like Adam and Noah have no place in the genealogies of real ones, like Jesus and oneself; and Hebrew legends don't set lightly in the New Testament as the analogues of crucial historical events like the Crucifixion (Romans 5:12-17) and the Last Judgment (Matthew 24:37-39), events which themselves furnish the basis of ethical injunctions, such as the appeal to lead godly and other-worldly lives (2 Peter 2:5-9; 3:5-13). So it's quite correct to argue that the legitimating power of the Genesis stories depends squarely on their historicity.

Secondly, consider the social context in which the interpretation of Genesis has become a matter of greater public concern for a longer period than, I believe, at any time since the middle of the nineteenth century. Whether the context is measured from school desegregation in 1954, from Sputnik in 1957, or from the apotheosis of Neo-Darwinism on the centenary of the *Origin of Species* in 1959—whenever you choose to begin tracing the forces that elicited Whitcomb and Morris's *Genesis Flood* (1961) and the Creation Research Society two years later, the subsequent period has witnessed the profoundest changes in American capitalist society. Recreational sex, open marriage, abortion-on-demand, gay pride, women's liberation, and the fission of nuclear families have gone hand-in-hand with the rise of the Pill and the decline of the work ethic, with ecological consciousness, ethnic consciousness, drug-induced consciousness, and a profusion of narcissistic therapies and fads. The cultural transformation has been aided and abetted by multi-national corporations engineering demand, and by the electronic media manipulating consent. These, too, have been sources of new work-time disciplines for new labor constituencies as new technologies have been deployed to exploit new markets. Within thirty years, in short, the mode and tempo of life have diversified bewilderingly as human beings have tried to accommodate or to resist the demands of capital; and the "third industrial revolution" portends still greater dislocations in our personal and collective lives.

Communism without and humanism within, the New Creationists tell us, are to blame for this plainly worsening state of affairs. What I think they mean is that men and women, East and West, have got it wrongly into their minds that human nature is not fixed, but can somehow change or improve by adapting to new environments. What I think *this* means, in turn, is that Neo-creationists represent certain values and interests crucially at odds with the liberalism and collectivism of the Super Powers. Show them the failure of liberal and collectivist nostrums, then look for a resurgence of classical political economy. Confront them with the pragmatic evolutionary assumptions of the professional élite who preside over our changing society— functionalist sociologists, behavioral psychologists, progressive educators, and now sociobiologists—then watch the new political economy take shape in terms of the moral and social imperatives of the Book of Genesis. Finally, offer Neo-creationists the status and emoluments that attach to scientific professionalism, East and West, then witness this moral minority with money create for themselves a science out of those stories in Genesis with ostensibly the greatest empirical evidence on their behalf, the global Deluge and the seven days of Creation.

So what's at stake in the interpretation of Genesis is not merely the historicity of ancient narratives, or the doctrine of biblical inerrancy, or even the systems of theology based on an inerrant historical record of Creation, Fall, and Deluge. These abstract, intellectualist preoccupations, it may be argued, are complex expressions of the turmoil and uncertainty of people's everyday lives. From the perspective of a critical hermeneutics what's ultimately at stake in the interpretation of Genesis is nothing less than the social order, its character and sanctions, as dependent on human nature, created and corrupt.

The third element of a critical hermeneutics is the interpreters themselves. Who are the parties contending for hermeneutic jurisdiction over the Book of Genesis? What segments of society, or class-fractions, do they represent? At ten years' remove on the far side of the Atlantic I can only offer my prejudices and suspicions, so I must leave others to investigate, for example, the background of Neo-creationist leaders in the defense industries, the striking affiliation with the physical, engineering, and information sciences among the movement's membership, and the financial and organizational links between the New Creationism and the New Right. I can, however, direct our attention, in the first instance, to the interpreters who last competed when the Book of Genesis was a political football, and this may prove salutary. I refer not to the controversies of the 1920s, when Fundamentalists tended rather to oppose evolution than to propose con-

structive creationist alternatives. Nor do I have in mind the more
limited debates in antebellum America, when southern exegetes commended the Hamitic curse of Genesis 9 as the sanction for a social
institution otherwise justified by spurious science. In some ways the
closest historical parallel to the New Creationism lies a century earlier,
when John Hutchinson and his High Church followers devised an anti-
Newtonian "biblical" natural philosophy, based on the opening verses
of Genesis, as an ideological response to the alliance of Latitudinarian
politics with Newtonian cosmology after the Glorious Revolution of
1688-89. But this episode from pre-industrial England is historically too
remote from the present controversies to shed much light on the
interests and identities of the participants. For this insight we need only
go back to the nineteenth-century debates among geologists and interpreters of Genesis.

## II

By the turn of the nineteenth century, when geologists first forged a
professional identity in the Geological Society of London, the doctrine
of the "two books," as formulated by Francis Bacon, had become
almost a shibboleth. For Bacon, heralding the scientific revolution of
the seventeenth century, the book of God's "works" in nature was "a
key" to understanding the book of God's "word" in Scripture. Students
of nature may instruct interpreters of the Bible. Biblical interpreters, on
the other hand, must not suppose that things in nature should conform
to their understanding of the words of Scripture. This, said Bacon, was
to "unwisely mingle or confound" the two learnings together. The
doctrine of the two books was of course a political compromise, a
compromise in which students of nature would illustrate the divine
omnipotence in natural phenomena, furnish the "true sense" of
Scripture, and aid recovery from the noetic effects of the Fall—all in
exchange for freedom from harassment by interpreters of biblical
texts. Commended by the sobering example of Galileo, and by the
supreme ones of Boyle and Newton, the Baconian compromise was
gradually consolidated in the nascent science of geology. At length, in
the geological profession itself, empirical and exegetical investigations
were to be carefully and explicitly distinguished. Geologists, however,
being Christian gentlemen, would gladly expound God's word and
exhibit God's works if left to get on with their job. Geologists, after all,
could prove the fact of a universal Deluge "had we never heard of such
an event from Scripture, or any other authority," the Reverend William
Buckland boasted in his inaugural lecture at Oxford in 1820.

The Baconian compromise, like all political compromises, could be
maintained only so long as the parties concerned fulfilled its terms and
otherwise pursued policies that made for social harmony. And to an

overwhelming extent they did this, from Bacon's time until the early decades of the nineteenth century. Interpreting the Bible was indeed a naturalist's legitimate avocation—the case of Newton is well known—and clergymen frequently took the lead in studying natural history. The "advancement of learning," as Bacon called it, was a gentlemanly pursuit to which the few were called and chosen from the upper reaches of society. But in the context of rapid industrialization, as geologists, like others, began to parade the independent authority of their hard-won expertise, the professionalism of their interpretations of earth-history, the Baconian compromise fell into jeopardy for several decades. The outcome was the dissolution of the doctrine of the two books into the division of labor that it had adumbrated from the start.

The thin end of the wedge was the three thick volumes of Charles Lyell's *Principles of Geology* (1830-33). Lyell, a student of Buckland's, undertook in his work to define the "principle of reasoning" in the science so as to exclude the possibility that geologists might have to concern themselves with the Book of Genesis. In formulating this principle of extreme actualism—only those causes have operated in earth history which are now observed to operate, and only with the intensities now observed—Lyell rewrote the history of geology as though every path of inquiry in the science had been blocked repeatedly with Noah's Ark, every thread of induction had been routinely snapped with a divine creative fiat. His polemics, in the *Principles of Geology* and elsewhere, were directed not only at certain colleagues, like Buckland, who looked over their shoulders at Genesis, but at a "certain class of writers" known as "scriptural geologists." These men, said Lyell, "denounce as heterodox the current opinions of geologists, with respect to the high antiquity of the earth and of certain classes of organic beings," yet they "do not scruple to promulgate theories concerning the creation and the deluge, derived from their own expositions of the sacred text, in which they endeavor to point out the accordance of Mosaic history with phenomena which they have never studied, and to judge of which every page of their writings proves their consummate incompetence." Lest such incompetence achieve popularity, to the detriment of professional geology, Lyell went on to commend *verbatim* Bacon's "admirable piece of advice" about the two books. In context it reads less like the political compromise it appears to be in Bacon's work than as a declaration of professional autonomy.

Much of the problem, as Lyell no doubt realized in the 1830s, was the enormous disparity between the skills of those who interpreted the past according to biblical texts, and the expertise of professional geologists, who studied the subject in the book of nature. In Germany the Old Testament had been studied professionally since the middle of the eighteenth century; and the initial chapters of Genesis had been among the first texts to be critically assessed. But in early-Victorian Britain and

America few of those who interpreted Genesis had any specialist skills. Professional clergymen, the most diligent and numerous of Bible students, possessed pastoral and denominational qualifications rather than scholarly ones. Not until the latter half of the century, and particularly after 1870, did Orientalists, Semitic philologists, and higher critics in Britain and America distinguish themselves from clerical exegetes of Genesis by their academic credentials and hermeneutic skills, professional qualifications which in most cases were acquired from Germany.

One of this vanguard was Benjamin Jowett at Oxford, who in 1860 declared in his contribution to *Essays and Reviews*, "On the Interpretation of Scripture," that one should "*Interpret the Scriptures like any other book.*" The purport of this statement was to claim biblical texts from amateur exegetes on behalf of those who possessed the critical expertise already developed, and deployed on "other books," by German philologists and historians. In other words, Jowett's "principle," if you will, served the professionalization of Old Testament scholarship in roughly the same way that Lyell's "principle of reasoning" had served the professionalization of geology. Lyell laid claim to the book of nature, Jowett to the Scripture, for empirical, actualistic, and specialist interpretation. From this point the two books could be studied professionally, in isolation, on the basis of common assumptions but according to an agreeable division of labor. Geologists and interpreters of Genesis need no longer compromise. Now they might freely cooperate or conspire.

Meanwhile, however, the Baconian compromise had fallen into jeopardy. The interval can be marked conveniently at 1832 by Lyell's adopted maxim, "The physical part of Geological inquiry ought to be conducted as if the Scriptures were not in existence," and at 1860 by Jowett's principle, "Interpret the Scriptures like any other book." This interval saw the main contests between the scriptural geologists and their opponents, the harmonizers of Genesis and geology. Scriptural geologists rejected the Baconian compromise with a radical assertion of their own competence to interpret earth-history from the Book of Genesis alone, sometimes with geological facts (usually obtained at second-hand) brought in by way of illustration. They were largely pre-professionals or members of the older professions—classically educated and genteel laymen, versed in polite literature; clergymen, linguists, and antiquaries—those, in general, with vested interests in mediating the meaning of books, rather than rocks, in churches and classrooms. To them a sound classical education, with logic, perhaps mathematics as well, and a proven ability at inductive reasoning, were the sole requisite skills, not only for interpreting Genesis, but for assessing the explanations of geologists and arbitrating among them. Thus the typical ploy of ransacking geological works for passages of which no real understanding is shown but which serve admirably to exercise and display the interpreter's own proficiency in logic and linguistics.

Many scriptural geologists no doubt were also deeply concerned that ordinary people should be able to extract a true history of the earth from the Bible, which was after all the most widely read and circulated book at the time. With an eye on the progress of infidelity among the restive workers, and a troubled glance at the rising and increasingly well-educated middle classes, they foresaw only too clearly the social consequences of a general questioning or abandonment of the literal historicity of the early chapters of Genesis. So for scriptural geologists to lay claim to geo-history in the name of biblical inspiration or some other doctrine was not just a matter of disinterestedly pursuing theological truth. Nor perhaps was it merely an attempt to insure continued recognition for their traditional hermeneutic skills. It was also arguably an urgent bid to maintain socially needful interpretations of the Genesis stories, interpretations which had previously depended on their own mediation and had lately come under threat by a band of upstarts, self-regarding professionals, who proposed to go about their work as if Genesis did not exist.

The obvious recourse for many older geologists, who as yet lived by the Baconian compromise, was to vindicate their profession by pointing out how little, or how edifyingly, the results of geological inquiry affected traditional interpretations. In recent years they had perhaps been negligent in proffering the "true sense" of the scriptures, too comfortable in the belief that the truth of both "books" would ultimately coincide. Now, for their own good and society's—geologists also feared incompetence and infidelity—they would have to show how the Genesis stories could be harmonized with the record in the rocks. "The earlier attempts, to square the facts to the narrative," as one commentator wryly observed, "have been succeeded by those to square the narrative to the facts."

The chief harmonizers of Genesis and geology were among the most eminent professional geologists of the early-Victorian period. In Britain Buckland, Conybeare, Mantell, Sedgwick, Whewell, and Hugh Miller did not each condone detailed schemes of reconciliation, but all were at pains on more than one occasion to reassure their audiences, by precept or example, that although the Bible had not been intended to teach scientific truths, its statements would always be shown to harmonize with properly demonstrated theories. In America the same conviction was advanced unremittingly through most of the century by a kind of apostolic succession of evangelical geologists—Silliman, Hitchcock, Guyot, Dana, and J. W. Dawson. Each of them labored in one or more popular books—Dawson in a dozen—to uphold established geological theories by reinterpreting the Genesis stories.

By dint of piety, prestige, and perseverance the harmonizers secured the independent authority of the geological profession and the prerogative of its members to interpret the Book of Genesis. After 1860 the fatuity and irrelevance of the scriptural geologists was plain for all to see. Whether geologists would now renew the Baconian compromise was, however, another matter. With their social role secure they could resume working "as if the Scriptures were not in existence"; and the majority of younger geologists found the prospect inviting. Also, as Darwin was relieving naturalists of the obligation, under the compromise, to glorify God from his works, the chief supporters of this obligation, the professional harmonizers, were rapidly becoming extinct. By 1873 all of them had died except Dana, who was becoming an evolutionist, and Dawson and Guyot. Thereafter the main body of harmonizers would be amateurs—popular preachers and miscellaneous writers—some of whom would now seek, ironically, to defend Genesis from higher critics by showing its accord with geology. Professionals had other interests and obligations, such as mutual defense against bands of marauding laymen.

*Essays and Reviews* first alerted professionals to the need for an alliance. The book, a collective effort by Jowett and six other Germanizing Broad Churchmen, was published in 1860, and it went through thirteen editions in the time that the *Origin of Species* passed through three. Two of the authors were taken to court on heresy charges, and when they were cleared nearly half the clergy in England and Ireland, together with 137,000 lay persons, signed statements of protest. About the same time, in 1864, a group of science students in London circulated a declaration affirming that it was impossible for the "two books," of God's word and God's works, ever to contradict one another. The declaration skirted the issue of hermeneutic jurisdiction—harmonizers and scriptural geologists could sign it with impunity; and eventually 717 men of mainly questionable scientific attainment attached their names. In 1865 a number of the signatories joined in founding "The Victoria Institute, or Philosophical Society of Great Britain," an organization intended to defend "the great truths revealed in Holy Scripture . . . against the oppositions of Science, falsely so-called." The membership at once became an epitome of evangelical amateurism, with the Earl of Shaftesbury and Philip Gosse, the famous scriptural geologist, presiding over them. In 1882 some of the members' names could be found in the list of subscribers prefixed to Samuel Kinns' pretentious volume, *Moses and Geology; or, The Harmony of the Bible with Science.* The list included 15 bishops, 10 other peers, 16 members of Parliament, 64 lesser clergymen, 18 military men, perhaps a dozen marginal scientists (two or three of note), and 341 other individuals of no particular distinction.

So the political threat was clear. "The ignorance of the so-called educated classes," as Darwin's defender T. H. Huxley would later call it, might well prevail over the theories of self-defining expertise if professionals did not join in upholding each other's authority. Accordingly, in 1861 the authors of *Essays and Reviews* received support from a group of prominent scientists who subscribed an address welcoming the essayists' "attempts to establish religious teaching on a firmer and broader foundation." Among those who signed were Darwin and Lyell. A year later, when Bishop Colenso of Natal was socially ostracised for publishing a "strict scientific" inquiry entitled *The Pentateuch and Book of Joshua Critically Examined*, it was Lyell who came to his rescue. He introduced Colenso at his club in London even as the bishop was being forced from office at the Society for the Propagation of the Gospel, and thereafter the Lyells remained the Colenso family's most faithful supporters in England. When Colenso sought redress from the Crown after an unsuccessful attempt to deprive him of his see, it was not only Lyell, however, but Huxley, who gave him financial support. Huxley had recently been advising a future bishop, the Hebrew scholar J. J. S. Perowne, in the preparation of an article on the Deluge for Smith's *Dictionary of the Bible*. So in 1864 he felt quite at home, one evening, cheering up the forlorn Colenso in the company of free-thinking colleagues like John Tyndall and Herbert Spencer, who had recently formed themselves into the "X Club." Twenty years later the same professional gentlemen, probably the most powerful and prestigious coterie in English science at the time, joined in entertaining Britain's first fully professional Old Testament scholar, the brilliant William Robertson Smith, who had just undergone the sordid litigation that deprived him of his chair of oriental languages and Old Testament exegesis in the Free Church College, Aberdeen.

Darwin's main contribution to the professional alliance came in proposing the clerical philologist F. W. Farrar for a Fellowship of the Royal Society, to which he was duly elected in 1866. In 1882 Farrar, now a canon of Westminster, paid his respects by negotiating Darwin's burial in the Abbey and serving as a pallbearer. Three years later he delivered the Bampton Lectures at Oxford, published as *History of Interpretation* (1886). Here was no censure, nor timid acceptance of science, but a celebration of its "irrefragable conclusions" in their bearing on biblical exegesis: a history of "the triumph of light over darkness, of truth over error, of faith and freedom over tyranny and persecution." Beginning in utter "incompetency"—witness the "foolish exegesis" of Genesis—biblical interpretation had passed in latter days, according to a "law" of "eternal progress," into the hands of German theologians and their English representatives. These, said Farrar, like the "great discoverers" of science, had been reviled and condemned by the "religious world." But withal "it remains certain that true science and true religion are twin sisters, each studying her own sacred book of

God." "Let them study in mutual love and honour side by side," he advised, "and pronounce respecting those things which alone she knows."

"Those things which alone she knows." And to think that at the very time, in the pages of a leading journal, Huxley was trying to upstage the octogenarian Prime Minister, W. E. Gladstone, that "copious shuffler" who had made "ignorance" a political force, by invoking the "assured results of modern biblical criticism" as to the interpretation of Genesis. "I need hardly say that I depend upon authoritative Biblical critics, whenever a question of interpretation of the text arises," Huxley confidently noted in another essay, appending a list of German names. The irony ascends when it is realized that this amateur exegete, if ever there was one, substantially devoted the last years of his life in the 1890s to preparing a series of working men's lectures, and a book for young people, on the history of biblical religion in the light of modern "scientific" scholarship. Two books and twin sisters indeed.

But ironies entertained too lightly obscure real contradictions or underlying continuities. The doctrine of the two books was ever a piece of ideology, the Baconian compromise a political settlement from the start. In reality the "sister" who successfully imposes her definition of what may be known, and how, defines what the other one knows. By 1890 Huxley and his professional colleagues could interpret Genesis on their own epistemological terms, with the full complicity of professional Old Testament scholars. A view of human nature and historical progress united them, and a concern to uphold the freedom and prerogatives of professional experts. Indeed, as keepers of the cosmology of an industrial and imperial social order, professional interpreters of the "two books" shared economic and social interests which, it may be argued, were well served by interpreting Genesis as a "primitive" account of the beginning of the world.

## III

The story might easily be carried forward by reviewing the rapid development of social anthropology and the "science of religions" in relation to the needs of colonial administration, and by considering in turn the impact of these disciplines on biblical hermeneutics within the context of expanding Protestant missions, which required a conservative but modernizing ideology both to justify their endeavors and to inculcate appropriate religious beliefs in "primitive" cultures. But all this must be left for another time. The importance of the account I've given of geologists and interpreters of Genesis is that it begins to trace the formation of the professional hegemony in the biological and human sciences against which the New Creationism can be seen as a social and intellectual protest. History is not repeating itself; nor am I using an historical analogy to understand the present. In the last century the Baconian compromise came to pieces in a contest between professional and pre-professional élites. Here as elsewhere in an industrializing society, the dominion of wealth and rank gave way slowly but inexorably to the hegemony of merit and expertise; and after 1860 professionals consolidated their gains in an alliance *against* the mass of meddling, censorious laypeople. In our day, by contrast, we have a contest between *established* professional experts on the one hand, and *aspiring* professional experts, on the other, whose bid for cultural leadership is based on a claim to speak *for* the mass of Christian laypeople in a so-called Christian country. This claim, needless to say, can only be made good by discrediting those who would still claim to represent Christian opinion by upholding the Baconian compromise.

The latter, at any rate, is what I take to be the meaning of two important monographs produced at about the time when a group broke away from the broadly evangelical and specialist American Scientific Affiliation to form the narrowly evangelical and more strictly specialist Creation Research Society. *The Origin of the Solar System* (1964) originated in an address delivered in May 1962 by John C. Whitcomb, Jr. before members of the Evangelical Theological Society. It is a sustained attack on what the author calls the "double-revelation theory": that is, the view alleged to be current among scientifically trained evangelical apologists that God has given two mutually consistent revelations, in nature and the Bible, and that when these two revelations appear to conflict the God-appointed interpreters of the Bible, theologians, must adjust their interpretations to harmonize with the conclusions of the God-appointed interpreters of nature, scientists. Whitcomb, an Old Testament exegete, of course opted to have it the other way around, and a year later he was supported by his engineering colleague, Henry M. Morris. "The Spirit of Compromise," a provocative address delivered by Morris in June 1963 before members of the American Scientific Affiliation, was a clarion call for evangelicals to choose between creation and evolution "on the basis of moral and spiritual considerations." It marked the separation of the modern Creationist movement from the evangelical mainstream, which, Morris claimed, had sought to "harmonize" the Bible with the Satanically inspired philosophy of "modern intellectualism." In conclusion he implored, "May God in these last days guard His people against this Spirit of Compromise which is today threatening to remove the last vestige of Biblical Christianity even from supposedly Christian America."

But if interpreters of Genesis alone, unaided by interpreters of nature, are to furnish the cosmology that makes for cultural renewal in "a nation founded largely on Christianity and the Bible," as Morris says elsewhere, then one might reasonably expect the New Creationism to give pride of place to its experts in hermeneutics. The leading Neo-creationists should be highly trained and accomplished Semitic philolo-gists, Egyptologists, Assyriologists, and other specialists in ancient Near Eastern history. There should be Neo-creationist institutes and research centers devoted to the full range of Classical and Oriental studies. Obviously, however, this is not the case. Hermeneutics is simply not problematic for Neo-creationists. Whitcomb calls it a "time-honored and God-honored science"; another Neo-creationist claims to be a "professional student" of the subject. But the body of Neo-creationist literature belies their views. Seldom if ever does a writer evince any insight beyond platitudes like "the meaning of texts is determined by their contexts" and "interpretation should be as induc-tive as possible." One reason—perhaps the main reason—for this is the populist appeal of the New Creationism. Meanings must be "obvious" to people of "average intelligence," according to the self-styled "pro-fessional student" of hermeneutics. Or as Morris puts it in a popular booklet, the Genesis record "was written to be understood and therefore is to be taken literally rather than mystically or parabolically. There is no need for some special 'key' of interpretation to be supplied by modern evolutionists."

Nor, it seems, by modern creationists either. For to pursue cultural hegemony on the consistently radical basis of hermeneutic expertise would no doubt alienate Neo-creationist leaders from their constitu-ency by depriving these ordinary people of direct personal access to the moral and social imperatives of the Book of Genesis. So, instead, the bid for ascendancy in American culture is made on the familiar and vastly more acceptable basis of speaking *scientifically* on behalf of the masses.

From its inception the New Creationism was at least in part a reaction against the triumphal positivism and overweening profes-sionalism of established scientific authorities. But now, under the banner of "scientific creationism" or "creation-science," it apes what it once abhorred. In the end all that the New Creationism has to offer society is, I believe, a countervailing professionalism, with its accredited institutions, approved textbooks, official media, and scholarly publications. The structure of creation-science is hierarchical, authoritarian, and dominated by men. The leadership are a self-reviewing and self-policing élite with their own Velikovsky-like victims. The ethos of creation-science is exclusive and dogmatic, naively empiricist in its approach to Scripture and increasingly positiv-ist in its conception of science. Those who caution against "mixing" creation-science with "creation-religion" are not just being disingenuous; at a very deep level they have already been defeated by their opponents. In repudiating the theories of established science the New Creationism is reproducing its practices, so it should not seem surprising if the theories reappear, as it were, through the back door. How then may the New Creationism be successfully challenged? Not, to my mind, by better and better evolutionary arguments or by a greater and greater weight of professional scientific authority. If society is what's at stake, this only leaves us advocating a more or less enlightened version of the status quo. By simply taking sides against the New Creationism we overlook the social sources of the movement, which are our common enemies: the realities of powerlessness, deprivation, uncertainty, and fear in ordinary people's lives that aspiring political and professional élites so easily manipulate for their own ends. The incoherence of Neo-creationist arguments must certainly be stressed, as well as their theological enormities. But people also need something better to believe in, something better than value-free scientific theories mediated by remote disinterested experts, Neo-creationist or otherwise. We need concepts of nature, human nature, and political struggle that will help us undermine the natural theologies of our day, the theories from whatever quarter which assert the naturalness and inevitability of an oppressive social order.

*Bibliographical Note*

This paper was presented at the teach-in on "Creationism in American Culture and Theology" held at the Lutheran School of Theology at Chicago, 9 October 1982. Portions of this paper closely follow an essay prepared for the Carner Foundation—University of Wisconsin Conference on "Christianity and Science: 2000 Years of Conflict and Comrpomise," held at Madison, 23-25 April 1981; this essay, "Geologists and Interpreters of Genesis in the Nineteenth Century," will appear in a collective work, edited by Ronald L. Numbers and David C. Lindberg, to be published by Harper & Row in 1983. Full documentation for section II will be found there.

On the Arkansas evolution trial, see Roger Lewin's suggestive report, "A Tale with Many Connections," *Science*, 215 (29 Jan. 1982), 484-87; Frank Viviano, "The Crucifixion of Evolution," *Mother Jones*, 6 (Sept.-Oct. 1981), 22-59; and "Creationism in Schools: The Decision in McLean versus the Arkansas Board of Education," *Science*, 215 (19 Feb. 1982), 934-43.

For some discussion of creationist and related views, see Henry M. Morris, *The Twilight of Evolution* (Grand Rapids, Mich.: Baker Book House, 1963); *Studies in the Bible and Science, or Christ and Creation* (Grand Rapids, Mich.: Baker Book House, 1966); *Evolution and the Modern Christian* (Grand Rapids, Mich.: Baker Book House, 1967); John C. Whitcomb, Jr., *The Origin of the Solar System: Biblical Inerrancy and the Double-Revelation Theory* (Philadelphia: Presbyterian and Reformed Publishing Co., 1964); *The Early Earth* (Grand Rapids, Mich.: Baker Book House, 1972); Arthur F. Williams, "The

Genesis Account of Creation," in *Why Not Creation? Selected Articles from the "Creation Research Society Quarterly," Volumes I through V (1964-1968)*, ed. Walter E. Lammerts (Philadelphia: Presbyterian and Reformed Publishing Co., 1970); and Wayne Frair and P. William Davis, *The Case for Creation*, rev. ed. (Chicago: Moody Press, 1972); cf. also Dan Wonderly (formerly of Grace College, Winona Lake, Indiana), *God's Time-Records in Ancient Sediments: Evidences of Long Time Spans in Earth's History* (Flint, Mich.: Crystal Press, 1977).

# SSSR MONOGRAPH SERIES

## Volume Number 1    Richard K. Fenn's
## TOWARD A THEORY OF SECULARIZATION
Focusing upon conflicts over the scope and location of the sacred in modern societies, this work presents a multi-phase model for the analysis of secularization process. Out of print.

## Volume Number 2    William H. Swatos, Jr.'s
## INTO DENOMINATIONALISM:
## THE ANGLICAN METAMORPHOSIS
Proposing a new typology of churches, sects and denomination, this work provides a socio-historical analysis of the development of Anglicanism in the U.S. and England.

## Volume Number 3    Gail Gehrig's
## AMERICAN CIVIL RELIGION: AN ASSESSMENT
Through a comparative analysis of divergent theories and research, this volume assesses the value of the civil religion concept for the social scientific theory of religion.

Available from:
SSSR Business Office                     Vol. No. 2    $5.50 postage paid
Box U-68A
University of Connecticut                 Vol. No. 3    $5.50 postage paid
Storrs, Ct. 06268

DIANE KIRKPATRICK

# RELIGIOUS PHOTOGRAPHY IN THE VICTORIAN AGE

The camera cannot compete with brush and palette—as long as it cannot be used in heaven or in hell.

Edvard Munch (1890)

The camera, being a supremely physical device, has not yet managed to operate in the heaven or hell to which the imagination of an inspired painter can transport his or her vision. However, during the second half of the nineteenth century, several artists used photography to depict the earthly manifestations of central characters in the Christian drama, with a few side forays into the Old Testament, the Apocrypha, and the lives of the saints. While most eyes of the 1980s regard these photographs of sacred subjects with laughter, distaste, or acute discomfort, Victorian viewers often responded with reverent enthusiasm. This essay will explore the aesthetic and cultural impulses that led to the creation of Victorian photographic religious images.

## I

As early as 1851, the religious impulse in photography was demonstrated when the American photographer Gabriel Harrison exhibited *The Infant Savior Bearing The Cross* and *Mary Magdalene* in the group of photographs shown at London's Crystal Palace Exhibition. Harrison's photographs have not survived, so we can only speculate about his aesthetic approach to these subjects. But among the Crystal Palace visitors who saw the pictures was O. G. Rejlander, a Swedish-born painter then working in England, who turned photographer a few years later. Of the photographs in the Crystal Palace Exhibition, Rejlander wrote: "They were all Daguerrotypes and awakened in me at the moment nothing but curiosity."

Rejlander moved beyond curiosity about photography to appreciation of the new process in 1852 in Rome, when he experienced the heady delights of using photographs to compare sculpture in diverse collections and discovered a coat sleeve in one photo portrait that was a perfect model for a detail in one of his paintings. Back in England in 1853, Rejlander learned the basic techniques of collodion photography. Before long he had turned his back almost completely on painting and joined the fight to prove the legitimacy of art photography "based on lessons learned from the great masters of the fine arts."

Although Rejlander would later turn his attention to documentary photography, in his High Art photographs he joined the "pictorialists" who believed that the highest form of photography was not a simple "straight" record of a scene in front of the camera lens, but rather the capturing on film of a composition in which the arrangement of models and props was inspired by great paintings. Rejlander's High Art photography contained little specifically religious subject matter, but his *The Head of John the Baptist* (Plate 1) warrants our consideration for its rare theme and its curiously haunting effect. The head was originally meant to be combined with the figure of a Salome in the kind of photographic combination print Rejlander used for works like his famous moral allegory *The Two Ways of Life*. For reasons best known to the photographer himself, he never completed the intended Salome print. Rejlander's *The Head of John the Baptist* would not have easily been combined with his photographic study of Salome, because the shallow empty platter in the study is held at right angles to Salome's body and the Baptist's head, when added, would be in profile, while Rejlander canted the tray in our print toward the viewer so we look down on John's "severed" head, which rests on a sort of drapery "bed" within a hollow resembling that of a soup plate.

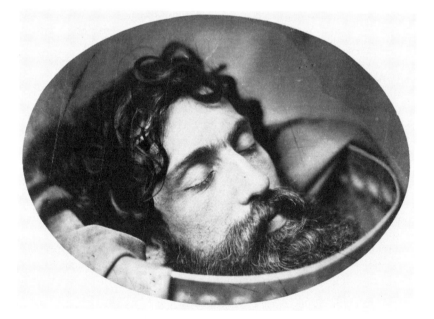

*Plate 1.* O. G. Rejlander. *The Head of John the Baptist.* Late 1850s. Collection of Royal Photographic Society, Bath, England.

Some viewers of *The Head of John the Baptist* were impressed by the expression of the bearded head with its closed eyes, but could not overlook a suspicious depth in the right side of the platter's concavity. As one contemporary critic wrote: "One of the feelings that I never can shake off when looking at this picture is the incongruous one of that hole in the charger through which the model must have popped his handsome head." The same writer also jibed at the subject as unsuitable for photography: "It is not every subject that is good in a painting that would therefore be good in a photograph. . . . In a painting the method would not be so obtrusive as here it is, and hence the suggestion of unsuitability." This objection, like those to the portrayal of any non-documentary subject in photography, is linked to the habit of most Western viewers to regard photographs as records of physical reality. As Susan Sontag elegantly puts it: "A photograph is not only an image (as a painting is an image), an interpretation of the real; it is also a trace, something directly stenciled off the real, like a footprint or a death mask." Only a viewer who can grant to photography the power of representation that we commonly give to the actors, props, and sets of movies and theatrical performances will be able to enter the kind of "truth" given us by Rejlander and others who attempt to see in a pictorialist way.

Despite the negative critical comments, Rejlander sent his photographic *Head of John the Baptist* on a successful independent journey of exhibitions and sales. What was there in the viewing climate of mid-nineteenth century England that prepared the ground for this work? Partly, the theme was a religious subject bound to stir tender Victorian pity at John's fate. As a photographic rendering, the image also carried the authority of John Ruskin's ideas on artistic truth and Augustus Welby Pugin's thoughts about sacred art. In *Modern Painters*, Ruskin argues that an artist who seeks the ideal truth within nature's variety and flux must never try to depict a realm of the purely ideal, because true ideal art

> concerns itself simply with things as they ARE, and accepts, in all of them, alike the evil and the good. . . . The inferior artists, the vulgar, the insensitive, see fact only partially: they often try to invent form. Genius, however, discovers it; genius sees the whole real thing. . . . A man who can see truth at all, sees it wholly, and neither desires nor dares to mutilate it.

In a related vein, Pugin wrote about religious art:

> No reasonable man would think of altering the proportions of the human so beautifully and wisely ordained by the Creator. . . . The finest productions of Christian Art are the closest approximations to nature, and when they failed in proportion and anatomy, it was not a defect of principle but of execution.

Ruskin's and Pugin's ideas were a nineteenth-century restatement of a fifteenth-century northern European Christian belief that because God was present in everything in the world, an artist must avoid distorting the appearance of even a blade of grass lest he or she be guilty of the sacrilege of rearranging divine truth. One could argue that photographers would succeed best in presenting the details of nature (without color, of course), because their apparatus was guaranteed to record such truth without "mutilating it." Certainly Rejlander, perhaps because of his painting background, worked like the Victorian painters who consistently saw in live models the features of sacred and classical figures of old. He had seen the head of his John the Baptist two years before he persuaded its owner to pose: "I always saw that head as you see it now. . . . That model never came before me without having his head in a charger."

## II

At the end of the 1850s, Rejlander closed his High Art eyes to concentrate on recording the world as it appeared around him. Almost immediately a worthy successor followed him into the pictorialist field—Julia Margaret Cameron. Born of English parents in Calcutta in 1815, Cameron already had a full life behind her as the wife of a British lawyer and official in India, with property in Ceylon, who retired early to England in 1848. After their return, the Camerons lived first near and then in London, where the spirited and intelligent Julia forged close friendships with many of the eminent people of her day, including the poet Sir Henry Taylor, the Poet Laureate Alfred Tennyson, and the scientist Sir John Herschel.

While Charles Cameron was in Ceylon in 1859, Julia visited the Tennysons at their home on the Isle of Wight, fell in love with the place, and acquired a home—Freshwater—there. When she was given a camera and darkroom kit by her daughter and son-in-law in 1863, she turned Freshwater's glass chicken house into a photographic studio, and transformed the coalhouse into a darkroom. Then she set out to learn the process of photography by attempting to capture on her large glass-plate negatives the faces of all the local people whose appearances took her eye.

Cameron was well read, emotionally enthusiastic, and tireless in pursuit of a photographic subject she had "seen." All her subjects attracted her by the echo of the divine she found in their features: "I longed to arrest all beauty that came before me, and at length the longing has been satisfied." The photographic process was for her so intense that it often became almost a part of her daily devotions. She wrote of her portrait session with the historian Thomas Carlyle: "When I have had such men before my camera my whole soul has endeavoured to do its duty towards them in recording faithfully the greatness of the inner as well as the features of the outer man. The photograph thus taken has been almost the embodiment of a prayer." The vision that informs many of Cameron's characters draws partially on the aesthetic of the Pre-Raphaelites, which she met most closely in the paintings of her good friend George Frederick Watts. The Pre-Raphaelites admired the clarity, truth and beauty of the painting of the Italian masters who were active before Raphael, and sought to create anew the expression of religious purity found in the early masters. In a similar spirit, Cameron created photographs which she titled *In the Manner of Perugino, A Study after the Manner of Francia,* and so forth. But she also was infused with the spirit that led Ruskin to conceive of his "*naturalist* ideal." In a catalogue of her work for an exhibition in Southampton in 1886, Cameron spoke of "photographs from the life, not enlarged, and all untouched prints from untouched negatives." And she titled one of her religious works *La Madonna (From life).* As Colin Ford put it:

> For Mrs. Cameron, the highest human achievement was to be an Artist, and the highest forms of Art were poetry and oil painting. After devoting much of her time to the former, she wanted her photographs to be . . . like the best portrait paintings, "From Life."

It was important to her that her viewers should know that her photographs contained the high truth of natural beauty.

Sometimes a sitter reminded her of the style of a master whose work she admired. For example, she wrote "Carlyle like a rough block of Michael Angelo's sculpture" on her portrait of the famous historian. But almost everyone who caught her eye reminded her most strongly of a character in a Shakespeare play, a Tennyson poem, or one of the stories in the Bible. Good friends were repeatedly imposed upon. As she noted:

> Our chief friend, Sir Henry Taylor, lent himself greatly to my early efforts. Regardless of the possible dread that sitting to my fancy might be making a fool of himself, he, with greatness which belongs to unselfish affection, consented to be in turn Friar Laurence with Juliet, Prospero with Miranda, Ahasuerus with Queen Esther.

Most often in the mid-1860s, Cameron's maid Mary Hillier became the Madonna in the artist's mental eye, while various neighborhood children were brought in to play the young Jesus. The titles of many of the Madonna studies reflect the photographer's Pre-Raphaelite tastes: *La Madonna Adolorata, La Madonna Aspettante* (Plate 2), *La Madonna Riposata,* and *La Beata.* Mary Hillier also represented the Virgin Mary in *The Return After 3 Days* (a vignette of Mary, young Christ, and two attendant women after Jesus' return from his discussion with the wise elders in the Temple) and posed for St. Agnes and for the central characters in such general sacred themes as *Faith,*

*Plate 2.* Julia Margaret Cameron. *La Madonna Aspettante.* 1865. Collection of The National Portrait Gallery, London.

*Divine Love, Goodness,* and *Heaven.* Another model, Cyllena Wilson, inspired Cameron to do two versions of *The Holy Family* (without St. Joseph, but with two children) and a depiction of *The Angel at the Sepulchre.*

Once Cameron settled on a vision, she selected the costumes for the scene and installed her sitter or sitters in her studio with a minimal background created by some of the cloth she draped over the windows to direct her light. Then, through sheer force of will, she stage-managed her charges into holding the desired mood during the four-minute exposures her equipment and materials required. (The infants who occasionally posed for the baby Jesus could only hold still for the long exposures when asleep, which limited any composition that used them.)

In Cameron's religious photographs, as in most of her other works, the figures are shown close-up and half length or less. The consistent mood of all these works is one of subdued tenderness and solemn, attentive love. The camera focus is soft and shallow (a characteristic of the lens Cameron preferred). Only occasionally, as in *Ahasuerus and Queen Esther,* do Cameron's figures act out a particular moment in a story. Most often her sitters hold poses that suggest their represented characters. In this they resemble the series of portraits Cameron produced of the people she considered important in her day. The main holy women wear a drape over their heads, one around their shoulders, and either a plain dress or one with banding at the neck and down the front that suggests the style used by some fifteenth-century Italian masters.

None of Cameron's religious compositions seem to have been based on specific painting compositions. Instead, the inspiration from painting seems to have been for overall "tone" and for the "look" of the models. Cyllena Wilson's delicate beauty embodied Pre-Raphaelite tastes, and even a modern viewer can be captured by the mood of sweetly sad serenity Mary Hillier projects before Cameron's lens. But the child models, perhaps suffering from the hard work of sitting still during the long exposures, seem more often bored or petulant than divine.

## III

Cameron's religious photographs are mainly typic images of great Christian heroines; Fred Holland Day created photographic representations of specific scenes from the Passion of Christ. As a young man Day participated in the Boston cultural world of his time as a bibliophile and co-founder of the publishing firm of Copeland and Day, which printed experimental American authors and brought to America the works of Maurice Maeterlinck, William Butler Yeats, Oscar Wilde, and Aubrey Beardsley and *The Yellow Book.*

Like most bibliophiles of the time, Day collected not only books but pictures of things connected with the authors he loved. He acquired a camera to document literary sites in Massachusetts, expanded to doing portraits of family and friends, and discovered that shy authors might open their doors to one bearing photographs of their homes or their faces. Increasingly Day became serious about his camera work, joining the ranks of those who were out to prove that photography is art. Such works were linked with Pre-Raphaelite beliefs, specifically, in John Nicoll's phrase, "Ruskin's development of the Lockean philosophy that ideas (which man shares with God) are nobler than senses (which he shares with beasts) and that therefore the greatest picture is that with the greatest number of good ideas."

Many artists in the late nineteenth century sought their great ideas in depicting the sacred figures of many religions: Christian, Buddhist, Egyptian. But to a devout Christian, the greatest of great ideas would be those connected with the Bible. Yet only a few American aesthetic photographers turned to such subject matter at the end of the century. Gertrude Kasebier (like Cameron earlier) took divine mother love as a theme in works like *The Manger* (1898 or 1899), while Frank Eugene did a nude *Adam and Eva* (1898) in which soft focus and scratches prepared the image for genteel eyes. In these same years Day was creating a controversial series of photographs of the crucifixion, resurrection, Seven Last Words, and entombment of Christ, with himself as the model for Christ.

What inspired Day to tackle this particular complex of sacred subjects? Estelle Jussim suggests that the theme was deeply interwoven with the photographer's personal beliefs. By 1896 Day was doing many works that suggested links with the occult Christian mystical ideas of the Order of the Hermetic Students of the Golden Dawn in England and Rosicrucian groups in western Europe. Jussim traces Day's connections with the British group through his friendship with the poet William Butler Yeats, and she establishes iconographical ties with elements of Golden Dawn ritual in such Day photographs as *The Vigil* of 1899. Most intriguing for our study is her statement that one of the initiating rituals for new members in the Golden Dawn was a "symbolic crucifixion in which [the initiate] was bound by ropes to the 'Cross of Suffering.'"

The desire to participate more deeply in the Christian mystery by sharing the sufferings of Christ was not a new idea. Many Christian mystics have written about the powerful experiences they underwent when they were able to bring Christ's suffering strongly enough before their mind's eye. St. Ignatius Loyola developed his *Spiritual Exercises* to help ensure that his followers could visualize clearly in this way. And artists like Roger van der Weyden in fifteenth-century Flanders and Matthias Grünewald in sixteenth-century Germany were among those who tried to depict Christ's wounds and pain so vividly that their art would help the faithful enter such meditation.

In addition the Christian faith has had persistent pockets of worshippers who believed that true union with Christ's suffering came only when their own bodies were scourged and beaten. Sometimes this physical reenactment took place in public ceremonies. More often the public ritual was transformed into the performance of miracle or mystery plays. The best-known survivor of the performance tradition is the Oberammergau Passion Play, still presented every ten years in the small south German village which promised to undertake this task in 1633 if God would spare the community further ravages from the plague. From the beginning, individual villagers have been elected to each of the roles for each new cycle, and the cast traditionally spends long months in preparation for the summer of arduous day-long performances.

During a trip to Europe in 1890, Day attended the Oberammergau Passion Play. Afterward he visited the Prado Museum in Madrid where he especially admired religious paintings by Van Dyck, Rubens, and Velàzquez. By spring 1891, Day was building a collection of photographs of great sacred works of art, writing a dealer:

Could you conveniently jot down the names of any *modern* sacred pieces which you may run across especially in Germany with the name of their artists, you would greatly oblige a caprice of mine which leads me into the collecting of reproductions of such works of this character as are really good.

Two years later he posed his friend, the poet Louise Guiney, for two half-length "studies" of *St. Barbara*. (In reproduction, they look more like "costume pieces" than the kind of religious photographic studies we are considering here.)

In 1895, Guiney sent Day data from England on the proper iconography for depictions of Christ, and Jussim dates Day's first *Study for the Crucifixion* a year later, 1896. Without Day's title for a clue, the pose of this shadow-bathed frontal study of a male nude would suggest Michelangelo's *Dying Slave* more than any traditional depiction of Christ on the Cross. But the final 1898 series of crucifixion photographs were clearly inspired by previous religious art.

Day prepared with great care for his project—an elaborate expedition into the countryside near his Norwood, Massachusetts, home to stage nearly two hundred photographs of the crucifixion (Plate 3), the entombment (Plate 4), the resurrection, and the Seven Last Words of Christ (Plate 5). Enormous energy went into ordering special sandals and cloth made in the Middle East. A wooden cross was imported from Syria. And the supporting cast was chosen from among the citizenry of Norwood.

Day's choice of himself to play Christ may seem as surprising to us as it did to some of his contemporaries, but the decision is quite in line with aspects of the photographic aesthetic that underlay his work. As Charles Caffin, an eminent American critic, put it in 1901:

> In the *genre* picture . . . the least self-consciousness stiffens, and . . . may jar upon the general feeling. . . . The artist may wish to . . . find a model that already corresponds to his conception, that may, indeed, have inspired it, . . . or as a final resort, act as model himself.

Having accepted the task, Day took it seriously. He went on a strenuous and lengthy diet to get his body in shape and let his hair grow to shoulder length. This physical conditioning was essential to his proposed compositions, for in all but one of them he appeared clad only in a loincloth.

At last, in July 1898, everything was in readiness, and Day took his equipment, his props, and his troupe of costumed players to the chosen site to photograph the crucifixion. Two years later, the critic Sadakichi Hartmann said: "The rehearsing of his company and the sacred tragedy was played more than a hundred times on the top of that hill while curious farmers on their wagons with their families came from far and near to gaze at the strange spectacle."

*Plate 3.* Fred Holland Day. *The Crucifixion.* 1898. Collection of Royal Photographic Society, Bath, England.

We only know a small portion of the work created for this series, because in 1904 a tragic fire in Day's studio destroyed all his negatives, a large collection of his prints, and much of his photographic research archive of art images. At least six surviving versions of the crucifixion have been published and two further variations exist in an artist's newspaper sketches. The compositions are varied and depict different moments in the crucifixion. One of the sketched prints shows a distant view of a hilltop where the three crosses carrying Christ and the two thieves stand at the right with a crowd of soldiers and mourners round the foot of the central cross. The most elaborate surviving published photograph has four voluminously draped figures grouped at the foot of the single central cross, two women at the left and two men at the right. The rest of the compositions are less ambitious, containing only the central cross, alone or with one or more figures at its foot. Most often Christ faces us or we see him in profile. One of the newspaper drawings shows a version depicting the moment when Longinus thrusts his spear into Christ's side. Here Christ is held to the cross with two sets of ropes around his torso. The ropes also appear in a surviving photograph (included, too, in sketch form in the newspaper report) where we see the cross from a three-quarter rear view with Mary Magdalene embracing its foot in grief and St. Longinus attentively leaning on his spear at the left. In all of the published photographs, a single huge "spike" "pins" Christ's feet to a jutting slanted platform and "blood" streams from "wounds" on his feet, hands, and brow. The crown of thorns is clearly visible in the surviving prints and a board with the traditional inscription is visible in all but one straight side view. Only in one surviving photograph is there a "halo."

The published images from Day's crucifixion series range in mood from early German art through Italian Early and High Renaissance paintings to the works of Velàzquez and Guido Reni. In most of Day's surviving compositions, his body recalls that of a German late-Gothic carved crucifix. Only in the work with the four flanking men and women is his figure grotesquely doll-like and thus totally unconvincing. With the series as a whole, it is as if, having filled himself with images of this sacred subject, Day was attempting to distill all the artistic visions of this drama into one set of visual works.

The compositions of Day's entombment photographs are less varied. At least three surviving versions have been published and a fourth variation exists in the newspaper sketch form. In all versions, the body of Christ is stretched laterally, left to right, before us on a bier-ledge. The general composition is reminiscent of Holbein's *Dead Christ*, but Day, unlike Holbein, does not suggest the body *in* the tomb. Rather we seem to see it lying outside, just prior to entombment. A ring-halo appears in all versions. Two photographs and the sketch version appear to have been taken in the same setting, indoors before a stone

*Plate 4.* Fred Holland Day. *The Entombment.* 1898. Alfred Stieglitz Collection, The Metropolitan Museum of Art, New York City.

*Plate 5.* Fred Holland Day. *The Seven Last Words of Christ.* 1898. Alfred Stieglitz Collection, The Metropolitan Museum of Art, New York City.

and plaster wall. The bier-ledge is covered with a cloth, and there are wounds in Christ's side and visible hand. In one of the indoor-site photographs, a wound also appears in Christ's foot, while the inscription from the cross and the crown of thorns are propped against the bier. In a second surviving photograph and the drawing after a lost photograph, these are gone but Mary Magdalene bends grieving over Christ's feet (from behind the bier in the photograph, from in front of the bier in the sketch).

The remaining entombment photograph (Plate 4) is strikingly different. Here Christ lies on a rocky ledge against a cliff wall, with his head raised slightly by a natural rock "pillow." As in the other versions, he lies on a cloth and has a halo. But there are no "wounds," which may indicate that this was a study, rejected for the final composition because it did not share enough with the iconography of past art.

Day's *Resurrection from the Tomb* apparently survives in only one version in which a robed Christ stands, his hand raised in blessing, within the open entrance of a stone-slab tomb-sepulchre (which looks rather as if a local cemetery monument was adapted for the occasion). What appears to be the same inscription panel used in some of the crucifixion photographs is fastened to a triangular slab of stone that forms a simple pediment. This entombment composition suggests not so much earlier art as a scene from a biblical play or pageant.

Perhaps most unusual of all Day's religious works is *The Seven Last Words of Christ* (Plate 5). There are seven individual closeup photographs of Day's head, wearing a crown of thorns and streamlets of "blood." Several viewers have noticed that the yearning upturned eyes which occur in many of the panels of Day's *Seven Last Words of Christ* recall the characteristic expression of Christ in Guido Reni's paintings. Whatever the inspiration, we know that the photographer fastened a mirror to his camera so he could capture the appropriate expressions to illustrate Christ's seven "words":

> "Father, forgive them; they know not what they do". "To-day thou shalt be with Me in Paradise". "Woman, behold thy son, son, thy mother". "My God! my God! why hast Thou forsaken me?". "I thirst". "Into Thy hands I commend my spirit". "It is finished."

The cropping around each head is tight. The result is a rather cinematic series of images, which the artist mounted for exhibition in a specially constructed architectural frame with the "seven last words" inscribed across the top.

Day's religious photographs received mixed response in his time. Louise Guiney had warned him: "The sacred exhibition scheme seems to me . . . too hazardous." But Day's initial experience with a private showing in Boston was, on the whole, positive:

Considerable argument and some protest naturally arose among those to whom the results were shown, and in November [1898], a private view of some thirty prints was arranged in Boston. To this exhibition there came people of all shades of religious belief—Quakers, Jews, Anglicans, and Roman Catholics, Nonconformists, Swedenborgian[s], priests and clergymen. Among them were many known to hold adverse opinions before seeing the prints, but with the exception of a single individual, these prejudices entirely disappeared.

Some initial public response was also favorable. Headlines in one 1898 newspaper read:

Sacred art modernized. Photograph of the Crucifixion from Living Figures. Mr. F. H. Day Finds a New and Important Work for the Camera. The Models for His Group Clothed with Historical Accuracy. Scene Selected in Norwood Represented as Nearly as Possible Natural Features of Calvary. Picture Completed Without Marring Either the Meaning or Spirit of the Subject.

Emboldened, Day showed *The Seven Last Words of Christ* and one version of the *Entombment* in the 1898 Philadelphia Salon. He exhibited a *Christ on the Cross* at the Second Philadelphia Salon in 1899. He included a number of his crucifixion compositions with the group of prints he sent for exhibitions in London in 1899. And he showed some crucifixion photographs in London at the Royal Photographic Society in 1900.

As his religious works were more widely seen, opposition developed rapidly. One photographer-critic, Joseph Keiley, called the central images "crude representations of the crucifixion stamped on the cheapest grade of German mortuary cards." But most of the hostility swirled not around artistic merit, but around Day's use of himself as the model for Christ. As one American writer said: "I can hardly associate the appearance of this man, carrying always a portfolio with prints under his arm . . . with the idea of his impersonating such an august personality, and yet his Christ in the sepulchre looks very much like him." A British reviewer was more pointedly virulent: "The crowning objection . . . lies in the fact that he himself poses before the camera as representing one whom so many millions of the earth's people revere as the Divine Founder of Christianity!" Even Day's sympathetic modern biographer, Estelle Jussim, says of his religious work: "The prints were, by and large, abominable. Only the studio-produced hand-manipulated prints of *The Seven Last Words* can be considered to have achieved any level of feeling or aesthetic effect beyond the imitative."

## IV

Our hearts and minds seem to have moved into a very different environment than that which encouraged Day to produce his Passion photographs. Indeed most modern Western viewers have difficulty responding empathetically to *any* of the Victorian religious photography. We recoil from what seems a misuse of the medium. We may be willing to accept the montaged visions of a present-day artist like Jerry Uelsmann as part of photography, but we still expect a "straight" photograph of physical things to be a record of the condition of those things, not a picture that uses those things as stand-ins for other things in other times or places. We do not expect the details of a photograph to reveal to us elements of divine truth. Nor do we any longer respond positively to a seemingly straight photograph of what we know to be a bygone scene. In this sense, the Western photographic viewing tradition differs from that of modern China. There, as Susan Sontag points out, "photographs are supposed to display what has already been described. . . . What makes an image true is it is good for people to see it." This aesthetic allowed the Chinese to create in the 1960s a "staged" photographic series of scenes from the life of an exemplary anonymous citizen, apparently giving the set increased power because of the "truth" of the photographic image. Such a series recalls the now-departed Victorian popular taste for staged photographic stereo-card series designed to bring moral lessons vividly into the home parlor. In the mid-twentieth century, large audiences did like the presentation of biblical themes with living models in elaborately researched and staged movies and television mini-series. But the action in film and television drama is akin to that on the stage, and we retain the habit of "seeing through" theater actors to the characters they represent. With moving images we may accept "stand-ins," but the concept of creating still photographs with Christian themes will probably remain locked in the era of Victorian taste and needs.

*Bibliographical Note*

On Rejlander, see Stephanie Laine Spencer, *O. G. Rejlander—Art Photographer* (University of Michigan Dissertation, 1981). On Cameron, see Helmut Gernsheim, *Julia Margaret Cameron* (Millerton, New York: Aperture, 1975), and Colin Ford, *The Cameron Collection: An Album of Photographs by Julia Margaret Cameron Presented to Sir John Herschel* (New York: Van Nostrand Reinhold, 1975). The basic source on Day is Estelle Jussim's *Slave to Beauty: The Eccentric Life and Controversial Career of F. Holland Day* (Boston: David R. Godine, 1981). Other information and examples of his work are given in Cecil Beaton and Gail Buckland, *The Magic Image: The Genius of Photography from 1839 to the Present Day* (Boston: Little, Brown, 1975); W. J. Naef, *The Collection of Alfred Stieglitz: Fifty Pioneers of Modern Photography* (New York: Viking, 1978); and Jean Gibran and Kahlil Gibran, *Kahlil Gibran: His Life and World* (Boston: New York Graphic Society, 1974).

On Ruskin, see H. A. Ladd, *The Victorian Morality of Art: An Analysis of Ruskin's Esthetic* (New York: Octagon, 1968). On other nineteenth-century esthetic theories, see John Nicoll, *The Pre-Raphaelites* (New York: Dutton, 1970); Quentin Bell, *Victorian Artists* (Cambridge: Harvard University Press, 1967) (on A. W. Pugin); and Vicki Goldberg, ed., *Photography in Print* (New York: Simon and Schuster, 1981) (for Charles Caffin). For a leading contemporary view, see Susan Sontag, *On Photography* (New York: Farrar, Straus, and Giroux, 1978).

*FOUR*

# NEW FICTION AND POETRY

JON SILKIN

# FOOTSTEPS ON THE DOWNCAST PATH

*As if it had tunnel vision, the poem narrates events crucial to the Jewish calendar, beginning with the destruction by the Romans of the Jerusalem Temple in 70 C.E., and finishing with the struggles of the Jewish Ghetto in Warsaw in 1943.*

*The narrator has a dogged interlocutor who is demonic, less jovial than Mephistopheles, with a colorless lethal vitality. In a mental sense, at least, this figure is bent on destroying the narrator, but this good liberal indignant Jew is to profit from his interlocutor—he who asks a few of the right questions if for the wrong reasons.*

1

The tormented in a sullen privilege. Now
they are captors, and bind a naked man
to a wood horse. Then, they beat his soldiers
to his body, dappled with fear.
And for sustenance, in any case,
they tear him, beseeching forgiveness.

        "Men at their torturing,"
a man said. "These troubled soldiers, gulping
their leader—does it disturb you?"

           The wood flinched,
as water flinches with wind; the aureole
is scratched off his chest.

        "Anguish cleanses,"
he said, "and it's anguish in these men, lapping
his blood. Come on, all it is is torture."

A tree shakes with ice, fear shags me;
the fir innocent, his sharp grin sagging.

"Look," he repeated, "at this feast,
the eye innocent, the hand not."

"I don't want to"

"but you should.
what a housewife you make. Doubting Thomas
passed into earth, and it got
a larger helping than he. These men
gasping, you can feel their pain, they feel it.
It's the way we are, each, contrite
for what's done."

We get a move on, patrolling
this city of steps with a soldier's
muddy anguish. On each side
house-walls shop-walls
with moustaches,
sold calico, silk, the desert's spiky
rambling wool, and the stone walls
quickened on one side of us, or the other: chiefly the left,
on the left, always. Here is the first
stone visitation,
a tableau. "Hear me, O Jerusalem," I mutter. You,
heavy, petrol-fumed
like silk. We watch,
with sweat panic'd into the buttery stone,
a stone picture, the slab growing quick.
Women are hiked onto blocks, soldiers
hold open their thighs, as Roman flesh comes
in the woken belly.
                     "Look," he said,
"they are beautiful"
                     while, at their back,
the temple sputtered like upright matches,
the doric'd flames a burst tangle
of burning cries, the folded paupery
of bodies flammable
with soldierly hatred and rage, curtains of torn light.

"All joys are sexual," he said, linking
his arm with mine.
                     "No," I said, "no."

"Are you virgin, the coy sabbath resumed
in prayer? or something"
                     still pumping my arm
as if to spurt a ragged juice.
                     "Yes."

"And not attractive to you?"

"Each woman has. . ."

"all women are; never dishonor a cunt."
And what else but squeezing the spirit
to tighten the candle's hot feather. "Oh, my God,
what is preferable?"

"This is torture"

"To not have is torture. To have nothing
is a mockery of creation."

We walked more downward through the city, its crustacean
vaulting ragged. There was a second picture
in stone: three boats—each, a round prow,
a breast lifted.
Raised up to the sun, that between it
and sea, the English pennant shook its cross,
I mean blood. As if waves caressed
the wood's creaking sussurations, two mailed figures
lift children, with their frail
nuptial of parents, in gentle unction
to the sea's usury. England expels Jews.
The date crouches on its flag: 1290.

That first picture undid the temple, seventy years,
its squat fragile ghosts.
"History," he mouthed, "is wonderful, is its own pentecost
the brain of God exhales. Such suffering,
such parleying in stone, that batters
a skull someone's hands have carefully,
with consideration, put at ease.
Look, you speak as if your fruits were sugared.
Are you a decent man? kiss your arse then,
your lumpish testicles frumpish and sinning
as any."
            I turned away justified;
and as his purposeful destruction of me
sustained, we saw a third picture—

                        a stony hill;
in it a ledge, two men on thrones wearing
their gold, each head fitting a heavy crown,
with white hair, floss conferring sanctity.

In the soft mouths of Fair Philip, and Charles,
a torn shout—"Juifs, Juifs—turn again, for you
pity is France." So the ragged speech,
as trucks judder, when a locomotive startles.
A troop of families, at the alpine face,
half-exiled, alive in exile,
start downwards, like spiders clinging
textured crystal. The movement, hardly
set into opposition to itself,
than the mouths, "Juifs, Juifs"—
stencilled a delicate "no, go away."
Families at the clambering seams. Two kings shout: "Juifs,
this is the kingdom; go. No, do not go yet;
I mean go." Open mouths at the dainty
air, the sun crashes onto a tor:
in cold desolations, splintered alps
speckle with figures. 1394, the date
freezes in air. Praise for my God
fills my mouth, frost, that spangles me.


2


In this hot country there is a dotted winter, hoar
baffling the mind of paraffin: a weak nucleus,
soft, hollowing forms of gas. The lamp fluxes a burning hand.

Virgins come, wisdom mingling with fools.
The big Hand strews its quartzes of terse life,
hard structures with soft fuels. Careless and intense.

Spilt wax itches the curious hand Psyche searched with; foolish body,
her person charged with curiosity—that waxy
illiterate conjunction. "There's no release
from foolishness." That's what he said. I answered
"let's have something to drink," "yes" he said "yes."
and we went.


3


Two separate events, two feet in two shoes . . .
the march, the slow protèstant amble;
a pair of feet, many, like pelting rain—but the sound
in the lamp is like ash, its dots identical
and every dot comes out of the same flesh.

Bruised puce, bruised heart, the sea pulsing in it;
the salt is the same, as water
crossing its bed. To the bed it's the same—many stones
uprooted in watery flight. These ruined facts—ah—
as, ah, ah, to a stethoscope's black cup.

A dais, with Torquemada, the face, plain,
its invariable smirk hot and boy-like. A tongue
pushes out lips pursed on mirth's quick. Quaint bi-sexual mouth
of lisped lippings, an orifice, a hollow jointure
of mouth on tongue. His candle the thick root
of his mind, a martyr's bed-light, singes so many.
Christ's proxy wets the hot earth,
staked into which not a cross, wood,—its projecting
metal length glansed, its tip a penis
on which men, the Jews, rest their genitals. Soot and melting,
the Vatican is ribbed vanes, a vacuous spirit
its night-piece, mucky fluttering angel. Weep,
like Ruth in the corn, having no home—weep
for Christ in innocence, for whom pain, they say,
and death were made. Jews sit on this metal jump,
corded by their necks to the upright—
a cross without arms— and their tongues protrude.
Look at the picture, if I seem to lie.

As the hands of the dark sisters death and night softly wash this soiled
        earth
the remnant searches a fresh portion of it,
as if who in this ambling soil could root. Who, and where.


4


This ragged city, a thalus on a pole,
blotches white the even-colored psyche; at its foot
it buries in our soft dust.
"You are what I need," the city spoke, like a girl
in the dormitory of a hostel.
The city spoken for by a single lamp, Jew or Arab.
"I need you," she demanded, hair
wisped on the sun-burned skin, the blanket rucked
on the hostel's black-painted iron, a bed
braced with dreams. This city is a hospital,
sickness pitting its joints, with its split bags
of lavender. Its matrons are ill-advised

and ill-fed, but, in the market,
jaunty with spice and fruit.

Dreams in a ruck-sack. "Oh, look," he said.

"You again?"

            "Yes," he admitted, "this city's
soft-spoken ouzo, like an old client
whose eyes are milky with pain, won't disperse me."

The stone devises another scene
as dust devises life, its shadow.
The lives of Jews dissolve in Russian, a lamp,
its flame lightly blue behind smoke. It bristles
with cherubim, a spume of exultation.
The Emperess Caterina's bronze candle-sticks
spatter.
            "Wax is blood." he said.
                              Her Cossacks—
her riders' legs riffle, and bridle bells
flicker, softly jangled. 1881.
The Russian tongue is a strand in the officer's braid,
in his zinc badge—its artifice
a cock on a weather-vane the wind shakes through.

And then a stairway of familiar
more recent likenesses. Of Poland, its wars.
An archway links two terraces of homes.
May frosts its eglantine
that is not maytime, spring,
dancing its thrush upon tawny grass.
Fire arrives, a horse brandishing flame—a mane
of thick steady arranged bands—catches
at shrieking wood and crevice. Girls
in a row, on fire. Hot sheen, blood
in ashes beside that. And wiring
that trails, then snaps—the blue cobbles slashed.
Armor's chain rickets on the flesh.
Sinewy cries, anfractuous crying; sweat, petals, shit,
and everything that one must do, to resist
in a Polish sewer. The House
up-ends its beard of flame, Warsaw, feathery
with soot; a fossil
gets smelted to a wall.

The working flesh of Polish gentlewomen
steps the downcast path. Spiny cats
trickle the streets, with lean inquiring faces.

5

For Jerusalem start the train with fifty lirot. Then, springy, dilgent as a
goat, the locomotive circles the hill's aureole—the buttery stone of
which has a nub of fudge-like decrudescence, viscous and sweet. We
spiral—as if, by reverse motion, we sank down; as though the down-
spent mind were, by stuttering connection, an *urbs* suckered with
flittering minds. Not so: sucked and dabbed at by moths we climb.

Under Jerusalem is a sea. I purchase an unattractive boat but the oars
are made of Galil Cedar and give off a wan dismissive smell. Lucifer
abandons this cavernous water, his fire dark; it is a cloak he has shed.
No littoral and no tide, but a number of crisp shells pallid for want of
light. I go to tie a hammock under the speckled orchards of citrus—
these fragrant cheerful lamps. This is a mendicant corner of the
Turkish empire, its moustache fine as an arrow-head.

At David Street, a man weighs heat, from fingers to forearms a soft hot
red, its greasy powder hairless as his skin. This fear of death on him
enflames a desire for more, hot life. My friend smiled faintly when he
heard this, as if he were my diary.

Returning once, we stopped to extinguish a fire that had seized another
bus. After, I was afflicted by the ragged viridian of Cypresses that,
notched with a grim demeanor, step uphill. If death tastes like this I
may find it bearable. The pepper-man dispenses his red, touchy
ounces. My friend laughs on David Street. The talk of the evening
sputters in Aramaic—Christ's year, with its wings of short stubby
feathers. No more trees with the hinged mechanism of the cross, no
more men springing fully armed into martyrdom: I want the cross to
fold into a featureless stick. On the Temple's Jebusite threshing-floor I
know that the wheat is about to explain, "I am eaten, I am alive."

6

A simple quantity of Hebrew spills.
"Is this a pogrom?"
                    "It is not" I say.

"Is all that finished with?"

The timbrel
in orthodox voices as they bind their shoulders
and pray. No, it is her hand dancing, her nails
that swish the light. If I'm alive, stone, not music
gives me my energy. I form a language
of chips and indentations in rock, scratches
and little pressings of momentary rest
the may-fly in her flight north left on it,
the bat of cherub wings, the family
pressure of angels disturbing the desert pebbles
in their variety communal. I form words
and become stone. Praise for this to the designer
of letters.
        Dropping through this hell to a shaded field
I scrape another stone. The jerboa
fixes its little teeth into the side
of something smaller. Sparse cindery flowers
rub bees that like the insides of the plant,
the sweet wax food, spiky fractures
of blue and lightning, each feathery spike holding
a flame inside its own. I wait beside
these acid pauses, flower-like, my eyes
wide with surprise. I fondle surface, and its veins
smoky with tenderness spread, binding themselves
with bitter strength.

My friend smiles faintly, and his smiling is
a patch of bleeding on the tufted sand.

Drink, nightly, a small measure of dry wine.

Jerusalem 1980—Newcastle 1982

JOYCE CAROL OATES

# LAST DAYS

...the Scourge of G-d. But perhaps he is born too late? A Messiah at any hour. For a while he is "into" Holocaust literature, for a while it is Wittgenstein who obsesses him ("Whereof we cannot speak, thereof we must be silent"—or words to that effect: Saul is too excited to get them 100% accurate), for a few unfortunate weeks in his senior year of college it is Kant's Categorical Imperative: "Do you realize," Saul says heatedly to his friends and to whoever will listen, even to his offended father at long distance, "—that whatever we do or say or *think*, it should be a moral imperative for *all of humanity*? Our slightest whim or action—a transcendental law for *all time*?" The semester of his first (official, recorded, historic) breakdown. Six frenzied mock-frothing-at-the-mouth hours in the infirmary.

Saul Morgenstern, the Wrath of G-d. The apple of G-d's Eye. He rips the letter to shreds from the Rhodes foundation, throws the pieces like confetti into the air. He walks away from the "minimum security" mental hospital at Fort Spear, Michigan. Not five weeks later he takes a lumbering exhaust-spewing bus, a wide-shouldered big-assed bus (Saul's own "surreal" images, he has taken to writing poetry feverishly in his last days) to Toledo, to buy a $15 pistol for $78.24 at the Liberty Pawnshop, from a clerk whose gold-rimmed innocently round eye-glasses resemble his own, and whose swarthy good looks (so Saul imagines) mirror his in an *almost* Semitic way. The Ohio laws governing the sale of rifles, handguns, and bullets are much friendlier than the laws of neighboring states. If you are a former convict or a former mental patient, if you are visibly agitated and "in the wings of" the hottest event of your life (so Saul has been gleefully warning his friends for weeks) you will not be turned away. "No doubt about it," says the youngish stoop-shouldered gentleman with the gold-rimmed glasses, Saul's smirking twin, "—a gun is your best friend these days. Of course I am speaking of an emergency. Have you ever found yourself caught up in the confusing flurry of an emergency?" Saul was turning the pistol over and over in his icy fingers. He hadn't counted on the object having such weight; such gravity. ("There is physicality here in all its surprising abruptness," he tells himself. For a brief while Wittgenstein's disciples toyed with the idea of calling his philosophy "physicalism" or a word to that effect: selling it to Stalin perhaps: but Stalin had been unimpressed, probably had his mind on other things.)

He hadn't counted on so much reality though he was the proud author of two articles on the subject of current "academic shibboleths" published precociously in *The New Republic*, and a one hundred sixty-five page seminar paper on the subject of Buber, Existentialism, Structuralism, Post-Structuralism, and the Holocaust as Text, a paper generally acclaimed as brilliant among Morgenstern's circle, though intemperately rejected as "unacceptable as either scholarship or poetry" by that Professor W_____ who had best remain nameless, as Saul is "contemplating" graphic revenge. Saul's fingers are shaking. He pays no heed. Nor does the pawnbroker's clerk. It is a workday like any other, a Tuesday perhaps. It is ordinary life "sliced" in a perfectly ordinary way. Saul could photograph with his eyes the crowded interior of the Liberty Pawnshop on Seventh Street, downtown Toledo, or is it Dayton?—the affable clerk bent smiling over the badly scarified glass counter, he has an unfailing "photographic memory" ("what a great device for cheating," his envious freshman-dorm roommate little Sammy Frankel said, Sammy set like a wind-up toy for medical school and a million-dollar practice: contemptible little Jewboy, Saul called him)—but why trouble to immerse himself in what is, after all, only *statistical* reality? (The police report will describe a Colt New Police model .32-caliber revolver, its original five-inch barrel sawed off to two, for pocket convenience; the usual six-shot cylinder. A weapon manufactured twenty-five years ago. Commonly sold over (and under) the counter. So badly in need of oiling, "surprising that it worked at all," one of the police will say.) Saul has been staring for some uncomfortable seconds at the amazing *object* in his hands, and his eyes, though customarily "dark, piercing, or brooding," have gone as blank and round and empty as his glasses. The clerk breathes warmly onto Saul's hands. He squints up companionably at him. "This material is chrome, if you are wondering," he says, "—that, zinc. A fine gun. The very best for emergencies. And if you had maybe a secret pocket sewed into your coat, I don't mean any big deal, or maybe you have one already?—it would be absolutely safe. And the price is right." Saul stares at the gun and the left corner of his mouth begins to twitch. Because he has seen this gun before, he has seen the scratched glass counter before, his own nail-bitten winter-reddened hands, the clerk's amiable ghostly reflection observing him from out of the glass. The forbidden thought arises: the Messiah has come and gone. Saul Morgenstern is too late. But "Right-o," Saul says in his deep bass voice, the most manly of voices, to deflect the clerk from suspicion. It is really a very ordinary very *routine* sort of morning. Rabbi Reuben Engelman is always telling Saul that it is the *routine* of life, the "happy dailiness" in which Faith and Practice are "wed," that constitutes the real challenge. Saul defeats the hypocritical old windbag with one loud slam of his hand on the desk top. And afterward re-enacts the scene for his table of undergraduate disciples in the student union cafeteria. ("I'm the Zen hand, the single Zen hand, that pounds and pounds and pounds my enemies to dust," he shouts. Saul Morgenstern the Scourge of G-d. Saul Morgenstern who rejected a Rhodes Scholarship. So forceful in the smoky interior of the Union, so Biblical, with his deep voice and flashing eyes and lustrous black wiry kinky hairs that curl from out of his clothes . . . no wonder the little WASP girls slit their eyes at him.) Now he turns the pistol in his fingers. Murmurs, "Right-o," while he tries to remember precisely why he is here. Murmurs, "But can't I 'jew you down' a few bucks, I have my doubts that this thing is worth $85. . . ." Several minutes of animated conversation. Saul says laughingly that he doesn't intend to kill his father: Ernest Morgenstern isn't worth killing: that kind of sloppy *personal* behavior ("acting out" the shrinks call it) has no class. The pawnbroker's clerk agrees. Or hasn't precisely heard. Saul turns the empty cylinder, sights along the barrel, licks his numbed lips, asks the clerk if he'd had any member or members of his family lost in the Holocaust, makes the comment (mildly, even sadly, smiling) that the family is a vanishing animal in the United States, doomed to extinction. "That's right," the clerk says agreeably. Saul stares blinking at him and sees that he isn't a twin at all, he's a morose ugly man in his late thirties, going bald, a queer sagging to one eyelid. He's an informant, probably. The pawnshop is monitored. ". . . a target like Kissinger," Saul is saying, ". . . from the point of view of the Jewish community. But of course it's too late. Years too late. I was only a high school kid then, I didn't know shit. Also I've always been a pacifist. Even when my father struck me in the face and cracked my nose—I didn't strike back." "That's right," the clerk says. He is making an unconscious "wringing" gesture with his hands. Pontius Pilate. Naturally. "David Gridlock" (the name on the purchase slip) files the image away for future reference. He has become feverishly interested in poetry lately; he begins to wonder if his real talent doesn't lie in that direction, and not in the direction of sombre meticulous mirthless scholarship. . . . Also, he hasn't yet settled upon the absolute sequence of events, to be enacted in the synagogue next Sabbath: whether, after performing the assassination, he will then commit suicide by firing a single bullet, calmly, into the base of his skull, or whether he will allow himself to be captured by his enemies and led away. At the moment he leans toward the former. But, if the latter, he will want to immerse himself in poetry. And certain images are so "haunting," so "clustering". . . . The bargain is made, the price is right, Saul pays in cash, that is, "David Gridlock" pays unhesitatingly in cash, though he wonders if he is being cheated—being so bookish, so obviously not a man of the world. The price of the bullets too is suspiciously high. But what can he do?—he plays it safe, buys three dozen.

Freddy C_____, Dale S_____, Sol M_____ discuss the problem of Morgenstern endlessly. "Frankly I'm afraid of him," says Freddy. "Also very exhausted. I wish he'd kill himself soon." But this isn't serious talk, this is sorrow, despair, cowardice. Vera R_____ (by simple and insignificant happenstance a niece of Mrs. Morgenstern's oldest sister-in-law) becomes emotional, sometimes very angry, when the others say such things. ". . . how do you think we'll all feel, if. . ." she says in a low trembling voice. Of course they agree. They absolutely agree. And the fact that Saul has been going about claiming his former housemates have cheated him of "six months' rent" and "invaluable rare books" cannot fail to add to their uneasiness. Denise E_____ has tried to make contact with Saul's former psychiatrists (Dr. Ritchie at the hospital, Dr. Mermelstein in the city) but since she is afraid of telling the gentlemen who she is, and hasn't been able to finish typing out a fifteen-page letter chronicling Saul's behavior in the past several months, her efforts have been unsuccessful. (Afterward, Denise will tell at least one reporter that Dr. Ritchie was "flippant" and "hurried" on the telephone, and told her that "if Saul's hostility was acted out, it would most likely be directed only against himself." This statement Dr. Ritchie has denied having made.) Dale thinks the police should be called and if Saul shows up at the house again he will call them himself. Sol thinks the parents should be told ("but they know all about it, don't they"), the hospital's administration should be told ("but they don't give a damn"), Saul's former professors at the university, Saul's former friends. . . . But maybe it's wisest not to get involved. Not to get involved officially. For Saul has already threatened to sue everyone from the Governor of the state on down to his former housemates at 18332 Twenty-Third Street if any terminology hinting at his "mental condition" is made public. He has told Rose P_____ (herself not altogether stable) that certain betrayers of his trust will soon "regret the day of their birth" as the inhabitants of the cities of Hiroshima, Berlin, and Pompeii regretted theirs. Rose P_____ thinks Saul is probably a saint. If he could be rooted in the earth somehow, brought into contact with his sensual primitive fundamental self. . . . "It's ideas and thinking and books that have made him sick," she says in a passionate reedy voice, which makes Dale explode nervously, "For Christ's sake Saul doesn't think at *all* these days, he's given up thinking for the past six months, he can't even sit still to *read* unless he's on medication," and Vera says over and over, ". . . if he's really dangerous and does something, and . . . how do you think we'll feel. . . ." However, it *is* a free country. Even if Saul has some sort of "infectious malaise" as Rose thinks, a "psychic virus" picked up out of the air of America. Even if he drives without a driving license. (His license has been suspended for ninety days.) Even if as rumor has it he has bought a gun. And probably he *is* a saint, Rose says, are there saints in the Jewish religion . . . ? Rose makes a nuisance of herself hanging out around school, dropping in at the house on Twenty-Third all hours of the night, hinting clumsily that she and Saul are "devoted lovers." The others will refute her angrily, saying that Saul hadn't ever made love to a girl, he basically detested girls, but Rose, ferret-faced little Rose, will make her grubby claim now and forever. After all she often accompanies Saul on his nocturnal wanderings about the city and at the Eastland Hills Shopping Mall where he sings so that his rich vibrating voice (a baritone voice?) echoes. He sings fearlessly, lustily, even in the library stacks, even in the Chippewa Tavern where the younger workers from the Chrysler plant hang out, even in the maze-like undulations of Abbey Farms, the "luxury custom-homes" development where the Morgensterns bought a house before the husband divorced the wife—easily worth one-third of a million dollars in today's inflated market: he isn't shy. Singing Leporello, singing Don Giovanni, singing sweet German lyrics by Schubert, shifting raucously into the sleaziest of Janis Joplin, while his spaced-out girl trots after him clapping until her palms burn. She loves him, she's crazy about him, why isn't her adoration enough to save him, why didn't he (if Fate and Karma pulled him in that direction) propose that they die together, snug in his Volkswagen overlooking the lake, while the snow dreamily falls and covers them up . . . ? Rose P_____ who wants to convert to Judaism, "the most orthodox kind." Rose P_____ who is the only person, apart from Saul's mother, to notice that his right eye is just perceptibly darker—a darker greeny-brown—than his left. Rose P_____ at whose tremulous bosom Saul had once cocked and fired a forefinger, chuckling, in front of five or six embarrassed friends. Rose P_____ whom Saul succeeded in "breaking down" by reading her harrowing selections from such Holocaust literature as *Survivors of Auschwitz, Voices of the Deathcamp, In the Ghettos of Warsaw and Lodz,* and *After the Apocalypse.* Rose P_____ to whom he confessed on the eve of the assassination/suicide, "The real thing is, God's curse on me is, *I was born too late. All the suffering is over—all the memoirs have been written. Every breath of Saul's has been breathed by someone else.*"

His senior year, Saul is editor-in-chief of the student newspaper and works on the average of fifty hours a week. He is known for his generosity. He is known for his "biting" sarcasm. He is locally famous for having published articles in *The New Republic* that bravely criticize the university from which he will graduate. An editorial on academicians who have "prostituted" themselves for federal grant money appeared on the op-ed page of the *New York Times,* and impressed even Mr. Morgenstern (at that time living on East Seventy-Sixth Street with his second and very young, or at any rate youthful, wife and her eleven-year-old son). He discovers that he doesn't require sleep as other people do. He runs for miles in the still dry winter night (temperatures as low as 5°, breath steaming, heart a wondrous unstoppable fist that opens and closes, opens and closes, absolutely triumphant—why for Christ's sake had he ever worried about his health, frightened himself that he had cancer of the rectum when it was only bleeding hemorrhoids)—he chins himself on railings, impresses those credulous WASP girls by climbing over walls, not minding the iron spikes and broken glass scattered about, he *is* invulnerable on certain days, and strong as an ox besides. He gorges on non-kosher food and never feels a tinge of nausea. He sits at the rear of the Adath Israel synagogue, that "eye-stopping" "eye-sore" that Rabbi Reuben Engelman dreamt up out of his shameless materialistic dreams, before (and after) the murder/suicide lavishly featured in national magazines— Saul sits quietly as any sweet little brainwashed Jew-boy, a yarmulke on his head, taking notes in his loose-leaf journal on the fixtures, the fur coats, the "masks of cunning and deceit" on all sides. He even takes notes in a short-hand of his own invention when Rabbi Engelman delivers his rousing patriotic take-pride-in-America-and-don't-look-back sermons. Sometimes he chuckles, but quietly. No one appears to notice.

No psychiatrist can help him because he's too smart—he knows the Freudian crap, the jargon, inside and out. His I.Q. has been measured at 168. Perhaps it is 186. No one at the hospital dares approach him *on his own terms* because his problems aren't trivial and personal: his problems have to do with life and death, G-d and man, the special destiny of the Jews, the contrasting fates of Vessels of Grace and Vessels of Wrath ("For twenty-two years I was a Vessel of Grace," Saul says with a bitter lopsided grin, "—and then I realized that was the wrong category.") Dr. Ritchie is an idiot, Dr. Merlmelstein a homosexual sadist, Professor W———— who handed back his paper covered in red ink is an impostor, a crook. "David Gridlock" was born one drizzly December afternoon while Saul ran panting through the hospital woods, his parrot-green canvas jacket unzipped and his tongue lolling, borne along on waves of elation so powerful, so exquisite, he knew they were the province of G-d: except of course he didn't believe in such superstitious crap. He never had, in fact. Even at his Bar Mitzvah, in fact, reading his prayers and singing his chants with as much solemn assurance as if he'd been doing it all his young life. ("If I were G-d," Saul tells his nervous housemates Freddy and Dale, "I would bless you all and suck away your oxygen and that would be that—before you had a chance to wake up and ruin everything. Of course I mean 'you' in a generic sense," he explains.)

The psychiatrists, the psychologists, the therapists, the self-appointed do-gooders, certain meddlesome members of the Morgenstern family . . . no one is qualified to give advice to *him*. He baffles Mermelstein with a recitation from Kafka which he asks him to identify

("If we are possessed by the Devil it cannot be done by one, for then we should live quietly, as with God, in unit, without contradiction . . . always sure of the man behind us"), he shocks a former philosophy professor at Ann Arbor by a late-night visit meant to "hammer out" the problem of Wittgenstein ("Is it true that 'what can be said at all can be said clearly, and what we cannot talk about we must pass over in silence'?—and how is this to be reconciled with the philosopher's compulsive homosexual promiscuity?"—delivered in a ringing triumphant voice), he dismays his father with an unannounced appearance in New York during spring break ("Van Gogh cut off his ear with a razor blade for atonement," he tells his angry bewildered father, "—if I castrated myself would that please you and the new Mrs. Morgenstern?"), he works long fevered idle hallucinatory hours on a prose-poem tentatively titled "Last Days" (". . .At the age of twenty-three I see that everything is falling in place at last and that there was no secret to its meaning all along, except that Saul Morgenstern 'saw through a glass darkly'"). He wakes in alarm, and sometimes in a sweating rage, with the conviction that he will be, *he cannot avoid being*, a belated Messiah. It is very late in the twentieth century. The sacrificial act has already been performed. Every syllable of his speech has been recorded on tape, even the gunshots, even the idiot screams of the congregation: and pirated (no doubt) for the local radio stations.

"I'm starving! Dying of hunger!" Saul accuses his mother when he chances to appear at the house on Sussex Drive. "I can't breathe," he accuses his housemates, who foul the air with their cigarettes, their solemn mirthless clichés, the unwashed heat of their bodies. Dale S_____ will remember an "uncannily lucid" conversation with Saul on the subject of the Holocaust and its significance for all of human history, past and future. The face of absolute evil, the anonymity of sin, Hitler as the Anti-Messiah, the "Final Solution" being the pollution of every cubic foot of oxygen—hence Saul's choking, his coughing spells. (Which certain of his acquaintances, grown less indulgent with time, saw as shabbily theatrical. "He was faking," they say. "He was always faking. Except—of course—at the end. But only at the *very* end.")

He graduates with highest honors, he is the only Rhodes scholar named this year in the state of Michigan, he will study history, politics, religion at Oxford: but sickness intervenes. Now he practices firing his Colt New Police pistol into a pile of stacked newspapers and magazines in the basement of his mother's (no longer his parents') custom-made house on Sussex Drive. His mother is away for the afternoon, fortunately. At the Club. At the hospital visiting an aged ailing female relative. "I cannot understand you, Saul," Mrs. Morgenstern has said many times. Sometimes she blinks tears out of her eyes, sometimes she stands sombre and stoic, not to be "broken down" (in Saul's own words) by the non-negotiable presence of her son. Her name is

Barbara, she is altogether American, assimilated. She bears very little resemblance to her dignified son except for the shade of her eyes—a queer muddy-green—sometimes enlivened with thought, sometimes merely muddy. Saul loves her, he readily admits, but he cannot bear her: not her voice which is so painfully *sympathetic*, not her touch which burns, not the faintest whiff of her expensive lethal perfume. All this he explains patiently to Rabbi Engelman in the rabbi's handsome panelled library in his home. All this he explains to Freddy, to Sol, to Vera, to Dr. Ritchie, to the contemptible Mermelstein, to passengers on the Greyhound bus returning from Toledo, to anyone who will listen: for, after all, as Saul reasons, isn't it the story of our (collective) lives? Stunning in its transparency, irrefutable as a mathematical equation, how can it be resisted—? Pulling the trigger, shocked and gratified by the simple loud *noise* of the explosion, Saul knows for the first time that though everyone is lying to him, everyone has agreed to "humor" him at least to his face, it no longer matters *to him* what they think.

Still, in his last days, he makes many telephone calls. He will become famous for his telephone calls.

Lying sleepless in his rumpled bed on the third floor (rear) of the "boarding house" at 3831 Railroad Avenue, a half-mile from the squalid southerly fringes of the university campus, some eleven miles south and east of the Adath Israel synagogue on the Hamilton Expressway. . . . Lying sleepless by day and night, "David Gridlock" plotting his revenge which will take the form of simple atonement. It isn't the sickish terror of insomnia that overcomes him. He has long been adjusted to insomnia. It's the bed rumpled and smelling of someone else's heated thoughts, someone else's turbulent nights, *before Saul lies in it*. It's the soiled sheets, the indentation of a stranger's head on the pillow, stray hairs, curly and dark but not his own. The unflushed toilet in the hall. Waste, foul and sickening and *not his own*. His fear is of being unoriginal, accused of plagiarism, exposed, ridiculed, cast aside as ordinary: "What's so special about *you*, that you have the right to persecute *me*?" Mr. Morgenstern shouts. As editor-in-chief of the student newspaper he *knocks himself out*, rewrites slovenly half-assed copy, his head buzzing with coffee, cigarettes, amphetamines. Often he hears the half-scolding half-awed exclamation: "Saul, don't knock yourself out!" And again, "Saul, why do you knock yourself out over this?—you don't even get academic credit." It is his responsibility to write three or four editorials a week. Provocative "controversial" pieces. The undemocratic nature of fraternities and sororities, discrimination even by self-styled liberals, *de facto* segregation . . . that sort of thing. One of his editorials is a passionate attack upon prejudice. He is actually moved as he types it out, very moved, agitated, close to tears. For the principle is—*can* human nature be changed, after all; what in fact is "human nature," that it might be "changed"; what hope is there after so many centuries . . . ? A bold editorial, Saul thinks. An attack. A frontal assault. And then comes a prissy sarcastic letter from a graduate student in engineering, *engineering* of all contemptible subjects, ignoring the thrust of Saul's editorial and accusing him of plagiarism. Plagiarism!—with reference to a (famous) essay by Sartre on anti-semitism which Saul has never read, or cannot remember having read, G-d as his witness. Fortunately Saul can get rid of the letter before anyone sees it. . . . Then again, not long ago, in his "Issues in Contemporary Thought" seminar, for which Saul wrote a fifty-page paper embellished with clever footnotes, he is accused of "not having adequately acknowledged" his sources: whole paragraphs, it seems, in the language of Camus, certain insights from Camus's "Reflections on the Guillotine" ("Capital punishment throughout history has always been a religious punishment. . . . The real judgment is not pronounced in this world but in the next. . . . Religious values are the only ones on which the death penalty can be based. . . ."), turns of phrase appropriated from Buber and Tillich: *which Saul has never read, or cannot remember having read.* The mortification, then, of pleading his case with the professor. Of uttering the truth in so shaky and childish a voice, it is transformed into a falsehood. I am innocent, Saul says, how can I prove my innocence, have I been born too late, have all the words been used, has all the oxygen been breathed . . . ? His heart pounds with the shame of it, the oppression, the humiliation not to be borne. Better to die, Saul instructs Saul, than to crawl like a dog into someone else's sheets, stare helplessly into the toilet at someone else's shit.

In general, however, he is happy; almost euphoric. He shakes the hands of strangers, helps derelicts across the wide windy streets, helps push a car out of an icy snowbank. He never exaggerates because there isn't the need. "Around me," he boasts, "the world itself exaggerates." In any case he knows the importance of maintaining a certain level of energy in his bloodstream, maintaining a certain gut strength. He's bookish but no fool. He's suffered the ignominy of electro-convulsive shock treatments but he has always bounced back. In his loose-leaf journal he writes as clearly as possible so that, after his death, he won't be misunderstood as he was misunderstood in life. *Around the hero all things turn into tragedy; around the demigod, into a satyr-play; around Morgenstern—clumsy farce.* The freshness of the insight and the vigor of its language excite him. Death promises not to be painful at all.

In the crappy little room on Railroad Avenue he finds himself thinking of Ft. Spear and the long dazed fluorescent-lit corridors, the fenced-in woods through which he ran with the intention of making his heart burst; but when he was in the hospital he thought of the house on Sussex Drive, the Abbey Farms sub-division, Rabbi Engelman and his wife Tillie seated in the living room, Mrs. Morgenstern serving them coffee and weeping. In one place he thinks of another. In one time-zone he yearns for another. Hence the frantic letter-writing, the telephone calls. . . . His father in Manhattan, Moses Goldhand at the University of Chicago, Professor Fox at the University of Michigan who had had such "high hopes" for him as a Rhodes scholar, Vera R_____ who "perhaps unconsciously" betrayed him, Dr. Ritchie the homosexual-charlatan, Dr. Mermelstein whom he will soon expose. It is a preposterous and almost unsayable fact that both his parents, united after years of bitter disagreement, conspired to so misrepresent facts to a Probate Court judge that Saul was "committed" to a state hospital: this truth must be acknowledged, turned fearlessly in the fingers like a rare poisonous insect, a lurid glaring jewel of an insect, *this truth the son cannot shirk.* "Rabbi," Saul says in a boy's abrupt voice, "I think I need help. It isn't that I feel sick or weak or anything . . . I feel too strong."

Saul's clothes don't exactly fit though he dresses with fussy self-consciousness: his Englishy tweed jacket with the leather patches at the elbows and the buttons covered in leather; his handsome silk tie, a tasteful dark red; his black silk-and-cotton socks, the very best quality. "He took pride in his appearance," says Rose P_____, "and why shouldn't he—? He was so beautiful sometimes, you could see his soul shining in his eyes." Vera R_____ says, "Well—he was a little vain, I suppose, when I first met him.. He said something strange once: that if he'd been able to sing, if he'd gone on the stage, his life would have been peaceful and dedicated to beauty." The girls adore him, his disciples in the coffee shop applaud, Morgenstern the Scourge of G-d with his wiry curly black hair, his semitic nose and eyes, the gold-rimmed glasses that give him so perplexed and scholarly and teacherly a look—one of those skinny dark-browed anarchists of Old Russia, a student out of Dostoyevsky, prepared to give his life in the rebellion against tyranny. But lately his clothes have grown so baggy he wonders if in fact they are *his.* Perhaps his housemates have hatched a cruel prank, sneaking into his new room, substituting someone else's clothes for his. Suddenly it seems very plausible. A Jew's worst enemy is another Jew, right? The swastikas scrawled on his poster of Freud with cigar (taped to the door of his library carrel) were doubtless the work of other Jews envious of Saul's success at the university and with WASP females in particular. Sol M_____, for instance. The Frank kid, what is his name, his physician-father hangs out with Rockefeller. . . .

"Rabbi," Saul says, "I think I need help. People are insulting me behind my back. It hasn't been the same since Ft. Spear, since my parents turned me in, I mean they gave me the highest dosage of drugs there, the highest legal dosage, and I lost count of how many shock treatments, which I believe are against the state law—I'm seeing a lawyer in the morning—I'm not going to let any of this rest—but from you I need help, they have begun calling me the 'worst kind of Jew,' *will you please tell them to stop?*"

He pays $78 in cash for two weeks in the boarding house (the flophouse) on slummy Railroad Avenue though he knows secretly that he won't be there that long. He won't be anywhere that long. Carefully he arranges a selection of his most cherished books, certain newspaper and magazine clippings, a slightly wrinkled but still dramatic poster-photograph of Ché Guevara ("Ché Guevara!" Freddy C____ will exclaim, "—I mean, since when, Ché Guevara and Saul Morgenstern?"), and the typed and heavily annotated manuscript of "Last Things." But the clean white dime-store envelope containing his denunciation speech is kept in the left pocket of his tweed coat. In the right pocket, the pistol. Its compact weight has become assimilated to his own in recent days: he rarely needs to think of it any longer.

His friends, his former friends, the frightened housemates, certain university acquaintances and gossipers—they debate the existence of the pistol, which no one has ever seen. Some are certain that Saul has a gun ("He keeps his elbow pressed against his pocket in a way, you know there's something dangerous there"), others are equally certain that he is lying ("All he wants is for us to talk about him—always to talk about *him*"), a few believe that his carefully stylized "crazy behavior" is the real thing and that he should be considered dangerous ("Maybe he was kidding around at first but now he's lost control—you can smell a really weird odor on him"). An unidentified young woman tells one of the campus security police that there is going to be trouble unless a certain "graduate student in history" is taken into custody, but she professes not to know his name, and refuses to give any further information. Mrs. Morgenstern telephones her former husband and leaves a message with his maid which is never returned: possibly because (so Mrs. Morgenstern says, she is renowned for always putting the best face on things) the maid spoke with a heavy Hispanic accent, and probably had not understood the message.

Saul aka "David Gridstone" jogs through the Abbey Farms sub-division one chill Sunday morning, wishing to see it with uncon-taminated (i.e., an anthropologist's) eyes. Essex Drive, Queens Lane, Drakes Center, Pemberton Circle, Shropshire Way, Sussex Drive. . . . An exemplary Jewish neighborhood, Saul thinks, panting, laughing silently, a real kike fantasy, all these English names, all the undulations of the lanes, ways, roads, drives, not a street among them, not a hint of urban origins. He runs, he swings his arms, he forgets not to breathe through his opened mouth, the fierce sunlight pours into him and swells him with energy, his very brain is tumescent, he realizes suddenly that he will live forever: a bullet from his own gun cannot stop him. Drakes Center and Shropshire and here is Sussex Drive and here is 18 Sussex . . . a custom-made house like all the rest . . . built by the same developer . . . dreamt up by the same architect. Saul "sees" for the first time since the Morgensterns bought the house eleven years before that 18 Sussex is . . . a remodeled barn: that all the houses in Abbey Farms are remodeled barns: made of wood specially treated to look "weathered," even slightly "rotted"; with narrow vertical windows designed to give the illusion of having been "cut out" of obdurate barn walls. He begins to laugh aloud as he runs. Perhaps he will succumb to a fit of laughing, wheezing, asthmatic choking, he can't help himself, it *is* hilariously funny, he will have to add a footnote to "Last Things," a sly dig at Abbey Farms the "restricted residential community" a few miles from Adath Israel, the private and domestic expression of that Jewish essence of which (he is straining for the most muscular but also the most mocking syntax) Adath Israel is the public and cultural expression. English lanes and circles and ways, gaunt gray-weathered Andrew Wyeth barns, hexagonal and octagonal "classic" shapes, rough unpainted fences, even "split-log" fences, even mock-silos with orange-red aluminum roofs adjacent to garages. . . . Disney Land! Fantasy land! Kike heaven! Saul jogs along the deserted wintry streets, his breath steaming, his lips and tongue going numb. "I will go until I am stopped," he thinks, elated, "—and I never am stopped. G-d be praised."

The Last Will & Testament of Saul Morgenstern: . . . *as I cannot and will not continue to live in this abomination of hypocrisy I will make you an outright present of my life to satisfy your bloodlust. As for my worldly goods . . . if it should be discovered that the debts lodged against me are fraudulent and I should possess after all some wealth I direct that it be given to the Lubavitcher Hasidim and not a penny to those who have betrayed me. My books, papers, personal possessions etc. to be burnt and scattered with my body.*

Saul's car breaks down en route to Adath Israel but he has learned to be affable (i.e., fatalistic) enough, he doesn't waste precious minutes shaking his fist at the skies, why despair when it's only a few minutes after eleven and in his tweed coat and red necktie and glinting gold-rimmed glasses he's an excellent candidate to be picked up and offered a ride by a passing motorist . . . ? In any case he is only about four miles south of the synagogue, on the Hamilton Expressway. And a weightless sensation pulses through him. *He cannot fail, he has entered History.*

A certain Judge Marvin McL_____ of the Probate Court receives a letter from Dr. Harold A_____ the Director of the Ft. Spear State Hospital, explaining that Mr. Saul Morgenstern, having left the hospital on "unauthorized leave," was now being granted the status of "convalescent" as he had initiated "therapy of a private nature" outside the hospital, with a certain Dr. Aaron Mermelstein, and had made a "reasonable adjustment" there. This, a bitter triumph for the forces of Justice after long haggling, begging, whispered pleading, the defiant restraint of the injured party to scream aloud the circumstances of his degradation. Mrs. Morgenstern is particularly alarmed to see that he's grown so skinny—a weight loss of fifteen pounds in two weeks—does this mean that her boy is *eluding her in the flesh*? Vera R_____ is also "alarmed" and "shocked" when by accident she encounters Saul in the university library, he looks so sallow, so "old," "not himself". . . . Speaking idly but lucidly in the coffee shop he reads to her selected passages from "Last Days," explaining the principles of desecration [DE-(reversal) + (CON)SECRATE]: these principles necessary in order that G-d be summoned back to the community. First, there is the desecration of the SABBATH, the holiest day of the week; then, the desecration of the SYNAGOGUE, the holiest place; if possible, the desecration of the BIMAH, the most sacred place in the synagogue; the desecration of the HOLINESS OF THE RABBI; The desecration of the PUBLIC RITUAL. . . . ("By which I mean that a 'counter-ritual' is performed not only in view of the members of the congregation, and by extension all the Jews of the world, but *the entire world of non- and anti-Jews itself*," Saul says.) Vera R_____ confesses that her underlying instinct was simply to escape her old (former) (doomed) (depressing) friend. She "maybe" told three or four people about the conversation. In truth she didn't take it altogether seriously because Saul had been talking along such lines for months and you didn't know whether Suicide to him meant an actual act or a metaphor (as in one of his favorite expressions, "the suicidal drift of our generation . . ."), you didn't know whether an elaborate exegesis of the principles of desecration was something he had dreamt up himself or appropriated from one of his masters, Buber, say, or Eliade. And in any case, says Vera R_____, he spoke in so calm and low-keyed and even *fatigued* a voice, it didn't seem that anything urgent was being pressed upon her. He said too as she was leaving that he probably wouldn't be seeing her again—he had been accepted as a tutorial student at the Jung Institute in Zurich and would be leaving the first of March.

Saul walks as many as eight or nine miles in the falling snow, in the cruel swirling winds. A "living snowman": hatless, gloveless, wearing only his shoes, lightweight socks. Is he cold? Are his teeth chattering? His skin is so hot that snow melts and runs down his cheeks in rivulets like tears. He arrives as if against his will at his married sister's house in Bay Ridge: ". . . with no explanation, just walking in and announcing he was starving, he hadn't eaten all day, I'd better prepare him something to eat or he'd collapse. Della and I were both terrified, he walked in without knocking or ringing the doorbell, we thought it was a madman at first. . . ." He arrives at the university library from which he has been barred by an "executive order" of the provost: he only wants to test the thoroughness of the security police. (The doors are unguarded. The librarians don't recognize him. No one "sees" him, in fact.) He arrives at Flanagans on Fifteenth Street where he sits with a group of (former) friends and acquaintances, a long rowdy table that shifts as the hours pass (from approximately nine in the evening to one-thirty in the morning), being most crowded and friendly around eleven. In the dim light he insists upon reading passages from an "obscene" and "outrageous" book titled *The Fallacy of the 'Final Solution'*—"some book by a writer no one had ever heard of, Saul claimed he's stolen it from the bookstore, the thesis being that the Holocaust had never occurred, it was only 'public relations' on the part of the Jews. . . . The book *was* fairly outrageous but when I asked Saul why didn't he just throw it away, who gives a damn about a nut like that, he didn't even seem to hear me, he just looked through me, then went back to the book, leafing and paging through it. . . . He said that someone had told him not to pollute his spiritual energy with sick people, it might have been a professor or a rabbi, or his father, Saul was never very clear who it was, only that he'd said in rebuttal, 'But it's *sick people* we have got to help.'" He is radiant with certainty, his eyes shine, his hands no longer shake. He says: "Some of the Holocaust survivors believed that simple survival was resistance but what does that mean for us . . . ? Simple survival is defeat now. It's succumbing to the enemy." No one argues, no one even questions him. Perhaps no one hears.

Saul arrives at the synagogue just as Rabbi Engelman is concluding his sermon. He has been sleeping a stuporous "David Gridlock" sleep for forty-eight hours. Reverently he puts a yarmulke on his head, unobtrusively he enters the sanctuary at the rear (left), makes his way along the aisle at the far left, walking slowly, calling little or no attention to himself. He takes his seat in the same pew with members of his mother's family but doesn't catch sight of his mother or sister at first. He has heard the sermon before and has no need to hear it again. All the words have been spoken, *all* the words, Saul clutches this excruciating truth to his chest and belly, a clawing beast, clawing and tearing and pulling at his guts, and sits slightly hunched over. He is breathing shallowly through his mouth. The pistol is comfortably in his pocket along with five or six Smith & Wesson cartridges. The speech in the envelope has been carefully prepared, typed, proof-read. *I make this congregation a present of my life, before you can take it from me.* The pawnbroker's assistant in Toledo will not remember him.

After the first breakdown in Ann Arbor his father said: You've been poisoned by books. (Saul had just read a passage from Kafka, in a high ringing accusing voice, and thrown the book down on a table.) According to friends who remember Saul's anecdote he shouted triumphantly in the (angry? frightened?) man's face: What should I have been poisoned by,—*you?*

The room is dimly and vaguely oval. There are no windows. There are queer and somehow frightening indentations in the walls. . . . When Saul approaches the wall it shrinks away. He knows he must escape because his oxygen supply is diminishing but there are no windows, no doors, no actual walls. . . . Suddenly he sees his own body lying at the front of the synagogue. His arms and legs are outspread, he is vomiting blood. Is he "conscious" or "unconscious," is he "in terrible pain" or "beyond pain". . . ? The commotion is distracting, the place is a madhouse, screams, wails, a stampede in the aisles, where is his mother . . . ? It is the dying rabbi the congregation mourns but Saul can't see where he has fallen. One shot in the side of the neck, the second in the upper left arm, the third into the left eye and into the brain. . . . Abruptly the image dissolves and Saul finds himself in an unfamiliar dark that isn't dark enough. The ghostly outline of his single window disturbs his sleep, a mottled patch of light from the street that falls slantwise across his ceiling. . . .

Once Saul confided in his closest friend Freddy C———— (who later betrayed him) that he was "afraid." "Afraid of what?" Freddy asked. "Just afraid," said Saul. After a long uneasy moment Freddy said, blinking and staring at his feet, "Well—I guess I am too." But now Saul isn't at all afraid because the Sabbath services are always taped and everything he says will be preserved for the record. His elegant speech of denunciation won't be distorted or mangled or misquoted. And he is well-informed enough to know that the crucial area of the brain is at the base of the skull, he won't fail to fire directly into it, he has always been something of a physical coward but this lies in the province of abstract logic. In "Last Things" he puzzles over the fact that in life *as it is actually lived* we feel very little genuine emotion: it is after an event, perhaps even years afterward, when we "remember," that we imagine we also "feel." *Hence an episode as it is actually lived (performed) may be without any emotion whatsoever.*

The elder of the two cantors has opened a prayerbook at the lectern and Rabbi Engelman has returned to his seat when Saul reasons that it is time to make his move. Lithe and unhesitating, though still somewhat hunched over, he rises and comes forward with the pistol in his hand. If he has worried that his voice won't be forceful enough, that it will turn shrill at the climactic moment, he was mistaken—it is vibrant and manly beyond his most intoxicated dreams.

*All who are gathered here this morning . . . an outrage and an abomination . . . a betrayal of the sacred heritage of. . . . Deceit, worship of false gods, mendacity, hypocrisy. . . . I alone raise my voice in protest . . . I alone utter the forbidden thought. . . . Did the Jews of Europe bring upon themselves the cruel justice of the Holocaust. . . . Do the Jews of the "New World" bring upon themselves. . . .*

He runs in the stinging swirling snow to hail the Greyhound bus as it is pulling away from the curb. He runs through the woods at dawn, in his green windbreaker, not minding how the branches of trees and bushes claw against his face. ("Don't be so faint-hearted, time is running out," he says when he meets one of his numberless girls in a coffee shop on State Street and she professes shock at his bleeding forehead and cheeks. "Don't you know we're in the *last days* of this era—?") He's exhausted, he wants to press his face against his mother's breasts and burrow in deep, deep. He's exuberant, trotting out to I-95 by way of the back fields of the Ft. Spear hospital grounds, an illicit $15 snug in his pocket. Who can stop him? What is the magic word that can stop him?

To the dazed congregation it must look as if Rabbi Engelman is welcoming him on the bimah. As if the performance has been rehearsed. "I know this young man," the rabbi says in a high stern courageous voice. "I know this young man and I trust him," he says, raising his voice to be heard over the murmurs, the isolated screams, the faint falling incredulous cries. Saul bounds up the steps to the bimah, to the sacred place, pistol raised like a scepter. He smiles calmly into a blur of light, a pulsing radiance in which no single face can be discerned. Why had he ever imagined fear, why had he ever imagined failure? He belongs to History now. Every syllable will be taped and preserved. "I know this young man and I trust him," the rabbi is saying, insisting. "I don't fear him. Please do as he says. Please do not anger him. Of course we are willing to listen to him, of course he may have the lectern and the microphone and our undivided attention. . . ."

The surrender of one generation to another, Saul thinks. The aged battered wolf, king of the pack, baring his throat to the fangs of the next king. "Thank you, Rabbi Engelman," he says in a strong formal voice.

He takes his speech of denunciation out of his pocket and begins to read.

Dale S_____, though not present at Adath Israel this morning, will write an article called "The Enigma of Saul Morgenstern, Sacrificial Assassin," to be published in late May in the Sunday supplement of the larger of the two local newspapers: a controversial piece that draws so much attention Dale is led to think (mistakenly, as it turns out) that he might have a career in journalism of a glamorous sort. Freddy C_____ will revise a doctoral dissertation on the subject of "American assassinations" in which Saul Morgenstern is eventually relegated to a lengthy footnote—a reasonably well-received academic study published by Oxford University Press. Sol M_____ tries for months to organize his thoughts on the subject of Morgenstern (did he despise Morgenstern from the very first, did he envy him his brash crazy style, did he think that "basically" Morgenstern was correct, did he think that in fact Morgenstern was insane?)—and eventually fails: *there is too much to say*. Denise E_____, though on the periphery of Saul's "circle," writes an overlong impressionistic piece for the university paper, "The Tragedy of a Lost Soul." Rose P_____ will stubbornly revise a short story over the years, presenting it in various awkward forms to writing workshops in the university's extension school, and rejecting all criticism with the angry rejoinder, "but it happened like this, *it happened exactly like this.*" Saul Morgenstern assassinated Rabbi Engelman of Adath Israel Congregation in full view of eight hundred people by shooting him point blank, three times: the fatal shot entering the brain through the left eye, at a slightly upward angle. Without hesitating he then turned the gun against himself, pressing the barrel just behind his right ear, and pulled the trigger. The impact of the blow sent him staggering backward. His legs spun beneath him, his wet shoes skidded, he fell heavily and never rose again. A witness cited in Rose's story says Saul Morgenstern "stood on tiptoe" when he pulled the trigger. His expression was tight and strained but "radiant." He fell about ten feet from the dying rabbi. His head was nearly touching the base of the Ark. A blood-tinted foam with bits of white matter began to seep from the wound in his head, and, dying, he started helplessly to vomit. At first he vomited bile and blood, and then just blood, a thick flow of blood, a powerful hemorrhage. . . . He was vomiting as he died. (But Rose P_____ wasn't a witness. She isn't Jewish, she never was Saul's lover, she must have read about the assassination-suicide in the newspaper, like everyone else.)

Saul Morgenstern, the Scourge of G-d. His style is outrage tinged with irony and humor. "Black Humor" perhaps but humor nonetheless. He is a marvelous talker, a tireless spinner of anecdotes, tall tales, moral parables. With enviable agility he climbs the steps to the "sacred" space before the congregation. With a burst of extraordinary energy he hauls himself over a six-foot wall (littered with broken bottles, it is afterward claimed) while his friends stand gaping and staring. He risks death, he defies death, knowing himself immortal. The entire performance is being taped. Not a syllable, not a wince, will be lost. He has penciled in last-minute corrections in his fastidious hand, the manuscript awaits its public, he can hear beforehand the envious remarks of his friends and acquaintances and professors. Am I the Messiah, he wonders, with so many eyes upon me?—standing erect at the lectern, the pistol in one hand and the microphone in the other.

ROBERT A. FINK

# MY SONS ASK WHERE GOD LIVES

When I was eight I asked Miss Reese.
She was long as her dresses, hair
thin as snakes dangling to her belt.
She read the Bible every hour just in case.
There was nothing she had missed.
Miss Reese kept me nights
when my folks were out of town.
She sent me off to sleep with prophets
calling flames from heaven, the earth opening
to swallow wicked kids, a pit of fire for unbelievers.
She made it easy to believe.

At Sunday School, they never mentioned this.
The picture on the wall was kind,
pretty as Wally Simpson's mother.
There were children come from everywhere,
all colors. Jesus hugged them like his own.
Every Sunday I would look for me
and the pit that must be in a lower corner
disguised—a well, water the color of sulfur.
I wanted to believe Miss Reese was wrong,
that Jesus never frowned, but I remembered
he had cleared a temple with a whip
and only picked one thief for heaven.

I realize this is no answer.
The pretty God lived on the wall in Sunday School.
I tried to find him in my heart
which is where they said he was. All but Miss Reese
who knew he hid in alleys waiting for a boy
slipped out from church, sneaking home to ride his Schwinn
or play *Army* or try Dad's pipe.
Her God smiled straight as the shiv
he'd slip between the first and second ribs
and twist until he hollowed out a pit,
fit habitation in the gut,
a dripping wound that never healed.

# ON JESUS, TAKING HIS WORD
# ON IMMORTALITY

It is not a question of belief.
The Bible says that even devils believe
and tremble, their humped backs smoldering
still, their horns curled black
recalling the jagged heat of light,
the length of a scream falling.
It is, instead, a matter of faith—
saying to the mountains, *Move!*,
telling a crippled man *rise up and walk*, or
doing what we do as if each poem,
each story told were being written down
somewhere in red letters. It is patience—
learning to watch for the sea
to sift the mountains down to size
thin enough for pockets
or skimming flat across the water.
It is waiting for the man to give it up—
the old alms game, eyes hard behind dark glasses,
one leg folded back until the night
and home down alleys narrow as the eye of storms
or the Red Sea walls. Can we count
the hairs of a head? Or clothe ourselves
in lilies? It is harder than belief.
It is what we pray to find at the end of poems.

THEODORE WEISS

# THE INN

He made it all to make Himself
some company? Why then did each
one, quickly crusted over, become
a creature self-engrossed?
                                    Apples,
luminous yet hard, pushing out
against the world, a bulged,
regardless gaze.
                          And gorging all
the days on juicy worms, the birds
wrapt up in bubbled warblings
of delight.
                    The waters which
reflected well enough, so seemed
to recognize, each feature glossed,
His face;
                and yet, no whore more
fickle, promptly they forgot as if
to make, like any well-run inn,
room for newcomers.
                              Or the mini
creatures and the mammoth, pulling
their shaggy hides over them,
content to burrow down
                                    inside
their shadowy, self-smelling holes.
And men and women, who might
have thrust out light
                              to honor
as it banks the light they bask in,
even more set on themselves,
evolving mazes.
                        Small company,
small comfort in all this! That is,
unless He feels, loving variety,
He's made well enough
                                    composing

such choice masterpieces that brim
over with themselves, He praised
in their complexities.


# THE INN II


First you thought you must
proceed a certain way, uncover
signs and clues this jumbled
world conceals; the mood, time,
place must be exactly right.
But now you see
                    the scapes
wasps are: that war-like star,
leathery, then slithering away,
a lizard makes: the holiday
your woman's eye proclaims:
deploying fireflies,
                    blown
higher and higher as though,
hurled up by their mite flame,
trying again and again to stake
some constellation, lighting
nothing but themselves.
                    Now
you see, wherever you may land,
a likely way is here, that place
you would arrive at: creatures,
woman, firefly, lizard, wasp,
impervious to whims
                    however
wilful, striking off redoubtable
sparks, by their very self-
preoccupation sites and sights
a seer might delight in, you,
like them, too occupied to see.

GLORIA WHELAN

# A DWELLING PLACE FOR DRAGONS

He chose four fish and placed them side by side so that he might admire their elliptical shape and the delicate yellow of their bellies. The rest of the morning's catch were for the alligator, George. In delivering his sermons over the years, the Reverend Donald Wangeman had made the usual gospel allusions to fishermen. It was not until his retirement to Florida that he had become one. And then it had not been his idea.

His doctor, baffled by the Reverend Wangeman's lack of progress and alarmed that a clergyman should despair, had suggested a hobby. The Reverend Wangeman's wife, Betty, agreed with the doctor saying she couldn't clean house properly with her husband underfoot. So each day after breakfast he dutifully set out for the pier with his fishing rod. The rod was one of too many gifts from a congregation whose generosity arose from a bad conscience over having had to insist on the Reverend Wangeman's early retirement. He was cast out. That was how he put it to himself. From long association his simplest thoughts fell into a scriptural mode.

"I'll clean the fish when I get back from feeding George," he said to Betty. He was glad to be through with the day's recreation. For years he had spent mornings in a church office with walls the color of dried leaves and afternoons in the company of the infirm and the grieving. Dazzling sun and sea and svelte, compliant fish should have been a pleasant change, but he could not learn to separate leisure from guilt. He envied his wife whose housekeeping saved her from vacant moments. He knew that in the back of her mind she carried with her, always, a resource of hidden bits of dust and dirt awaiting her attention.

"You're going to have to stop feeding that animal," Betty warned him, not without sympathy. "Evelyn Ackerman said she'd call the sheriff next time she saw George and she means it too. She's worried about George eating Bitsy."

"Evelyn Ackerman is a busybody. George wouldn't touch that foul-smelling, yapping poodle of hers." He was ashamed immediately of his harsh words. Mrs. Ackerman was probably as attached to her dog as he was to George and doubtless for a more wholesome reason, but the thought of something happening to George nudged awake a fear that had lain dormant for many blessed weeks.

Ever since his breakdown, when Donald had become for a time quite irrational, Betty had undertaken the task of bringing gently to his attention as much reality as she thought he could stand. Now she said, "Alligators *have* been known to eat dogs. You shouldn't have named George. Once you start calling something by a name you're bound to become attached to it. I don't know what you see in that creature. It looks like something out of a medieval bestiary. It's . . . " she groped for a word, "excessive."

"There's nothing dangerous in an old man having a foible or two," he was pleading although he knew perfectly well his wife would not be moved by pity where a principle was at stake.

"The sooner you forget about George, the better. There are plenty of other things to do around here besides feeding reptiles. You could start by helping me carry down a load of wash." He had the impression Betty worked at keeping him moving, as though he were a volleyball to be passed rapidly along lest he fall to earth.

In the laundry room they shared with the other residents in their complex, Betty sorted clothes while Donald read the notices taped above the stationary tub. The Questers announced their tours for the month: a local Air Force base, Sanibel for shelling (brown bag lunch), a two-day bus trip to Disneyworld (wheel chairs available). "Mrs. Morgan's having a sale?"

"She's going into a nursing home."

He shook his head. "Her things won't sell. No one has room for them." It was true. Retirees moving south brought with them everything they owned so that in many of the condominiums you had trouble squeezing in and out of the rooms. The residents might have been anticipating the pronouncement of some future anthropologist that their history lay in their possessions. "Don't wait lunch." He kissed the top of his wife's head. "I may take a little walk." He had decided on a plan.

The path to the lagoon led Donald through garden patches available to any resident who cared to tend one. Their neighbor, Mrs. Gutherie's, was full of fleshy roses flourishing beyond decency in the lush climate and blooming long after you tired of their beauty. Here and there a plot held nothing more than a tangle of weeds and a moldy zinnia or two that had outlived the gardener who planted it.

Beyond their own complex, Donald could see other complexes wrested from the surrounding wilderness of cypress swamp. The condominiums appeared identical as if mirrors had been cleverly placed to reflect, endlessly, one single building. Florida was pocked with these havens as though a new glacial age were roaring down, sweeping before it the entire population of the north.

The developer of their own complex had seen in a stream meandering through the swamp a possible advantage. By damming one of the branches he had created a lagoon which he then ringed round with ornamental shrubs bearing flowers in florid reds and yellows. The setting gave the appearance of a crudely tinted photograph, but it brought higher rents.

Donald thumped the bank of the lagoon with a large board he kept hidden beneath the drooping branches of a Norfolk pine. Each day while he waited for George to appear, he worried that something might have happened to the alligator: poachers, poisoned meat, the sheriff's patrol. Mrs. Ackerman was not the only one who wanted to do away with George. There were tenants with visiting grandchildren and those who preferred not to know what lounged in the backwaters.

He did not see the alligator approach until his back parted the water. The landscaped lagoon showed him off to good advantage as an ornate frame will sometimes enhance a primitive painting. The blunt snout with its stockade of teeth swung open to receive Donald's fish. When the fish were gone, George sunk slowly beneath the water, not like the sinking of a ship which is final; but like an orchestra lowered into a pit—the movements below promising future performances.

The alligator's hooded eyes remained above the surface staring at Donald who returned the look. In this daily exchange the alligator tacitly acknowledged his true identity to Donald. It was a little joke between the two of them that he should be nurtured by a man of the cloth. For his part, Donald believed as long as he had the alligator eating out of his hand the rest of the world was safe.

Like many in his profession, Donald had come late in life to the certain knowledge of evil. Though he often spoke of evil from the pulpit, the faces that looked up at him were as against it as he was. Wretchedness, disappointment, suffering were all comfortably familiar to them, but evil was alien, even outlandish. A soldier on the ready, Donald found no enemy to oppose. The battlefield appeared to lie elsewhere and so little by little he began to disarm. He spoke of Paul's charity and John's love. He abandoned the churlish prophets and their endless tales of doom.

Then a year ago a member of his congregation had asked for help for a daughter involved with drugs. "Pastor, I'm ashamed to say this in front of a man like yourself who shouldn't have to hear such things, but she's out on the streets supporting her habit. It's killing me and her mother." The man had covered his face with his hands and sobbed. Donald, in all the years of his ministry, had never put his arm around a parishioner. This was not from any lack of compassion, but because he was afraid the parishioner might flinch. Now he walked over and embraced the man. The daughter had been in one of Donald's confirmation classes. He remembered with regret that he had not succeeded in making her understand the difference between con-substantiation and transubstantiation. Surely, he thought, that had nothing to do with what she had become?

He had promised to call on the girl and learning her address, thought she might find his visit less embarrassing if he were casually dressed, but as he walked through the ruinous neighborhood, Donald found himself longing for the protection of clerical clothes. He dismissed his uneasiness, telling himself a man in his calling had a responsibility from time to time to go unprotected. He reproached himself for not knowing that area of the city and considered how he might do a better job of bringing the misfortune of others to his congregation.

He had difficulty locating the apartment. Many of the decaying buildings lacked numbers. This anonymity seemed to him the worst part of their neglect. When at last he found the address, he mentioned the girl's name to a young man lounging in the doorway. Because the man wore thick glasses Donald believed he would be helpful. Looking more closely, Donald saw eyes so full of malevolence the glasses appeared a protection for others. The man leered knowingly at Donald and pointed to an apartment below street level.

Donald began the descent of a stairway that exhaled garbage and urine. Its darkness was the darkness of the basement stairway of his childhood. As then, he had to discipline himself to keep from looking back over his shoulder. He concentrated on what he might say to the girl. His thoughts ran to Mary Magdalene and even to Paul whose deliverance had been so felicitous. When he knocked at the girl's door, it swung open at once. Donald was shocked to see the girl had dwindled to little more than a wraith; her thin body was a light pencil mark, her hair clotted strings, her eyes large and feverish. She didn't recognize him, but she smiled and drew him into the room.

A backpack rested on a chair. Its contents had spilled to the floor and lay in a silky light-hearted heap. The bed was unmade, the sheets soiled. He thought how shocked Betty would be. On one wall of the basement room someone had painted an orange sun fringed round with rays like a kindergartener's picture. On the opposite wall was the moon with a face drawn on it, but the face was not one a child would draw.

Before Donald could introduce himself, the girl slipped off her light robe and stood naked before him. It was not her corruption that appalled him, but the purity of her slight body. As he fled, she called after him in a desperate voice, "Whatever you want."

The girl began to appear in his dreams. At first she came unbidden, poised and diminutive like the ornament on the hood of an expensive car. Then he found he had only to seek sleep and she was there. This seemed an act of the will and he stopped sleeping.

Shortly after this he had a breakdown, which he did not think of as a breakdown at all, but as a time when everything inside of him was scraped clean, as you would run a spoon around the rind of a melon, scraping away the last bits of flesh. In the months that followed he had tried to replenish himself and was terrified to learn that although the Lord made him the first time, this time he was on his own.

Something dark and shapeless filled the emptiness, creeping up into his head and spilling out of his eyes so that his congregation began to avoid him. When Donald gave the Sunday school lesson the younger children sometimes cried. Reluctantly the vestry took over the running of the church and sent him away lest his derangement become contagious.

The darkness settled in Donald's mind like an incubus. Then one day, shortly after their move to Florida, a miracle occurred. He had been looking out over the lagoon when an alligator surfaced and the sinister presence he had been harboring lifted, gathered itself, and entered the body of the alligator. In his joy and relief he thought of Christ driving the devils into the swine. Donald's only worry was that should something happen to the animal, the devils would be released to re-enter the world. Feeling a terrible responsibility, he began to feed the animal so that he might see him each day and be reassured. Mrs. Ackerman's threat to call the sheriff meant Donald must now find a more remote place where his transactions with the alligator could be carried on in secret.

When the alligator surfaced, switched its tail and began to swim back the way it had come, Donald followed along on the bank. The lagoon narrowed into a stream and the flowering shrubbery and smooth green lawn became thickets and tangles of sawgrass. The alligator moved through the sluggish water just beneath a dense green mat of water hyacinths. When it surfaced, as a wave rolls occasionally on a still sea, the long scaly body was festooned with a cloak of dainty yellow flowers like an ugly old woman in a girlish dress.

Donald made his way through the tall grass, stepping around the little humps of soft mud excavated by crawfish so as not to undo their work. Once he saw a yellow rat snake like a thick coil of hemp lying indolent and satisfied in the sun. Donald's canvas hat with its jaunty plaid hatband protected his head from the noon sun, but his shirt stuck damply to his arms and back. He told himself he was on a fool's errand and was glad Betty was not there to judge him.

There were gaps in the water hyacinths where he could look down into dark water at the darker shapes of black acara swimming in flighty schools. His shoes were wet and reeked of decaying mud. George led him into a cypress swamp, a shadowed, cool place where the footing was treacherous. Donald had to clamber over fallen trees and watch for springs that oozed up through the spongy ground. There was a sharp fetid odor which he could not identify. He knew he had only to follow the river to find his way back, yet he felt lost and worried that he had come too far.

The river petered out into a labyrinth of shallow runnels. The alligator, moving slowly through the muddy broth, was making his way toward a mound of vegetable debris—grasses and sedges. The mound was nearly three feet high and perhaps six to seven feet across.

An alligator, somewhat smaller than George, was draped over the dome of the mound like a modeled handle on the cover of a soup tureen. When the alligator saw Donald, it made little guttural noises. A number of what Donald had taken for sticks lying partially submerged in the swamp, began to writhe toward the grunting mother. There were too many to count. When he looked for George he saw the alligator's snout stretched into a wide paternal grin. Donald trembled. Here in the dark backwaters George had copulated and now there were legions of alligators. Donald saw he would never be able to keep track of them all. People must be warned. Unwatched, the legions would escape into the world.

Although he retraced his steps, nothing was quite familiar; while his back was turned, the terrain had been subtly transformed. When at last he neared the rows of condominiums he thought of Betty ascending the stairway, in her arms a neatly folded pile of clean, fresh-smelling linen. He considered what Betty's reaction would be to the warning he brought and foresaw for himself further appointments with the doctor. What if they put him away? Still he hurried on with his message. They had flung Jeremiah into a dungeon but the old man had not ceased his prophesying. He had admonished Babylon, Damascus, Kedar and Elam. He had warned Hazor it would become a dwelling place for dragons.

Donald stumbled against a shrub. An orange butterfly detached itself and unexpectedly flew at him. Donald ducked out of its way, but the encounter left him shattered and close to tears. It was insupportable that he should be threatened by something so small and delicate. He fell to his knees and waited like Jeremiah for the Lord to deliver him.

DAVID LEHMAN

# FOR I WILL CONSIDER
# YOUR DOG MOLLY

For it was the first day of Rosh Ha'shanah, New Year's Day, day of
remembrance, of ancient sacrifices and averted calamities.
For I started the day by eating an apple dipped in honey, as ritual
required.
For I went to the local synagogue to listen to the ram's horn blown.
For I asked Our Father, Our King, to save us for his sake if not for
ours, for the sake of his abundant mercies, for the sake of
his right hand, for the sake of those who went through fire
and water for the sanctification of his name.
For despite the use of a microphone and other gross violations
of ceremony, I gave myself up gladly to the synagogue's
sensual insatiable vast womb.
For what right have I to feel offended?
For I communed with my dead father, and a conspicuous tear rolled
down my right cheek, and there was loud crying inside me.
For I understood how that tear could become an orb.
For the Hebrew melodies comforted me.
For I lost my voice.
For I met a friend who asked "is this a day of high seriousness" and
when I said yes he said "it has taken your voice away."
For he was right, for I felt the strong lashes of the wind lashing me by
the throat.
For I thought there shall come a day that the watchmen upon the hills
of Ephraim shall cry, Arise and let us go up to Zion unto the Lord
our God.
For the virgin shall rejoice in the dance, and the young and old in each
other's arms, and their soul shall be as a watered garden, and
neither shall they learn war any more.
For God shall lower the price of bread and corn and wine and oil, he
shall let our cry come up to him.
For it is customary on the first day of Rosh Ha'shanah to cast a stone
into the depths of the sea, to weep and pray to weep no more.
For the stone represents all the sins of the people.
For I asked you and Molly to accompany me to Cascadilla Creek, there
being no ocean nearby.
For we talked about the Psalms of David along the way, and the story

of Hannah, mother of Samuel, who sought the most robust bard to remedy her barrenness.

For Isaac said "I see the fire and the wood, but where is the lamb for the offering?"

For as soon as I saw the stone, white flat oblong and heavy, I knew that it had summoned me.

For I heard the voice locked inside that stone, for I pictured a dry wilderness in which, with a wave of my staff, I could command sweet waters to flow forth from that stone.

For I cast the stone into the stream and watched it sink to the bottom where dozens of smaller stones, all of them black, gathered around it.

For the waterfall performed the function of the chorus.

For after the moment of solemnity dissolved, you playfully tossed Molly into the stream.

For you tossed her three times, and three times she swam back for her life.

For she shook the water off her body, refreshed.

For you removed the leash from her neck and let her roam freely.

For she darted off into the brush and speared a small grey moving thing in the neck.

For this was the work of an instant.

For we looked and behold! the small grey thing was a rat.

For Molly had killed the rat with a single efficient bite, in conformance with Jewish law.

For I took the rat and cast him into the stream, and both of us congratulated Molly.

For now she resumed her noble gait.

For she does not lie awake in the dark and weep for her sins, and whine about her condition, and discuss her duty to God.

For I'd as lief pray with your dog Molly as with any man.

For she knows that God is her savior.

JOHN BRAND

# DROPPINGS

Last night we broke bread while it rained. "This-do-in-remembrance-of-me." Why does He need re-membering? Does He think He's Humpty Dumpty? The world has its share of droppings.

During this Holy Thursday worship I prayed for sleep. At night our stained-glass windows turn black, and black was the sleep I prayed for.

> Lord, make the hearts of this people fat,
> And make their ears heavy,
> And shut their eyes . . .

Rain fell on the rain-soaked town. Words fell. I preached on the Fall of God. God rules by falling until He is man. Jesus saves by falling; he kneels and washes the feet of the twelve. I preached all this. Then she had to go and do likewise.

She awaited me after worship in the dark of my study. She of the seven devils I had cast out was calling herself my Magdalene. My first words to her had broken her spell. What could I have said? You are dying of yourself, I said, you do not even know you are cursing the day you were born. Those words broke her spell, she said. Cast out her sins, so she said. Afterwards she came bearing gifts, and this night awaited me in the dark of my study, waited until I had taken off my clerical gown and collar before she stepped out of her corner. I had sweated while preaching and was beginning a chill. She was in her usual wet heat, weeping and begging me to see her again. I said No and she asked Why. I said Because why. She seized my wet shirt at its buttons and begged me to assure her we would be together in the Afterlife. I could assure her no such thing. "Then may I bow before you?" she said. Before I could back off she covered my feet. Lust? Lust, but only for Holy Ground, a pair of feet to fall upon. Hell is being unable to love. Nevertheless, I did not want her devotion near me.

She just had to hear the Good News. A pox on preaching. May my throat become an open sepulchre, for my sermons actually yield returns: hearts are not near heavy enough, stupor is not thick enough. Someone always hears, goes and does likewise—goes down on me. Always on me. Do not misunderstand: I believe in God the Father Almighty, and in Jesus Christ His Only Son—wouldn't you find offensive the mortal who kneels and slobbers over your shoes? Do not misunderstand: Jesus saves, but does not tidy up after Himself. Enter

His chosen: I collect droppings. Every civilization has its collectors and I collect droppings. Somebody has to.

It is still Good Friday and I am awake after dreaming of more prostration, another heat stroke. We were processing towards the Lord's Table when there fell a figure. Her face touched her knees, her hair draped her knees and our crimson carpet. I veered away from the Feast we were there to keep, with its broken loaf, its teeming chalice. The weeping woman grew perfectly still, and it is still Good Friday.

More seepage. And then more. That sodden woman—she is either one who was or is to come. She's to come: this is because droppings always come in threes.

I tried, Lord knows I tried. Grant them hearts of stone, I prayed. Next I pared the liturgy: draped table, pulpit and pews with black ribbon; shut the Book; hid the chalice—only dry heaves allowed. I withheld my voice . . .

The manna that night's rains brought us was sleet. Our church's sloping roof was white, thick and quiet with sleet. Stained-glass windows were black, and we grew black with sleep. It grew on us, it and darkness grew. The nodding began. I nearly nodded for joy until I heard someone about to happen again, about to drop. I always know when.

My wife was angry at me for omitting my sermon. There was no sign of sleep in her black, dilating eyes. She asked why I had denied her. Deny her? Holding fast the sleeve of my gown, she said, "You know I hang on your every word." She held fast until I synopsized what I had intended to preach. The usual: Love is stronger than Death. The crucifixion is a victory because Jesus leaves Death nothing to claim. No booty, no plunder. All has been lavishly let go so that the dead Jesus is empty and therefore conqueror. My wife released my full sleeve, its black rayon spotted with her tears. "I thank my God for every remembrance of you," she managed to say. She wearies me with her love of God.

What had I done to lower her so? I obviously said something again. Old habit: in the beginning is the word and my words do not return unto me void. Preaching? It's spitting in your own face. As I recall, it was not preaching I was doing when I met the woman who would become my wife, but I was speaking, with those words that keep bringing women to my knees. Do not misunderstand: they do not drop their pants, my Magdalene never dropped her pants, they do not drop their pants or mine, they just drop.

We met after a funeral in our sanctuary, where instead of the Lord's Table there was only a coffin. Atop it was no floral spray, no glossy magnolia leaves. Atop it sat a loaf. Next to the loaf, a full chalice. I began the service by breaking the loaf. "If we are united with Him in a death like His," I began. I said Death is the dance God invites us to join.

That day I loved her at first sight, loved her high, sloping cheek-bones, the nape of her erect neck, loved the way she pursed her glacial lips and passed me without saying a word. She was a perfect Winter Beauty. Easy to violate. First sight, first blight.

While others got in the cars forming the procession to the cemetery she lingered in the foyer to the clammy sanctuary. She then approached me and touched my wrist with the tip of her gloved finger. The words conveyed to me by her cool breath were cooling to my cheek. "Will someone please tell me why I bothered to attend?" She called my service a wake, and called me morbid. I turned my other cheek in the direction of her minted breath. "You, Sir, I do not need," she said. If you don't need me, I said, why are you still here? We argued again the next week, and after a while we married.

My Beauty lost her cool bloom. She now weeps with those who weep, and even rejoices with those who rejoice. I infected her, imperfected her. It is not easy to speak to a believing age. I have no one but myself to blame. Once she neared me I knew she was about to drop. I should have joined the funeral procession sooner—wiped the wet from my feet and walked off. The least I could have done was let someone else collect her. I suppose I collected her for the same reason I preach: I'm good at it.

Easter Eve. Lord, now lettest thou thy servant depart in sleep—have I not loathed them that love thee? Cover me with snow. I just dreamed my wife fell out of our bed. I reached for my glasses on the nightstand but by the time I got them on she had fallen away again. She fell out of the house and out of the church-house to the bottom of the high steps leading from the street to our sanctuary. From the depths, she cried, "It is not I who live but Christ who lives in me." I removed my glasses. That seemed a long way to go to collect her.

PETER ORESICK

# RECEIVING CHRIST

after St. John Chrysostom

Not like Judas with a kiss,
but like the good thief
whose broken bones rejoiced.

"The glory of God,
that God *be* God,
is that the poor live."

It is a circumcision
made without hands:
sloughing off the body of flesh,
putting on the body of Christ.

"The glory of God,
that God *be* God,
is that the poor live."

It is to stand
like good Nicodemus and accept the body
as it is lowered down from its cross.

MARGARET AVISON

# THE BIBLE TO BE BELIEVED

The word read by the living Word
sculptured its shaper's form.
What happens, means. The meanings are not blurred
by Flood—or fiery atom.

     He reads: a Jewish-Egyptian
     firstborn, not three years old;
     a coal-seared poet-statesman;
     an anointed twelve-year old.

The Word dwells on this word
honing His heart's sword,
ready at knife-edge to declare
holiness, and come clear.

     Ancient names, eon-brittled eyes,
     within the word, open on mysteries:
     the estranged murderer, exiled, hears at last
     his kinsman's voice;
     the child, confidingly questioning, so close
     to the awful ritual knife,
     is stilled by another, looking to His Father—
          the saving one, not safe.

The Word alive cherishes all:
doves, lambs —or whale—
beyond old rites or emblem burial.
Grapes, bread, and fragrant oil:
all that means, is real
now, only as One wills.

     Yes, he was tempted to wash out
     in covenanting song
     the brand on the dry bone;
     he heard the tempter quote
     the texts he meant and went embodying.

The Word was moved
too vitally to be entombed
in time. He has hewn out
of it one crevice-gate.

His final silencing endured
has sealed the living word:
now, therefore, He is voiceful, to be heard,
free, and of all opening-out the Lord.

# THE BIBLICAL PRESENCE
# IN MODERN ART

Eric Gill (English, 1882–1940). *Eve*. Wood engraving. 4⅞″ × 9⅜″. Courtesy
of the University of Michigan Museum of Art, Gift of Jean Paul Slusser.

Leonard Baskin (American, born 1922). *Ruth and Naomi*, 1978. Bronze. 52″ high. By permission of the artist and courtesy of Kennedy Galleries, Inc., New York.

Leonard Baskin, *Lazarus*, 1959. Bronze. 30.5″ high. By permission of the artist and courtesy of Kennedy Galleries, Inc., New York.

Jacques Lipchitz (French, 1891–1973). *Hagar I*, 1948. Bronze. 35″ high. Courtesy of Marlborough Gallery, New York.

Jacques Lipchitz, *Return of the Prodigal Son*, 1930. Bronze. 8″. Courtesy of Marlborough Gallery, New York.

David Sharir (Israeli, born 1938). *Jacob's Dream*, 1970. Lithograph. 25½″ × 18″.
Courtesy of Michael Hittleman Gallery, Los Angeles.

Jacob Epstein (English, 1880–1959). *Jacob and the Angel*, 1940. Veined
Alabaster. 84″, base 43″ × 46″. Courtesy of Granada Television Collection,
on loan to the University of Liverpool.

Jacob Epstein, *St. Michael Defeating the Devil*, 1958–1962. Bronze. 25 feet.
Coventry Cathedral, Coventry (U.K.)

Graham Sutherland (English, 1903–1980). *Christ in Glory in the Tetramorph*
(final cartoon), 1957. Oil on hardboard. 74″ × 40″.

Max Pechstein (German, 1881–1955). *Vater unser* (from the series *Das Vater Unser*), 1921. Hand-colored woodcut. 16″ × 12″. Courtesy of The University of Michigan Museum of Art.

Max Pechstein, *Dein Reiche komme* (from the series *Das Vater Unser*), 1921.
Hand-colored woodcut. 16″ × 12″.

Michail Grobman (Israeli, born 1939). *Aaron's Cane*, 1976. Screenprint. 22″ × 30″. Courtesy of Michael Hittleman Gallery, Los Angeles.

Karen Rasco (American, born 1956). *Moses Descending Mount Sinai*, 1982.
Photo collage. 7″ × 9″. Courtesy of the artist.

Giacomo Manzù (Italian, born 1908). *Variations on a Theme, One* (from the series "Variations on a Theme," 1955–65). Bronze bas-relief. 32″ × 16″.

Giacomo Manzù, *The Death of Stephen* (study for the Vatican door), 1963.
Study for bronze bas-relief. 37″ × 25″.

Ernst Barlach (German, 1870–1938). *Der Erste Tag* (from the series "Transformations of God," 1920). Woodcut. 14⅜″ × 10¼″. Courtesy of The University of Michigan Museum of Art.

*FIVE*

# THE POLITICS OF
# THE HOLY LAND

CAROL MEYERS

# THE ISRAELITE EMPIRE:
# IN DEFENSE OF KING SOLOMON

## I. Evaluating the Israelite Empire

For a fleeting period of time in the millennia of human existence and civilization in the ancient Near East, the narrow strip of land between the Jordan River and the Mediterranean Sea was united under a centralized government and controlled by indigenous rulers. With its core settlements in the hill country of Ephraim and Judah, the kingdom of ancient Israel spread out northward into Galilee, westward to the coast, and eastward along the Transjordanian plateau. These territories constituted the domain of the Davidic Monarchy, which was superimposed over the tribal organizations that had held sway over this portion of the Levant during the several hundred years preceding David's accession to kingship around the year 1000 B.C.E.

The fragility of such a unified governing system in the pre-modern Levant is apparent from the minute place it occupies in the register of political configurations that rose and fell in the Fertile Crescent. The tenuousness of such a system is also abundantly clear from the major, virtually the only, source for our knowledge of its existence, the Hebrew Bible. The historical books of the Bible record the difficulty with which the Davidic dynasty was established in its rule over the twelve tribes and describe the agony that marked its breakdown into the tiny southern Kingdom of Judah after only one other monarch, David's son Solomon, had occupied the Davidic throne.

The concern of the biblical sources for the emergence and the dissolution of the United Kingdom tends to obscure the fact that that kingdom was not a simple self-contained national state but rather was the seat of an empire. To be sure, it was an empire of modest proportions in comparison with the empires that normally held sway in Egypt to the south and in Syria and Mesopotamia to the north and east. Indeed, it was to some extent the faltering of those superpowers that created the power vacuum which enabled the Israelite kingdom to secure its short-lived hegemony over neighboring polities. Yet Israel during the time of David and Solomon, during the Golden Age of the United Monarchy, was nonetheless a minor imperial power.

That fact has rarely been properly appreciated in the ongoing scholarly efforts to evaluate the Davidic dynasty. Since the international scope of affairs was not the primary concern of the biblical historiographers, modern historians have quite naturally focused upon the internal working of the monarchy and upon the individual characteristics of the various rulers. In particular, because the United Monarchy consisted of the reigns, each roughly four decades in duration, of only two kings, evaluations of any kind—theological, political, sociological—have tended to consist of comparisons of the reigns of David and Solomon. (The antecedent reign of Saul is a different matter.)

David was the first Israelite "emperor"—the initiator, the brilliant and perhaps charismatic warrior who brought all the tribes together under unified rule and extended his sovereignty over a succession of surrounding territories. Solomon was the second and also the last "emperor," who held the disparate territorial components together for an unprecedented period of stability, who created a glorious cosmopolitan capital and built up a series of royal cities throughout the land. Is it not fair to ask, then, whether the very fact of Solomon's being the terminating figure in this brief and uncharacteristic Levantine political configuration predisposes both ancient sources and modern investigators to favor David over Solomon?

In the ancient sources David is clearly favored. He looms large as the dynastic figure *par excellence*, against whom all subsequent rulers are measured and on whom the eschatological model of a messianic ruler is based. In examining the biblical sources for the monarchic history, the two books each of Samuel, Kings, and Chronicles, one is struck by the preponderance of Davidic material. In those six biblical books, 151 chapters deal with 434 years of dynastic succession in Israel and Judah. Sixty of those chapters, or nearly 40 percent of biblical historiography, focus on the reign of one figure, David, whose reign of about forty years constituted less than 10 percent of the duration of the dynasty he founded. Solomon, with eighteen biblical chapters reporting his reign, comes in a poor second. In another kind of quantitative reckoning, we see David's name mentioned nearly 800 times in the Hebrew Bible; Solomon's name appears fewer than 300 times.

There are complex reasons for such discrepancies, not the least of which is that David as a warrior and a man of violent actions was involved in a sucession of deeds which, by their very nature, provoked literary activity in a way that the manifold activities of Solomon, for whom no personal military action is recorded, could never have achieved. David's exploits and accomplishments on the battlefield, and his dramatic victory in the power struggle between rival kinship factions, constitute success stories appealing to a popular audience. One wonders how that fact skews historical perspective, favoring the perpetrator of violence and slaughter, which are the concomitants of the successful wielding of military power, over the manipulator with symbols and words, even while recognizing that Solomon's ability to wield power with words was contingent upon Davidic military achievements.

The modern scholar nonetheless must utilize the overwhelmingly pro-David biblical sources in considering the reigns of the only two indigenous emperors ever to have ruled from a Jerusalem throne. A tendency to aggrandize David and to be disparaging of Solomon understandably characterizes many scholarly treatments of the monarchy and of Israelite history. While the Bible has clearly built the pedestal upon which David has been placed, it does not provide evidence of the Oriental despotism and monarchical tastes for grandeur, or disdain for simpler times and traditions, that are often ascribed to the Solomonic reign. The tendency to depict Solomon with such negative constructs draws not simply from the biblical predominance of David but also from the complexity of western religious traditions and biblical scholarship. The seeming materialism and burgeoning economic development of the Solomonic era have been pulled out of their ancient imperial context and measured unconsciously against western puritanical and democratic modes.

By acknowledging these subtle influences on evaluations of David and Solomon, we can go back to the biblical sources and reconsider more fairly the relative contributions of the two Israelite emperors. In addition, recognition of the empire status of the domains of these two figures is essential to a proper perspective on their respective merits. Precisely at that point, understanding the Israelite kings as emperors, the value of social scientific research for analyzing ancient polities, with their various social organizations and ideologies, becomes relevant. The biblical imbalance of information can be overcome to the extent to which the actions of David and Solomon can be related to what social scientists have observed about the dynamics of empires of various kinds.

The use of social scientific methodologies and data to flesh out and evaluate critically the theologically-oriented stance of most of the biblical sources for ancient Israel is hardly an innovative endeavor. The name of Max Weber stands out among the giants of sociology as one who investigated Israel through the lens of sociological analysis. But he hardly stands alone. The beginnings of Israelite existence in the pre-monarchic tribal era have most recently and most thoroughly been subjected to and illuminated by the kind of investigation that sociological and anthropological methodologies and models can bring to biblical studies.

The monarchy too has long been subjected to institutional analysis. However, as we have already hinted, such analyses suffer from the distortion of the internal perspective of the biblical sources themselves, which focus on the national and religious aspects of the kingdom rather than on its international configurations, as well as from the biblical bias towards the exaltedness of David. In addition, the recent close attention to the tribal period has led naturally to a concentration upon the dynamics of the actual emergence of a nation-state rather than upon the dynamics of organization and operation within a nation-state with a supranational domain.

Political theorists and sociologists with an historical interest have been active in their descriptions and classifications of expansionist societies, or empires, and various criteria which characterize imperial powers have been identified, even if they have not yet been studied in a sufficiently systematic way. Such criteria suggest we must place the Davidic state within the category of a pre-modern empire, that is, a supranational state with a centralized bureaucracy ruled by a monarch with claims to traditional-sacred legitimacy.

The definition of empire is no less a problem for the monarchic period than is the matter of the definition of tribe for the pre-monarchic period of ancient Israel. Much of the difficulty in defining empire lies in describing the motivation in the establishment of an empire. Since certain negative connotations attach themselves to the notion of empire, which necessarily involves exploitation, there is a certain amount of bias in considering motivation. Thus it seems important to ascertain first if a given power sought to expand territorially from an ideology of its own superiority and concomitant right to extend its domination. Such a situation would seem to constitute a policy of pure aggression, and, if it does exist, might properly be designated "imperialistic." The Macedonian empire of Philip and Alexander may be an example.

Alternately, other expansionist powers can be shown to have constructed their positions of supranational domination from an initial aim of self-defense or for the procurement of additional resources when their own territories did not provide sufficient productivity to meet internal population demands. Such origins of empire have sometimes been dubbed "accidental imperialism," in which initial success in wars of defense gained momentum and led to extensions of the need to protect ever-widening frontiers. "Defensive imperialism" would be another descriptive term applied to such conditions. Early Rome is a case in point.

## II. Davidic Expansion and Rule

The Davidic expansion clearly can be classified among the empires arising from the defensive or accidental sort of empire-building. It should thus escape some of the opprobrium that attaches to imperialistic states. The Davidic monarchy arose at least in part as a result of David's wars against the Philistines; accounts of this turbulent struggle occupy a major portion of the military narratives of the books of Samuel. The Israelite tribes and the Philistine city-states, after nearly two hundred years of coexistence, had each prospered internally and grown enough so that control of the fruitful grain-producing Shephelah, the lowland region which constituted their common border, had become critical, especially for Israel. The Philistines seem to have had an Egyptian liaison which perhaps stimulated politically their growing expansionism and upon which they could rely to some extent for military aid or economic assistance. Israel had no such support.

David's course of action exhibited characteristics common to most, if not all, empires in their stages of formation. Founding dynasts need not be noble born; David, as the poor son of a farmer, was hardly among the leaders of his people. Lower-class origins are not at all unusual, considering that the overturning or superseding of the previous political system is typical of the beginnings of an empire.

Normally a period of increasing internal turmoil, accompanying external threats or pressures, is the grounding for the emergence of a leader whose rise to power is predicated upon his ability to resolve acute unrest and to establish security and order. David's career surely demonstrates such an ability. He pulled the Israelite tribes out of the murky anarchy into which they had sunk and proceeded to establish both unity within and security along the borders. The remarkable Davidic achievement required a monopoly of the decision-making processes and the authority to draw upon human and material resources which the old form of tribal confederation could not provide. The monarchic system, perhaps built upon an intermediate chiefdom stage under Saul, was indispensable to Davidic successes on the battlefield.

Such centralization of power is rarely unchallenged, and the so-called anti-monarchic component of the Samuel books is witness to the existence of such a challenge in Israel's case. The opposition of traditional groups is characteristically met by a successful ruler in his utilization of key portions or features of the old order. David seems to have been extraordinarily successful in incorporating tribal traditions in the integrated religio-political sphere into the vastly different centralized system of a monarchy. His loyalty to the Yahwistic ark traditions may have stemmed from deep personal convictions that he held, yet the political expediency of centering his dynastic formation upon this ancient symbol and its attendant values should not be overlooked. The traditional-sacred legitimacy claimed by David as ruler afforded him the support of traditional tribal leaders whose authority and autonomy would otherwise be threatened by the authority of a centralized monarchical government.

The Davidic war machine did not stop at the task of securing the immediate borders of the unified Israelite tribes. Successful warfare in and of itself, in some ways, leads to further territorial expansion. The economic needs of supporting an army and then the newly-acquired arsenal lead to acquisition of new lands, of new sources of revenue. More personnel and increased quantities of support materials are required as the conqueror acquires both territory and the accompanying need to provide for the administration of that territory. The emotional flush of victory likewise propels the warrior on to further conquests, which then provide the material means either for additional advances and/or for domestic development. This combination of economic and personal factors is reflected in the abbreviated account in 2 Samuel 8 of Davidic victories over neighboring states. David extended his economic power base with the tribute and the booty of foreign conquests: "And David took the shields of gold which were carried by the servants of Hadadezer, and brought them to Jerusalem. And from Betah and Berothai, cities of Hadadezer, King David took a great deal of bronze (2 Sam 8:7, 8)." Such were the economic rewards of conquering Aram Zobah, the domain of Hadadezer. David acquired similar spoil, silver and gold, "from all the nations he subdued, from Edom, Moab, the Ammonites, the Philistines, Amalek" (2 Sam 8:11–12). In addition, David's supremacy and might were acknowledged by states that he did not directly defeat: Toi, King of Hamath, sent a delegation led by his son and bearing "articles of silver, of gold, and of bronze" (2 Sam 8:10). All those goods are reported to have been collected and "dedicated to the Lord." David combined political with traditional, sacred orientations and thus provided continuity with the Yahwistic base of tribal Israel.

This extraordinary success, and the attendant economic benefits to his kingdom, allowed David to establish "justice and equity for all his people" (2 Sam 8:15) and to provide the internal security which is the immediate and motivating goal of an emergent imperial ruler. However, along with this security came the need to establish a bureaucracy to handle the territories and revenues generated by the territorial acquisitions as well as to provide the mechanisms of the internal administration of a state-level political organization. David had to establish garrisons in the conquered states and set up procedures for the collection and redistribution of the revenues of empire. It is no accident that the description of military subjection (and slaughter) in 2 Samuel 8 is coupled with a schematic delineation of the administrative structure he initiated. Empire brings with it the need for bureaucracy. The specialization of tasks under administrators personally loyal to the ruler, so that he controls the administrative power, is a requisite feature of an expanded nation-state. David fits such a pattern in his establishment of a small cabinet of officers responsible for military, political, economic, and cultural affairs. 2 Sam 8:15–18 enumerates the officers of David's incipient bureaucracy. While the specific identity and function of each of the officers is not always clear, their combined role as the top level of a bureaucratic structure is evident.

From a period later in his reign, a somewhat altered set of officers is listed in 2 Sam 20:23–26. As much as possible, continuity with the old loyal ministers was an evident goal. As in the first listing, the general of the armies appears first in the order of the ministers, attesting to the primacy of military affairs in the Davidic organization. Further, the military faction appears to have been tightened during the course of David's reign. The leader of the mercenary troops of Cherethites and Pelethites, listed near the end of the first roster of ministers, has been placed immediately following the name of the commander-in-chief by the time of the second list.

The scattered bits of information about Davidic administration that can be gleaned from the biblical record, such as these lists of officers, reveal the preliminary stages in the establishment of the necessary organs of management to handle the various activities of a supra-national state. The organization is still oriented internally and traditionally as far as possible while allowing David the flexibility of independent decision and action. There is no indication that David reorganized the unified tribes internally, despite what he may have superimposed upon their long-established patterns of communal structure. By his personal command of the loyalty of their leaders, he could rely upon and utilize existing patterns of organization.

David's foreign policy was by and large identical with his military activities. He appears to have allowed the internal political systems of the states he conquered to have continued to function, especially with respect to the expanded Aramean kingdom of Hadadezer, which was not contiguous with Israelite borders and which stretched to the Euphrates, as well as to the territory of Hamath. The repute of David's military might was evidently strong enough to elicit, without undue restructuring of the conquered territories, the revenues demanded by his growing kingdom.

The military dimension of the establishment of the Davidic empire must be emphasized. Any imperial subjugation is essentially a system of unbalance, of coercion, whereby the productivity of subservient groups is transferred for the benefit of distant consumers, i.e., the imperial power. The setting up of such an exploitative system is normally achieved at the level of physical action, by military brutalization and through the fear of such. Military power in the initial stage of empire overcomes the resistance of a population in order to transfer the products of its labor to a distant and alien group. Battlefield victories are closely followed by the establishment of garrisons within the conquered territories to extend the threat of destruction and thus the coercive power of the conqueror. David's reign, his energies and his interests, belongs rather consistently to this effective, initial dimension of supranational subjugation.

## III. Solomonic Expansion and Rule

With the accession of Solomon to the throne, the momentum of Israelite military conquest was terminated. The "conquest phase" which characterizes the beginnings of empire and constitutes the very manner of its establishment had been so successful under Davidic direction that Solomon was left with full arsenals, a well-organized military structure, and secure borders at least to the north and east. Solomonic rule, freed from the preoccupation with warfare, belongs to a distinct subsequent stage of imperial activity.

One generation removed from the personal loyalty which had allowed the charismatic David to command the cooperation and support of existing tribal government, Solomon needed to impose stronger administrative and economic control over internal matters. A new position was introduced to the Solomonic version of the cabinet, delineated in 1 Kings 4:2–6. A man named Azariah was put in charge of the tribal districts. While the relative tribal autonomy of Davidic times was thereby diminished, Solomon does seem to have retained old patrimonial allotments as far as possible in the redistricting he organized. He apparently sought to draw new revenues from within Israel to offset his mammoth expenses and yet assure the well-being and stability of his kingdom.

The most remarkable feature of Solomonic imperial rule is the international aspect of his long occupation of the Davidic throne. The biblical record of Solomon's reign provides ample evidence of this. For example, his extensive marital ties, described in the stylized language of 1 Kings 11:4 as "seven hundred wives, princesses, and three hundred concubines," involved largely foreign women. He established trading routes and commercial ties with distant lands in Africa and Asia. Representatives of other countries, such as the Queen of Sheba, came from far and wide and with elaborate retinues to visit the royal complex that Solomon constructed in Jerusalem.

These and other related aspects of Solomonic rule are the source of the criticism, going back to the biblical account itself, that tends to permeate discussion of David's successor. The international community that Solomon established in Jerusalem was seen by the biblical author as diluting time-honored Yahwism: "When Solomon was old his wives turned away his heart after other gods, and his heart was not wholly true to the LORD his God as was the heart of David his father" (1 Kings 11:4). There may in fact be justification in questioning Solomon's values. However, to follow in the evaluative footsteps of the biblical editor by appraising materialism and grandeur, to say nothing of dealings with foreign nations, as independent and self-designed features of Solomonic rule is to look at them in meaningless isolation. Within the context of the empire that David had established, the commercial and material accomplishments of Solomon were as essential a set of instruments of rule as were the weapons and warriors of David's court. Solomon's projects and policies, internal and external, belong to a post-conquest phase of empire and are inextricably connected with the results of Davidic conquest.

The physical imposition of Israelite unity and dominion in the Levant achieved under David through charismatic leadership and warfare at the beginning of the tenth century B.C.E. was sustained by Solomon for another forty years through diplomacy and ideology. The coercion introduced by military might was continued by ideological pressure, whereby both Solomon's bureaucrats and the foreign representatives with whom they dealt were convinced of the legitimate right of the Solomonic national state to withdraw resources from the dependent or conquered states.

The immediate and essential component of that ideological framework was divine legitimization of the monarchy. David had already accomplished such legitimization internally by unifying the tribes around the Ark of the Lord and by his covenant with tribal leaders "before the Lord" (2 Sam 5:3) at Hebron. Establishment of a capital in Jerusalem, acceptable to both northern and southern tribes, was concretized by the transfer of the Ark of the Lord to the City of David and by the public ceremonies accompanying that event.

Solomon was challenged to extend that legitimization to a supra-national level. It was incumbent upon him to maintain the loyalty of his bureaucracy and also to sustain the tributary status of his vassals by promulgating an ideology that legitimated his imperial rule. Jerusalem became, not simply the capital of a nation state, but rather the "center" of an empire and the locus of activities and structures that impinged upon the "periphery," upon territories removed from the Israelite state in which Jerusalem was located. The impact of that center on the local population of the periphery mainly took the form of exaction of tribute; little internal restructuring of peripheral communities seems to have been effected. Yet the ability of Solomon to extract taxation rested upon the notion of his dynastic supremacy.

The process of holding the notion of the supremacy of the center, in the post-conquest phase of empire, rests to a great extent upon the establishment of the symbols of identity of the conquering power, normally the deities to whom the imperial ruler attributes his success. For Israel, this meant that the national legitimization of Davidic rule under Yahweh needed to be extended internationally. Solomon's construction of an elaborate temple building and cultus in Jerusalem served such supranational aims. The temple provided on an international level what the ark had provided on a national level; it was the symbolic representation of Yahweh's presence in Jerusalem.

To be effective, the royal ideology of a divinely-chartered kingship had to be communicated, both to Solomon's Israelite administrators and also to representatives of the foreign populations under Israelite subjugation. The message of divine sanction of Solomonic rule in Jerusalem required both vehicles of communication and modes of expression. The immediate audiences for this message were the bureaucracy and the royal court. Rather than being the products of a macho personality, Solomon's foreign wives, with their entourages, brought persons close to the subjugated monarchs into the royal citadel and under the direct influence of the palace. With this audience at hand, the construction of a temple and palace were as essential to the functioning of an empire in its second stage as were the military campaigns of the initial stage. The elaborate temple building was the dramatic visual statement of Yahweh's legitimation of Solomonic rule.

The Jerusalem temple, in a sense, came into being not from any internal impulse for the centralized ark tradition to find permanent housing but rather from the pressure on an international capital to demonstrate to the representatives of the conquered peoples that Israel had the right to dominate. Jerusalem, in erecting a temple, acquired the visual means of communicating its status of center in a language that would be readily comprehended by Near Eastern populations. If the artistic embellishments of the temple as they can be understood from the biblical description seem closest to the architectural and artistic traditions of the major Syro-Hittite cities, it is because those cities held precisely the populations that Solomon needed to reach with his message of Yahwistic supremacy.

Temples in the ancient Near East, the Jerusalem temple among them, both represented and stood at the center of the cosmos. Through various architectonic practices, temple buildings created a microcosm of the universe and provided for the regime with which they were associated its *raison d'être*. Although not a trace of the Jerusalem temple is available archeologically, an elaborate account of its construction in 1 Kings 6–8 provides plentiful information about its size and character. In comparison with other Syro-Palestinian sacred structures of the end of the Late Bronze Age or the beginning of the Iron Age, for which ground plans have been recovered through excavation, the Jerusalem building seems to have been the largest and probably the grandest (although comparison of embellishments is less feasible, since few of the furnishings and little of the superstructures of those other temples have survived). This striking fact is fully in accord with the Solomonic empire's unique position as the most extensive polity to have existed in ancient Syria-Palestine.

The existence of the temple of Yahweh in the palace complex was the typical and effective Near Eastern manner for communicating to the palace officials as well as to foreign emissaries that the king was carrying out Yahweh's will in his dominion over Israel and all the conquered territories. On the visual level, it proclaimed to those who saw it the message of royal Israelite supremacy under divine sanction. That a foreign audience, perhaps even more than the domestic one, was intended for the temple structure, is perhaps indicated by the place that the temple-building project occupies within the structure of 1 Kings. The descriptions of the Jerusalem temple (and palace) and its dedication appear in 1 Kings 5–9, immediately after the account of the extent of Solomon's political empire in 1 Kings 4:20–34 and before the Queen of Sheba episode and the listing of Solomon's trading connections in 1 Kings 10. The centrality of Jerusalem thus holds together the concept of empire, which includes both the politically dependent states as well as those with more mutual commercial ties.

The trading empire of the Solomonic regime is not unrelated to the symbolic role of the capital as center, politically and symbolically. As microcosm, a center should contain all the elements of the world. Therefore, it must bring into itself elements of the remote corners which it controls and also with which it has less direct, or commercial, contacts. The use of a variety of imported materials in the construction of the Solomonic temple and palace and also the accumulation of goods in the royal or sacred treasuries constituted the concrete portrayal of the center's domination of the periphery. It was not simply a demonstration of exotica and wealth that Solomon effected; it was a message of Jerusalem's cosmic centrality and therefore of its right to dominate. If imported monkeys and rare ivories, among other precious commodities, were part of the Jerusalem scene, according to the information in 1 Kings 10, the whole of creation was thus contained within the center of creation.

The royal capital in Jerusalem, with its splendid temple and even more resplendent palace, was the visual centerpiece of Solomonic imperial ideology. But were temple and palace the only means by which Solomon's message of Yahwistic/Israelite supremacy reached the peripheral populations and their leaders or representatives? As important as visual statements and concrete monuments were for the preliterate world, they cannot be deemed the sole modes of communication. Not all the world was literally present in Jerusalem, despite the fact that the dedication of the royal complex was celebrated in a great feast attended by "Israel [and] a great assembly, from the entrance of Hamath to the Brook of Egypt" (1 Kings 8:65).

Written or literary accounts, to be read or to be divulged orally, no doubt constituted a complementary form of communication. The official description and interpretation of events had to be organized in texts that could traverse, whether on papyrus and tablets or in the heads of messengers, the distances between the center in Jerusalem and the peripheral polities. The hypothetical nature of such documents is given some suggestive support by the fact that the biblical historiographer points to a distinct and discrete source for his information about Solomon.

The nine chapters, 3–11, of 1 Kings that deal with the Solomonic era constitute a self-contained and highly-structured work. These chapters, with their unifying themes of Solomonic wealth, honor, and wisdom, stand out as unique in biblical historiography even though they are carefully integrated into the narrative of the Book of Kings. In addition, the biblical editor himself has cited as a source for these chapters an independent extra-biblical (and non-extant) work, called the Book of the Acts of Solomon (1 Kings 11:41), which is the only such extra-biblical work associated with a single Israelite king. Not even for David is such a source mentioned.

Other biblical narratives dealing with the monarchy cite what appear to be royal annalistic records, the "Book of the Chronicles of the Kings of Judah" or the "Book of the Chronicles of the Kings of Israel." Yet those sources, both because of their titles—the use of the word "chronicles"—and because of their comprehensiveness in that they were probably ongoing court records, seem to have been of a different order from the Solomonic source. The nature of the Solomonic source is given in its citation: "all that he did, and his wisdom." Unlike other biblical citations in Kings, "wisdom" is part of the contents of the work cited. This parallels the fact that the biblical Solomonic narrative is permeated by the theme of royal wisdom and so differs from the subsequent narratives dealing with the succeeding kings of Israel and Judah. Consequently, the source upon which the Solomonic section is based can be deemed an independent work, different from the annals which supplied materials for the rest of the monarchic history.

The nature and purpose of the source of 1 Kings 3–11 can be inferred with a certain legitimacy from the character of those biblical chapters which drew from it. The wisdom theme predominates but the international dealings and diplomacy of Solomon are the central and consistent issues of the Solomonic narrative; there is an intrinsic connection between international diplomacy and wisdom.

Even the long central segment, chapters 5–9, which describes the construction and dedication of the Jerusalem temple-palace complex, does not have an internal, Israelite purview as its sole focus. The international propaganda significance of the buildings is clear. Indeed, the supranational scope of the Jerusalem project is communicated and prefigured in the opening episode fo the Solomonic narrative, 1 Kings 3:4–14. In this text God appears to Solomon in a dream and grants him wisdom, which he immediately demonstrates in the tale of the two harlots and which he then uses in his decision to build the temple. Typologically, this sequence is comprehensible in the context of the royally-dominated Near Eastern world, where gods communicated to rulers through dreams in a sanctuary and where temple building was the task of victorious kings. Such dreams are rather alien, if not forbidden, to Israelites. The dreams of Daniel and Joseph take place in

Babylonian and Egyptian contexts. And this vision of Solomon, while taking place within Israel at the high place at Gibeon, is an element common to Near-Eastern temple-building narratives, an element meaningful to a broader audience than the Israelite hierarchy or people alone.

Solomon's international orientation is visible in other ways. Embedded in the narrative of his reign is a third version in 1 Kings 4:1–6 of the listing of the royal cabinet. The officers of this executive council are no longer called "servants" ('ăbādîm), which seems to have been the term for such senior bureaucrats during the Davidic conquest phase of empire. Under Solomon the word for these cabinet members is "officials" (śārîm), a designation for high royal officers which appears to be part of the international bureaucratic vocabulary of the day.

The character of the cabinet has also shifted somewhat. The chief army officer is no longer first, as he was in both Davidic sequences; the military officer is now fourth on the list, indicating a decrease in importance of military affairs. Furthermore, there are no longer separate officers for the army and for the mercenary forces; the military component evidently was consolidated as the conquest phase of empire came to an end. On the other hand, the overall administration of affairs appears to have become more complex. The office of "scribe," held by one man under David, is now shared by two incumbents and must be related to the expanded international affairs of state. The district or prefect head is an addition. A "house" officer or major domo now appears, presumably to oversee the elaborate palace complex, with its many foreign inhabitants and visitors, and perhaps also the royal estate. Finally, a kind of personal counsel to Solomon, a "friend" of the king, joins the cabinet ranks. In short, the organization of Solomonic rule testifies to a post-conquest phase of empire: the civil bureaucracy is elaborated and the military bureaucracy is streamlined.

The ability of Solomon to retain the holdings acquired by his father and to sustain the support of the northern tribes can be related in significant measure to his personal diplomatic skill. Once the conquest phase of booty and plunder had filled the royal coffers and produced captive workers, the maintenance of Jerusalem as a center—not only of a nation state but also of an empire—demanded taxation and tribute and also forced laborers, corvée. In addition to the development of Jerusalem itself, the mechanics of empire depended upon the construction of store cities, administrative centers, and military outposts throughout the land. The cost to the Israelite population as well as to the conquered peoples was considerable, for most of the territories they inhabited were not naturally suitable for yielding economic surpluses. It is no wonder that, following Solomon's reign, the nation as well as the empire fell apart, with the royal heirs no longer able to exploit the overextended resource base of the Israelite empire in the manner required for the maintenance of that empire.

Solomon's ability to sustain the empire rested on more than the riches and regions acquired by David his father. His "wisdom," his personal gifts in dealing with the subjugated peoples, surely contributed to his long and relatively peaceful reign. Solomonic diplomacy on the international scene is expressed in the biblical sources by the wisdom theme of the narratives in Kings. They laud in the most superlative tones the wisdom and understanding of this Israelite emperor. One of the hallmarks of such sagacity is the ability to achieve, diplomatically, through discussion and "indirection," through skillfully persuasive speech, what otherwise might have to be achieved through force. Embedded in the biblical account are sporadic examples of such activity. Insofar as proverbs are associated with wisdom, the use of proverbial sayings is consistently connected with indirection in the non-violent accomplishment of conflict resolution. Gideon, for example, uses a traditional saying and successfully defuses the near-explosive ire of the Ephraimites (Judges 8:13). The attribution to Solomon of 3000 proverbs (and 1005 songs; in 1 Kings 4:32), however exaggerated that figure may be, must be considered a sign of his extraordinary diplomatic skill.

The art of persuasive speech seems to have been Solomon's métier, providing during his long reign the means to subjugate conquered peoples that military brilliance had supplied for David. If a context is sought for the composition of the unique source (The Book of the Acts of Solomon) for the biblical Solomonic narrative, perhaps it can be found in the propaganda machine of the Solomonic bureaucracy. For those not able to see firsthand in Jerusalem the visual statements of Solomonic legitimacy, i.e., the elaborate temple and palace, the written account of his rightful imperial reign and of his superior regnal wisdom would help convince outlying peoples to continue their subservience. The temple and palace descriptions in particular would have provided the means for distant officials to conceptualize Jerusalem as legitimate center. Unlike the elaborate tabernacle texts in Exodus, which seem to have been part of a priestly handbook or archive, the temple texts of Kings constitute a diplomatic position paper. If the temple-palace complex was the concrete centerpiece of the empire in the material realm, the description of that complex would have been the keystone of the diplomatic activity that connected the peripheral territories to the center. In Solomon's dedicating temple speech, he mentions parenthetically (1 Kings 8:41–42) that foreign peoples hear of Jerusalem's supremacy. The Queen of Sheba episode itself is predicated upon reports of Jerusalem's splendor and Solomon's wisdom having reached distant lands.

The achievement of Solomon in international diplomacy is measured not only by his success in holding the Davidic empire together but also by his expansion of its territorial extent. His foreign policy was not simply one of retention; there is evidence of at least one major annexation. Although Saul and David before him had incessantly dealt with the Philistines on a military level, neither of his predecessors seems to have actually taken control of Philistia itself. The Solomonic acquisition of Philistine territory is directly related to his dealings with Egypt.

The Philistines had served as Egyptian mercenaries and as representatives of Egyptian rule in Canaan. The weakened state of the Egyptian empire by the time of the Israelite monarchy meant that the Philistines could not draw upon Egyptian aid in their wars with Israel. On their own, the Philistines retained their core territory but their expansion was attenuated while Davidic territory expanded northward. One of Solomon's first diplomatic acts appears to have been a pact with Egypt in which Gezer and other regions of Philistia were ceded to Israelite control. The Egyptian pharaoh handed over to Solomon his Philistine vassal lands and also his daughter in an unprecedented act of acknowledgment of Solomonic supremacy. Never before had a Pharaoh given his daughter in marriage to an outsider. This unique arrangement (1 Kings 3:1) provided Israel with its title to the Egyptian-dominated Philistine holdings to the west and south of Israel. Solomon thereby, through diplomacy, completed the territorial control of the eastern Mediterranean coast that David had initiated through warfare.

### IV. Reevaluating Solomon

The Solomonic era thus represents a continuation of Davidic imperial expansion. However, it constitutes a second, post-conquest phase of that expansion. What Solomon achieved in his bureaucratic and material development was predicated upon and necessitated by the remarkable territorial expansion that preceded his accession to the throne. If it took the charisma and genius of a David to create an empire, against major economic, political, and historical odds, the maintenance of that empire for another regnal span rested upon Solomon's unique gifts of wisdom and of successful diplomacy.

Wisdom in the biblical world had clear international connections. Its material, derived from the cultural systems of common sense and everyday life, was comprehensible to Egyptians, Syrians, and Israelites alike. It thus could rise above the particular and constitute a universally understood mode of discourse, at least within the boundaries of a larger shared cultural world such as the ancient Near East. Solomon achieved his reputation as a master of wisdom by virtue of his skill in maintaining authority over an international court as well as Israelite leaders without the use of force. Both domestic and foreign representatives had increasing reason to resist Solomonic rule. Yet he held their submission to the Davidic throne without, so far as we can discern from the biblical information, using the military resources available to him. It is no accident that wisdom as a theme virtually disappears from the historiography of Kings after the death of Solomon and the dissolution of the Israelite kingdom and empire.

The termination of the United Monarchy and its imperial holdings seems to have brought an end to the reliance upon words and wisdom as the keys to peace and stability. The maintenance of a court, of a center in Jerusalem that could concretize the legitimacy of an Israelite emperor, became far too costly in economic and social terms. The population had increased during Solomon's reign, after a decline at the end of David's rule; and the Israelites themselves could no longer afford to siphon off the products of their labor to support the Jerusalem court. Without a local, domestic power base of men and materials the far-flung empire could only crumble. The ruins of empire carried with them the mode of its Solomonic character. The presence of Solomon the internationalist, relying skillfully on a universal vocabulary, gave way in the tradition to the primacy of David the warrior.

The demise of Israelite unity and hegemony after Solomon cannot be separated from the economic hardships and social disruption that imperialism imposed on the fragile resources of the eastern Mediterranean region. However, responsibility for the exploitative aspects of empire cannot be separated from the dynamics of empire maintenance. Solomon did not create the empire; he only, brilliantly and in his own way, did what needed to be done in order to sustain what he had inherited. While the biblical history writer condemns Solomon for not always walking in the ways of David his father, in many aspects he followed all too loyally the political path his father had paved. He took seriously the supranational span of his realm, and he accomplished through effective visual and verbal communication what was necessary to protect that realm. The materialism, the enforced servitude, the conscription, the bureaucracy—in short all the negative concomitants of Solomonic achievement—must not be isolated from the context of empire.

The narrative in 1 Kings 3 that describes Solomon's dream at Gibeon relates God's praise of Solomon for not asking for "riches or the life of your enemies." Instead, Solomon at the outset of his reign recognized that, given the immensity of his realm, he could only be successful through the exercise of great diplomatic skill. He asks God for "an understanding mind to govern my people, that I may discern between good and evil; for who is able to govern this, thy great people?"

Ironically, God's response not only praises Solomon for requesting neither wealth nor military might; it also grants him the former and not the latter, along with the discerning mind that Solomon had specifically requested. Solomon's individuality, what he sought for himself, thus lay in his wisdom and not in his wealth, according to the biblical narrative. Indeed, in language reminiscent of the evaluation of Moses at the end of Deuteronomy, where Moses' mighty deeds and his unique relationship to God are heralded ("and there has not arisen a prophet since in Israel like Moses," Deut. 34:10), Solomon is said to have possessed "a wise and discerning mind" such that no one like him had existed before him nor would anyone like him arise after him. Reevaluating Solomon means reasserting this unique dimension of Solomonic individuality and recognizing, as does the biblical author, that the riches and honor which characterized his realm were not of his choosing.

*Bibliographical Note*

A good example of the standard modern treatment of Solomon is provided by Martin Noth's *The History of Israel* (trans. Peter Ackroyd; New York: Harper and Row, 1960): "Solomon represented the decadent successor who has entered upon a great inheritance and administers it with an outward show of brilliance but who in reality allows it to fall into decay because he fails to acquire afresh for himself through his own skill and efficiency what he has inherited from his fathers." See also E. W. Heaton, *Solomon's New Men: The Emergence of Ancient Israel as a National State* (New York: Pica Press, 1974). The basic work for the sociological study of early Israel is George Mendenhall's *The Tenth Generation* (Baltimore: Johns Hopkins University Press, 1973); Norman Gottwald's *The Tribes of Yahweh: A Sociology of the Religion of Liberated Israel* (Maryknoll, New York: Orbis, 1979) extends the study. Readings in the history of empire are furnished in S. N. Eisenstadt's anthology *The Decline of Empire* (Englewood Cliffs, New Jersey: Prentice-Hall, 1967).

EDNA AMIR COFFIN

# THE BINDING OF ISAAC IN MODERN
# ISRAELI LITERATURE

The story of the *aqedah* is the greatest, most magnificent and deepest in meaning of all stories. It is the story of our generation. . . . In each generation Divine Providence, be it called whatever it may be called, promises us that if we sacrifice our Isaac, we will be granted the covenant and the promise will be kept. In every generation we are tempted anew and send our Isaacs to the battlefields of each nation and of each class, and it is not the ram that is caught by its horns in the bush, but we who are trapped. In every generation the nation of fathers yields to the voices of its fathers and sends its sons to the slaughter.

Moshe Shamir (1960)

There have been many attempts to apply the greatest and most important of Jewish myths, the myth of the *aqedah*, to Israeli reality. In spite of the many attempts in this direction and in spite of the the the fact that indeed it has been used both in art and in literature, I am of the opinion that on the whole this myth is not suitable for Israeli reality. There is no pious father who sends a passive son to slaughter. The myth of the *aqedah* is much more suitable to the acts of martyrdom of the Middle Ages in Exile. There the model of this myth is applicable, while here it has no real significance.

A. B. Yehoshua (1981)

These opposing views suggest the preoccupation of Israeli authors with the theme of the *aqedah*, the biblical story of Abraham binding Isaac over for sacrifice. This theme has emerged as central in Modern Hebrew literature at least partly in response to historical events which have affected the Jewish community in the twentieth century. The two sets of ethical questions associated with it are those raised by the struggle for the modern Jewish State, which demanded great sacrifice, and those raised by the Nazi Holocaust, which claimed millions of victims. In psychological fiction, father-son conflicts have been treated in the narrative vocabulary of the *aqedah* story. Unlike medieval authors, modern writers do not simply retell the story in order to reflect existing conditions; rather, they use its basic structure, or parts of that structure, to provide frames of reference. The ethical questions are raised not so much in a religious context as in the context of concerns over survival, whether national, group, or familial. In this essay three major thematic uses of the *aqedah* will be discussed in reviewing works by Moshe Shamir (born 1921) and A. B. Yehoshua (born 1936), both fiction writers, and the poets Amir Gilboa (born 1917) and Chaim Guri (born 1923). Shamir's novel centers on fathers and sons in the struggle for a Jewish national home; the poems of Gilboa and Guri provide responses to the Holocaust; and Yehoshua's fictional works use fragments of the *aqedah* story in portraying basic human drives.

## I. Biblical and Rabbinic Background

According to the narrative in Genesis 22, God calls Abraham in order to test him, asking him to offer his son Isaac as a sacrifice. Abraham proceeds to implement God's wish, and only through divine intervention is he prevented from carrying out the sacrificial act: a ram is provided as a substitute offering. God then promises Abraham that he and his offspring shall inherit the earth. Both the incident and the story are referred to in Jewish tradition as the *aqedah*, a noun meaning "binding"; the form implies the existence of both an actor and a recipient of the act. The event, when seen as fundamentally involving Abraham, is referred to as Abraham's Trial; when viewed primarily as Isaac's ordeal, it is called either the Binding or the Sacrifice of Isaac.

It is useful to explore briefly the biblical and rabbinic versions of the episode before proceeding to the modern works, since all forms of the story are relevant. The biblical narrative is introduced by a mitigating statement to assure the reader that the entire story is to be regarded as a trial or test for Abraham and that the ensuing events must be understood in these terms only. The five major participants come from the divine realm, the human world, and the animal kingdom. The divine presence is represented both by God and an angelic messenger. The two main human participants are Abraham and Isaac; they are accompanied in their journey by two anonymous and silent servants. The animal figure, the ram, is central to the story, as it provides a resolution of the dilemma by becoming Isaac's surrogate in the sacrificial act.

The biblical narrative reveals little about the emotional state of its participants; there are, however, a number of stylistic devices which serve to enhance characterization. The use of apposition, in a progression from the general to the specific, indicates the enormity of the sacrifice asked of Araham: "Take your son, your only one, the one you love, Isaac." Each reference further emphasizes Abraham's special attachment to his son. The description of the journey as lasting three days accentuates the agony of Abraham's trial. The account of Abraham's leaving his servants behind emphasizes the loneliness of the trial. The fact that Isaac is made to carry the firewood for his own slaughter heightens the irony of the situation. The phrase "And the two of them went together" summarizes the event succinctly, just as the brief dialogue immediately preceding underscores the major issues. The question "Where is the lamb for the sacrifice?" reveals Isaac's concern, while Abraham's ambiguous answer, "God will see to it," indicates a moral dilemma facing Abraham which is not fully evoked in the biblical text: is it Abraham's belief that God will provide a substitute for Isaac, or does this statement indicate that Abraham is transferring responsibility to God's domain? The simple rhetorical device of repetition when the angel calls for Abraham to stop the sacrifice communicates urgency to the reader. The biblical narrative is thus rendered tersely; the reader participates in the experience by raising basic questions for which no answers are given.

Because rabbinic literature fills in some of the textual gaps, modern authors often use it for source material. The cast of characters is expanded and includes in the superhuman category a Satan or tempter figure as well as God and the angel; the *aqedah* is presented as a test not only for Abraham but also for God when God is challenged by Satan, as in the story of Job.

Satan serves not only as the instigator who triggers the entire chain of events but also as a disturber; he actively tries to foil the mission by appearing to Abraham and Isaac in various guises, trying to dissuade them from carrying out the act, as well as by erecting physical barriers to prevent them from reaching their destination.

The protective mother Sarah also enters the picture. Her welfare is very much the concern of both Abraham and Isaac; in some of the rabbinic tales she becomes the victim of the trial, her death ensuing when Satan informs her of the journey's purpose, revealing what Abraham and Isaac have tried so hard to conceal. The two servants are mentioned by name, Ishmael and Eliezer; they are pictured as vying for the position of Abraham's heir subsequent to the anticipated demise of Isaac.

Isaac is seen as a martyr, carrying the firewood just as a person about to be crucified carries the cross on his shoulder. The connection made between the Isaac figure of rabbinic literature and the figure of Jesus is echoed in Modern Hebrew literature, in, for example, Aharon Appelfeld's celebrated Holocaust story "Kitty." In some of the rabbinic tales Isaac is actually sacrificed and then resurrected, forcing Abraham to attempt again to carry out God's command. One of the most touching details in rabbinic retellings describes Abraham at the moment of his trial as nearly drowning in a pool of tears. The Abraham of the rabbinic tales is not acquiescent—he demands to hear God's own voice, insisting that the voice of the angel is not sufficient to stop the trial. These and other features of the retellings expand the emotional dimensions of the story and add structural features, as well as posing additional questions. The appropriateness of the entire notion of the trial itself is questioned.

## II. National Concerns

Israeli literature of the 1940s and 1950s is for the most part dedicated to visions of a new social order and the realization of the Zionist dream. Writers of this generation (often referred to as the Generation of 1948) focus on distinctly Israeli realities, believing that Israeli literature must be "a responsible literature, concerned above all with the individual and the community, with the people and the country"; writers are "heroes of a national struggle, of a class-war, of culture; people of conviction and responsibility" (H. Hazaz).

It was in this tradition that Moshe Shamir, at the time a member of a kibbutz as well as of the Palmach (the strike units of the Jewish defense forces in Palestine), began his literary efforts. His first novel, *He Walked through the Fields* (1948), poses the questions which pre-occupied his generation. The novel asks whether ideological commitment to national goals supersedes the needs of individuals. The heroes include both founders and sons; from both, a readiness for ultimate sacrifice is demanded. The novel reflects a structural affinity to the *aqedah*, but unlike the biblical story and like many other modern works of fiction which have used this theme, in this *aqedah* the sacrifice is carried out, and there is no divine presence or interference. The lack of such a presence shifts the responsibility for the outcome to individuals and their community. The relationship between a demanding ideology and the individual who must suffer its consequences constitutes the central concern for Shamir, who views the writer's responsibility as "not necessarily . . . revolutionary in literary terms"; rather the work must be bound to historical circumstance and therefore should "follow the revolution of life." The balance between duty and desire, between life and death, between fathers and sons, is viewed in a historical framework, where the protagonists are actors who participate in the making of a secular history.

The story is set on a kibbutz in the 1940s, where communal interests outrank those of individuals. The plot involves the breakup of a family and ends on a note of tragedy when the only son is killed in a military training accident. The nuclear family is part of the larger extended family of the kibbutz, which in turn belongs to the larger family of the *Yishuv* (the Jewish community in pre-state Palestine), which is bound to the goals not only of a new morality based on social justice but also of Zionism.

Willy, the Abraham figure in the story, is a typical '40s hero, one of the founders of the kibbutz and a central figure in the *Yishuv*. He is constantly performing service for the community, at first bringing

Jewish refugees to Palestine and later volunteering to fight in the British army against the Germans. He is perceived by others as a heroic figure, though his own family sees his community service as a convenient excuse for escaping the routine challenges of kibbutz and family life. Rutka, like the rabbinic Sarah, is an overprotective, loving mother who places above group interests her instinct to guard her only child from all dangers. In the early days of the kibbutz Rutka had taken her son Uri and fled with him to Tel Aviv; the lack of adequate medical care at the kibbutz (pointed up by the death of one of its three children) seemed to pose a threat to her son's life. Though she is brought back to the kibbutz, her flight is not forgotten; it is considered a betrayal of principle, a sign of her inability to show total commitment to ideology. "Willy is zero, I am zero, the kibbutz is zero," says Rutka, "compared with Uri what is all this high talk, what is all this kibbutz compared to his life?" Echoes from the language of the rabbinic tales can be heard as Rutka-Sarah justifies to herself her course of action: "She heard the voice within her calling: Rutka, save, save Uri, save him. . . . There are more important things than all of these . . . values, or whatever you call them: Life itself!" Willy brings Rutka back to the kibbutz, persuading her of the necessity of direct commitment, not expecting others to make the sacrifice. Shamir deviates from the "moral" of the biblical *aqedah*; in the modern form of the story there are no substitute sacrifices: all people must be ready to give the ultimate offering, not only their own lives, but the lives of their children as well.

Uri is faced with Isaac's problem, of living in the shadow of his father, the founder of a new religion. He is preoccupied with finding his own identity. Since Willy constantly puts himself in situations where his commitment is tried and tested, Uri feels compelled to understand the meaning of such trials. At first he sees the test as an undramatic but necessary challenge:

> You will not be tested to see whether you are the first born of the kibbutz, or a graduate of an agricultural school, or Willy's and Rutka's son, but you will be tested in the simple way, on a daily basis: will you get up again for work tomorrow morning?

His rivalry with his father moves Uri to action. First he starts courting Mika, one of the refugee girls his father brought to the kibbutz; she has a strong attachment to Willy. Sexual rivalry with his father is as much a motive in Uri's courting Mika as his attraction to her. She is "another success, sought in order to overcome another distance."

Eventually, the contest in love gives way to a contest in death. Uri concludes that in order to prove his worth as a man he must outdo his father in the only way left for him: to make the sacrifice of his own life. Willy has joined the army, though he is no longer young; Uri sees

Willy's action as an attempt to escape not only the constricting life of the kibbutz but also a failing marriage (Rutka has taken a lover). Uri is dismayed at the dissolution of his family and overcome by a sense of guilt, feeling that he was partly to blame for this outcome.

> Willy . . . will die before you and for you, just as up till now he lived before you, took a wife before you, founded a kibbutz before you, and did all the difficult things that you are not sure you could do. . . . You could not possibly live before him, but you can die before him, you can leave this world with Willy, Rutka and without Uri. . . .
> Now Uri should be taken out of the picture, he should die before them, let them suffer the entire weight of pain. . . . He wants to be better and more saintly than the two of them, to suffer more, to be a victim, to return to them all at once. . . .

Uri comes to believe that how a man dies and not how he lives is most important. He is convinced that after his death his parents will reunite. Unwittingly the father is involved in responsibility for his son's death, having set himself up as an uncompromising and awesome model.

Uri is soon called to his task, when he is drafted. As he leaves he echoes his father's words: "I will not have other people defend me or you or the kibbutz. . . . Everybody must bear their own responsibility." Uri is another hero in the War of Independence literature: young, somewhat irresponsible and insensitive to others in personal relationships, unsure of identity and historical role, yet willing to accept responsibility for communal goals and willing to face death. The manner and meaning of Uri's death, however, remain ambiguous: he is killed not while defending his community but in an accident. He challenges the weakest member of his unit, who is too paralyzed by fear to throw a grenade. When the grenade is thrown and falls short, Uri must cover it with his own body to save the rest of the group from the explosion.

Uri leaves Mika with a child, so that the continuity of the family, of the kibbutz, and of the nation is assured. While the sons are put to the test of death, their offspring is destined to inherit the land, as in the biblical promise. Shamir sums up his own feelings about the meaningless death in Rutka's and Willy's comments on the meaning of sacrifice:

> "Years of life will pass and everything will look so small, all the tragedies, the upsets, the difficult parting hours, the unions set for life, the family room, the desire, handsome young men, moments of ecstasy—only one thing will remain dear and inviolable—the son."
> Willy came to the same conclusion: he knew the whole truth. "This child [Uri's son] is the only thing that will be left to us of Uri" . . . and it became the most important thing to preserve.

The notion of sacrifice for the good of the community has been perverted by a misunderstanding, a fatal mistake, but out of this trial the heroes emerge with a new understanding of the importance of preserving life. Continuity supersedes the notion of sacrifice. While borrowing structure and metaphors from the *aqedah* story, Shamir substitutes secular content for religious ideas and reexamines the values of life and death in his own frame of historical events and ideological drives.

## III. Responses to the Holocaust

A different approach to the theme of the *aqedah* is taken in many literary responses to the Holocaust; these view the sacrifice not as an offering but rather as a tragic and senseless event in a world devoid of moral values. The victims of the Holocaust, unlike the intended sacrificial offering of the biblical narrative, have no divine cause which justifies their senseless death. The biblical tale promises a miracle, a divine intervention against the forces of death. Without the miraculous salvation the myth is viewed as a broken promise.

Amir Gilboa and Chaim Guri belong to a group of poets often referred to as the "Native School." While some of these poets were actually native born (Guri was born in Tel Aviv), others were either brought to Palestine in their childhood and educated there, or were deeply involved in Zionist and Hebrew causes abroad (Gilboa was born in the Ukraine and came to Palestine in 1936). Like Moshe Shamir, their contemporary, both Guri and Gilboa were members of the 1948 Generation, and their poetry reflects the social concerns and ideology of that generation.

Gilboa's poem "Isaac" was published in 1953, in his third collection of poems. In typical Gilboa fashion, it blends the biblical motif with surrealistic dreamlike elements, in order to create a strong identification of the poet's voice with that of the biblical Isaac.

### Isaac

Toward morning the sun strolled in the forest
Together with me and with father;
My right hand was in his left.

Like lightning flash, a knife between the trees
And I fear the terror of my eyes opposite the blood on the leaves.

Father, Father, come quickly and save Isaac
That no one may be missing at the noon meal.

It is I who am slaughtered, my son,
And my blood is already on the leaves.
Father's voice choked.
His face grew pale.

And I wanted to scream, writhing not to believe
And I opened my eyes wide.
And I awoke.

Bloodless was my right hand.

(trans. T. Carmi)

At first using the voice of the child, the poem describes, as if telling of an ideal world in which all things exist in their proper order, a father and son walking in the woods hand in hand. The emphasis is on calm and complete trust. The sun in the woods and the light of the early morning contribute to the idyllic picture.

In the second stanza the knife image introduces the *aqedah* motif. Isaac's reaction, unspecified in the biblical episode, is stated clearly in this modern version: "And I fear the terror of my eyes opposite the blood on the leaves." It moves the reader from a world of childhood where parents protect their children, to a reality in which danger is ever-present and trust can no longer be assumed. In the third stanza the rhetoric shifts from storytelling to an urgent address to the father, but still in a child's language: "Father, father" is reminiscent of the repetition in the biblical story when the angel calls Abraham twice to stop the sacrifice. Here the repetition and urgency are communicated by Isaac. The reason for the plea is childlike: the speaker wants no one to miss the midday meal; he is a helpless child who instinctively senses danger, without being able to fully grasp its shape.

There is a surprising reversal in the fourth stanza, when the voice of the father enters the poem. This shift in voices accompanies a shift in structure, both in person and grammatical tense. The victim is not son but father, and the act of sacrifice is not about to take place but has already taken place. The father's choking voice and pale face introduce the actual killing of the father. Another voice enters in the fifth stanza, the voice of the dreamer, the adult Isaac filled with terror at the sight of blood in his dream, only to awaken to a far more frightening reality, that of helplessness and guilt in the face of what has occurred. The poem ends with the power line, "Bloodless was my right hand." This line can be taken in physical terms: the dreamer, who has gone to sleep lying on his right hand, awakens to find it tingling and bloodless. On another and more important level it refers back to the line, "My right hand was in his left." The intimacy and trust between father and son in early childhood are no longer a reality in the adult world, where the son is helpless to aid the father. The right hand, symbol of power and the ability to act, of trust and closeness, now proves to be impotent. In addition, the line echoes Psalm 137: "If I forget thee, O Jerusalem, may my right hand wither."

Gilboa expresses feelings of terror, guilt, and impotence in the face of the European disaster. The community of fathers has been betrayed

by sons who have been consigned to the role of bystanders unable to
fulfill their filial obligations. Their responses are those of involved and
horrified spectators. Thus Gilboa brings twentieth-century reality into
the paradigm of existing *aqedah* interpretations. Some of the participants in the story, the father and the son, are present, but there is no
sign of God's presence, no ram to serve as the substitute victim, and no
angel who can intervene at the last minute to bring about the miracle.

Chaim Guri, like Gilboa, saw extensive military service in the '40s,
and his poetry reflects the national concerns of his time. Using biblical
sources and ancient Jewish legends as well as figures from Greek
mythology, Guri commonly relates the events of the present to past
literature. He too responds to the Holocaust experience with metaphors from the Binding of Isaac.

### Heritage

The ram came last of all.
Abraham did not know that it
came to answer the boy's question—
first of his strength when his day was on the wane.

The old man raised his head.
Seeing that it was no dream
and that the angel stood there—
the knife slipped from his hand.

The boy, released from his bonds,
saw his father's back.

Isaac, as the story goes, was not sacrificed.
He lived for many years,
saw what pleasure had to offer, until his eyesight dimmed.

But he bequeathed that hour to his offspring.
They are born
with a knife in their hearts.

(trans. after T. Carmi)

Guri's point of departure is Isaac's question in the biblical story,
"Here are the fire and the wood, but where is the lamb for the
sacrifice?" Abraham is portrayed as if in a dream; he acts in a trancelike
state when faced with the terrible task of sacrificing his son; perhaps he
even intends to complete the act. Guri portrays Abraham's act of
dropping the knife not as an assertion of his will, but rather as an
involuntary response to the angel's call. Like the biblical storyteller,
Guri refrains from describing the emotions of the participants. It is
through simple images that the intensity of feelings is portrayed. In
contrast to the rabbinic literature, in which, at the moment of sacrifice,

"the eyes of Abraham were on the eyes of Isaac, and the eyes of Isaac were on the heavens," Guri paints a different picture: "The boy, released from his bonds,/ saw his father's back." There are no words adequate to describe the emotions of the father, who has been given a reprieve as much as Isaac has.

An anticlimax follows this dramatic moment, focusing on Isaac, who went on to lead a long and uneventful life. It is only in the last line that Guri describes the true nature of Isaac's bequest. In the biblical story Abraham is promised that his offspring will be as numerous as the stars in the heavens and sands on the seashore; the actual bequest, Guri says, is that each of the offspring is fated to be born with a knife in the heart.

Guri's understanding and resolution of the modern *aqedah* stands in stark contrast to the biblical promise and constitutes a powerful protest against the fate of the Holocaust victims. The *aqedah* is perceived to be both a unique event as well as an eternally ongoing occurrence. Each generation is fated to go through the trial and test of the *aqedah*—this is the true bequest, the true promise.

### IV. Fathers and Sons

While the Generation of 1948 was oriented to social reality and national ideology, the generation of writers that followed took a new direction. This generation (referred to as the New Wave or the Generation of the State) is concerned with the psychological dimensions of characters, with their inner worlds, rather than with the relationship of the individual to society or with historical mission. The approach to national reality and historical role is often ambivalent. Heroes no longer have definite ties to their environment; rather, existential concerns of growing estrangement and alienation from society as well as ontological isolation preoccupy them. There is a tendency to erase the clear lines which separate the realistic plane of fiction from the fantastic. A. B. Yehoshua, for example, employs allegorical and symbolic modes in mapping the inner experiences and conflicts of his protagonists. Yehoshua in his early fiction creates a world removed from immediate local concerns, one in which the primary urges and drives of the individual are paramount.

Yehoshua uses the *aqedah* motif to explore relationships between authority figures and their intended followers: fathers-sons, teachers-students, religious and political prophets-followers, and so on. Rather than involing the *aqedah* tradition in its entirety with all its ethical and religious implications, Yehoshua dwells on the Oedipal aspects of the story. The attempts of the generation of fathers to exercise authority and godlike control over their sons, as well as the rebellion of the younger generation in the face of such domination, lend themselves to a treatment based on the biblical myth.

In the novella "Three Days and a Child" (1968), several features of the *aqedah* story aid in illustrating the primary ambivalence of fathers toward sons. Yehoshua uses as his frame the span of three days from the time that Abraham sets out on his journey with Isaac to the time he arrives at the sacrificial site. The main characters are a child, three-year-old Yali, and his surrogate father for three days, a student to whom the boy is entrusted for this period. Behind the story stands Yali's mother. The student has in the past vied with others for the mother's affection; he is now vying with her child. There is a faint suggestion that the student may even be the biological father of the child whose life is literally in his hands. During the three days the student swings from one emotional pole to its opposite—from hate to love, from jealousy to compassion, from the wish to kill to the wish to preserve life. Yehoshua sees the voices of God, the angel, and Satan, conflicting urges and emotions within the individual.

Yehoshua's work changed in the late '60s from a predominantly psychological and metarealistic use of symbolism to include political dimensions as well. Several fictional works use the *aqedah* motif extensively, but I will discuss only the story "Early in the Summer of 1970," which is set during the War of Attrition (1969-1970). The characters reflect the absurd and near-grotesque features of the world in which they live. Time, place and plot all contribute to the sense of disintegration of fixed orders and known values. An old teacher is informed that his only son, who had returned from abroad only to be sent to the war, has been killed. The son is no longer very young—he is thirty-one years old—and he has brought back with him a wife and a son. The teacher travels to Jerusalem to identify his son's body, only to find out that it has all been a mistake—the body is that of another soldier with the same name. The father then embarks on another journey to the desert to find his son, and upon discovering him alive returns to Jerusalem to bring the tidings to his son's wife.

This story is repeated three times, and in each version the protagonist views the events in a different state of consciousness. Symbols are reinterpreted, bringing a growing knowledge of the elusive truth. In the first two versions the journey includes the discovery that the victim is not the teacher's son; the third version is interrupted at the point when the father receives the notice about his son's death.

> Five or six hours ago—
> In the Jordan Valley—
> Killed on the spot—

The interruption suggests that perhaps in the last and possibly truest version of the story, death has indeed occurred, the intended sacrifice has been completed.

The repetition of the story with interruptions also points up the cyclical nature of the *aqedah* myth; its concerns are repeated throughout history, time and again. In each generation fathers are confronted with their inadequacy in assigning a meaning to the senseless sacrifices demanded of sons in the name of the established order. Each generation of fathers gives way to a new generation of fathers, who like the biblical Abraham come to the Promised Land with a new religion. When one god is dead, new gods arise to replace him. The father leaves "a dead, distant, biblical deity among the arid hills," while his son brings with him a new religion from abroad concerned with "Prophecies and Politics," delivered in a jargon of half-English and half-Hebrew. The gap between the old order and the new is unbridgeable, and the attempt of the father to find in the "confusion of generations" some usable meaning is destined to fail.

These questions are posed in the story in two parallel plots. One is the thrice-told story of the son's death. The other, which also involves a triple narration, centers on the father's life as a retired teacher. He has forced himself back on the system, using the war and the consequent death of pupils as reasons for returning to his old position as Bible teacher. Others do not see a connection between his role as a teacher and the war, but he imagines the two as inseparable: "I did not see how I could leave them, now that we were sending them to their death." He sees his function as preparing his students for death, as he has been prepared for the sacrifice. He puts his students to several tests, preparing them and rehearsing for the ultimate trial. A distorted fusion of God and Abraham, who because of age has lost much of his authority, the teacher derives whatever strength he has from his students. It is his reflection in their eyes that endows him with power. When the reflection dims, he must acknowledge his loss of influence. The signs are there from the start, when he finds his students at the blackboard "rubbing out wild words—a distorted image of myself," but still "silent." Age gives him authority: "For the present my gray hairs still subdue them." In one retelling of the story, the loss of control is more visible; he must resort to force rather than teaching or persuasion: "White sheets of paper spread on their desks like the flags of surrender, Bibles shelved deep inside. The tyranny I enforce by means of the Bible." In the third version, he comes to the realization that he has lost his relevance to them: "I realize: I am not important to them any more, have lost my power over them, and they are done with me, I already belong to the past."

In the context of the classroom, the Isaac figures, like the teacher-God-Abraham, undergo transformations in role and attitude throughout the three versions. Seen initially as "wild-haired, red-faced. . .dropping Bibles, the desk tops covered with blank sheets of paper, ready for the examination," they change into quiet revolutionaries. When faced with the test, "they are stunned, fail to see my purpose," and slowly begin to react: "Someone rises and leaves the room . . . another follows, and a third, and suddenly it seems as though they are up in revolt." These "long-haired, inarticulate, slightly obtuse students, vague graduates without ideals," are the Isaacs who "have the strength and readiness to die . . . so young, and in fact so disciplined, amazing us over and over with obedience." In the final version, the teacher is faced with the void once the students are sent to the war: "They are abandoning it all soon, leaving empty classrooms behind them, a pile of chairs in a corner, a clean blackboard, and traces of their names scored on desks as on tombstones." Faced with their presence and their disappearance the teacher is brought to ask himself: "Am I here or am I not?" As in the *aqedah* story this is not a historical dilemma but an existential one. "Am I setting a trap for them?" asks the teacher, who is no longer in a position to change the *aqedah* construct; he has fulfilled his role and is no longer necessary for the equation.

The pathos with which the old teacher delivers his imaginary message to the graduating class reveals his vain attempts to rationalize the human role in a senseless world and give meaning to history. In rehearsing the speech in his mind, the narrator states his main point: "All this has been nothing but a prelude. . . . Forgive me but I feel the need to say a few words to those among us who may disappear. On the face of it, your disappearance is nothing, is meaningless, futile. Because historically speaking, however stubborn you are, your death will again be but a weary repetition in a slightly different setting. . . . But the blood is the same, and the pain is familiar. Yet another glance reverses it all, as it were. Your disappearance fills with meaning, becomes a fiery branch, a source of wonderful, lasting inspiration." He is unconvinced by his own words: history will not come to his aid and give meaning to death, and so he concludes: "It remains shrouded with a sense of mystery. For to say it plainly and clearly, there is no history. Only a few scraps of text, some potsherds. All further research is futile. Everything fills with mystery again."

The search for the missing, presumably dead son, which occupies the father-son part of the story, is also replete with symbolism of the *aqedah* theme, and raises the same existential questions in a different context. The announcement of the son's death puts the father, who previously had no vital role in society, back in a central position: "They were all coming back, some with tears in their eyes, surrounding me, a whole tribe breaking my loneliness." The father, in a ritualized act which gives new order to his disintegrating existence, begins his social and historical role as the bereaved father: "I cleanse myself, put on fresh linen, find a heavy black suit." He derives renewed authority from his new status, and begins his imaginary address to the students from this vantage point: "I am not speaking to you as senior teacher, but as one who was a father and is a father no more." Advising others to prepare for the sacrifice, he remarks: "I ask you to look at me and guard yourself against surprise, because I was prepared for his death in a manner, and that was my strength in that fearful moment." With heroic and dramatic gestures he links his personal tragedy to the common fate of the nation and of mankind: "Out of my private sorrow a common truth will illumine us all," a statement which will prove as false and absurd as it sounds.

Father and son are portrayed as mirror images and as totally alien. The son, like the old teacher, is presented as "a husband, father and near professor," and is seen by others as resembling his father. The father prepares his students for the wars that will ensure the kingdom of peace, and the son-turned-father is also preoccupied with such endeavors. The efforts of the father have proven useless, those of the son will come to the test at a future time. Like the biblical Isaac, the son is referred to as "my son, my only son" even though he is no longer young and is himself a father. Like the biblical Isaac, he is reprieved at the last moment, for it was all a mistake, he never was the real sacrifice, there was a substitute, only the name was the same. He cannot be the sacrifice, for he has already been transformed from son to father, taking on a new identity, preparing for his own historical role.

In depicting the son as the possible victim Yehoshua relies not on the basic narrative in the Bible, but on later rabbinic stories in which Abraham kills Isaac on the first try, but Isaac is resurrected; thereupon Abraham attempts to kill him again, but the angel intervenes and saves Isaac. Similarly, when the father encounters the son in the desert, it is as if he had died and been resurrected. The two are surrounded by others who want to hear of the miracle which spells out hope or reprieve for all: "The ring around us tightens, the men cleave to us. The story of his death and resurrection thrills them. . . . We both stand trembling and smiling." Echoes of Kierkegaard's *Fear and Trembling* can be heard in this scene as well. This Isaac, the adult son, asks no questions, but rather comments on the absurdity of the trial: "You can see for yourself, such a loss of time . . . so pointless," leaving his father unable to rise to the task of giving him "some point, some meaning"; consequently he "disappears at the vague nightly lines of the desert."

Yehoshua confronts the reader, through the aging father, with the despair of sending sons and students to "distant deserts" from whence "there are those who do not come back. . . . Some disappear." A deep sense of betrayal is felt by those who return to resume life after their trial: "Even those who come back, though they walk with their children and their shopping baskets, there is something veiled in their eyes, they stare at me blankly, almost ignore me, as though I had deceived them somewhere. I mean, as though with the material itself I had deceived them. As though it had all collapsed for them out there, in the dust, the scorching fire, the lonely night, had all failed the test of some other reality. But what other reality: Lord of Hosts, Lord God—what other reality for heaven's sake?" It remains to be seen whether the son's new message will contain any answers to the questions posed by the father, who says "'There is my son,'. . . as if he had brought some new gospel, tidings of a revolution of some other reality, wonderful and unknown. . . ."

Enhancing the *aqedah* theme is the use of various symbols from the biblical tale, such as the knife, which appears with all three generational figures; father, son and even grandson are portrayed holding the knife at various crucial points in the story, for each must assume the Abraham role in turn. In keeping with Yehoshua's ambiguous use of symbols, the knife contains several meanings: a potential weapon, it appears in the story as a decorative object on the son's desk, with the word PEACE engraved on it. The grandson is seen playfully pounding a can with a knife, whereas the father holds it with great deliberation, eventually letting it drop from his hand. The number three also appears several times in the story, which itself is told three times. Other biblical allusions in the text remove the story from the realm of the "here" and "now" of the War of Attrition to a greater and timeless reality.

## V. Conclusion

The *aqedah* story does not belong to the literature of antiquity alone; it is equally relevant in modern times. In its entirety as well as in its parts, it informs different historical contexts and a variety of philosophical and religious questions. Some Modern Hebrew literature written in Israel links the biblical text with the new reality of Zionism; but the strength of the biblical and rabbinic texts lends beauty and truth to all the modern works. As Shamir comments, "It is the greatest, most magnificent and deepest in meaning of all stories." He claims it is not a historical text, but a text for all generations and, indeed, "it is the story of our generation." While Yehoshua rejects the literal application of the *aqedah* myth to modern Israeli reality, he has used the myth in grappling with the deepest issues and questions of the human condition. Guri and Gilboa both find the *aqedah* to be the most powerful construct with which to record their anguish and protest at the catastrophic events of the Holocaust. Elie Wiesel has rightly observed of the *aqedah*: "Terrifying in content, it has become a source of consolation to those who, in retelling it, make it part of their own experience."

*Bibliographical Note*

The poems quoted are both given in T. Carmi, ed., *The Penguin Book of Hebrew Verse* (London: Penguin, 1980); see also R. F. Mintz, *Modern Hebrew*

*Poetry* (Los Angeles: University of California Press, 1968). Some of A. B. Yehoshua' fiction is available in English: *Three Days and a Child*, trans. Miriam Arad (Garden City: Doubleday, 1970) and *Early in the Summer of 1970*, trans. Miriam Arad (Garden City: Doubleday, 1977). Moshe Shamir's novels are not. Recent treatments of the *aqedah* include Erich Wellisch, *Isaac and Oedipus* (London: Routledge & Kegan Paul, 1956); Emil Fackenheim, *Encounters Between Judaism and Modern Philosophy* (New York: Basic Books, 1973); Eli Weisel, *Messengers of God* (New York: Random House, 1976); and Silvano Arieti, *Abraham and the Contemporary Mind* (New York: Basic Books, 1981).

YEHUDA AMICHAI

# THE TRUE HERO OF THE *AQEDAH*

The true hero of the *aqedah* was the ram,
unaware of the connivance of others.
It seemingly volunteered to die in Isaac's place.
I want to sing a tribute to its memory,
its curly wool and its human eyes
and its horns, so quiet on the lively head,
which were made into trumpets after its slaughter
for them to sound their war blasts
and to broadcast their vulgar joy.

I want to remember the last picture
like a nice photo in a refined fashion magazine:
the spoiled tanned youth in his fancy clothes
and next to him the angel in a silk robe
for a festive reception.
And the two of them with vacuous eyes
staring at two empty spots.

And behind them, like a colorful background, the ram
caught in the thicket before the slaughter,
and the thicket his very last friend.

The angel went home.
Isaac went home.
Abraham and God went home too.

But the true hero of the *aqedah*
is the ram.

(Trans. Edna Amir Coffin)

PAUL RABOFF

# ALTAR

Its countless stone potential
Makes the land a ready altar.
I see rainbows in its dust
Thrown to quench gray embers.

On my back I carry fuel
From Egypt, fire from Babel.
In the coming world disaster,
When the one ignites the other,
My going up the mountain
Leaves vacuum for contention.

Father walks and prophesies,
Thinking all the things he says
To comfort me are lies.
I believe: a vision fortifies.

Nations burning, fire in wood,
Smoke like columns of suet;
The whole land banked and piled
As an altar; at its summit
I, face up, bound hand and foot.

Above, the saving dispensation
Looms like a virgin continent:
Its sand's flat inclination
Cuts successive waves of light.
I await the interdiction unafraid.

RICHARD L. RUBENSTEIN

# THE BESIEGED COMMUNITY
# IN ANCIENT AND MODERN TIMES

## I

The terrible events that culminated in the slaughter of unarmed
Palestinians between 14 and 16 September 1982, in Beirut's Sabra and
Shatilla refugee camps remind us once again of the awesome links
between religion, politics, and violence, ties clearly manifest in the
Bible and other documents of ancient Near Eastern civilization.
Christian Lebanese slaughtered Muslim Palestinians with the acquiescence if not the toleration of Israeli military authorities. One of the
more depressing aspects of the massacre is that it occurred in a part of
the world that has witnessed ethnic, tribal, and religious violence since
the dawn of human history.

During the summer of 1982, West Beirut was in effect a city under
siege. Although the siege was ultimately less destructive of both life
and property than similar contests in the Eastern Mediterranean in
ancient times, it is my belief that we can better understand the
significance of what happened in Lebanon if we consider briefly the
biblical traditions pertaining to the capture of a besieged city and the
siege in ancient times of Melos and Troy, cities located not far from
contemporary Beirut.

The story of the Athenian siege of the island polis of Melos during
the Peloponnesian War is recounted in Thucydides' history of that war.
The Athenians attempted to gain control of the sea by forcing the
island colonies of the mainland Greeks to become Athens' tributaries.
Initially, the Melians, who had been allied to Sparta, assumed a posture
of neutrality, hoping thereby to avoid Athenian attack. Rejecting the
Melian offer of neutrality, the Athenians demanded that the Melians
surrender and become tributary. This the Melians refused to do, with
disastrous consequences for themselves.

Thucydides offers an account of the dialogue between the Melian
emissaries and the more powerful Athenians as the latter attempt to
persuade their foes to surrender and accept dependent status. The
Athenians argue that such a course is not dishonorable and that any
other will prove suicidal. The Athenian arguments are marked by
unsentimental political realism typified by the observation that ". . . the
strong do what they can and the weak suffer what they must." The

447

Athenians are prepared to be magnanimous, but only if the Melians surrender.

The Melians are far less realistic. They attempt to gain through persuasion what they cannot gain through power. They are, however, unable to do the one thing that offers them a viable future, namely, to submit to the Athenians. When Melos finally collapses under siege, the fate of the Melians is sealed. Thucydides tells the story tersely:

> . . . the Melians surrendered unconditionally to the Athenians, who put to death all the men of military age whom they took, and sold the women and children as slaves. Melos itself they took over for themselves, sending out a later colony of 500 men.

According to Xenophon, there were a few male Melian survivors. Nevertheless, Thucydides' account accurately reflects the customary treatment of the defeated enemy in the Eastern Mediterranean in ancient times. It is my conviction that the story is not irrelevant to the 1982 war in Lebanon or to the wider Arab-Israeli conflict.

Perhaps an even more dramatic example of the treatment of a defeated enemy is the fate of Hector's son, Astyanax, at the fall of Troy, as depicted by Euripides in *The Trojan Women*. That drama was performed in Athens for the first time only two years after the slaughter at Melos. Euripides' drama is thus as much a reflection on the fate of Melos as it is on Troy.

The drama begins with the men of Troy already slain, often before the eyes of their women, and their city in ruins. The high-born women of Troy have been reduced to the status of captives and slaves. Awaiting imminent enforced departure from their native city, the captive women belong wholly to their victorious masters. Few, if any, of the women are compelled to endure a worse fate than Andromache, widow of Hector and mother of Astyanax. She has been informed that she is to become the wife of the son of Achilles, her husband's killer. When Hecuba, her mother-in-law, bewails the death of her daughter Polyxena, who has been offered up as a human sacrifice by the victors at the tomb of Achilles, Andromache replies:

> Mother, listen—I will explain something
> to you, so you will be happy.
> I want to give you some words of comfort, if I can,
> and to lighten your heart, already too heavy:
> I tell you this—not to have been born
> is the same as death: but to die,
> that is better than living in sadness;
> but the lucky man, sometimes called "the happy,"
> when his luck changes and goes bad,
> wanders in mind far from his former state.
> . . . . . . . . . . . . .

... mother, when the Greeks heard
that there was a woman and a wife like me,
[it] destroyed me and laid me open: Pyrrhus,
Achilles' son, wanted me to wife,
to make me a slave in a murderer's home:
for if by rejecting Hector and his ghost,
I offer my heart to my new husband,
I will appear unfaithful to a dead man,
but on the other hand, if I spurn Pyrrhus
I shall win my master's hate.
. . . . . . . . . . . . .
Now do you think that Polyxena's death,
for whom you were mourning just now,
is a greater thing than my misfortunes?
That which is left over for all men
is denied me: hope is no comfort in my life,
and I do not delude myself, thinking
I will attempt something useful—
but it is sweet to dream, and nothing more.

If Andromache sees no hope in the future, Hecuba does. She
counsels her daughter-in-law to be submissive and compliant to her
new master so that Astyanax, the young son of Andromache and
Hector, may grow to maturity and perhaps save Troy. However, as
Hecuba speaks, Talthybius, the messenger of the Greeks, informs
Andromache that the Greeks have resolved to kill Astyanax purely for
reasons of state:

Odysseus, addressing the assembly, put the motion through,
affirming that it was not in our best interests
to permit a Trojan hero's son to live in Greece.

Talythybius goes on to warn Andromache against resistance:

Think for a moment:
we have put an end to your city, your husband;
we hold you in our power: how can one woman
think to fight us? therefore it is my wish
that you give up this desire to fight about it,
and to do what would be disgraceful for you
and shame for you; and above all, to stop hurling curses
at the Greeks.
If you turn the army against you because of these insults,
your child will rot unburied, no one will pay him
the customary funeral rites: keep quiet and hope for the best,
give in to the pressure of events: in this way you will at least
insure your son a ritual death, and perhaps because of your
decorum
at this critical moment the Greeks will become your better
friends.

As we know, denial of a proper burial was the ultimate indignity for the Greeks. Andromache has only the choice of total submission or the horror that her child will lie unburied as so much refuse. Understandably, she submits.

The decision to slaughter an innocent child such as Astyanax has been repeated both singularly and en masse from time immemorial. We have seen a horrible example of this in Lebanon in September 1982. The slaughter of the innocent, especially a child, has always kindled a special sense of horror. Our sense of justice expects a measure of symmetry between an individual's behavior and his or her fate. Even Talthybius wants to have no part in the child's murder though he knows it must be done. He addresses first the child and then a Greek accomplice:

> Come on, lad, let go of your mother;
> she has her own sorrows: you must come
> with me to that embrasured ancestral tower
> where it has been decreed you shall die.
> Take him: matters such as this
> should have the services of a herald
> who pitiless and shameless understands
> the king's wisdom more than I.

Nevertheless, throughout history the slaughter of the innocent has been coldly and deliberately perpetrated by responsible political leaders pursuing what they considered rational ends as often as such slaughter has been the rampaging act of mob passion. The Greeks were acting with cold deliberation when they decided that, however innocent the child Astyanax might be, "it [is] not in our best interests/ to permit a Trojan hero's son to live in Greece." Their motive was to complete the destruction of the community of the defeated enemy. To the victors, such a decision appeared rational. They had risked their lives for the survival of their own community. They knew that in war neither mystical nor ontological status but victory in combat alone defines the difference between a king and a slave. They understood that their good fortune could easily have gone the other way. They also understood, as did Hegel and Nietzsche, that in defeat the enslaved captive remains an enemy who hopes some day to reverse the wheel of fortune. They understood the vanquished because they understood themselves. In their eyes, the personal innocence of little Astyanax was irrelevant because of his potential as a leader and savior of the defeated community.

There is a striking similarity in the traditions concerning the treatment of the vanquished enemy in the ancient civilizations of the Greeks and the Hebrews. This is evident in the following passage in Deuteronomy:

When you approach a city to make war on it, you shall offer it peace. If the city accepts the offer and opens its gates to you, then all the people in it shall be put to forced labor and shall serve you. But if it does not make peace with you, but wages war against you, then you shall besiege it, and Yahweh your God will deliver it into your hands. You shall kill all the males with the sword. But the women and the little children and the cattle and all that is in the town, all the plunder in it, you shall seize for yourself. You may consume the spoil of your enemies which Yahweh your God gives you (Deut 20:10–14).

The passage is followed by what appears to be a later gloss which had the effect of limiting application of the injunction to enslave the adult males to "cities at a great distance" (Deut 20:15). In the case of neighoring communities, the law as given in the gloss was far harsher:

In the cities of those nations whose land Yahweh your God is giving you as a patrimony, you shall not leave any creature alive. You shall annihilate them—Hittites, Amorites, Canaanites, Perizzites, Hivites, Jebusites—as Yahweh your God commanded you, so that they might not teach you to imitate all the abominable things that they have done for their gods and so cause you to sin against Yahweh your God (Deut 20:16–18).

There is scholarly debate concerning the degree to which the indigenous Canaanite population was actually proscribed in different periods of Israelite history. Undoubtedly, there were instances, well attested in Scripture, when proscription of the enemy did take place, but Deuteronomy's insistence on universal proscription seems to be motivated by an ideological desire to keep the community free of foreign influences rather than a realistic demand for the extermination of the neighoring peoples. The author of the passage was fearful of the religio-cultural consequences of contact with the Canaanite world. He regarded Canaanite paganism as utterly incompatible with the values of his own community. What was at stake was the preservation of Israel's religio-cultural world rather than simple hatred of the stranger. This is evident in the fact that Deuteronomy also prescribes the same harsh treatment for both the individual Israelite and the Israelite city that permit the introduction of pagan customs (Deut 13:6–11) In the case of the Israelite city, the prescription is as follows:

If after diligent examination, the report proves to be true and it is shown that this abominable thing has been done among you, you shall put the inhabitants of the city to the sword; you shall lay the city under solemn ban together with everything in it. You shall gather all its goods into the square and offer both city and goods as a complete offering to Yahweh your God; and it shall remain a mound of ruins, never to be rebuilt.

Nevertheless, the demand that an enemy city be put under a solemn ban—the Hebrew word is *herem*—is consistent with the biblical conception of the nature of war, especially in the period before

Solomon. In the biblical worldview war is more than the extension of diplomacy "by other means" as Clausewitz had argued. War continues diplomacy by other means only when the combatants more or less share the same fundamental civilization and values, as was the case with the warring states of Christian Europe before the twentieth century. War between peoples of incompatible values can also be relatively moderate in aim when neither side has the capacity to annihilate the other. In the Bible, war between Israel and her neighbors was normally seen as a conflict between two radically different "worlds" in the sociological sense of the word. Such a conflict is a religious or holy war par excellence and is the kind that can result in extermination or, at the very least, the total destruction of the hostile community. The Danish biblical scholar Johannes Pedersen captures the spirit of this kind of conflict: "The hostile armies meet in battle, each bringing its entire world with it. Each people appears in all its strength, with its history, and its God." Given the radical incompatibility of the worlds in conflict, there was no way the victor could absorb the defeated enemy into its midst. Unless the victor had imperial interests, as did Solomon, Alexander, and the Roman Caesars, the defeated could expect expulsion, enslavement, or death.

An important example of the biblical conception of the Holy War can be found in the call for the extermination of Edom in Isaiah 34, believed by some scholars to have been written during the period following Israel's return from Babylon:

> For the sword of Yahweh appears in heaven.
> See how it descends on Edom,
> On the people whom he dooms to destruction. . . .
> For the Lord has a day of vengeance,
> The champion of Zion has a year when he will requite.
> Edom's torrents shall be turned into pitch
> And its soil into brimstone,
> And the land shall become blazing pitch,
> Which night and day shall never be quenched,
> And its smoke shall go up forever.
> From generation to generation it shall lie in waste,
> And no man shall pass through it ever again. . . .
> No king shall be acclaimed there,
> And all its princes shall come to nought (34:5–12).

The picture presented here is one in which God causes the utter destruction and extermination of Edom, its people and its institutions. Moreover, the author of this passage was no ordinary writer but was one of the founders of the religious civilization of the western world. In the face of bloodthirsty passages of this sort, liberals tend to adopt an intellectual strategy relegating them to the domain of "primitive" values from which our "higher" ideals have evolved. Such a strategy aims to preserve the legitimacy of the biblical text by placing it in an evolutionary continuum. There is, however, greater evidence of the perennial than the "primitive" character of these terrible ideas. For example, there was little that was "primitive" in the successful wars of expulsion and extermination waged by the Puritan settlers against the Indians. Faced with a civilization incompatible with and unassimilable to their own and convinced that they were God's New Israel, the Euro-American settlers proceeded to eliminate the Amerindians, in some cases by confining them to segregated precincts, in others by outright extermination. The first concentration camp in North America was set up in 1675 during King Philip's War when most of the inhabitants of the Indian towns near Boston were incarcerated on Deer Island in Boston harbor.

Those Euro-Americans who required religious legitimation for their actions, and there were many, easily found it in Scripture. As the religio-cultural foundation of Puritan civilization, the Bible legitimated the expulsion and extermination of the indigenous population by those who considered themselves "God's New Israel." As the Indians ceased to be necessary to the New England economy, the Puritans turned on them with a ferocity and a thoroughness the Indians had never before experienced. In May 1637 the entire Pequot tribe was exterminated. Captain John Underhill, the Puritan leader in the slaughter, observed that, unlike the Puritans, the Indians fought each other "more for pastime than to conquer and subdue enemies." Lazar Ziff has written about the lessons learned by the Indians allied to the Puritans on the day the Pequots were exterminated:

> "Conquer and subdue" was the Puritan goal, and consequently the English entered into the skirmish with such a will that their Indian allies cried out to them, "Mach it, mach it; that is, It is naught, because it is furious and slays too many men." Victory and annihilation were not the same thing in their [the Indians'] outlook. But English war, the Mohegans learned that day, was not symbolic and exemplary of the superior art of the victor; it was massive and aimed at annihilation. . . . The Indians came to see the English as incredibly furious, bent on the kill at the expense of all else.

Regrettably, in their thoroughness and their systematic destructiveness, there is nothing "primitive" about wars of extermination.

## II

When we reflect on the tragic events in Lebanon during the summer of 1982, it is evident the situation in that country began to fall apart with the collapse of the central government in the civil strife of the nineteen-seventies. As long as the central state retained some credible authority, the country did not disintegrate into a collection of warring tribal or feudal groups, each with its own private army. Because of the religious split between Christians and Muslims, state authority could not rest on a religious foundation as it did in the ancient world. The modern state can be seen as an abstract institution that has attempted to fill the vacuum left by the demise of the integrated religio-political community of an earlier period. Lacking sacred authority, the modern political state rests upon two related foundations, the consent of its citizens and its monopoply of the instruments of coercion within its territory.

The dual foundation of the modern secular state was understood by Thomas Hobbes in the seventeenth century. As is well known, Hobbes argued that men covenant to place a sovereign with absolute power over them in order to escape the radical insecurity of the "state of nature." According to Hobbes, without the coercive power of the sovereign to guarantee public order, men would be locked in an intolerable state of universal hostility

> ... where every man is Enemy to every man; ... wherein men live without other security, than what their own strength, and their own invention shall furnish them withall.

The proliferation of private militias in Lebanon demonstrates the abiding validity of Hobbes' thesis. When the secular central government failed to provide effective political authority by guaranteeing the security of its citizens, the Lebanese had no alternative but to submit to those who did possess a monopoly of the instruments of coercion in whatever area they were domiciled or to band together and form such groups on their own. As is known, in parts of Lebanon, the PLO, aided by a generous infusion of foreign money and armament, possessed the monopoly of force. In other areas it was the Syrians, or the Israeli-backed Christian militia of Major Haddad, or the various other Muslim or Christian militias. Community, security, and authority all tended to narrow to whatever small circle of mutual trust and obligation remained credible. In general, one's community of trust and obligation was based on either common origin or comon faith. Indeed, in Lebanon as elsewhere, differences of faith often reflected tribal and kinship differences.

When the PLO was negotiating the terms of its departure from Beirut, one of its principal concerns was the fate of the Palestinian community after the departure of the PLO armed forces. The PLO leadership understood that neither shared trust nor obligation existed between the Palestinians and the Lebanese, whether Christian or Muslim. They further understood that a defenseless Palestinian community would be wholly dependent upon Lebanese groups who had every reason to want to eliminate them from the Lebanese body politic and would have the means to do so. The PLO understandably sought guarantees from disinterested third parties such as the United States that the departure of their armed forces would not leave the remaining Palestinians at the mercy of their enemies. Put differently, the PLO attempted through diplomacy to prevent its community from paying the full price of defeat in war. If, as appears to be the case, the United States gave the PLO assurances that Palestinian civilians would be safe, then our first withdrawal from Beirut appears to have been premature if not irresponsible. The situation of the Palestinians after the destruction of their military capability left them in the situation of any defeated enemy community in the ancient Near East. As we have seen, whether the community was destroyed by the enslavement of all its members, the extermination of adult males, or total extermination, defeat spelled the end of the vanquished community. It is, however, important that the reason for such harsh treatment be kept in mind. Having risked everything in war, the victors were determined to prevent the vanquished from having a second chance to enslave or exterminate them.

It is interesting to note how different the real situation of the Palestinians was from the way the PLO departure was depicted in the media. Had there been no television crews to record the event for the hundreds of millions of onlookers throughout the world, it is doubtful that the departing Palestinians would have left with public demonstrations of celebration and triumph as they did. Millions beheld theater on their screens, but it was not truthful theater. The ancients would not have been deceived. They would never have regarded the fall of a besieged city as anything but a disaster for the vanquished. The departure of the PLO was in reality a catastrophic defeat. The bravado and the gunfire could not alter the predicament of the remaining Palestinians. They had become defenseless against their enemies, as the brutal massacres at the Sabra and Shatilla camps demonstrated. Moreover, the full scope of their helplessness was revealed only after the massacres, when Lebanese authorities announced their intention to reduce the size of the Palestinian presence in their country by ninety percent.

Once it became known that the Lebanese intended to encourage the departure of the Palestinians, the rationale behind the slaughter at Sabra and Shatilla became apparent. The massacres in the camps were a traditional pogrom, that is, mob violence against a target population tolerated or encouraged by public authorities. The pogroms are regarded by authorities as a means of putting the target population on notice that, whatever their previous status, they are now considered strangers who can expect none of the normal legal protections of the community, even if they continue to be law-abiding. Public authorities usually resort to pogroms when they do not wish to exterminate a target population but are nevertheless determined to eliminate it by effectively encouraging its departure.

There is great irony in the fact that at the time of the Beirut massacre, the public authority consisted largely of the descendants of the victims of the pogroms of Europe. The pogroms that took place in Tsarist Russia from 1881 onwards were tolerated, if not welcomed, by public authorities because they were enormously successful in encouraging the target population to depart. Between 1881 and 1930 over 4,000,000 Jews left Russia. A similar motive was involved in the pogrom known as Kristallnacht which took place in National Socialist Germany in November 1938. The public authorities sought to encourage mass emigration. As we know, shortly thereafter the National Socialist government decided that mass extermination was a more effective means of eliminating the target population.

In the summer of 1982, like the original inhabitants of Canaan and the Indians of North America, the Palestinians of Beirut were a population targeted for elimination. Moreover, even the departure of the Israeli army from Lebanon is not likely to alter their fate. In the ancient world, overt violence was normally the method employed to eliminate a defeated community. In modern times, bureaucratic strategies, such as concentration camp confinement or the deportation of men and women with "irregular" or "invalid" indentity papers, have proven equally effective. Lebanese authorities may be less noticeable and overtly less violent than were the Phalangists who massacred the unarmed Palestinians. Nevertheless, by means of police and bureaucratic harassment they have the power to bring about the departure of the majority of the Palestinians. Unfortunately, there does not seem to be any community willing or able to absorb them.

Under the circumstances, the Palestinian demand for a state of their own in Palestine is altogether understandable. It is noteworthy, however, that President Reagan's recent peace proposals exclude that possibility for reasons that are equally understandable. Sovereignty is ultimately a matter of possessing a monopoly of force. Neither the Israelis nor the Jordanians are likely to permit the creation, in territory between them, of even a miniscule power that might some day have the capacity to make war. Just as the Greeks refused to permit Astyanax to grow to manhood, so too neither the Israelis nor the Jordanians are likely to permit a savior or a saving community to nourish the hopes of the defeated Palestinians that they can someday reverse their fortunes. The Palestinians, first defeated in their homeland and then outside of it, have become the new wandering Jews, while the old wandering Jews are resolved never to permit their enemy the chance to exile or exterminate them yet another time.

## III

At the beginning of the 1982 war, the Israelis stated that they were entering Lebanon to put an end to the shelling of northern Israel by the PLO. This may have been their original war aim, but the objective of the invasion quickly became the destruction of the PLO mini-state in Lebanon. After the dissolution of the Lebanese government as an effective political authority during the civil war, possession of a monopoly of force, even in a small territory, was sufficient to create a mini-state. Whether recognized as such by other nations, the PLO was in fact such a state.

As long as the PLO state survived, Palestinians in Lebanon were in no danger of deportation or wanton slaughter. All this changed with their defeat by the Israelis. Thereafter, their very existence was dependent upon hostile strangers. Ironically, the fate of the Palestinians offers grim evidence of the reasons the Israelis felt compelled to risk all they had to create their own political state, even at the cost of displacing the former inhabitants of the territory. It is also the opinion of this writer that the fate of the Palestinians points to the ultimacy of the political dimension of human existence.

Neither of these opinions are shared by one of Israel's most implacable academic critics, biblical scholar George E. Mendenhall. Nevertheless, Mendenhall's opinions are to be taken seriously even when they are stated, as they sometimes are, with intemperate hostility to Zionism as an ideology and the State of Israel as a political entity.* To the best

---

*For an example of Mendenhall at his most intemperate, see his article in *The Ann Arbor News,* Sunday, July 18, 1982. Mendenhall characterizes the Israeli invasion of Lebanon as "a disaster unlike any since the barbarian Mongol invasions of the 13th century," ignoring the far greater loss of life the Lebanese, Palestinians, and Syrians inflicted on each other during the 1975 civil war. Mendenhall suggests that if America has a "moral commitment" to Israel as the only democratic state in the Near East, "then we should have had a moral commitment to Nazi Germany. . . ." Mendenhall writes of the Israeli "Anschluss" of Jerusalem and the Golan Heights, using the term employed by the Nazis to characterize their invasion and seizure of Austria in 1938. Mendenhall thus equates the Nazi threat to use overwhelming force in order to overrun independent Austria, which was no threat to Germany, to the Israeli capture of Jerusalem during the 1967 war *after* King Hussein had joined Syria and Egypt in their war against Israel and after the king had publicly declared that his objective was to drive the Israelis into the sea. This writer visited the West Bank and the Golan Heights in July 1967 and saw the comic books which had been distributed to Arab soldiers before and during the war by Syria and Jordan. They depicted Tel Aviv in flames and hook-nosed Jews drowning in the Mediterranean. A particularly revealing comment was made to me at the time by a young Palestinian: "You Jews have long memories. We are your cousins. What makes you think we have shorter memories? Sooner or later we shall return and destroy you." One wonders what realistic suggestions Menden-

of my knowledge, no other scholar has spelled out as clearly as he the profound difference between the political values implicit in the biblical theology of covenant and election and the classical political values of western civilization. Mendenhall sees the root of this difference in the conflict between the sacralized kingdom of the Pharaohs and the covenant made by Moses with Yahweh, the God of history. According to Mendenhall, Yahweh's insistence on exclusive worship was a revolutionary ethical and political challenge not only to Pharaoh but to all of the sacralized kingdoms of the ancient Near East. The functions and the authority that had normally been ascribed to human rulers were claimed at Sinai to be the prerogative of God alone.

By declaring their rulers to be gods, sacralized kingdoms in effect make the claim that the state and its institutions are self-legitimating. Yahweh's claim to Israel's exclusive loyalty is thus as much a political as a religious demand. According to Mendenhall, the covenant at Sinai makes the ascription of ultimacy to political institutions a blasphemous form of idolatry. The covenant at Sinai affirms the unqualified sovereignty of God and the subordination of all human institutions to the ethical obligations demanded by him. Mendenhall expresses the conflict of values in the following passage:

---

hall might have concerning the conditions under which the Israelis might turn over territory to such implacable enemies. Throughout Mendenhall's attack outraged denunciation follows denunciation but nowhere does he offer a single constructive suggestion concerning how the Israelis and the Palestinians, so deeply and bitterly distrustful of each other, might resolve their differences without mutual self-destruction. Apparently, it never occurs to him that after Hitler Jews are not likely to dismiss as hyperbole anybody's promise to exterminate them.

Mendenhall also complains that when the United States ignores the overwhelmingly anti-Israel sentiment of the United Nations, that organization is "slandered and vilified," as if there were anything sacrosanct about the UN. For a contrasting view of the United Nations, see Leo Kuper, *Genocide* (New Haven: Yale University Press, 1982), pp. 175–76, where Kuper comments on the dismal, partisan record of the United Nations in dealing with the phenomenon of genocide: "The performance of the United Nations Organization in the suppression of the crime of genocide is deeply disillusioning, particularly against the humanitarian ideals which inspired its founding, . . . ideals in which the suppression of . . . genocide were quite central. But of course the United Nations is not a humanitarian, but a political, organization, and its humanitarian goals are at the play of political forces, pressure blocs, in an arena where delegates pursue the divisive interests of the states they represent. . . . Above all, it is the rulers of the states of the world who gather together at the United Nations, and it is mainly, though not exclusively, the rulers who engage in genocide." It is difficult to read Mendenhall's abusive observations on Israel without concluding that he is far more interested in diatribe and denunciation than in making constructive suggestions that might be applicable to the real world where lives are at stake.

At Sinai there was made real in human experience the fact that there was an alternative to the deification of the state as the infallible cause of human well-being and security, and the final arbiter of human obligation. It is difficult to imagine a more perverse and vicious ideology than the notion that ethical obligation is a mere function of a social or political boundary line, but, unfortunately, there is little evidence of any other concept in the ancient world.

Given his commitment to the biblical theology of covenant and his uncompromising hostility to the ascription of primacy to the political order, it is hardly surprising that Mendenhall casts in a negative light the values he opposes. Nevertheless, it is simply not the case that ethical obligation in the ancient political community was "a mere function of a social or political boundary line." As we have noted, ethical obligation was a function of a religiously-legitimated circle of mutual trust and trustworthiness. The stranger was excluded from the circle of mutual trust because there was no credible assurance he could be trusted, especially in crisis situations. Far more was involved in ethical obligation in the sacralized societies of the ancient world than boundaries.

Nor, given his theological commitments, is it surprising that Mendenhall sees ancient Israel's ultimate downfall as the direct consequence of its failure to keep the Sinaitic covenant and its ascription of ultimacy to the interests of the political state. This position is, of course, the classical prophetic position. Mendenhall offers the following analysis of the defeats of ancient Israel:

> Before two centuries had passed, the newly formed community found ways in the pre-Mosaic paganism to substitute rituals for obedience under the pretext of political necessity. The consequence was division in 922, destruction in 917, 722, and 597, and finally the mass suicide of Masada in A.D. 70. Fortunately, the latter did not represent the sane opinion of most Jews of the time who evidently felt that the rule of God had nothing to do with the madness of power politics.

Mendenhall is, of course, correct in regarding the ethic implicit in the biblical theology of covenant and election as profoundly anti-political. A theocracy is simply not a polity. For those who accept such a theology with full understanding of its implications, the political state can have only a relative, instrumental value. Insofar as it conducts itself in accordance with God's commandments, the state has a legitimate role as the human institution capable of guaranteeing the security and well-being of its citizens; insofar as it deviates from the will of God and fails to take heed of God's warning chastisements, it deserves to be destroyed. Within the theology of covenant, there is nothing ultimate about the state. It is merely an instrument whose survival depends upon its utility.

As Mendenhall fully understands, such a position runs counter to the way the state was viewed by the great political philosophers. Even when Socrates was convinced that the polis had unjustly condemned him to death, he rejected flight and exile and accepted its judgment against him. According to Aristotle:

> . . . as all associations aim at some good, that one which is supreme will aim at the supreme good. That is the association we call the Polis, and that type of association we call political.

In contrast to the biblical view, Aristotle did not see the political order as an instrument of a higher principle. It alone aims at the supreme good. Similarly, Hegel saw the state as an absolute. One of his most controversial statements held: "Es is der Gang Gottes in der Welt, dass der Staat ist." Walter Kaufmann has translated Hegel's statement: "It is the way of God in the world, that there should be (literally: is) a state." Although careless readers have taken Hegel's statement to be a blind glorification of state power, in reality Hegel was interested in reminding us that the existence of a viable political order makes freedom, civilization, and, indeed, even religion possible. Although Hegel was as aware as any prophet of ancient Israel of the abuses political leaders can perpetrate, he was nevertheless convinced that "the state is the actuality of concrete freedom."

Hegel's view of the state as the guarantor of civilization is not unlike that of Hobbes who reminds us of the likely condition of men without a political order:

> In such condition, there is no place for Industry; because the fruit thereof is uncertain: and consequently no Culture of the Earth; no Navigation, nor use of commodities that may be imported by Sea; no commodious Building; no Instrument of moving and removing such things as require force; no Knowledge of the face of the Earth; no account of Time; no Arts; no Letters; no Society; and which is worst of all, continuall feare, and danger of violent death; And the life of man, solitary, poore, nasty, brutish and short.

Having experienced the anarchy of civil war in England, Hobbes understood that without a viable political structure, there could be security for no human institution. In reality, for any appeal to human rights to be more than pious rhetoric, a person must be a member of a political community with the power to defend his rights. As the grim history of the twentieth century has amply demonstrated, the groups which have been successfully targeted for elimination have invariably been those who could turn to no political power willing or able to defend their rights. An important reason for the establishment of the State of Israel was that the extermination camps convinced Europe's surviving Jews that, without a political structure of their own capable of effectively guaranteeing their right to exist, no other political structure and certainly no European religious institution would manifest any greater interest in guaranteeing their survival than these institutions had done during World War II.

Nor was the experience of Europe's Jews unique. A particularly graphic example of the intimate connection between political status and human rights can be seen in the fate of the Vietnamese "boat people" who were persistently attacked at sea by Thai pirates between 1978 and 1982. In the aftermath of its victory, the communist government of Vietnam decided to use its bureaucratic structure to encourage the emigration of over 1,000,000 predominantly ethnic Chinese members of the middle class. As members of the bourgeoisie and as Chinese, these people were regarded as doubly unassimilable to the new communist order. Initially, the refugees set out in small boats of doubtful seaworthiness, hoping to find a haven by hugging the coast and traveling northward to Thailand. Few succeeded. The vast majority were set upon by Thai fishermen turned pirate whose record for unspeakable cruelty and sadism has few parallels in the history of piracy. Tens of thousands of boat people were systematically robbed, the men viciously murdered, women gang-raped in front of their children, and the boats disabled. It soon became apparent that as long as the pirate activities were confined to the stateless boat people, no nation was concerned. Moreover, the attacks were tolerated, if not encouraged, by the Thai government as a means of discouraging the movement of the boat people to Thai ports. The boat people were without protection and wholly at the mercy of the pirates because they had ceased to be members of any political community willing or able to defend their elementary rights. Without meaningful political status, they were simply prey to be disposed of as their attackers desired.

Undoubtedly, after they settled on the land, the men and women of ancient Israel came to understand the necessity of giving priority to the maintenance and defense of their political structures. As Mendenhall correctly points out, settlement in the land meant compromising with or abandoning the old Sinaitic covenant. An institution that served the purpose of liberating the Hebrews from Egyptian and Canaanite political structures which had degraded and enslaved them was hardly a suitable vehicle for creating a new polity of their own. Where Mendenhall's analysis is open to question is his assertion that the major defeats of the Israelites from 597 to 70 were a direct consequence of their having turned away from the covenant. Given the power equation between the Israelite kingdoms and their imperial adversaries, does Mendenhall really think that the Israelites could have been victorious in any circumstance? Is it not more likely that ancient Israel was foredoomed to its defeats by its relative military weakness rather than the quality of its relationship with its God?

Predictably, Mendenhall sees the current State of Israel as a repetition of what he regards as Israel's ancient mistake, commitment to a political structure as the ultimate value. Passionately committed to the cause of the stateless Palestinians and convinced that Zionism is a pagan ideology, Mendenhall has even gone so far as to liken the actions of the State of Israel to those of National Socialist Germany.

Apparently it has never occurred to Mendenhall that both the Israelis and the Palestinians might be locked in a tragic encounter offering both adversaries little hope of a fortunate outcome. Although Mendenhall angrily attacks the Zionists as pagan, nowhere does he offer a realistic alternative to a political state as the institution capable of guaranteeing Israelis even the minimal right to exist as human beings. Moderate members of the PLO claim that such rights would be guaranteed were a secular, democratic state established in the entire land of Palestine. However, this is a proposal lacking in credibility to the Israelis, who understand that, in a state with an Arab majority, the monopoly of force would inevitably pass to the majority. This would leave the Jews wholly at the mercy of the Arabs for their survival. Given their bitter history, especially in the twentieth century, Israelis see no alternative but to trust in their own monopoly of force for their survival. It is, of course, entirely possible that the Israeli monopoly of force may some day be destroyed by Arab enemies and that Israel may some day become as Troy and Melos, but that is the risk a small state must be prepared to take.

The Palestinians have now been forced to learn the same bitter lesson the Jews and other defeated peoples have learned in an earlier age, namely, that the loss of the power to defend oneself can be equivalent to the loss of one's place in the world of men. As long as the Palestinians were protected by their own weapons, there was no talk in Lebanon of deporting refugees with irregular identity papers. Nor did bulldozers level refugee camps in the face of the oncoming winter, as took place in the fall of 1982. Without the capacity to defend themselves, the Palestinians have become the new wandering Jews. Like the old wandering Jews, if they do not assimilate within the countries of their diaspora, they will have little choice but to dream, and perhaps to plan, for a time when they can restore their own state in what they regard as their homeland. Should they succeed, no matter what promises they now make, the happiest fate that would await the Israelis would be to become unwelcome wanderers once again. Like Antigone and Creon, the Israelis and the Palestinians are locked in hopeless combat.

*Bibliographical Note*

The quotations from *The Trojan Women* are from Charles Doria's translation (in *An Anthology of Greek Tragedy*, ed. Albert Cook and Edwin Dolin; Indianapolis: Bobbs-Merrill, 1972); those from Thucydides, where the story of Melos is told in Book 5, are after *The Peloponnesian War*, trans. Rex Warner (Harmondsworth: Penguin, 1980). Johannes Pedersen's treatment of *herem* is given in his *Israel: Its Life and Culture* (Copenhagen: Branner og Kroch, 1940). Larzer Ziff discusses the American treatment of Indians in *Puritanism in America: New Culture in a New World* (New York: Viking, 1973). The Vietnamese boat people are treated in Rubenstein, *The Age of Triage: Fear and Hope in an Overcrowded World* (Boston: Beacon, 1983). The quotations from Mendenhall's writings on ancient Israel are from his *The Tenth Generation* (Baltimore: Johns Hopkins, 1973).

*SIX*

# THE RELIGIOUS TRADITION

JACOB NEUSNER

# ACCOMMODATING MISHNAH TO SCRIPTURE IN JUDAISM: THE UNEASY UNION AND ITS OFFSPRING

From the formation of ancient Israelite Scripture into a holy book in Judaism, to begin with in the aftermath of the return to Zion and the creation of the Torah-book in Ezra's time (ca. 450 B.C.), the established canon of revelation (whatever its contents) presented a considerable problem to coming generations. As new writers came along, what they wrote had to be set into relationship with the established, authoritative Scripture. Otherwise, in the setting of Israelite culture, the new writings could find no ready hearing. Over the next six hundred years, from ca. 400 B.C. to ca. A.D. 200, four conventional ways to accommodate new writings to the established canon of received Scripture came to the fore. First and simplest, a writer would sign a famous name to his book, attributing his ideas to Enoch, Adam, Jacob's sons, Jeremiah, Baruch, and any number of others, down to Ezra. Second, he might also imitate the style of Biblical Hebrew and so try to creep into the canon by adopting the cloak of Scripture. Third, he would surely claim his work was inspired by God, a new revelation for an open canon. Fourth, at the very least, someone would link his opinions to biblical verses through the exegesis of the latter in line with the former, so Scripture would validate his views.

The authors of the pseudepigraphic books of the Old Testament took the first route; the writers of the Dead Sea Psalms and other compositions, the second; some of the pseudepigraphs, the third; the school of Matthew, the fourth. From the time of Ezra to the second century A.D., we have not got a single book clearly claiming religious sanction and standing as a holy book and authority over Israel, the Jewish nation, that fails to conform to one or more of these conventions. In these ways the new found its place in the framework of the old. Accordingly, we may describe how Israelite culture over the period of six hundred years dealt with the intimidating authority and presence of Scripture. We find essentially two modes of accommodation: imitation and augmentation. The newcomers would either imitate the old or they would link the new to the established.

To skip ahead in my story, from the third century to the eighteenth century, the normal mode of expressing creativity in Israelite culture—in all contexts of Judaism—remained precisely the same. Either people would imitate established conventions of literature, or they would link their compositions to existing ones in the guise of commentary and exegesis. In that long period of time in which the Hebrew Scripture reigned unchallenged as arbiter of Judaism in all its forms, from the formation of the Torah-book by Ezra to the advent of modernization in the nineteenth century, the only important alternatives available within the circle of the faith and the framework of the community of Judaism were imitate or augment: in either case, avoid the appearance of innovation. The Zohar, a mystical work composed in the thirteenth century, attributed its materials to second-century authorities. The composition of collections of biblical exegesis (*midrashim*) in the name of Talmudic sages constituted an ongoing convention of Jewish writing to the eighteenth century. Above all, like contemporary Christians and Moslems, Jewish writers composed their ideas into commentaries on established works of classical (Judaic) antiquity. Accordingly, the profoundly conservative and traditional traits of the ongoing culture of the Jewish people masked the equally deep-seated creative capacities of minds that were open and capable of imagination and innovation. Given the condition of Israel, a small group absorbing within its life the diverse cultures of Oriental Islam and European Christendom, superficially rigid constraints on creativity hardly present a puzzle. You could say anything you wanted, so long as it did not look new—not much of a limitation.

When, therefore, we come across an exception to the rule established by the literary conventions by which ancient writers made their way into the canon of Judaism, we must find the case remarkable. There was one document in which all of the established modes of saying the new in the guise of the old and enduring proved useless. I speak, further, of a document that, for its part, rarely cites Scripture and furthermore admits to no antecedents except for Scripture itself. The work at hand claims no point of contact with any book written by a Jew from its own day backward for nearly seven hundred years, to the time of Ezra (as we should say), or to the time of Moses (as its framers would allege). Further, from the document at hand, for the next eighteen hundred years to the present day, important expressions of Judaism flow forth. The work at hand followed no models, but itself served as a model for many. So all roads lead back to this book, but the book at hand leaps back to Sinai alone. Now if we want to know the exception to the iron rules of how in Judaism people say fresh and new ideas, we have therefore to confront the one document that violated all the rules and therefore established, from its time to ours, a whole new set of rules.

I refer to the Mishnah, a collection of exquisitely composed philosophical essays on various legal problems. Framed in carefully formalized and patterned sentences, put together within a nearly uniform set of literary conventions and redactional patterns, the Mishnah was established, from its time onward, as the principal source of Jewish law and mediator of the law of Scripture. In form, it is a construction in six divisions, themselves comprised of sixty-three tractates. All divisions take up the issue of the sanctification of Israel, the Jewish nation, through provision of the laws of holiness as they touch these six successive dimensions of the national life: the (agricultural) economy, the division of time and seasons, the conduct of the life of the family, with special attention to women and their rights, the construction of government and the conduct of civil law, the correct conduct of the service of God through the cult, and the protection of the life of the cult and the bed and table of the ordinary Israelite from the contagions of uncleanness and, so, for the possibility of sanctification.

## I. The Mishnah as a Crisis

Let me now explain why the Mishnah presents us with so stunning a literary anomaly and then raise the question of how the document was received by its continuators and brought into relationship with Scripture. When these two questions have been worked out, we shall have a fair picture of how the Hebrew Bible was received and mediated into the religion of Judaism, as that religion came to full expression in the Mishnah, the first definitive and normative document of Judaism, and the authoritative works that flowed from it. For when we recall that Judaism is the religion not of the Old Testament alone, any more than is the case with Christianity, but of the Old Testament as mediated by a second and central document, the issue at hand takes on considerable weight. Judaism is the religious tradition framed by the Hebrew Scriptures (called "the written Torah") and the documents beginning with the Mishnah itself (later on called, all together, "the oral Torah") which comprise (after the Mishnah) "the one whole Torah of Moses, our rabbi." So at issue is the birth of Judaism as we know it, in the age of the formation of the first document of Judaism after the Hebrew Bible itself. Judaism as we know it is the offspring of the uneasy but enduring union between Scripture and the Mishnah.

What the framers of the Mishnah did not do, to recapitulate, was what everyone else had done for well over a millennium. That is to say, the authorities in the Mishnah did not sign biblical names. Sayings in the Mishnah mainly bear the names of sages of the late first and second century A.D. Accordingly, we find not the slightest pretense of claiming antiquity for the document's allegations. The Hebrew of the Mishnah is totally different from the Hebrew of the Hebrew Scriptures. Its verbal system, for instance, makes provision for not only completed and continuing action, but also for past and future times, subjunctive and indicative voices, and much else. The syntax is like that of Indo-European, in that we can translate the word order of the Mishnah into any European Indo-European language and come up with perfect sense. None of that crabbed and artificial imitation of Biblical Hebrew that makes the Dead Sea scrolls an embarrassment to read characterizes the Hebrew of the Mishnah. Mishnaic style is elegant, subtle, exquisite in its sensitivity to word order and repetition, balance, and pattern.

The Mishnah moreover contains no allegation that any of its statements derives from God. Nor are the authors of the document alleged to have received revelation. To be sure, a rather odd and singular tractate, Abot, different from all other tractates of the Mishnah, begins with the allegation that "Moses received Torah at Sinai." The implication may be that part of the Torah—the Mishnah—was handed on orally, not in writing alone. But even here there is no explicit claim that the Mishnah, in particular, is *that* oral Torah of Moses at Sinai to which reference is made. Perhaps that is what is meant. Many suppose so. But it is not said in the way in which, for example, some writers of Old Testament pseudepigrapha say God spoke to them. Finally and most striking, unlike the first gospel, the splendid exegetical composition of the school of Matthew, the Mishnah contains remarkably little exegesis of the antecedent biblical writings. We discern no systematic effort to link laws and statements in the Mishnah with biblical verses.

The absence of such explicit links to Scripture as well as failure to provide some sort of myth of the origin of the law of the document together present a truly astonishing fact. The standing and authority of the Mishnah, the sanctions attending enforcement of the law, the reasons people ought to keep it and listen to the sages who enforced it—these are questions denied all attention. Perhaps the framers of the document, rather subtle philosophical lawyers, never imagined they should have to explain why people should obey the laws they made up, because they never imagined people would do so. Perhaps to begin with, the founders conceived their book as a kind of theoretical and speculative collection. Every paragraph of the Mishnah bears its share of contradictory opinions, framed as disputes about a common point, and that may mean the framers had not the slightest expectation that their book would serve as a lawcode. Arranging contradictory possibilities—*sic et non*, so to speak—may have served to turn abstract thought into concrete problems for future reflection. Accordingly, why invoke the authority and inspiration of Heaven for discourse on philosophical possibilities? But if that was the plan, it was never grasped by the successors and continuators of the document. For almost as soon as their work of framing the Mishnah was completed, it found its way into the service of the Jewish government of the Land of Israel of the day. The Mishnah enjoyed the political sponsorship of the head of that government, Judah, patriarch of the Jewish nation in its Land and recognized by the Roman government as ethnarch of the Jews of the Holy Land. It became the constitution and bylaws of the Jewish nation.

Accordingly whatever the original, theoretical character intended by the authors (if that is an accurate guess of what they had in mind), the Mishnah almost immediately demanded what its framers had denied it: a place within the canon of Judaism. In the nature of things, there were only two possibilities. Since no one now could credibly claim to sign the name of Ezra or Adam to a book of this kind, and since by ignoring Biblical Hebrew, the authors had provided themselves no apologetic through aesthetics, the only options lay elsewhere. The two were, first, provide a myth of the origin of the contents of the Mishnah, and, second, link each allegation of the Mishnah, through processes of biblical (not Mishnaic) exegesis, to verses of the Scriptures. These two procedures, together, would establish for the Mishnah that standing that the uses to which the document was to be put demanded for it: a place in the canon of Israel, a legitimate relationship to the Torah of Moses.

There were several ways in which the work went forward. These are represented by diverse documents that succeeded and dealt with the Mishnah. Let me now state the three principal possibilities. (1) The Mishnah required no systematic support through exegesis of Scripture in light of Mishnaic laws. (2) The Mishnah by itself provided no reliable information and all of its propositions demanded linkage to Scripture, to which the Mishnah must be shown to be subordinate and secondary. (3) The Mishnah is an autonomous document, but closely correlated with Scripture. The first extreme is represented by the Tosefta, a corpus of supplementary information about the Mishnah, a small part of it deriving, indeed, from the same period as the Mishnah's own composition. The second extreme is taken by the Sifra, a post-Mishnaic compilation of exegeses on Leviticus. The Sifra systematically challenges reason (= the Mishnah), unaided by revelation (that is, exegesis of Scripture), to sustain positions taken by the Mishnah, which is cited verbatim, and everywhere proves that it cannot be done. The third, and mediating, view is that of the Talmud of the Land of Israel, among the various documents produced by the Jewish sages of the Land of Israel between the end of the second century and the sixth. The Talmud of the Land of Israel (a.k.a. "Palestinian Talmud," "Yerushalmi"), like the one made up at the same period, in the third and fourth centuries, in Babylonia, was organized around the Mishnah. It provided a line by line or paragraph by paragraph exegesis and amplification of the Mishnah. Produced in sages' schools in Tiberias, Sepphoris, Lud (Lydda), and Caesarea, the Talmud of the Land of Israel developed a well-crafted theory of the Mishnah and its relationship to Scripture.

The Talmud of the Land of Israel forms the focus of the exposition to follow, on how the sages received the Mishnah and naturalized it into the framework of Scripture. The reason is that it is the most important holy book produced in the Land of Israel from the closure of the Mishnah to the beginning of the composition of collections of exegesis formed not around the Mishnah but around Scripture itself. These later collections, beginning in the fifth century with Genesis Rabbah, at the outset carried out with reference to Scripture precisely those procedures of exegesis and amplification established with regard to the Mishnah in the pages of the Talmud of the Land of Israel. They constitute therefore a literary echo of the controversies of the third and fourth century, debates precipitated by the peculiar character of the Mishnah, on the one side, and necessitated by its powerful political status and capital historical importance, on the other. So the Talmud is the centerpiece in describing the reception and explanation of the Mishnah.

## II. The Talmud's Theory of the Mishnah

The proper interpretation of the Mishnah in relationship to Scripture served as the ultimate guarantee of certainty. We therefore should anticipate a splendid myth of the origin and authority of the Mishnah, on which, for sages, all else rested. Yet, so far as I can see, the Talmud presents no explicit theory of the Mishnah as part of the Torah, that is, the revelation of Sinai. Implicitly, however, the Talmud's judgment of the Mishnah is self-evident, hardly demanding specification. After Scripture, the Mishnah is the authoritative law code of Israelite life, the center, the focus, the source. From it all else flows. Beyond the Mishnah looking backward to Sinai, sages see only Scripture. At the same time, the very implicit character of the expression of this fundamental judgment is puzzling. While nearly every unit of discourse of the Talmud—90 percent of the whole—pays its tribute to the importance of interpreting a cited law of the Mishnah, seldom does a passage of the Talmud speak about the Mishnah as a whole, let alone about its origin and authority. It is rare even to find an allusion to a complete tractate or even to a chapter as such. Accordingly, if we want to know how the sages of the Talmud, in the third and fourth centuries, explained to themselves the status and standing of the Mishnah as Torah, we are at a loss to find out. All is implicit, with views of the whole rarely expressed.

To be sure, in other documents contemporary to the Talmud at hand, the Mishnah is described as "oral Torah," Torah revealed by God to Moses at Mount Sinai and formulated and transmitted through a process of oral shaping and memorization. The myth of the two Torahs, one in writing, the other transmitted orally but now contained in the Mishnah and its continuations in the Talmuds, plays no substantial role in the Yerushalmi's treatment of the Mishnah. That myth does find expression in the Babylonian Talmud. To be sure, it is easier to say what is, than what is not, in either of the Talmuds. But it suffices at this stage to observe that the myth of the two Torahs is not invoked to account for the striking and paramount trait of the Yerushalmi: its consistent interest in the exposition and amplification of the Mishnah's laws. Nowhere are we explicitly told why that exercise is necessary.

Admittedly, the Yerushalmi knows full well the theory that there is a tradition separate from, and in addition to, the written Torah. But this tradition it knows as "the teachings of scribes." The Mishnah is not identified as the collection of those teachings. An ample instantiation of the Yerushalmi's recognition of this other, separate tradition is contained in the following unit of discourse. What is interesting is that, if these discussions take for granted the availability, to Israel, of authoritative teachings in addition to those of Scripture, they do not then claim those teachings are contained, uniquely or even partially, in the Mishnah in particular. Indeed, the discussion is remarkable in its supposition that extra-Scriptural teachings are associated with the views of "scribes," perhaps legitimately called sages, but not in a book, such as the Mishnah, to be venerated or memorized as a deed of ritual-learning.*

*Y. Abodah Zarah* 2:7:

III. A. Associates in the name of R. Yohanan: "The words of scribes are more beloved than the words of Torah and more cherished than words of Torah: 'Your palate is like the best wine' (Song 7:9)."

B. Simeon bar Ba in the name of R. Yohanan: "The words of scribes are more beloved than the words of Torah and more cherished than words of Torah: 'For your love is better than wine' (Song 1:2)." . . .

D. R. Ishmael repeated the following: "The words of Torah are subject to prohibition, and they are subject to remission; they are subject to lenient rulings, and they are subject to strict rulings. But words of scribes all are subject only to strict interpretation, for we have learned there: *He who rules, 'There is no requirement to wear phylacteries,' in order to transgress the teachings of the Torah, is exempt. But if he said, 'There are five partitions in the phylactery, instead of four,' in order to add to what the scribes have taught, he is liable'* [M. San. 11:3]."

E. R. Haninah in the name of R. Idi in the name of R. Tanhum b.

*In the following, M. indicates a passage from the Mishnah (ca. 200 A.D.), Y. a passage from the Talmud Yerushalmi (ca. 400–500 A.D.), and T. a passage from the Tosefta (ca. 200–400 A.D.). The abbreviations of the tractates are the standard ones.

> R. Hiyya: "More stringent are the words of the elders than the words of the prophets. For it is written, 'Do not preach'—thus they preach—'one should not preach of such things' (Micah 2:6). And it is written, '[If a man should go about and utter wind and lies, saying,] "I will preach to you of wine and strong drink," he would be the preacher for this people!' (Micah 2:11).
>
> F.  "A prophet and an elder—to what are they comparable? To a king who sent two senators of his to a certain province. Concerning one of them he wrote, 'If he does not show you my seal and signet, do not believe him.' But concerning the other one he wrote, 'Even though he does not show you my seal and signet, believe him.' So in the case of the prophet, he has had to write, 'If a prophet arises among you ... and gives you a sign or a wonder ...' (Deut 13:1). But here [with regard to an elder:] '... according to the instructions which they give you ...' (Deut 17:11) [without a sign or a wonder]."

What is important in the foregoing anthology is the distinction between teachings contained in the Torah and teachings in the name or authority of "scribes." These latter teachings are associated with quite specific details of the law and are indicated in the Mishnah's rule itself. Further, at E we have "elders" as against prophets. What conclusion is to be drawn from this mixture of word-choices referring to a law or tradition in addition to that of Scripture? The commonplace view, maintained in diverse forms of ancient Judaism, that Israel had access to a tradition beyond Scripture, clearly was well-known to the framers of the Yerushalmi. The question of how these framers viewed the Mishnah, however, is not to be settled by that fact. As I said, I cannot point to a single passage in which explicit judgment upon the character and status of the Mishnah as a complete document is laid down. Nor is the Mishnah treated as a symbol or called "the Orah Torah."

Still, there is ample evidence, once again implicit in what happens to the Mishnah in the Talmud, to allow a reliable description of how the Talmud's founders view the Mishnah. That view may be stated very simply. The Mishnah rarely cites verses of Scripture in support of its propositions. The Talmud routinely adduces Scriptural bases for the Mishnah's laws. The Mishnah seldom undertakes the exegesis of verses of Scripture for any purpose. The Talmud consistently investigates the meaning of verses of Scripture and does so for a variety of purposes. Accordingly, the Talmud, subordinate as it is to the Mishnah, regards the Mishnah as subordinate to, and contingent upon, Scripture. That is why, in the Talmud's view, the Mishnah requires the support of prooftexts of Scripture. That fact can mean only that, by itself, the Mishnah exercises no autonomous authority and enjoys no independent standing or norm-setting status. The task of the framers of the Talmud is not only to explain Mishnah-law but to prove *from Scripture* the facticity of rules of the Mishnah. Accordingly, insofar as the Talmud has a theory about the Mishnah as such, as distinct from a theory about the work to be done in the exposition and amplification and application to the court system of various laws in the Mishnah, it is quite clear. To state matters negatively (and the absence of articulate statements makes this the wiser choice), the Mishnah does not enjoy autonomous and uncontingent authority as part of "the one whole Torah of Moses revealed by God at Sinai." That conclusion is made ineluctable by the simple fact that one principal task facing sages, as I just said, is to adduce prooftexts for the Mishnah's laws. It follows that, without such texts, those laws stand on infirm foundations. We now turn to the ways in which the Yerushalmi does this work of founding, upon the secure basis of the written Torah, the fundamental propositions of the Mishnah's laws, taken up one by one.

### III. Scripture Behind the Mishnah in the Yerushalmi

Most units of discourse in the Yerushalmi, as I said, take up the exegesis and amplification of the Mishnah. Exegesis for the Talmudic sages means many things, from the close reading of a line and explanation of its word choices to large-scale, wide-ranging, and encompassing speculation on legal principles expressed in, among other places, the passage at hand. Yet two attitudes of mind appear everywhere.

First, the sages rarely, if ever, set out to twist the meaning of a Mishnah passage out of its original shape. Whatever problems they wish to solve, they do not resort to deliberately fanciful or capricious readings of what is at hand in the statement of the Mishnah's rule. Now that is an entirely subjective judgment, since one generation's plain sense is another age's fancy. What it means is (merely) that our sense and their sense of straightforward reading of a passage are the same. By our standards, they were honest men, because they thought then the way we do now. That fact is so ubiquitous and blatant as not to require further specification. Since a common heritage of intellectual procedures, a single view of the correct hermeneutics for a sacred text, read with philosophical clarity and honesty, joins us to them, we may reasonably express puzzlement with another paramount aspect of the Talmud's exegetical program.

The Talmud's sages, second, constantly cite verses of Scripture when reading statements of the Mishnah. These they read in their *own* way and framework. Let me spell this out. References to specific verses of Scripture are as uncommon in the Mishnah as they are routine in the Talmud. For the framers of the Talmud, certainty for the Mishnah's rules depended upon adducing Scriptural prooftexts. The entire system—the laws, courts, power of lawyer-philosophers themselves—thus is seen to rest upon the written revelation of God to Moses at Sinai, that alone. What this means for the sages' view of the Mishnah is that the details of the Mishnah depended for validity upon details contained within Mosaic revelation, in the written Torah. While, as we saw, some traditions, deemed entirely valid, were attributed to scribes of olden times, these enjoyed an explicitly subordinated status, quite separate from the statements of the written Torah.

The Mishnah, to begin with, was treated only as a collection of rules, each to be faithfully read by itself as a detail. That is why Scriptural prooftexts were cited to support one rule after another, without any large-scale thesis about the status of the document containing those discrete rules. Just as the sages of the Talmud read the Mishnah bit by bit, so they adduced evidence from Scripture for its rules, bit by bit. There can then have been no consideration whatever of the proposition that the Mishnah stood alongside of, and next to, the written Torah, as the oral part of "the one whole Torah of Moses, our rabbi." If that version of the Torah-myth found its way into the Yerushalmi at all, as I said, it played no considerable role in the approach of the Yerushalmi to the question of the authority and certainty of the principal document, the Mishnah itself. The Talmud's fragmented vision of the Mishnah accounts for the character of the Yerushalmi's approach, through passages of the Mishnah, to verses of Scripture.

Let us now proceed to review the types of ways in which the Talmud presents prooftexts for allegations of passages of the Mishnah, a sizable repertoire. We begin with the simplest example, an instance in which a passage of the Mishnah is cited, then linked directly to a verse of Scripture, deemed to constitute self-evident proof for what has been said. The Mishnah's rule is given in italics.

*Y. Abodah Zarah 4:4:*

III. A. [citing M. A.Z. 4:4:] *An idol belonging to a gentile is prohibited forthwith,* in line with the following verse of Scripture: "You shall surely destroy [all places where the nations whom you shall dispossess served their gods]" (Deut 12:2)—forthwith.

B. *And one belonging to an Israelite is prohibited only after it will have been worshipped,* in line with the following verse of Scripture: "Cursed be the man who makes a graven or molten image, an abomination to the Lord, a thing made by the hands of a craftsman, and set it up in secret" (Deut 27:15)—when he will set it up.

C. There are those who reverse the matter:

D. An idol belonging to an Israelite is prohibited forthwith, as it is written, "Cursed be the man who makes a graven or molten image."

E. And one belonging to a gentile is prohibited only after it will have been worshipped, as it is written, "You shall surely destroy all the places where the nations whom you shall dispossess served their gods."

F. R. Isaac bar Nahman in the name of Samuel derived that same view [that an idol belonging to a gentile is prohibited only after it will have been worshipped] from the following: If one has inherited [the idol] when it [already] is deemed a god, "in fire will you burn it," and if not: "whom the nations whom you shall dispossess . . . their gods." [You shall tear down their altars and dash in pieces their pillars and burn their Asherim with fire . . .] (Deut 12:2–3).

The instance shows the convention. A statement of the Mishnah is given, followed by a verse of Scripture regarded as proof of the antecedent conception. All we have are sentences from the one document, the Mishnah, juxtaposed to sentences from the other, the Scripture.

Along the lines of the foregoing, but somewhat more complex, is the case in which the language of the Mishnah rule is not cited verbatim, but the underlying proposition is stated, then provided with a proof-text. Here is one example of this phenomenon. Again, the Mishnah passage is in italics.

Y. Baba Mesia 2:1:

A. *What lost items are [the finder's], and which ones is he liable to proclaim [in the lost-and-found]?*

B. *These lost items are his [the finder's]:*

C. *"[If] he found pieces of fruit scattered about, coins scattered about, small sheaves in the public domain, cakes of figs, baker's loaves, strings of fish, pieces of meat, wool-shearings [as they come] from the country [of origin], stalks of flax, or tongues of purple—lo, these are his," [the words of R. Meir].*

I. A. [Since the operative criterion in M. B.M. 2:1 is that, with undistinguished items such as these, the owner takes for granted he will not recover them and so despairs of them, thus giving up his rights of ownership to them, we now ask:] Whence do we know from the Torah the law of the owner's despair [of recovering his property constitutes relinquishing rights of ownership and declaring the property to be ownerless, hence available to whoever finds it]?

B. R. Yohanan in the name of R. Simeon b. Yehosedeq: "'And so you shall do with his ass; so you shall do with his garment; so you shall do with any lost thing of your brother's, which he loses and you find; you may not withhold your help' (Deut 22:3)—

C. "That which is [perceived as] lost by him and found by you, you are liable to proclaim [as having been found], and that which is not [perceived as] lost by him [because he has given up hope of recovering it anyhow] and found by you, you are not liable to proclaim.

D. "This then excludes that for which the owner has despaired; which is lost to him and to any one."

What is striking in the preceding instance is the presence of a secondary layer of reasoning about the allegations of a verse of Scripture. The process of reasoning then derives, from the verse, a principle not made explicit therein, and that principle turns out to be precisely what the Mishnah's rule maintains. Accordingly, the Mishnah's law is shown to be merely a reversal of the Scripture's, that is, the reverse side of the coin. Or the Scripture's rule is shown to deal only with the case pertinent to the Mishnah's law, rather than to what, on the surface, that biblical law seems to contain.

We proceed to an instance in which a disputed point of the Mishnah is linked to a dispute on the interpretation of the pertinent verses of Scripture. What is important now is that the dispute in the Mishnah is made to devolve upon, not principles of law, but readings of the same pertinent verses of Scripture. Once again the net effect is to turn the Mishnah into a set of generalizations of what already is explicit in Scripture, a kind of restating in other language of what is quite familiar—therefore well-founded. The Mishnah passage is in italics.

*Y. Makkot 2:2:*

A. *[If] the iron flew from the heft and killed someone,*

B. *Rabbi says, "He does not go into exile."*

C. *And sages say, "He goes into exile."*

D. *[If] it flew from the wood which is being split,*

E. *Rabbi says, "He goes into exile."*

F. *And sages say, "He does not go into exile."*

I. A. What is the Scriptural basis for the position of Rabbi [at M. 2:2D–E]?

   B. Here it is stated, ". . . [and the head] slips [from the handle and strikes his neighbor so that he dies . . .]" (Deut 19:5).

   C. And later on, the same verb root is used: "[. . . for your olives] shall drop off . . ." (Deut 28:40).

D. Just as the verb root used later means "dropping off" so here it means "dropping off."

E. What is the Scriptural basis for the position of the rabbis [at M. 2:2F]?

F. Here the verb root "slipping" is used.

G. And later on elsewhere we have the following: ". . . and clears away many nations before you . . ." (Deut 7:1).

H. Just as the verb root "clearing away" refers to an [active] blow there, so here too it speaks of an [active] blow [by an object which strikes something, e.g., the ax, not chips of wood].

We see that both parties to the Mishnah's dispute read the same verse. The difference then depends upon their prior disagreement about the meaning of the verse. The underlying supposition is that the Mishnah simply restates in general language the results of the exegesis of biblical law.

We consider, finally, an instance in which the discussion of the Talmud consists wholly in the analysis of the verses of Scripture deemed to prove the point of the Mishnah. The upshot is that we deal not with a mere formality but a protracted, sustained inquiry. That is to say, the discussion of the Talmud transcends the limits of the Mishnah and becomes a well-developed discourse upon, *not* the Mishnah's rule, but Scripture's sense. What is important in the next item is the fact that the search for prooftexts in Scripture sustains not only propositions of the Mishnah, but also those of the Tosefta as well as those of the Talmud's own sages. This is a stunning fact. It indicates that the search of Scripture is primary, the source of propositions or texts in particular to be supported by those Scriptures, secondary. There is no limit, indeed, to the purposes for which Scriptural texts will be found relevant. The Mishnah's words are in italics, Tosefta's in bold face.

*Y. Sanhedrin 10:4:*

II. A. *The party of Korach has no portion in the world to come and will not live in the world to come,* [M. San. 10:4].

B. What is the Scriptural basis for this view?

C. "[So they and all that belonged to them went down alive into Sheol;] and the earth closed over them, and they perished from the midst of the assembly" (Num 16:33).

D. *"The earth closed over them"—in this world.*

E. *"And they perished from the midst of the assembly"—in the world to come* [M. San. 10:4D–F].

F. It was taught: **R. Judah b. Batera says, "[The contrary view] is to be derived from the implication of the following verse:**

G. "'I have gone astray like a lost sheep: seek thy servant [and do not forget thy commandments]' (Ps 119:176).

H. "Just as the lost object which is mentioned later on in the end is going to be searched for, so the lost object which is stated herein is destined to be searched for" [T. San. 13:9].

I. Who will pray for them?

J. R. Samuel b. Nahman said, "Moses will pray for them:

K. 'Let Reuben live, and not die, [nor let his men be few]' (Deut 33:6)."

L. R. Joshua b. Levi said, "Hannah will pray for them."

M. This is the view of R. Joshua b. Levi, for R. Joshua b. Levi said, "Thus did the party of Korach sink ever downward, until Hannah went and prayed for them and said, 'The Lord kills and brings to life; he brings down to Sheol and raises up' (1 Sam 2:6)."

We have a striking sequence of prooftexts, serving, one by one, the cited statement of the Mishnah, A–C, then an opinion of a rabbi in the Tosefta, F–H, then the position of a Talmudic rabbi, J–K, L–M. The process of providing the prooftexts therefore is central, the differentiation among the passages requiring the prooftexts, a matter of indifference.

### IV. Conclusion

We began with the interest in showing how the Scripture is made to supply prooftexts for propositions of the Mishnah, with consequences for the Talmud's theory of the Mishnah now requiring no repetition. But we see at the end that the search for appropriate verses of Scripture vastly transcended the purpose of study of the Mishnah, exegesis of its rules, and provision of adequate—Scriptural—authority for the document and its laws. In fact, any proposition to be taken seriously will elicit interest in Scriptural support, whether one in the Mishnah, in the Tosefta, or in the mouth of a Talmudic sage himself. So the main thing is that the Scripture is placed at the center and focus. A verse of Scripture settles all pertinent questions, wherever they are located, whatever their source. That is the Talmud's position. We know full well that it is not the Mishnah's position.

If the sages of the second century, who made the Mishnah as we know it, spoke in their own name and in the name of the logic of their own minds, those who followed, certainly the ones who flourished in the later fourth century and stand behind the Talmud, took a quite different view. Reverting to ancient authority like others of their age, they turned back to Scripture, deeming it the source of certainty about truth as they knew it. Unlike their masters in the Mishnah, theirs was a quest for a higher authority than the logic of their own minds. The shift from age to age then is clear. The second-century masters, who made the Mishnah, took commonplaces of Scripture, well-known facts, and stated them wholly in their own language and context. Fourth-century masters phrased commonplaces of the Mishnah or banalities of worldly wisdom, so far as they could, in the language of Scripture and its context.

But, as we saw at the end, this quest in Scripture for certainty far transcended the interest in supplying the Mishnah's rules with ample prooftexts. On the contrary, the real issue turns out to have been not the Mishnah at all, nor even its diverse sayings vindicated one by one. Once what a *sage* says, not merely a rule for the Mishnah, is made to refer to Scripture for proof, it must follow that, in the natural course of things, a rule of the Mishnah and of the Tosefta will likewise be asked to refer also to Scripture.

In other words, in phrasing matters as I have, I have turned matters on their head. The fact that the living sage validates what *he* says through Scripture explains why the sage *also* validates through verses of Scripture what the ancient sages of the Mishnah and Tosefta say. It is one, undivided phenomenon. The reception of the Mishnah constitutes merely one, though massive, testimony to a prevalent attitude of mind, important for the age of the Talmud, the third and fourth centuries, not solely for the Mishnah. The stated issue was the standing of the Mishnah, as I said. But the heart of the matter turns out to have been the authority of the sage himself. It is he who identified with the authors of the Mishnah and who claimed authoritatively to interpret the Mishnah and much else, specifically including Scripture. So the appeal to Scripture in behalf of the Mishnah represents simply one more expression of what proved critical in the formative age of Judaism: the person of the holy man himself, this new man, this incarnate Torah. When revelation—Torah—had become flesh, Judaism was born.

*Bibliographical Note*

On the relation between intellectual life and Judaism, see Neusner, *The Glory of God Is Intelligence* (Provo, Utah: Brigham Young University, 1978). On the Mishnah in particular, see *Judaism: The Evidence of the Mishnah* (Chicago: University of Chicago Press, 1981) and the Yale translation, *The Mishnah* (New Haven: Yale University Press, 1982). For selections from the Palestinian Talmud, see *Judaism: The Evidence of the Yerushalmi* (Chicago: University of Chicago Press, 1983). On the Babylonian Talmud, see *Invitation to the Talmud* (New York: Harper & Row, 1973). Other relevant ancient sources are surveyed in *Approaches to Ancient Judaism*, ed. W. S. Green (Brown Judaic Studies 1. Chico, California: Scholars Press, 1978), and *The Study of Ancient Judaism*, ed. Neusner (New York: KTAV, 1981), 2 vols.

AIDAN KAVANAGH

# SCRIPTURE AND WORSHIP IN
# SYNAGOGUE AND CHURCH

The purpose of this essay is to offer only a few trenchant observations on the role of scripture in the worship lives of those who participate in the Judeo-Christian religious tradition. The category of "scripture" is a large one which is constantly overflowing its boundaries. Here, it will be restricted to those works which each of the two parts of the common tradition generally has recognized as canonical: the Hebrew Bible's Law and the Prophets, the Christian Bible's gospels and apostolic writings. The category of "Judeo-Christian tradition" is no less large and not uncontroverted. From certain points of view, it is not one tradition but two. Here, it will be regarded as a tradition not without sharp distinctions between its two parts, but as a common tradition nonetheless. When all is said and done, Jew and Christian are more like each other than either of them are like Hindus and Buddhists or Pygmies and secularists. Christians have never been entirely easy to explain, but without Judaism Christianity is inexplicable.

## I

Standard procedure, especially among academics, has been to begin with scripture as the constitutive norm of the common tradition and finally, if there is time, to add some parenthetical remarks on how worship derives from the scriptural norm. This sequence is unsatisfactory because it is unable to account for the influence worship has had in constituting the scriptural norm in the common tradition. The following are contrary theses offered in order to modify the standard procedure.

1. *Judeo-Christian worship is worship of the Utterer of the divine Word, but it is not worship of written scripture.*

While the Judeo-Christian tradition accords the written scriptures marks of deepest veneration, it has never regarded the written scriptures, whether in Torah scrolls or in gospel book, as the object of liturgical cult. The object of Judeo-Christian worship has always been God alone. Anything less than this has received the vigorous criticism of apostle no less than of prophet. This exclusivity concerning the object of the common tradition's cult does not rule out loving care and

480

veneration of all those creatures which proceed from God's creating hand, nor does veneration of some thing or person obliterate the distinction between Creator and creature. Much less does it reverse their order of precedence or make the creature an object of worship on a par with God.

2. *Judeo-Christian worship is steeped in scripture but is not derived from it alone either in general or in detail.*

Neither Jews nor Christians waited to worship until the writing of their scriptures was complete. Their worship, on the contrary, antedates or is at least contemporary with the writing of every one of the books of the Hebrew and Christian Bibles. Indeed, the presence of already well-elaborated worship structures is often visible in these books themselves and cannot but have functioned in giving shape to the community of discourse which the books presume and seek to foster. The gospel of John, for example, is apparently structured not around the chronology of Jesus' life so much as around major feasts in the Jewish calendar of the time, from Sukkoth to Passover. These feasts appear to form the backdrop for interpreting the significance of what Jesus did and said. To be ignorant of Jewish festivals thus reduces one's ability to grasp what the author of the gospel wishes to say about Jesus, his life and work. The point for emphasis here is that it is not the writing of scripture which makes worship possible; it is assembling for worship which makes the writing and canonizing of scripture inevitable. The common tradition has never restricted itself to elaborating the structure or details of its worship from its canonical scriptures alone.

3. *Judeo-Christian worship is not scripture's stepchild. It is scripture's home.*

The assembly which worships is, under God, the "ecological" context of scripture's origination and sustenance. It is that assembly which, by its myriad transactions with divine and human reality, sustains a continuum of discourse within which the Word is uttered intelligibly for human consumption, written intelligibly for human pondering, and proclaimed intelligibly for human response. In this view, scripture and worship are not diverse and static categories but dynamically related aspects, in word and act, of a single dialectic between divine and human agents in which the divine has transcendent priority but the human is never shut out or reduced to brute passivity. God indeed judges human acts, but in doing so recognizes that the very basis of judgment lies in our being free and responsible in whatever we do. We are never irresponsible passives in the hands of an arbitrary deity. God's way may not be our ways, as the story of Job illustrates. Even so, humanity remains God's creature and the object of God's graceful solicitude, as the stories of Isaac, Jacob, and Jesus make clear.

## II

The purpose of the three foregoing assertions is not to demonstrate but merely to assert that the force which drives Jews and Christians to write scripture is the same force which drives them first to assemble for divine worship, and that it is the worshiping assembly which is both the genesis point and ongoing milieu of the assembly's liturgical ritual no less than of its canonical scriptures. In this perspective the assembly specifies God's Word in literary and intellectual ways just as liturgical worship specifies the same Word in communal actions and in the affections of the worshippers. From this it seems to follow that what is affirmed of scripture must be affirmed *mutatis mutandis* of liturgical worship. Thus if scripture is more than just words about God—that is, if scripture is in some real sense the Word of God—then the liturgical worship of an assembly of faithful Jews or Christians is not merely words and gestures about God but in some real sense the Word and *gestes* of God. The phenomenon of the common tradition's sustained need to canonize its liturgies no less than its scriptures stands as witness to this.

Such a statement does not fall easily on modern minds, which have been conditioned to regard liturgical ritual as antithetical to true worship, to regard public worship at best as some sort of tableau illustrative of the doctrinal or ethical content of a scriptural passage. Those of us who write or lecture about such matters from within academe, where we have been deeply influenced by modern scientific method and the worldview of professional educationalism, foster such attitudes. We turn the proclamation of God's Word in scripture into exegesis, the liturgy into a setup for didactic instruction more often on works' righteousness than on faith and its religious implications. One finds nothing of such attitudes, and nothing of such academical applications of them, in the sources of the common tradition.

One could maintain that this tendency originated in the clerical culture of medieval western Christianity with the development of the university. It continued into the Renaissance as those universities were increasingly secularized and theological effort withdrew into seminaries, those newly founded bastions of apologetics and clerical discipline necessitated by the schisms consequent upon the Reformation movements both Catholic and Protestant. *Sola fides* and *sola scriptura* provided a greatly simplified and powerful apologetic for those who wished to escape from medieval complications and embrace the emerging modern world of trade, industry, and enlightened thought presided over by a middle class of increasing financial means. A necessarily "learned" ministry was required to service such a community, a need which spurred evolution of the Jesuit-founded seminary into a new kind of college of sacred learning such as Harvard and Yale were at their origins. From these the typically American "divinity school" would emerge as a post-graduate institution of ecclesiastical arts and biblical science. Given this development, the learned Protestant minister could increasingly be perceived as a professional certified by academe to practice the religious arts along with his peers in law and medicine. The perception allowed him to shed many of the life-style requirements which had been involved in being not merely a religious professional but a living icon or sacrament, as it were, of religious faith and asceticism for the masses.

Those life-style requirements remained strongly entrenched in Catholic seminary polity due to Catholicism's greater iconic or sacramental perception of church and ministry. These requirements, such as celibacy and obedience to authority, tended in Catholic seminaries to overshadow academic requirements and standards which rapidly became native to Protestant divinity schools. Within the present generation's memory, in fact, one usually entered a Catholic seminary straight out of primary school, grew up there, and was *not* granted an academic degree on ordination to the presbyterate some twelve years later. While not lacking academic rigor, such seminaries stressed as much if not more the iconic and sacramental necessity of becoming *alter Christus*, another Christ, in order to represent God to the masses and bring them to God. The Catholic priest consummated his ministry not in acts of learned professionalism but in ritual acts of saying Mass and granting sacramental absolution from sins, acts that were iconic of the Lord and sacramental of his Body, the Church.

If Protestant ministers tended to become professional teachers and Catholic priests iconic sacramentalists, it remains nonetheless true that both groups generated a similar hieraticism in what they did which effectively removed them from, and placed them above if not over against their people. Increasingly priests and ministers were regarded as Christians who, because of their academic learning or their iconic and sacramental proximity to Christ, were raised above the level of ordinary Christians to first-class rank. They brought the message of Word and Sacrament to the proletariat of the merely baptized, and the message was presented in worship contexts which resembled theological skull sessions (among Protestants) or ceremonial *tableaux vivants* representing salient points of Counter-Reformation doctrine and piety (among Catholics).

This is, of course, an oversimplification of exceedingly complex matters. I resort to it simply to give the sort of point which only caricature can to the convoluted process by which some forms of western Christianity gradually lost their hold on and patience with symbol, myth, and ritual—and consequently lost access to their own historic memory and cultural subconsciousness. We thus thought, for example, that Rousseau's fable of the Noble Savage had set us free of social constraint, only to discover ourselves snared into other slaveries for which we had no name. This was only one of a succession of such jarring discoveries the cumulative effects of which upon our inherited social contracts have been both demoralizing and explosive. And a neat little lesson tucked away in all this is that as the West was canonizing its savage nobility, totalitarian states were putting the noble savage at the top of their most wanted lists and creating *gulags* to receive them. This inexorably widened the notion of the noble savage far beyond the image of an innocent afrolic upon the breast of nature and invested this fabulous creature with the sinister cloak reserved for socio-political subversives. At this point it seems to have occurred to some tyrant that while his own noble savages were to be kept in Siberia, those of opposing states might well be used to advantage. Their savagery might be unleashed, their nobility created by propaganda. Tarzan was transmuted into the freedom fighter of international terrorism, his purpose being to save his Blue Lagoon by destroying it. The benign image we accepted from the Enlightenment without remembering our historic experience with savagery has turned on us who prefer not to relearn that wolves have teeth—rather as eighteenth-century European seamen of Rousseau's own generation preferred to ignore the fact that the South Sea paradise they discovered was riddled with venereal disease, to which they promptly succumbed in large numbers.

Quite apart from the theological claims we have tended to make for the liturgical worship of the common tradition—Jewish, Catholic, or Protestant—its very ritualness performs one indispensable and natural human service: it puts us in touch with ourselves corporately and historically. When its ritualness is diminished or removed, whatever theological or ideological gains may accrue are vitiated by its remnant's consequent inability to put us in touch with ourselves. A human being is more than a brainpan filled with correct doctrine. A human being is the product of myriad transactions with reality which are given shape and contour for worse or better through patterns of contact with others of the same species. The process has been called socialization: its patterns have been called ritual and they include everything from toilet training to schooling, play, language speaking, theater, politics, religion, and conceptualization. Whatever else it may be, the liturgical worship of the common tradition is a species of the genus ritual.

This is a general fact, and I take it that the more general a fact is, the more precious it is. It is also a rather simple fact (which may account for its being regularly overlooked by seminary-trained minds, which tend to be very complex indeed), and I take it that the simpler a fact is, the more recurrent it will be. It turns up always in the extremes of greatest and smallest, where simple facts are easiest to discern. Finally, it is an interesting fact because it yields much insight otherwise unobtainable into why Jews and Christians think and behave they way they do. For all this, however, the fact that the liturgical worship of the common tradition is a species of the genus ritual does not usually yield quick and easy conclusions any more than acts of ritualized language such as *Beowulf* or the sonnets of Shakespeare, or acts of ritualized sound such as the Bach corpus, provide ethical messages or political comment. As important as ethics and politics are, everything is no more reducible to them than to economics. Some levels of human discourse run deeper and reach farther than bottom lines which can be acted upon without further ado.

## III

So far I have made three assertions concerning the common tradition's position on the relation between scripture and liturgical worship. It is clear, at least to me, that the connection between scripture and liturgical worship cannot be made from either of them, but only from the fact that both scripture and liturgical worship are correlative functions of that fundamental entity, the worshiping assembly. Neither scripture nor liturgy write or enact themselves; they are things which a group of people who share common patterns of belief do when they come together to worship God. In this view scripture is the oral and written account of the assembly's historic faith experience, liturgy the enactment of that same experience in a complementary medium. It is the latter medium which, due to its ritualness, puts believing people in touch with themselves in the first instance, rendering them capable of being an assembly and thus of gaining perspective on their whole human experience. And perspective is what enables past experiences to be seen as history which can then be codified in oral and written form.

This puts liturgical ritual prior to scriptural process in religious assembly just as social bonding necessarily precedes literary effort in society. But it in no way implies a superiority of liturgical ritual, or of scripture itself, for that matter, over the Word of God. It asserts only that scripture *derives* from God's creative and unsubordinated Word within a structured social context which provides the very words, concepts, and perceptions the writers of scripture must have in order to be obedient to their divine inspiration. Liturgical ritual is already present in that structured social context; indeed, it is a major factor which bestows meaningful cohesion upon that context, permitting it perspective upon its experiential past. To be ignorant of the society's liturgical ritual is to be ignorant also of the society's motives in composing and canonizing its scriptures.

It is precisely at this point, I think, that our own being out of touch with ourselves does us in as we try to account for the holistic complementarity of liturgical worship and scripture in the common tradition. Our academic thrust toward precise analysis sunders the whole into discrete parts. Our professional ministries are often unable to appreciate the fact that the untutored Mrs. Murphys in our assemblies regularly comprehend the real religious point of a scriptural reading as well if not better than their clergy, whose training has diminished their own hold on and patience with symbol, myth, and ritual. One does not have to listen to the sermons of such clergy for very long to sense this and to be impressed with how the allegedly enlightened, certainly romantic, notion of nobility of the asocial has penetrated the modern clerical mind to produce a benign optimism about human nature unwarranted by a steady hold on reality.

But liturgical ritual, no less than the sort of speech which scripture is, is an intrinsically social matter. Ritual and speech inexorably make a people. The idea that reducing ritual and simplifying speech make a people somehow better is widespread. The idea that eliminating ritual altogether, as in patterns of etiquette and precedence and address, and that speech reduced to the basics of word processing machines is more just, less oppressive, and vastly more democratic seems to be gaining ground. Yet it can be maintained that such reductions or eliminations make a people neither better nor worse: they only unmake it by rendering the effort at communication so difficult, so politically charged, or so ambiguous, that the continuing need for social bonding is frustrated. A people without discipline in such matters will not long remain a people.

This is an anthropological and social fact. It is not theological speculation. It can be verified among human societies generally and in Jewish and Christian assemblies specifically. The liturgical changes introduced into Roman Catholicism since the Second Vatican Council, for example, even though they have taken place over two decades and under the closest control of ecclesiastical authorities, have greatly loosened the social faith-bond in a church which was noted for its tight cohesion. The Catholic Church is today a more diversified body, even in matters which lie close to the very heart of its faith, than it has been in the past four centuries. And this has occurred with only a change in its patterns of ritual and speech which is relatively modest compared to many other Christian bodies. Some of those which have gone much further in this direction have suffered unprecedented declines in lay membership even as, predictably, their numbers of ministerial candidates have remained the same or increased. This paradox led one commentator to observe that if the trend continued, a certain church would have more clergy than laity by the early part of the next century. This would represent a fundamental social change of only slightly less magnitude than that of the church's going out of existence altogether.

## IV

It would be wrong to imply that there are no other factors involved in such shifts than those of changes in a religious group's patterns of speech and ritual. But these two patterns nonetheless focus many other shifts in themselves, and they intensify the effects of those other shifts often to the point of critical mass. Nor, as recent Roman Catholic experience suggests, can any one person or set of ecclesiastical bureaucracies adequately ride herd on the process once it is unleashed. It escalates, socially, into a sort of force of nature. One may flee to apparently safe ground by schismatic reaction. One may batten down in an attempt to reduce losses and survive—which is to some extent what Counter-Reformation Catholicism did after the upheavals of Renaissance and Reformation, what Jews did for centuries in response to pogrom and persecution. One may also succumb and take up mutual funds as a way of life.

But one may also stand up in the storm's teeth and relearn some old lessons at the same time that one is learning new ones. I doubt that the latter will be as numerous as the former; I suspect that many old lessons will come as very great news to many. Some of these may be the following:

1. *Human nature does not change very much.* For some this is consoling; for others it is a monstrous truth to be discounted or overturned. For me it is a fairly grim fact of life which ought not to be ignored. The common liturgical and scriptural tradition of Jew and Christian seems to accept it as a given in need of as much alleviation as possible with divine aid. This may account for the tradition's rather remarkable stability over the past four millennia. It has regarded with the greatest wariness suggestions from whatever source that human nature is in fact different from what conventional wisdom has held it to be, namely, basically good since it is a creature of God, but infested with a tendency to wickedness which stems from our misuse of the freedom with which our nature is endowed. Israel's prophets found human nature no more intrinsically evil than Jesus Christ found it to be without sin and basking in original innocence. Both found it capable of significant good but not without great difficulty. Each insisted that justice was its basic discipline, whether by Law or grace, that mercy was its constant need, that charity or love is its only true consummation.

This sort of outlook is deeply distrustful of sudden revelations to the contrary. It is also rather "low church" when it comes to ritual—a mode of activity it has regarded as necessary for assembling in order to work out and sustain common identity, but which needs constant vigilance lest it degenerate into an occasion for humbug and collective fantasy.

And while the common tradition has felt itself free to absorb ritual elements from all the diverse cultures through which it has passed, it has at the same time bent and subordinated all these elements, from images and ceremonies to incense and sacrifices, under its own rigorous polity centering on the Word of God disclosed in written scripture and in the flesh of an incarnate *Logos* who gave himself to humankind in a group of people whose central symbols were only water and oil, bread and wine, used in only two constitutive acts, a bath and a dinner. In a profound sense the common tradition of Jew and Christian together says that human nature does not change very much, and that its basic needs are met by contemplation of the law of God's Word, by bathing in that Word and dining upon it and it alone. If there is any hard core to what might be termed Judeo-Christian orthodoxy (which means "right worship"), this is probably it.

2. *The demands of social assembly remain much the same and are inexorable.* Assembling is not something which was invented by Jew or Christian. It is a basic *social* need of humankind, and its fundamental purpose seems to be the working out of a secure sense of identity both individual and corporate. Assembly is thus a basic *human* need, especially when that assembly takes the form of divine service. In their worship Jew and Christian work out a secure and distinctive sense of social and individual identity which is faithful to the imperatives of the divine Word. With them as for any other human group, therefore, the rules of human assembly not only pertain but reach a level of importance for the good of the world unmatched elsewhere. For the Word which summons Jew and Christian to assemble is not content that they come together merely for their own good but for that of the world. The worship of the common tradition is therefore accountable not only to its own assemblies; those assemblies are themselves accountable to God and to all God has created.

The demands and rules of assembly are neither complex nor arcane. When people assemble there must be a certain good order and due process observed, things which imply canons of justice, mutual respect, precedence, and reverence. The assembly's acts, in order to elicit participation by its members, must be formal and stable in order that the way they work may be easily entered into by all. This implies that the assembly's acts are repetitious and rhythmic, rhythm being the way repetition is organized and a powerful element in galvanizing individuals into a social unit. All these few demands and rules of assembly may be observed in action no less in religious worship than in public sporting events or political and judicial sessions. And while the demands and rules of assembly are neither complex nor arcane, they are inexorable. When a certain good order and due process lapses, the assembly is rendered incapable of constituting itself or of transacting its business—something which revolutionaries apply well in their

tactics of assaulting first the social canons of mutual respect, precedence, and reverence. When the formality and stability of the assembly's acts disintegrate, the individual members of the assembly are barred from participation in those acts—rather as when secret changes in the rules of play result in confusing the spectators' ability to determine when a score has been made. When the repetition and rhythm of the assembly's acts become dissipated, access to the meaning of those acts on the part of the assembly's members is reduced or blocked entirely, for the more diverse the membership the more repetition is needed and the more essential the unifying effect of rhythm becomes.

There is nothing theological in any of this. It is pure social dynamics and applies no less to religious than to any other sort of human assembly. It can become a strong maintenance for status quo or even reaction, and for collective fantasy. It can also be profoundly anti-structural, thus constituting a benign and ongoing revolution built into the very core of the social process. Some societies accomplish this by separating the powers of their executive, judicial, and legislative assemblies, as in the United States. Other societies accomplish this by having systemic recourse to the archaic as represented in a hereditary monarchy or other sacral form. In this sense the archaic is not the obsolete, as Victor Turner has pointed out; it represents the unconscious memory of a society and is tapped by various mechanisms for rendering that memory publicly accessible and overt under present circumstances. The evocation of such memory is regularly antistructural since it stands in critique of present structures for worse or better. It is most pronounced in religious societies such as Judaism and Christianity, which appeal not to an atemporal philosophical *mythos* but to a concrete history of divine revelation and salvation which is coterminous with, and indeed constitutive of, the story of the religious society itself—as one can see clearly, for example, in the intimately related feasts of Passover and Easter. Here by *haggadah* and *midrash* the past is evoked and interpreted as a judgment upon the assembly's present state and structures, something which suffuses the Christian Bible's accounts of the Last Supper and flows over into the weekly eucharists of Christians no less than into the yearly Seder of Jews to this day.

The demands and rules of social assembly remain much the same and are inexorable. Both Jew and Christian agree that God does not need liturgical worship (or anything else, for that matter), and that God does not issue ceremonies but Word. But they would also both agree that, given the way people have been created by God as social beings, we do need assembled worship and therefore tend to liturgical and scriptural composition.

3. *"Future shock" is real and debilitating, but no less so than "past*

*shock."* The popular book by Alvin Toffler has suggested to some that future shock is a peculiarly modern phenomenon and that its presence renders us exceptional in the history of the world. While some aspects of future shock may well be peculiarly modern, there is not much reason to regard the phenomenon itself as exclusively ours. The barbarian invasions set up a similar set of shocks in both eastern and western Europe over a period of four hundred years, a period of perpetual emergency which disrupted social structures and sapped cultural morale more deeply than anything we have perhaps yet experienced. One doubts that the atomic destruction of our ten most important cities would have a more traumatic effect on the modern world than the sack of Rome had on the civilized world of the fifth century. The Goth on the Palatine was a concrete and appalling icon of an encroaching future which even the best minds of the time (such as Jerome and Augustine) could not see beyond and which quite unmanned most of their contemporaries.

The fact seems to be that future shock is a fairly regular phenomenon at times when significant socio-cultural shift takes place. It is something people learn to deal with or they succumb to it. And a case might be made that "past shock" is a no less regular occurrence which represents a real and debilitating problem inverse to that of future shock. Some societies, especially traditional ones, seem at times to be shocked into near immobility by their pasts, which they serve with narrow and obsessive repetition to the point of being unable to function in any other way. This makes them richly textured but brittle and thus highly susceptible to minor viruses—a single new social idea, a natural calamity, or even a tilt in some balance of power such as Cortez caused in central Mexican and Pizzaro in Peruvian societies in the sixteenth century.

The question is what is to be done about both forms of shock. No healthy society can ignore them except at the risk of its own survival, and religious societies are no more immune to them than any other. The history of Judaism and Christianity suggests that future shock is best resisted by strong doses of hard-nosed insistence on ritual and speech forms because these deeply rooted social media provide the most easily accessible and effective routes to a sense of coherent social identity for the most people. In times of social stress both ritual and speech systems tend to stiffen and undergo canonization, a process which is conservative in direct ratio to the perceived seriousness of the stress. Thus sixteenth-century Catholicism responded to the stress of religious schism by conservatively reforming its worship system and then locking that reform in by law for four hundred years, a state from which Catholicism is only now beginning to emerge. Only time will tell whether the most recent liturgical reforms by the Second Vatican Council, reforms which are widely regarded as liberal but which in fact are deeply conservative of an almost forgotten tradition of slow and steady liturgical growth, come to be regarded as a restoration to normalcy after four hundred years or as a static criterion for reaction against what might be perceived increasingly as debilitating social stress.

The risk canonization runs is that it may slip imperceptibly into past shock should the social "drag" produced by the process become too great. The absorption of late Counter-Reformation Catholicism with the middle ages, something that began to occur only with the Industrial Revolution, would thus probably have happened even without nineteenth-century Romanticism, and may even have caused it. It is notable that such an absorption was absent from the sixteenth into the eighteenth centuries, when Counter-Reformation Catholicism was at the forefront of contemporary movements such as the baroque and rococo in art, music, and architecture. As social stress in the form of political and intellectual revolutions began to sap morale, however, Church officials called for the restoration of medieval forms of music (the so-called Gregorian chant) and thought (neo-Thomistic theology and philosophy) and implemented this call in church law. So canonized had this polity become by the middle of the present century that many Catholics on all levels doubted that another church council would ever again be called or that such a thing would even be possible. The Second Vatican Council, summoned in 1959, snapped the Roman Catholic Church out of whatever degree of past shock it may have been in. It might turn out that this was all it did or needed to do.

What the Second Vatican Council did at base seems to have been what any healthy society does when it senses past shock to be setting in. It administers strong doses of optimism and affirmation meant to loosen up fixations on the past and to emphasize those obligations the group has to present and future. This is a slippery business, and it is easier by far to open some windows in a house than it is to keep the fresh air admitted from blowing both furniture and occupants out. Having administered a dose of optimism it is often difficult to make clear that its scope is long-term, perhaps even eschatological, and that in the view from long experience it was a wary dose to begin with. Similarly, having administered a dose of affirmation of present values it is often difficult to make clear that this does not cancel all old values as well.

The upshot of this for the purpose at hand seems to be that ritual and speech forms modulate according to the state of the assembly using them. One can no more inquire into the condition of scripture and worship in Judaism without grasping something of its assemblies' historical circumstances than one can generalize about the same matters in Christianity apart from asking which Christian church one is talking about and when. For neither Jews nor Christians have ever worshiped or perceived God's Word in exactly the same way at all times and in all places. While forbidden by the Second Commandment, graven images adorned the Temple throughout its history, and painted images filled the synagogue at Dura Europas in the third century of the common era. Some Catholics have regarded the sacramental presence of Christ in the bread and wine of the eucharist as flatly carnal, despite the great weight of theological tradition to the contrary, and some Protestants have denied his presence there altogether. Yet Jews have had no trouble in recognizing Passover night and its Seder to be different from all others, and Christians have had little trouble over confusing baptism and eucharist with Saturday bath and Sunday dinner.

Future shock is real and debilitating, but no less so than past shock. A society's ritual and speech structures act as cultural ballast to give some needed stability under the pressures of such stresses, as Toffler recognizes. But he is mistaken in thinking that future shock requires old rituals to be jettisoned and new rituals created to deal with the problem. A ritual system cannot be "invented" any more than a spoken language can be, for neither system exists unto itself. Their genesis and maintenance is tied to countless other social, psychic, and cultural transactions which artificial changes in the ritual and speech systems by themselves are able to touch only rarely if at all, as the fate of Esperanto demonstrates. The change native to ritual and speech is a more subtle, "organic," long-term process; it works so slowly and on so many levels prior to that of the conscious that it is difficult to comment upon except well after the fact. Furthermore, rituals like languages may die, but they are extremely hard to kill. Attempts to do so, as during the French Revolution, often result in social tumult worse by far than future shock itself. Cultural revolutions are hard on the body social: they are easily called for, difficult to precipitate, impossible to control, and the sheer quantity of violence they entail numbs the mind.

## V

I began this essay with three observations on the correlative relation between scripture and liturgical worship in the common tradition. The relationship appears to me to be more subtle than the usual academic approach to such matters has tended to indicate. We often forget that prior to Gutenberg scripture was experienced by ordinary Jew and Christian as an oral event which took place regularly in relation to, or in context of, public worship. The study and memorization of sacred text was undertaken to tell its story amid a believing assembly as it worshiped the ultimate Author of the story which constituted the assembly as a peculiar People. In this perspective scripture and liturgical worship appear to be less two different enterprises than a single effort carried out in distinct but deeply related modes by a group of people sharing a common trust in the validity of what they were doing.

Nor were scripture and liturgical worship regarded then as a single effort unto itself. The assembly's public transactions with its story in word and act catalyzed all other aspects of the assembly's life both inside synagogue or church and outside them, flowing over into instruction for the young in the common life no less than into ethics, business, family life, law, folk literature, economics, politics, music, and all the arts. All this produced a total sense of community most moderns find too intense and confining even as they hanker after it in secular guises such as those offered by B. F. Skinner and others. Jews and Christians of orthodox persuasion distrust such offerings not so much, one suspects, because they fear the unknown (the deity with whom they claim to be on intimate terms is, after all, regularly described in their scriptural and liturgical systems as unspeakable, inconceivable, invisible, incomprehensible, and unknown), but because they find those offerings' suppositions unwise, their prescriptions inadequate, their promises dubious. They presuppose a human innocency and good will that no firm grasp on reality supports. They prescribe a *Gemeinschaft* or communal association shorn of obvious conventional sanctions but undergirded by obscure sanctions without seasoned or alleviating checks and balances which would protect the group from inadvertent allotheism. They promise a cheap eschatology available through therapeutic or state systems.

The whole story of Judaism and Christianity as told in scripture and carried in the worship traditions is one of steady disillusionment with such suppositions, prescriptions, and promises. Jew and Christian thus regard the world as a far stranger place than Marx or B. F. Skinner did, and they regard humanity as rather less predictable than any behaviorist seems capable of imagining—as angelic at one extreme and devilish at the other, with the vast majority of people somewhere in between and in constant trek back and forth from one end of the spectrum to the other. And if, as many claim, Jews and Christians have merely projected their idea of God from their common social experience with themselves, that idea represents the deity to be, if such a thing were conceivable, even more odd than humanity itself. To a cleanly unprejudiced mind this in itself might constitute a reasonable sociological datum which, since it has been derived from the intense social experience of many generations living over the course of four millennia, might be taken at least as seriously as the theories of one man or one school of social scientific thought.

Be this as it may, the disillusionment which Jew and Christian suffer results not in cynicism but in a sense of awe at the vast unknowable, but not unintelligible, mystery of it all—an awe that is not very different from that of a Zen Buddhist before Tao, that nameable but unnameable way all things follow with an inexorability which consummates those who are obedient to it and destroys all others. There is a Zen, a necessary discipline, in the maintenance of a motorcycle no less than in discovering one's self, in studying the Word, in worshiping God, in believing amid one's peers in faith, or in concluding a business deal. The Way will not be brooked, and at every point consummation and destruction come at one, hand in hand. This is as awesome as it is mysterious. Neither humbug nor unwarranted assumptions gain one anything but brief comfort before dissolution sets in. Only the truth, the fruit of a Zen which is learned only at immense cost, results in freedom and consummation of what one is, even if, as in the case of prophet or Messiah, it means throwing one's life away.

This is why I concluded this essay with three observations on human nature, social assembly, and shocks both future and past as these seem to relate to the scriptural and liturgical enterprises of the common tradition. The three observations attempt to reflect old lessons which each generation cannot afford to ignore but must always learn cleanly and anew for itself. These old lessons counsel that no assembly of people, no matter what the presence or absence of stress upon it, should reasonably expect to continue long in existence without recourse to ritual and speech forms. Nor should it reasonably expect those forms to yield up unalloyed peace and joy on demand. The scriptural and liturgical tradition of Jew and Christian in fact suggests that peace and joy are not simple commodities easily had, and that when they are had they often come to one in disturbing guises and from surprising quarters—peace as often as not out of war, joy as often as not from the depths of suffering. Judeo-Christian scripture and liturgy offer no one a cultural or religious Disneyland; only a real world where truth, hope, faith, and above all charity heal at the same time that they take their toll. When this happens one may be sure that scripture and liturgical worship have kissed and embraced each other in the lives of a peculiar people who exist by divine pleasure for the life of the world.

*Bibliographical Note*

Some relevant anthropological perspectives are given in Mary Douglas, *Natural Symbols: Explorations in Cosmology* (New York: Pantheon, 1970), and Victor W. Turner, *The Ritual Process: Structure and Antistructure* (Chicago: Aldine, 1969). For a sociologist's view see Erving Goffman, *Behavior in Public Places* (New York: The Free Press—Macmillan, 1963) and *Interaction Ritual: Essays on Face-to-Face Behavior* (New York: Anchor—Doubleday, 1967). Christian liturgical studies offer Alexander Schmemann, *Introduction to Liturgical Theology* (Portland: American Orthodox Press, 1966); Geoffrey Wainwright, *Doxology: The Praise of God in Worship, Doctrine and Life* (New York: Oxford University Press, 1980); and Aidan Kavanagh, *Elements of Rite: A Handbook of Liturgical Style* (New York: Pueblo Publishing Company, 1982).

C. H. SISSON

# THE PRAYER BOOK CONTROVERSY:
# AN INSULAR VIEW

The circumstances which have led the authorities of the Church of England to encourage the progressive dereliction of the Book of Common Prayer and the Authorized Version of the Bible are of so much complexity that any statement of them is likely to be challeneged in one quarter or another. It is hardly for me, who have a modest notoriety as a defender of the old books, to attempt to explain the matter to an American audience. The bare facts, as regards the Prayer Book, are that in 1974/5 the Parliament at Westminster, which had bothered its head little enough with such matters for the last forty or fifty years, relaxed its grip on the national church. It did so in such a manner that the Church has since been able to manage its own liturgical affairs without the risk of being overruled as happened in 1928, when a revised Prayer Book proposed by the Church, after much study and discussion, was rejected by Parliament. Lest anyone unacquainted with the habits of the island should imagine that this meant that no one ventured to use the new book for fear of inquisitorial interventions by the state, it must be said that many parish priests went their own way and that variations from the Book of Common Prayer, including material from the 1928 book, have been used with impunity ever since. It would probably be uncontroversial to say that the clergy of the Church of England have for many years been an undisciplined lot. In 1955 the Church set up its own Liturgical Commission and in 1965 authorized new services "for experimental use." "Since then the Commission has prepared revised forms, sometimes as many as three distinct series, for almost every aspect of the Church's worship." That is a quotation from the preface to the *Alternative Service Book, 1980*, an inconvenient volume which has been authorized, without reference to Parliament, in the manner which has been legal since 1975, "for use in the Church of England in conjunction with *The Book of Common Prayer.*" Parliament did not leave the Church free to abolish the latter book, and the "in conjunction with" is in recognition of that fact. The whole weight of ecclesiastical authority has, however, been put behind the *Alternative Book*, and the *Book of Common Prayer* has rapidly fallen from use and even from sight, in most places. At the same time, and in accordance with what appears to be the conviction of the ecclesiastical authorities that people can no longer understand the

English of the seventeenth century, a variety of contemporary translations of the Bible has largely replaced the *Authorized Version*, which is
the King James Bible.

It is not my purpose to inquire into the theological significance of
these events. Whatever it may be—and there is more to be said than
that "new forms of worship do not erode the historical foundations of
the Church's faith," which is how the Preface to the *Alternative Book*
puts it—these changes mark a change in the cultural, and it may be
political, history of England, none the less important because it has not
been generally understood. The politics are a subject in themselves,
perhaps a rather insular one and, except to the extent indicated below,
hardly relevant here. The cultural consequences of the dereliction may
themselves be only of secondary interest outside the United Kingdom;
they are however of such a nature as to offer, if not parallels, then at
least matter for reflection, to people with different political and
historical perspectives. Cranmer's books of 1549 and 1552 were the
outcome of theological and political developments—the general
European phenomena of the Reformation and the emergence of
national states. They were the outcome also of the related pressures for
a diminution of clerical exclusiveness and for a Bible and liturgy in the
vernacular. Cranmer's books and the revision of 1662 drew on earlier
matter in English as well as on the Latin service-books; the King James
Bible drew on versions from Tyndale's onward. Both Prayer Book and
Bible were in response to a popular demand to know what was going
on. From repeated and uniform use in parish churches, their phrases
went home to generations of English people, illiterate as well as
literate, and they became the first and sometimes the only reading
matter of those who could read. In the sixteenth century the Church of
England was conceived of as the successor, more or less contested, of
the medieval Church and the sole heir, in England, of the purer faith
imputed to earlier times. At all the subsequent stages of dissent and
emancipation from these conceptions, the Authorized Version of the
Bible retained its central position, expounded in every tabernacle and
read or read at by everyone who knew his letters. Jonathan Swift
attributed the continuity of ordinary language to these central books:
"if it were not for the *Bible* and *Common-Prayer-Book* in the vulgar
Tongue," he said in 1712, "we should hardly be able to understand
anything that was written among us an Hundred Years ago. . . : For
those books being perpetually read in Churches, have proved a Kind of
Standard for Language, especially for the Common People." The
language of the books was a common possession, an aid to understanding backward and forward in time and, at any given time, to understanding between different classes and localities. The extent to which it
has entered into the texture of the literary language, to Hardy and
Kipling and indeed beyond, is well understood, even though there are

assuredly every year fewer people who recognize the sources. It is not too much to say that the diminishing familiarity with the Bible and Prayer Book—which, of course, did not start with the antics of the Synod after 1975—has brought with it an impoverishment of the common language and a diminution of common understandings.

In the towns in particular, the reach of the Prayer Book and the Bible has long not been what it was. One can easily exaggerate the attachments of the past, yet until a few decades ago the Authorized Version was regularly used in state elementary schools for Scripture lessons which were an ordinary part of the curriculum, and there were still, for Church of England children and dissenters alike, a large number of Sunday schools. Since the Second World War, there has been a rapid collapse. Now the main source of popular superstition is the radio and television, both using for the most part a language debased beyond anything publicly available in the past. These developments give what plausibility there is in the plea that the older language is no longer a general medium of communication, though they do not, as they are usually supposed to do, give any ground for supposing that the listless and lifeless language of the *Alternative Service Book* and of the inferior translations of the Bible has any general intelligibility. In fact, very little that is apposite has been said, by the apologists of the new books, about the real problems of understanding which face the historic religions at the present time. The situation has been complicated by issues which carry one far beyond the domestic English scene. There has been an aspiration, on the part of some of the clergy, for an approximation of the liturgy to that used by Roman Catholics, a pressure which has naturally increased since Rome took up the fashion of vernacular liturgies and the Roman Church in the United Kingdom acquired its own depressing and inept English forms. More important is the pressure on the language of England which comes from all sides, in a world in which many more millions speak some version of it, either as a first or a second language, than there are inhabitants in the whole of what used to be called the British Isles. A certain disorientation, as compared with even recent times, is inescapable, the more since the ethos of the age, and the steep political decline of England itself, have led to a loss of confidence in the superiority of the mother tongue; and the process has been assisted by the decline in the domestic prestige of the language of the upper classes.

Seen in this context, the problems presented by the Bible and Prayer Book are closely related to those of literature as a whole. Is the authority of lateral comparisons to be greater or less than that of the local tradition? It has to be remembered that the local tradition is far from being exclusively local; it is rather the funnel through which foreign influences, Latin, Greek, Hebrew, French, Spanish, Italian and German, have played upon those who have written in English in these islands. Each generation continues to assimilate more or less matter from abroad including, of course, that of other English-speaking traditions—which, however, on this view of things, fall into place as something less than major influences. Those who seek to make the most of the lateral influences are emphasizing the value of the contemporaneous. There is a strong political and ideological element in this view of the matter; what is most in evidence is the desirability of understanding between societies scattered across the world. In ecclesiastical terms, this means that the Anglican communion uses English almost as the old Roman communion used Latin, as a *lingua franca*, with the difference that Canterbury lacks the political authority which the Pope's Rome inherited. The former imperial authority of England is a debit, not a credit, in the contemporary world, so that the Church of England itself, so far as it thinks of itself as a member of the Anglican communion, has to be endlessly apologetic and defensive. The favoring of translations of the Bible in what has been called a "mid-Atlantic dialect" is certainly not uninfluenced by this situation and so—though to a less degree—are the bolder flights of the *Alternative Service Book*, though in fact those flights are not very bold and there are some odd provincial relics, such as the borrowing from the Church of South India of a hymn which turns out to be by a British Poet Laureate (Robert Bridges, 1844-1930). All this is a distraction from what will be "understood of the people," here and now. As against this, attention to the local tradition should mean to the whole recognizable past through that tradition—which surely must be right as a matter of theology as well as from the point of view of making that tradition intelligible to contemporaries. Had the authors of the A.S.B. worked in that way, they would have been content with a very conservative revision of the Book of Common Prayer, realizing that their chances of adding material which *contained as much* as Cranmer's words were—to put it no higher—limited.

The issue—significant for literature at large as well as for biblical and liturgical studies—is that of the centrality of the master texts, the recognition that they *are* master texts. No one but a fool would set about rewriting Shakespeare, or would pretend that a translation of Dante superseded the original. The Authorized Version does not supersede earlier texts of the biblical books; it enhances the importance of those texts for us to the extent to which it effectively assimilates them to our local tradition. The politics of the day assert that Jack is as good as his master, and there are some who will have it that theology asserts the same. These doctrines are wholesome in their proper context. However that may be, those who consider that the day's newspaper or the winner of the latest poetry prize is more to be considered than the master texts should reflect soberly upon Dante's submission to Virgil. So should those who think that the most exalted matter can be dressed up in the language of journalism and of the contemporary poetry trade.

*Bibliographical Note*

For a fuller treatment of the Prayer Book Controversy, see *Crisis: For Cranmer and King James*, a special issue of *PN Review* edited by David Martin (*PN Review* 13; Manchester, 1979). C. H. Sisson discusses topics related to the controversy in his collected essays, *The Avoidance of Literature*, ed. Michael Schmidt (Manchester: Carcanet, 1978), and more specifically in *Anglican Essays* (Manchester: Carcanet, 1983).

CLAYTON LIBOLT

# PROTESTANTISM AND PREACHING

> . . . The pulpit is ever the earth's foremost part; all the rest comes in its
> rear; the pulpit leads the world. From thence it is the storm of God's
> quick wrath is first descried, and the bow must bear the earliest brunt.
> From thence it is the God of breezes fair or foul is first invoked for
> favorable winds. Yes, the world's a ship on its passage out, and not a
> voyage complete; and the pulpit is its prow.
>
> *Moby Dick*

For those like Ishmael who grew up in "the infallible Presbyterian
Church," the metaphor which placed the Protestant pulpit on the bow
of the Good Ship Earth was apt, for Protestantism led the world, and
the pulpit led Protestantism. Today the hyperbole is unbearable; the
century and a third since the publication of *Moby Dick* has not been
kind to Protestantism or the Protestant pulpit. To conjure the causes of
Protestant decline is to call up the causes of the decline of the West—
Protestantism, capitalism, Western imperialism, and whaling are related phenomena—but such long views are beyond the scope of this
essay and perhaps beyond contemporary observation.

If, as we must, we take shorter views, we can say that the crisis in
Protestantism now a long century old is a crisis in a particular view of
religious authority. The flashier tokens of the crisis, whether death-of-
God theologians or creationists, are distracting when they are taken as
particulars by the popular press, which takes shorter views still, rather
than as parts of a broader difficulty within the fragmented body of
Protestantism itself. It is a good long way from Ishmael's sober
hyperbole to the equally sober question of the conservative Lutheran
theologian Helmut Thielicke: "Does Protestantism have any future at
all or must we honestly confess that we have come to the end of the
road?"

Thielicke's question cannot be answered by those with less than
divine insight into the future, though plainly there is trouble in the
churches that Luther and Calvin built. They are fragmented, split along
modernist-fundamentalist lines, and in the American heartland they are
losing confidence. If one is pessimistic about the future of Protestantism, the past century can be understood as the last glow of what
Thielicke has called a "salutary fever in the body of Christendom."
Central to anyone's view of the future of Protestantism must be the
special relationship between the Bible and preaching which lies at the
heart of the movement. The Protestant perspective on religious author-

ity rests on the Word written and the Word spoken, the text and the proclamation of the text.

The issues raised by the relationships among religious authority, canonical scripture, and preaching are among the most interesting and important in our culture. Behind these issues (or adjacent to them) are the issues raised by fundamentalist reactions to contemporary culture, in the moderate form they take in the United States and in the immoderate form they have taken elsewhere. The basic issues can be put abstractly as issues in hermeneutics, though it should not be forgotten that hermeneutical theory describes how we perceive the world and that how we perceive the world has some relationship to how we act in it. In this essay, I will begin by abstracting from the history of Protestantism a set of general considerations relating to the Bible and preaching; in the end, I will address the issues to the times.

## I. The Protestant Reformation—*Typography*

The transformation of medieval Christianity into Renaissance Christianity was accompanied by, and perhaps created by, a powerful yet subtle transformation in the significance of the word in Western culture. The transformation was not effected by the Protestant Reformation, though Protestantism is both evidence of the change and, later, an engine of it. Tridentine Catholicism belongs equally to the story of the transformation, as do the varieties of enthusiastic Christianity of the same era. The movements were all various responses to what Walter Ong has called "the intense chirographic preoccupation of the Middle Ages" and its product, typography. The modern transformation in the technology of transmission of human words from typography to electronic media has thrown the sixteenth century into deeper perspective, and Walter Ong in particular has seized the opportunity to illuminate the fundamental features of the typographic revolution.

Ong has located the effect of technological change in the transmission of words in the influence that it has had on the psychology of the human sensorium—the interrelationships among our senses. Of the five senses, only hearing and sight are heavily used for verbal communication. Ong has collected considerable evidence to show that the typographic revolution effected a shift in Western culture from the ear to the eye; in the modern age there is far more reliance on perception in general while in the periods before typography was invented there was more reliance on what was heard. That basic shift has ramified throughout the culture in ways that surprise us only because they are so deeply imbedded in our consciousness. Of the daunting array of examples mentioned by Ong in *The Presence of the Word*, I will mention only a few.

The first is the gradual displacement of dialectical discourse in the

Western culture in favor of the descriptive style. In general, the features of the shift—from partisanship in scholarship toward neutrality, from deduction to induction in logic, from subjectivity to objectivity—have been well-studied. They are, after all, some of the more obvious data of Western intellectual history. The surprise comes when Ong notes the concomitance of psychology and technology.

> The reason for the development of modern science much more profound and real than the displacement of deduction by induction was the shift from the old oral-aural, conversational, disputatious, semianimistic, personalized feeling for knowledge, entailing a proclivity for auditory syntheses, to a feeling for knowledge as aligned with vision much more unequivocably than it had been in the past.
>
> The struggle in which the disputatious oral approach to existence and knowledge lost much of its hold, was a struggle between hearing and seeing. Seeing won. With the shift in the sensorium by print, the large scale campaign for the "clear and distinct" soon began, led by Ramus and focused by Descartes—a campaign for visually conceived cognitive enterprise.

Modern objectivity, if Ong is correct, is a psychological realization of a technological possiblity. The fundamental techniques of modern scientific scholarship—induction, close observation, hypothesis testing—were known from antiquity, but they were restrained by the lack of accurate information storage and dissemination methods until the invention of print. Chirographic cultures, those that rely on handwriting, remained strongly oral. The shift in technology brought a change in the human sensorium: the world was experienced differently. In fact, Ong argues, the human sensorium came in some respects to resemble the technology which extended it: the non-personal, visual aspect of print came to characterize the mindset of the culture. Knowledge, even in the chirographic cultures of the Middle Ages, was personal, partisan, inherently subjective. The world was, accordingly, "vaguely animistic." But in typographic cultures, knowledge becomes abstractable from living persons and the world, "something sighted and measured." Persons, by the time one reaches Enlightenment thought, are "unaccountable intrusions."

Typography made it possible for knowledge to exist independent of community. In a purely oral culture, "knowledge is a tribal possession, not a matter of individual speculation." Even in a chirographic culture, knowledge is most readily available in oral form and, therefore, requires a community. Reading is largely an oral act: silent reading is a feature of the typographic age. In the silencing of Western culture, a new sense of interiority was born. Learning, like reading, became a private matter. In the modern age, knowledge individuates. It is proprietary, received and disseminated over signatures. The psychological consequences of that change are enormous; alienation, for example, is a remote product of typography.

The Protestant Reformation began in the first century of typography. The concomitant psychological shifts were well underway, though it was still an age dominated by orality. The power of the theologies of the Reformers—their charismata, to use Weber's terminology—lies in the compatibility of those theologies with new realities. They spoke to the new human sensorium. The evangelical slogans *sola gratia* and *sola fide*, for example, can claim the authority of St. Paul and of St. Augustine, but they had a very different effect in the age of Luther. It is not so much that Luther discovered the priority of faith over works as that he discovered the priority of individual faith and grace over communal faith and grace. The opposition of faith and works has a different meaning in the context of the largely oral, chirographic cultures of late antiquity than in the nascent typographic culture of the sixteenth century. Although Luther insisted that faith was a response to the *hearing* of the gospel, it is not insignificant that he came to his own faith through reading. It is not far from the Reformation idea of *sola fide* to the individual offer of salvation in the teaching of Jacobus Arminius and, eventually, in the pleas of twentieth-century evangelists.

At the same time, the Reformers resisted the effects of some of their teachings. The response to Arminius at the Synod of Dort (1618–19) returned faith to community by the device of double predestination. Faith was not after all an individual choice; it was the choice of God, who habitually chose along family and communal lines. The Westminister Federal Theology (1640) reinterpreted the Hebrew idea of covenant to the same effect: children until the age of discretion were included with their parents in God's covenant. The difficulty that this doctrine later led to in American Puritanism with the "halfway covenanters" illustrates the problems of trying to preserve community when faith is understood individually.

## II. The Reorganization of Authority—*Sola Scriptura*

On the face of it, the third *sola* slogan from the Reformation, *sola scriptura*, is the quintessential typographic slogan—only what is written. But the slogan must be placed, first of all, not in the context of concerns about writing but in the context of authority. I have already intimated that writing and authority are related, but it is best that we understand authority before we deal with its relationship to writing. In this matter, I will have to begin at the beginning.

Authority in the Christian Church is always, theologically speaking, the authority of Christ. It is a personal authority, mediated in the first place through the Spirit of Christ. The early and fundamental Christian confession, "Christ is Lord," expresses that idea clearly. Immediately, however, even in that short confession, a question arises about tradition and community. How is the lordship of Christ to be understood? On the one hand, the confession "Christ is Lord" appropriates for Christianity the authority of the Hebrew Bible. It makes a claim over a tradition. On the other hand, the confession seems to make a claim for the manifest and living authority of the resurrected and spiritual Christ. These are clearly different kinds of authority. A tradition is always limiting: if it is to be a final authority, it cannot be superseded. Personal authority is not so restricted: new things can be spoken.

The relationship between James of Jerusalem and Paul can be understood in these terms. James felt more strongly the restrictiveness of tradition than did Paul, or, in other terms, Paul allowed more authority to the community than did James. A similar conflict was played out in the early Church between the bishops and the Gnostics. The Gnostics held that tradition could be superseded; the authority of Christ was not limited to what could be remembered. The bishops (notably Clement of Rome and Ignatius), on the other hand, argued that the authority of Christ was mediated to the Church through the Apostles. The bishops won. The authority of Christ was henceforth held to have been definitively manifest only in the apostolic tradition.

Apostolicity, however, was defined in a distinctively oral manner even though there were also apostolic writings. The primary sense of apostolicity was achieved traditionally within the received succession of teacher and pupil. The whole question of what writings are canonical, which has been subjected to intense scholarly scrutiny in our age, was a relatively minor aspect of the question of authority in the Patristic period. Only occasionally was the question important and then only to some persons in the Church, largely as a reflex of the need for editions of the New Testament. A noteworthy example is the flurry of activity in the fourth century associated with Constantine's request for fifty copies of the Scriptures. The invention of the codex was perhaps the most important stimulus for canon lists.

The notion of apostolicity created the first distinction in Christian authority, marking final authority as traditional. Charismatic authority, of course, did not go away—there were still prophetic voices—but charismatic authority was subjected to the test of apostolicity. If the new message could not be understood as an interpretation of the old message, it could not be accepted. Apostolicity introduced the idea of closure and limitation.

To *sola scriptura*, we owe a second distinction in the authority of Christ—between the Bible and the apostolic representative, the bishop. The first distinction was hierarchial—apostolicity is authority at a higher pitch but not different from charismatic authority. The second distinction is generic—the authority of a book is different from the authority of a living institution. The recognition of the independence of the Bible from the Church, thus, created two kinds of authority, each of which existed in two pitches. Traditional authority was present in apostolic weight in the canon itself; it also existed in the written and unwritten traditions which had accumulated since the beginning of the Church. Living and institutional authority existed in apostolic weight in the Roman Church (in the West); it also existed in other gatherings of believers outside the bounds of the official Church. The significance of *sola scriptura* cannot be understood without taking account of both forms and both pitches in Christian authority. Many of the confusions about the difference between authority in the Protestant churches and post-Trent Catholicism are due to the failure to understand properly the interrelationships among the various authorities in each tradition.

In taking the side of the Bible, the Protestant Reformers did not reject the authority of the instituted Church entirely. They rejected the apostolicity of Church authority, the sense of closure which distinguished clergy from laity. In Protestant thought, all believers are priests, and clergy are considered prophets. The Church is described as "invisible," which is to say, not institutionally expressed. Institutional expressions of Church, the "visible church" in the language of the Reformers, are capable of being true or false and must be judged according to the "marks of the true Church." Thus, the Reformers soften the lines between the institutional church and non-institutional gatherings of believers; in doing so they opened the way to denominationalism. At the same time, the Reformers drew the line between the Bible and other traditions more firmly than it had been drawn before.

Tridentine Catholicism responded to the Protestant Reformation by reversing the relationships. Trent recognized the authority of "written and unwritten traditions" so as to soften the line (though not so effectively as Protestants softened the line between instituted churches and gatherings of believers) between the Bible and later traditions. On the other hand, Tridentine Catholicism drew the line very firmly between Church and sects. In Catholicism, the Church decides between true and false traditions; in Protestantism, the Bible decides between true and false churches.

In these relationships, Protestantism took the side of modernity. The Tridentine formula "written and unwritten traditions" was hard to credit in a culture where the Bible circulated in print; the Protestant formula "visible and invisible church" more easily accommodated the rising individuality of the new culture. Catholicism became the religion of submodern societies and of postmodern individuals. Protestantism became the religion of modern typographic culture. The conflict which the Roman Church saw between its version of Christian authority and dissemination of vernacular Scripture was real. Print is destructive of community, and in that sense, it destroys the Church.

### III. Reification of the Bible—*Canon*

The Protestant reorganization of Christian authority requires a major rethinking of the process of canonizing Christian scriptures. It goes beyond canonization, for it partially removes the Bible from the rulings (canons) of the Church. The first stage in canonization required the development of a sense of closure; sixteenth-century developments required a reification of the Bible, separation between text and interpretation. This new form of canonization demanded a sense of the primacy of the written text and a sense of alienation between the text and the Christian community. The first stage marked off an authoritative tradition; Protestantism marked off an authoritative form of the tradition.

Work on the text of the Bible had begun earlier than Luther. Erasmus published his Greek New Testament in 1516, and the printing of the Hebrew Bible was well underway nearly a half century earlier. The great Complutensian Polyglot (with Hebrew, Latin, and Greek columns in the Old Testament section) was issued in 1522. The Reformers contributed a hermeneutic to go with the new sense of textuality which had developed in the West. Their hermeneutic remains fundamental, in outline, to hermeneutical discussions still underway. It is intricately related to the reorganization of church authority just reviewed, which is not surprising in view of the function of the Bible in Protestantism— the Reformation hermeneutic had to show how a book could rule a religion.

The Reformation hermeneutic has two major parts. One is related to the text itself, and it can be called, though without the whole freight of post-Kantian hermeneutics, explanation. The question here is what the text *says*. The second part of the Reformation hermeneutic is related to the reader, and it can be called appropriation. The question here is what the text *means*, specifically what it *means for me*, the reader. The analogy to the structures of Christian authority is apparent. The first part of the Reformation hermeneutic treats the text as an object, to be analyzed or, at least, read; the second part of the Reformation hermeneutic treats the text as a subject which addresses the reader. The labor of explanation treats the text as a tradition. The experience of appropriation recognizes the magisterium of the text; it is the text (and not the Church) which rules the conscience of the believer.

Although the distinction between explanation and appropriation has hermeneutical consequences, many of which have been explored since the Reformation, it must be remembered that the Reformers' statement of the fundamental hermeneutic was innocent of many of those consequences. It was especially innocent in the matter of explanation of the text. The simplest statement of the Reformers' hermeneutical direction for the labor of reading is that the text should be read in its plain sense. By itself, that dictate is comprehensible primarily as a repudiation of multiple senses, allegorical readings, and other interpretive devices which had grown up from antiquity. As Ong has noted, multiple senses are probably best understood as features of orality; in oral discourse, text and interpretation are not firmly separated. More precisely perhaps, in oral discourse, explanation and meaning are not separated, and the nonhistorical senses—allegory, anagogy, and tropology—all have to do with understanding the meaning of the text. The primacy of the historical or plain sense is much more significant in a typographic culture than it is in an oral culture, even a chirographically intense culture with oral features like the medieval period.

The doctrine of the plain sense can be more subtly expressed in terms of two more specific hermeneutical directions from the Reformation period. The broader of the two falls under the rubric of the *perspicuitas* of Scripture, its capacity to be understood easily. This teaching, which goes back to Luther, has created no end of difficulties for later theologians. It is quite apparent that the Bible is not, in many places, clear or perspicuous at all. The usual explanation of the Reformers' claim about the clarity of Scripture is that they were claiming clarity in a limited sense, clarity with respect to the central message of salvation. But that is not quite accurate to Luther's or other Reformers' ideas of clarity. Luther distinguished between external and internal clarity: "The clarity of Scripture has a double aspect, as also its obscurity: one is external, in the word as ministered, the other exists in the attitude of the recipient." Internal clarity is a property of the reader (we will take up that matter presently); external clarity is a matter of the words, and that is our concern here. Clarity for Luther meant that the Bible was open to ordinary means of reading; obscurity was a temporary failure, owing to the lack of expertise in the languages and literature of the period.

At stake in this matter of the clarity of Scripture is whether ordinary persons equipped with the ordinary qualifications for reading could understand the words of Scripture. The Reformers alleged that Scripture was open in just this sense and that no special power of the Church was required. Against Erasmus, Luther defended the notion of the public meaning of the words of Scripture, and so created the climate for biblical studies in the academic sense.

The second part of the doctrine of the plain sense is the hermeneutical directive contained in the Reformation slogan "Scripture is its own interpreter." This directive does not refer primarily to the unity of the Bible (which stipulates that one interprets Scripture by Scripture), though that was assumed and led to the development of typology as a distinctively Protestant form of exegesis. The basic sense of the directive is well stated by Gerhard Ebeling:

> We have, first of all, to do with an apparently purely formal and general rule of interpretation, namely, that interpretation is nothing else but allowing the text to speak for itself; it is the process of making clear and

establishing what the text actually says, and thus enabling it, as it were, to interpret itself.

The idea that Scripture is its own interpreter served to mark Scripture off from the history of interpretation and to require that the exegete go to the text itself.

The difficulties here, which are transparent to the modern reader, were not so obvious to the Reformation reader. Erasmus's doubts that text and interpretation could be so firmly separated were prescient, but that does not negate the importance of the Protestant achievement, which was to create the possibility of a nonsectarian and public approach to the interpretation of the Bible.

Explanation of the text in the Reformation hermeneutic is a matter of reading the plain sense; appropriation is a greater mystery. This is how Calvin explains it:

> ... Scripture indeed is self-authenticated; hence it is not right to subject it to proof and reasoning. And the certainty it attains with us, it attains by the testimony of the Holy Spirit.
> We seek no proofs, no marks of genuineness upon which our judgment may lean; but we subject our judgment and wit to it as to a thing far beyond any guesswork.

Although Calvin does go on to list a few "marks of genuineness," he does so apologetically; the marks he adduces carry little weight today. The point that Calvin makes, and the point which was often lost sight of in post-Reformation Protestant orthodoxy, is basic: the conviction that the Bible is the Word of God (i.e., the conviction of the truth of the Bible) is not the conclusion of an argument. One believes the Bible because, in the words of Paul, "the Spirit himself bears witness with our spirit." Explanation of the text is a public matter, formally outside of faith; appropriation is a private matter, the testimony of the Spirit which creates belief. Explanation treats the text as an object; appropriation treats the text as a subject which addresses the soul of the believer.

Thus the central paradox in the Reformation hermeneutic is created. Stripped of its religious clothing, it is the paradox that appears in the naive question about the relationship between what the text means and what the text means to me. Explanation and appropriation remain fundamental terms. The work of Paul Ricoeur on hermeneutics, to use a contemporary example, is an attempt to overcome the dichotomy between explanation and understanding or, in the terms he sometimes prefers, distantiation and appropriation. He identifies the dichotomy with post-Kantian Romanticist hermeneutics, claiming that "Kantianism represents the nearest horizon of hermeneutics." But it has deeper roots, in the Reformation doctrines we are discussing.

The Reformation notion of appropriation has two parts. The first is the testimony of the Holy Spirit, which has to do with the objective address of the text to the believer—the magisterium of the text. The doctrine of the testimony of the Holy Spirit arose in answer to the question of canonicity: if the Bible rules the Church, how could the Church have the authority to rule on the canon? The Protestant answer was that the Church recognized in its rulings on canon the testimony of the Spirit to the canonical books; the testimony is tied to the texts, not to the hierarchy. Technically, that is not a satisfactory answer: the question was not whether the Bible was objectively the Word of God, for on that there was agreement among all parties, but whether the recognition of the Church was to be trusted.

The Protestant answer to that question was typically individual: the Church can be trusted because I also recognize the Word of God in the text of the canonical scripture. Calvin says, "I speak of nothing other than what each believer experiences within himself." This idea became known as the "analogy of faith" (cf. Romans 12:6). Before Karl Barth early in this century elevated it as *the* Protestant principle, the analogy of faith was understood in a more restricted way, as a fundamental limitation on appropriation of the Bible. The truth can be understood only in proportion to one's faith in Christ. There can be no appropriation without faith, and all reading of Scripture is therefore inherently Christological.

As we have said, the Reformation hermeneutic imitates the structure of Christian authority. The two elements of explanation, the doctrines of the clarity and of the self-interpreting character of Scripture, are respectively the objective and subjective aspects of the authority of tradition, here defined narrowly as the canonical text. The two elements of appropriation, the testimony of the Holy Spirit and the analogy of faith, are respectively the objective and subjective aspects of the authority of the living presence of Christ, here defined without reference to Church. In a sense, the Reformation heremeneutic first imitates and later replaces the understanding of Christian authority that we earlier described. *Sola scriptura* comes alive in the Reformation hermeneutic.

## IV. The Resurrection of God's Word—*Preaching*

In any formal hermeneutic of reading, the difficulty lies in understanding the relationship between explanation and appropriation. The difficulty can be put in the following terms. Reading is a matter of text and reference, or, to put it otherwise, a matter of comment and subject. The text comments on or modifies a field of reference. We can take that modification of the field of reference as the meaning of the text. Explanation can be understood in these terms as an attempt to read the text against the field of reference proper to the text. If the text is a nineteenth-century text, the field of reference proper to the text includes features of nineteenth-century civilization that can be adduced as proper to the text. The goal of explanation is to distance the field of reference of the text as far as possible from the field of reference of the reader. What is different about the nineteenth century from the twentieth is important to the reader; what is the same is not important. We cannot be naive about reading the text against the nineteenth century, for none of us can in fact know the nineteenth century. We can, however, and do construct methodologies, historical and linguistic, which enable us to describe differences and, therefore, to reconstruct a field of reference for the text.

All recent critical approaches to hermeneutics, including structuralist approaches, aim to reduce the field of reference of a text to the text itself. This goal is an illusory one which can only be sustained with relatively modern texts. The stranger the linguistic and historical frames of reference are to the reader, the more important the labor of explanation becomes. For the Bible, which is both old and strange, the labor of explanation is very important. (It is also necessary to reject the goal of Romanticist hermeneutics, which attempted futilely to recover the subjectivity of the author.)

If explanation is a method of distancing the meaning of the text from the reader, the outcome of explanation is skepticism about the ability of the reader to know the meaning of the text at all. By distancing the text from the reader, it tends to trivialize its meaning. Appropriation, on the other hand, is reading the text against the field of reference proper to the reader. Meaning for the reader entails a modification in the reader's perception of the world. Paul Ricoeur puts it in terms of the text opening up new possibilities of "being-in-the-world." Appropriation seeks to assimilate the difference of the text into the field of reference of the reader. The goal of appropriation is, in this sense, precisely the opposite of explanation—overcoming the difference instead of accentuating it, making the text important instead of trivial.

In the reading of ordinary books, the tension between explanation and appropriation is interesting. It produces English departments. In the case of a sacred book, the difference is crucial. The Church has an inherent interest in what Hans-Georg Gadamer calls the "fusion of horizons." The hermeneutical situation which Ricoeur and Gadamer consider fundamental to understanding the processes of reading is that of dialogue. According to Ricoeur, reference in spoken language is ostensive: "That to which a dialogue ultimately refers is the situation common to the interlocutors, that is, the aspects of the reality which can be shown or pointed to . . . ." Written language is non-ostensive, but in the place of ostensive reference comes the fusion of horizons (*Horizonverschmelzung*) of the world opened up by the text and the world of the reader. Gadamer takes this one step farther. He claims that "to understand a text is to understand oneself in a kind of dialogue. This contention is confirmed by the fact that the concrete dealing with a text yields expression only when what is said in the text begins to find expression in the interpreter's own language."

Compared to Ricoeur's and Gadamer's solutions to the conflict between explanation and appropriation, which are private, the Protestant solution is public.

For Protestantism, the distance between explanation and appropriation is overcome in preaching. Preaching is the supreme sacerdotal act in Protestantism because it overcomes the crucial difficulty with *sola scriptura*, the distance between explanation and appropriation or, in Reformation terms, between the plain sense and faith.

In his essay "Maranatha," Ong approaches the question with which we have been struggling in a different way. He begins with a description of the "retrospectivity" of narrative. Narratives are always, in some sense, preterite, "once upon a time." He notes the relationship between death and writing, especially print. "The writer has produced a 'body' because he has 'executed' his work." He quotes Ricoeur's personal observations that "to read a book is to consider its author as already dead" and to meet the author is to "experience a kind of disturbance." Ong notes, further, the possibilities which are opened up by the text when it dies: "It can be freed from the surface, resurrected, variously." The fecundity of the text, however, can be realized only when it is made oral again. "For texts are there to produce words, which are irreducibly sounds, realized orally either in internalized utterance or in exterior imagination." In that sense, as Revelation 10:9–10 has it, the word must be "eaten." The text is resurrected only when it becomes proclamation. It is that insight which the Reformation institutionalized in the form of preaching. Preaching is the resurrection of the text.

## V. The Task of Preaching—*Mystery*

If I have represented the function of preaching correctly, it is impossible, or at least a hermeneutical *tour de force*. Explanation and appropriation are not to be combined in preaching but transcended. Preaching becomes in Protestantism an act of revelation. Calvin calls preachers "the very mouth of God." The two principal parts of Christian authority, the tradition and the living voice, are combined in a single person and a single voice. Clearly, this is too much to expect; not every preacher is a prophet. Most are priests, servants of the institution and purveyors of institutional religion. The Protestant hermeneutic requires charismata which are not always available in seminaries. The Protestant Church has responded in various ways to this problem.

The first response has been the substitution of a much more naive hermeneutic for the Reformation hermeneutic. Protestant orthodoxy very early reduced the meaning of the clarity of scripture from public meaning to ecclesiastical meaning. In the sixteenth century, creeds and catechisms were written and quickly institutionalized as authoritative documents; ministers were required to assent to them as equivalent to true readings of Scripture. The Synod of Dort, to which I have already referred, published a formula of subscription which said, among other things, that

> The undersigned . . . do hereby, sincerely and in good conscience before the Lord, declare by this our subscription that we heartily believe and are persuaded that all the articles and points of doctrine contained in the Confession and Catechism of the Reformed Church, together with the explanation of some points of the aforesaid doctrine made by the National Synod of Dordrecht, 1618–'19, do fully agree with the 'Word of God.'

This is an attempt to hold explanation and appropriation together by creating a new document which avoids the difficulties of the Bible. It is arguably a new stage in the history of canonicity. Binding explanations of this sort, however, could not be solutions for long, for immediately *they* were subject to interpretation and thus to the same difficulties as the primary text.

A more important response to the difficulty of preaching has two related parts. The first, partially due also to restrictions of confessionalism, was the development of biblical scholarship outside of the Church. The basic facts are well known. The plain sense was claimed by academic scholarship and lost to the mainstream of Protestantism. Explanation of the text became the province of scholars who labored to rediscover the frame of reference of the text and to understand the text against that frame.

The second part of the development, more recent, is the creation of a new community based on an essentially oral understanding of the text. Although intellectual apologists for fundamentalism insist that the movement is based on a reading of the biblical text, the oral bases of the movement are clear. The text is not so much read as recited, often memorized. It is not used so much as a source of knowledge as a confirmation of what is already known. Nothing new can be learned from the text, for true knowledge exists in the community and the words spoken in community, not in the text itself.

We have, thus, a split between the original terms of the Reformation synthesis. To scholarship goes the plain sense, which has turned out to be less and less plain. To the fundamentalist sects goes the testimony of the Holy Spirit, the living Word. But the two sides are not the same for having once been together. The doctrine of the clarity of Scripture can no longer be understood without awareness of its tendency to trivialize the meaning of the text. Indeed, reactions against the historical understanding of the text are the order of the day, even among scholars. On the other hand, repristination of the fundamentalist variety can no longer be innocent. It requires a great effort to deny the contextuality of the Bible in a post-typographic age.

The effect of the reification of the text was felt most concretely in the abortive death-of-God movement. Ong says, near the end of the *Presence of the Word:*

> The story told in the foregoing chapters suggests that a certain silencing of God may have been prepared for by the silencing of man's life-world. The ability to respond directly to the word enjoyed by early oral-aural man has been attenuated by objectifying the human life-world through hypotrophy of the visual and the obtrusion of the visual into the verbal itself as man moved through the chirographic and typographic stages of culture.
>
> In these perspectives, the religious problem of modern man is far deeper than secularization.

The effect of the reification of the text is felt also in the creationist movement. Creationism presents itself as a science—a visually conceived enterprise. It is not. It survives not by its appeal to the eye but by its appeal to the ear. Creationism is immune to evidence precisely because evidence is an eye-concept. Immunity, however, is costly these days.

The contemporary preacher is caught amid these developments. No traditional handbook on preaching is much aware of the difficulty or helpful in overcoming it. The history of Protestantism does not, to use the handbook terminology, allow us to go easily from exegesis to application. History suggests instead that they are irreconcilable. There remains, however, the original formulation: the preacher paradoxically, even mystically, is caught between explanation and appropriation. I suspect that it was the mystery of the act of preaching that Karl Barth had in mind when he wrote:

> . . . How energetically Calvin, having first established what stands in the text, sets himself to re-think the whole material and to wrestle with it, till the walls which separate the sixteenth century from the first become transparent! Paul speaks, and the man of the sixteenth century hears. The conversation between the original record and the reader moves around the subject-matter, until a distinction between yesterday and today becomes impossible.

Mystery, however, is a theological term. It does not excuse the preacher from responsibility either to the text or to the people; it simply denies the reduction of one to the other.

*Bibliographical Note*

The literature on preaching is huge; preachers not only talk, sometimes at more length than the audience will willingly bear, they write, especially books on preaching. Hermeneutics, the other major focus of the essay, is also burdened by a sizable bibliography.

*On Preaching.* Abingdon has recently begun publishing an uneven set of essays on preaching under the general title *Abingdon Preacher's Library*, edited by William D. Thompson. By the editor himself is *Preaching Biblically: Exegesis and Interpretation* (1981), a generally disappointing study, occasionally even silly. Elizabeth Achtemeier's *Creative Preaching: Finding the Words* (1980) is a study of the relationship of creativity and authority in preaching. Robert Duke in *The Sermon as God's Word: Theologies for Preaching* (1980) presents small sketches of five theologies of preaching. A short history of preaching is presented in DeWitte T. Holland, *The Preaching Tradition* (1980). Preaching in a traditional Protestant perspective is especially well presented by John R. W. Stott, *Between Two Worlds: The Art of Preaching in the Twentieth Century* (Grand Rapids: Eerdmans, 1982). Walter C. Kaiser, Jr., *Toward an Exegetical Theology: Biblical Exegesis for Preaching and Teaching* (Grand Rapids: Baker, 1981), is acquainted with modern developments in hermeneutical theory but adopts the traditional (Puritan) view of exegesis nevertheless. See also his *The Old Testament in Contemporary Preaching* (Grand Rapids: Baker, 1973). Small studies on preaching from traditional Protestant approaches are James Daane, *Preaching with Confidence: A Theological Essay and the Power of the Pulpit* (Grand Rapids: Eerdmans, 1980) and Edmund P. Clowney, *Preaching and Biblical Theology* (Nutley, New Jersey: Presbyterian and Reformed, 1977).

An odd lot of other books on preaching includes the classic study by H. H. Farmer, *The Servant of the Word* (Philadelphia: Fortress, 1942); a book of practical advice, well-done by James Earl Massey, *The Sermon in Perspective: A Study of Communication and Charisma* (Grand Rapids: Baker, 1976); an odd but effective book which mixes sermons and essays by Edmund A. Steimle, Morris J. Niedenthal, and Charles L. Rice, *Preaching the Story* (Philadelphia: Fortress, 1980); a typical handbook is James W. Cox's *A Guide to Biblical Preaching* (Nashville: Abingdon, 1976).

*On Hermeneutics.* Anthony C. Thiselton's *The Two Horizons* (Grand Rapids: Eerdmans, 1980), is a good introductory survey of the most important questions, and it includes a dissertation-size bibliography. The works chiefly consulted for this paper were Gerhard Ebeling, *The Word of God and Tradition*, translated by S. H. Hooke (Philadelphia: Fortress, 1964); Hans-Georg Gadamer, *Philosophical Hermeneutics*, translated and edited by David E. Linge (Berkeley: University of California, 1976); Paul Ricoeur, *Interpretation Theory: Discourse and the Surplus of Meaning* (Fort Worth: Texas Christian University, 1976); and Ricoeur, *Hermeneutics and the Human Sciences*, edited and translated by John B. Thompson (Cambridge: Cambridge University, 1981). The fullest statement of Walter Ong's unusual approach to hermeneutics is found in *The Presence of the Word* (New Haven: Yale University, 1967). See also *In the Human Grain* (New York: Macmillan, 1967) and *Interfaces of the Word* (Ithaca: Cornell University Press, 1977).

CHARLES P. R. TISDALE

# EASTER WORDS

In leafing through this dusty book
Eyes follow the printed letters
Like stalks in a winter garden.
Once margins were white, and flowers
Bloomed each page as though a thought
Could catch its own seed, a word
Not spoken except in some fertile phrase
Intent on resurrection.

Have not these fingers pushed
A pencil in mind's broken furrow,
Left the impression of its flesh
Counted out in rhythm's rows?
So fingers once again in final
Gathering rub the spine, run down
The rectos of the risen lords
For sunlight's bright arrangement.

Bloom, then, the petals of a book's
Survival, not so much sign
Of ever living after,
But in a verbal heaven
Proof of touch putting two hands
On what was said, feeling maker
Live again for what he made,
Words beyond tampering or change.

# THE JOURNAL OF RELIGION

Since 1882, when it was founded by William Rainey Harper, **The Journal of Religion** has promoted critical and systematic inquiry into religion. Recognizing that "religion" is an enormous and complex area of study, the **Journal** is not limited by content or ideological orientation, but embraces all areas of Protestant, Catholic, and Jewish theology as well as other types of religious studies.

## NOT JUST FOR THEOLOGIANS

The articles listed below illustrate the scope of the **Journal.** At the same time, the subject categories are not meant to be definitive: many of the essays could be placed under more than one heading. Rather, the categories serve to suggest the extent of the **Journal's** search into the meaning and import of religion.

### HISTORICAL THEOLOGY
Michael Morgan, The Curse of Historicity: The Role of History in Leo Strauss's Jewish Thought

### LITERARY RELIGIOUS STUDIES
Jeanne Clayton Hunter, "With Winges of Faith": Herbert's Communion Poems

### PSYCHOLOGICAL RELIGIOUS STUDIES
Peter Homans, A Personal Struggle with Religion in the Lives and Works of the First Psychologists

### CONSTRUCTIVE THEOLOGY
Ronald F. Thiemann, Revelation and Imaginative Construction

### PHILOSOPHICAL RELIGIOUS STUDIES
Jure Kristo, The Interpretation of Religious Experiences: What Do Mystics Intend When They Talk about Their Experiences

**The Journal of Religion** is published quarterly and is edited by B. A. Gerrish, David Tracy, and Anthony C. Yu.

**The University of Chicago Press**

# HISTORY OF RELIGIONS

**Edited by Mircea Eliade, Joseph M. Kitagawa, Frank E. Reynolds, and Wendy D. O'Flaherty**

**History of Religions** is the only English-language scholarly journal devoted to comparative historical religious studies. In promoting an understanding of religious phenomena in their various cultural manifestations, the journal has attracted its authors and audience from among scholars not only in the field of religious studies but also in the disciplines of psychology, textual analysis, anthropology, archaeology, history, phenomenology, sociology, and linguistics.

## Defining a Humanistic Approach to the Study of Religion

### MYTH AND SYMBOLIC LANGUAGE
**Jorunn Jacobsen Buckley,** A Rehabilitation of Spirit Ruha in Mandean Religion
**Emily B. Lyle,** Dumezil's Three Functions and Indo-European Cosmic Structure

### RELIGIOUS THOUGHT AND EXPRESSION
**Rodney L. Taylor,** Journey Into Self: The Autobiographical Reflections of Hu Chih
**Richard C. Martin,** Understanding the Qur'an in Text and Context

### RITUAL AND RELIGIOUS PRACTICE
**Helen Hardacre,** The Transformation of Healing in the Japanese New Religions
**Henry Pernet,** Masks and Women: Towards a Reappraisal

### COMPARATIVE STUDIES
**John Irwin,** The Sacred Anthill and the Cult of the Primordial Mound
**Cristiano Grotanelli,** The King's Grace and the Helpless Woman: A Comparative Study of the Stories of Ruth, Charilla, Sita

## THE UNIVERSITY OF CHICAGO PRESS